Praise for *The Participating Citizen*

"...truly reflects the expansive presence and influence of Schutz's thought in the social sciences ... a biographical portrait that puts the complex circumstances of Schutz's life into perspective..."

— *Human Studies*

"Not only is this book interesting to read, it is also a passionate account of Schutz's life and times that draws the reader directly into those life and times. The use and organization of a vast amount of unpublished material pertaining to Schutz, his friends, colleagues, and contemporaries is exemplary."

— Fred Kersten, author of *Phenomenological Method: Theory and Practice*

"Michael D. Barber impressively situates Schutz's philosophical ideas and commitments within the context of Schutz's own life, providing an immense amount of historical detail and insight into the broader intellectual and social history of the early half of the last century."

— Richard M. Zaner, author of *Conversations on the Edge: Narratives of Ethics and Illness*

THE PARTICIPATING CITIZEN

SUNY series in the Philosophy of the Social Sciences
Lenore Langsdorf, editor

THE PARTICIPATING CITIZEN

A Biography of Alfred Schutz

Michael D. Barber

State University of New York Press

Published by
State University of New York Press, Albany

Printed in the United States of America

For information, contact State University of New York Press, Albany, NY
www.sunypress.edu

Production by Diane Ganeles
Marketing by Susan Petrie

Library of Congress Cataloging-in-Publication Data

Barber, Michael D., 1949–
The Participating citizen : a biography of Alfred Schutz / Michael D. Barber.
p. cm. — (SUNY series in the philosophy of the social sciences)
Includes bibliographical references and index.
ISBN 978-0-7914-6141-9 (alk. paper)—978-0-7914-6142-6 (pb alk. paper)
1. Schutz, Alfred, 1899–1959. 2. Sociologists—Austria—Biography.
3. Phenomenological sociology. I. Title. II. Series.

MH479.S38B37 2004
301'.092—dc22
[B] 2003060488

10 9 8 7 6 5 4 3 2 1

For Pat, who loved children,
and
For Devin and Ollie, whom she would have loved

Maternity, which is bearing par excellence, bears even responsibility for the persecuting by the persecutor.

Emmanuel Levinas, *Otherwise than Being*

Then a child opens its eyes and sees a tree for the first time. And people seem to us like walking trees.

Czeslaw Milosz, "Into the Tree"

Contents

Preface

Years ago, I was intrigued by Professor Lester Embree's observation that the only biography of Alfred Schutz, Helmut Wagner's "intellectual biography," while thoroughly documenting Schutz's interactions with philosophical and sociological colleagues, had left out much of his interesting life. Ironically, the everyday life of the quintessential philosopher of everyday life remained anonymous.

To remedy that deficit, I embarked upon writing this biography, seeking to uncover the "subjective activity," i.e., the biographical doings, underlying the "objective meanings" that constitute the theoretical work of Schutz. Throughout the project, I have been impressed above all by his moral excellence. He lived an exemplary life as a husband, father, and friend; as a lawyer/businessman assisting hundreds to escape Hitler's domination; as a peacemaker in the fractious international phenomenology movement; and as a participant with other committed intellectuals in the incipient civil rights movement. He expressed his moral character in what he wrote, particularly in his lifelong concern for the intricacies, quandaries, and limits of intersubjective understanding. His life was linked to his thought.

While this biography will present Schutz's character and correlate it with his writings, it is also a *philosophical* biography, that is, it seeks to engage Schutz philosophically and critically. It looks for lacunas in his thought, weaknesses that might accompany his strengths, and the fault lines that others and even he himself might have detected. I stumbled on such a fissure when, after graduate school, I delivered my first paper, relying heavily on his thought, before an audience of philosophers who accused me of being mired in relativism and lacking any grounds for universal ethical claims. I went on to investigate the absence of ethics in his thought and discovered an ethics behind that absence of ethics: Schutz was all too aware of how moral codes and ethical theories can be used to bolster an in-group's folkways and further exile out-groups. While I had reached a "resting place," as James called it, on this issue, the writing of this biography has reopened it.

Although the care for others that Schutz demonstrated in his life found its way into his writings in their preoccupation with understanding the viewpoint of the other person, this preoccupation is only *implicitly* ethical, especially since throughout most of life he showed himself reluctant to endorse *explicitly* any normative ethical principles or theory. This book traces this reluctance to a philosophical version of the social scientific "value-freedom" that all his intellectual mentors shared, including Max Weber; the proponents of "Austrian economics," such as Ludwig von Mises; and the legal theorist Hans Kelsen. Moreover, insofar as this project has brought me into a philosophical community with Schutz's own interlocutors, I have found my concerns about Schutz's noncommittal approach to ethics and relativistic tendencies confirmed; as it turns out, his lifelong friends Aron Gurwitsch and, in particular, Eric Voegelin had raised similar objections to him during his lifetime. In fact, I will show that Voegelin challenged him for adopting what would now be identified as an *observer viewpoint*, cataloging the different relevance-rankings of actors and groups, without espousing, as a *participant*, any ranking of his own.

But it was even more a surprise to me working through his papers to discover that after *Brown* v. *Board of Education* and in concert with a group of ethically committed intellectuals he finally *did* end up espousing certain normative commitments about how democracy ought to be practiced. To be sure, in the essay "The Well-Informed Citizen" he had affirmed a kind of epistemic normativity insofar he affirmed that the opinion of the well-informed citizen ought to take precedence over that of experts and the uninformed. But in archival writings subsequent to that essay and recently published by Lester Embree, he asserted that democracy needs to be assessed in ethical terms of how well it allows the point of view of its individual citizens to be heard or recognized, particularly in small public forums. Although vague and unarticulated, this normative standard reflects his continual social scientific and philosophical theoretical concern to rescue the subjective viewpoint of actors from anonymity and, by this standard's formality, it preserves the pluralism of perspectives he had defended in correspondence with Voegelin. Furthermore, by basing democracy more on the active participation of individual citizens than on the anonymous votes of majorities, Schutz developed in the *political* sphere the Austrian insight that the economy needed to be understood in terms of the activities of individual entrepreneurs and consumers rather than of anonymous economic laws.

One can trace the strands of this philosophical argument through chapters 2, 3, 8, and 12, but the argument simply shows Schutz coming to a philosophical position that mirrors more adequately the kind of ethical life that becomes patent in the surrounding chapters. He did not live his life value-neutrally.

I have relied on four principal sources in writing this book. First, I have utilized and presented the contents of all of his published writings, including the posthumous ones. Second, I have consulted The Papers of Alfred Schutz at the Yale University Beinecke Rare Book and Manuscript Library. These papers contain fourteen boxes of published works, unpublished drafts of those works, and never-published manuscripts; five boxes of notes on courses given and books read; and seventeen boxes of correspondence with hundreds of interlocutors. Third, I have examined the unpublished manuscript, three thousand pages long, from which Helmut Wagner produced his *Alfred Schutz: An Intellectual Biography*. From this source, I was able to follow thoroughly Schutz's exchanges with his philosophical interlocutors and become thoroughly aware of the literature available to Schutz. Fourth, Ms. Evelyn S. Lang owns hundreds of folders of personal correspondence, The Personal Papers of Alfred Schutz, to which she generously allowed me access and of which Wagner's biography, written before such letters were available, made no use. I would like to thank Ms. Lang for permission to cite from The Papers of Alfred Schutz and The Personal Papers of Alfred Schutz, over both of which she holds the literary rights.

I am indebted to more people than I can ever thank. I am grateful to the College of Arts and Sciences of St. Louis University for a summer Mellon grant to read The Papers of Alfred Schutz and to Evelyn S. Lang and the Center for Advanced Research in Phenomenology for a grant to read The Personal Papers of Alfred Schutz. I acknowledge appreciatively the assistance of the Beinecke Rare Book and Manuscript Library and, in particular, of Mr. Vincent Giroud for their continual assistance with my study of The Papers of Alfred Schutz. I am most thankful to Lester Embree for suggesting the idea of this biography, and to him, Fred Kersten, Evelyn Schutz, Ilja Srubar, and Richard Zaner for their thorough, careful, perceptive reading of this manuscript. Their suggestions for improvement and encouragement have been invaluable. It has meant a great deal to me that those who knew Schutz personally, such as his daughter Evelyn, Fred Kersten, and Richard Zaner, have informed me that this book accurately captures the life of the man we admire together. I am also in the debt of Rev. Theodore Vitali, C.P., for giving me time off from seminars to complete this work and for his continual support of it. Thanks to editors Victoria Newman and Faith Glavey. Eleonore Stump and David Barber have shown constant interest in the manuscript and given me continual support in its production, as did my recently deceased mother, Patricia Barber. I could not have produced this work without the patience of the Leo Brown Community and without the continued friendship of my brothers, Tim and Terry, and their families; Susie Duckworth; Tom Kelly; Ollie Roundtree and his sons, Ollie and Devin; Gary Seibert; and Charlie Shelton.

Chapter 1

Maturing in a Troubled Vienna

Schutz's Youth

Alfred Schutz (in German, Schütz) was born April 13, 1899 to Johanna Schutz (born Fialla, of Czechoslovakian parents) and Alfred Schutz, of Vienna. The latter had died on January 19, 1899, before his son was born, and two years after his death Johanna married her husband's brother, Otto, also of Vienna, who acted as a father to Alfred throughout his life. Otto's father, Moritz, had been a grocer in Vienna, and Otto himself served for over forty-five years as an executive of the time-honored Vienna banking firm Ephrussi and Col. The Schutz family lived in the Mariahilf neighborhood adjacent to the Innere Stadt, which, surrounded by the Ringstrasse, contained the empire's public buildings, such as the Parliament, University, National Theater, Opera, and Stock Exchange.[1]

Johanna never informed Alfred that his biological father had died before his birth, and she accompanied Alfred to the school he attended to fill out forms for him so that he would not know that his father had died. Alfred discovered this fact when he applied in Vienna to join the military at age seventeen and his mother turned over to him official legal documents. He was not angry with his mother, especially since he came to learn that his mother had been very much in love with his father, who had been a *Schöngeist,* interested in poetry rather than science. Schutz even wondered whether he would have been able to get along with his father, since he himself was, according to his wife Ilse, "so very thorough and so very scientific."[2]

The discovery of his true parentage in fact augmented his love for Otto, as he would reveal twenty-five years later in an affidavit filed on behalf of his father's visa for entry into the United States:

> That from my youth the warmth of father and son was a natural development between myself and my mother's husband, Otto Schutz, and that after learning the family history an unusual degree of

> attachment was created considering the treatment of the past years that was given to me by my father's brother, moreover the possibilities of education and social standing he desired me to have.[3]

At Alfred's request, Otto had consented to adopt him legally as his son in 1920, and Alfred admitted

> [T]hat I know no other man who served me so loyally and faithfully throughout my life, and my undivided attention and devotion under present abnormal conditions is a natural feeling toward him and there is nothing short of sacrificing my own life that I would not do to assist him in any troublesome situation that he may be faced with.[4]

There was every indication in Schutz's correspondence as a child and young man that he maintained with both his parents the same kind of close relationship that he, as a man of forty-two, described as having had with his stepfather. For instance, the young Schutz regularly composed poetry for his parents on New Year's Day, Christmas, their birthdays, and Mother's Day, dating from as early as January 1, 1909. Letters from summer vacation with his uncle, Otto Weissberger, who lived near Pilsen, Austria, revealed the warm, playful relationship between the teenage Schutz and his parents. In describing the train trip to Pilsen, he depicted himself as a suave adult beyond his years, reading a paper, smoking a cigarette, and being the last traveler left on the train before his uncle met him and placed him in a horse-drawn wagon. In addition, he displayed his musical proclivities in commenting on the double bass (*Kontrabass*) and percussion instruments (*Schlagwerk*) employed by a chamber orchestra entertaining in the village. However, he concluded on a humorous note, describing the "brave musicians" as "loud farmers" who were noteworthy in their activity (*Tat*) and tempo and who played according to notes in an atmosphere filled with wine, cigars, and the much-cherished money tossed their way.[5]

In addition to composing poems on special occasions for his parents, he produced whole volumes of poetry, one of which was dedicated to his parents on Christmas 1914, when he would have been only fifteen years of age. This volume included poems expressing childhood pieties as well as a dialogue between Don Quixote and Sancho Panza, who urged his master to live everyday life (*Alltagsleben*) instead of losing himself among the clouds of idealism. The book also contained a series of poems, not dedicated to anyone in particular and dubbed "Songs of an Egoist," in which the voices of Max Stirner or Friedrich Nietzsche resounded in a poem entitled "Ich":

Pray to me, you weak,
You, who still deny
That you are gods,
Sink to your knees before the strong.
I have my fate
In my hand,
I forge myself
My own lot,
I am alone for all myself
The only God
And I am strong.[6]

Whether Schutz here vented adolescent rebelliousness or parodied egoism, it is significant that at age fifteen he was able to set aside any moralizing scruples to take on a point of view starkly at odds with the familial tone of his other poetry. It was as if he used his poetry to practice a kind of free imaginative variation, adopting perspectives quite foreign to his own.

Another instance of such free variation appeared when he composed "Vera's Diary," an essay of about ten pages in length, which pretended to be a diary dictated by the six-month-old daughter of his cousin Elly to "Uncle Freddy" on July 25, 1916. Vera told Uncle Freddy that people were horrible to her on her first day in this world, laughing and making faces at her when she cried, as if they were enjoying themselves over her psychological pain. She gave vent to her suspicion of the world only to find that this behavior infuriated her nurse. She thought that the large gray house in which Freddy lived would have soured even his most beautiful day. She described philosophical problems pressing upon her and decided to devote her life to answering questions about her foot in relation to her body—in other words, to study philosophy. Schutz utilized the diary to poke fun at family members and philosophy itself, even as he explored the misinterpretations possible between a newborn child and her family.[7]

His mother supervised his education, fostering in him a deep and lifelong love for music through piano lessons that he received from an orchestra trumpeter. In addition, he attended the Esterhazy Gymnasium, also known as Staatsgymnasium VI, at which he did better than all his classmates, taking eight years of Latin and Greek and graduating in January 1918, summa cum laude.[8]

The gymnasium system up until 1904 had been the only form of secondary education in the monarchy that enabled entry into the university and a consequent career as a doctor or lawyer. Gymnasium education contrasted with that of the *Realschule*, which provided a more practical education—it taught, for example, the modern languages instead of the classics—but it must be added that Ludwig Wittgenstein and Arnold Schoenberg attended a *Realschule*. In 1957 when Schutz was drawing up a proposal for a Ford Foundation Grant for the New School, he compared his own gymnasium education unfavorably with the high school education his children received in the United States:

> [i]t is one of the most gratifying aspects of American education that children are encouraged at a very early age to participate in the life of the nation by discussing freely the major problems connected with daily events and to try to formulate sensible and well-founded opinions on these issues. I well remember the school regulations at the Austrian "Gymnasium" where I studied under the Habsburg Monarchy: students up to the age of 18 years who engaged in any kind of political discussion were threatened with immediate expulsion. On the other hand, I had the good fortune of watching how my own children, who were educated in American schools, enjoyed full freedom of opinion and were guided to good democratic citizenship not by authoritarian dogmas, but by unfolding the faculties of their own judgment.[9]

The authoritarian character of the gymnasium education may have resulted from academic rigor, its character as the training ground for the Josephinist bureaucracy, or the prevalent mood of the country under the monarchy. It is significant that Schutz's own appreciation for democratic process—a theme to be developed later—was shaped by a lack of democratic experience in his own education.[10]

At age seventeen and with Austria involved in the world war, he completed his education with a comprehensive emergency examination, one year before he should have taken the *Abitur*, or *Matura*, examination to qualify for the university. According to Ilse, Alfred had passed through an adolescent crisis in which he had entertained thoughts of suicide, but, she noted, "he never would have committed [suicide] on account of his mother." He joined the army's artillery division in order to be killed, even though he could have been exempted from military service because of a chronic ear inflammation he suffered from since childhood. Holding the rank of lieutenant in the artillery, Schutz performed assorted dangerous military services on the Italian front, including reconnaissance, poison gas protection, signaling, and the reparation of disrupted communications. Although he had intended to end his life, according to Ilse "when the first bombs came, he was among the very first ones to lie down on the ground protecting himself from being killed." After he spent ten months at the front and witnessed great carnage, the time for his first furlough arrived, and he took the last train returning to Vienna. The rest of his regiment were taken prisoners, the war ceased, and the Central Powers had been defeated.[11]

In a letter to Ilse of May 8, 1938, three months after Hitler's *Anschluss*, he described his military service in World War I in order that she might apply for an exit permit. He mentioned with pride that he had served in the trenches in the midst of gas at the battle of Montello and that he had comported himself bravely in war, earning silver and bronze medals for bravery, the Karl Truppenkreuze, and the War Memorial medallion with swords. There was a pathos to Schutz's proud appeal to his valiant military service as a sign of his patriotism for the same country that required of him ten days later a signed promise to emigrate and to prevent his children from ever again setting foot on its soil.[12]

The Austrian/Viennese Context: Up to World War I

In discussing the war, I have been presupposing the cultural, political, and economic events in Austria and Vienna that furnish the context of Schutz's maturation and his subsequent philosophical work. Let me try to describe some of them.

When Count Rudolf IV, chosen by the imperial electors as king, established his power over the Danube Basin in 1278, the Habsburg dynasty commenced a reign that would last for six and a half centuries. In spite of the Austrian monarchy's frequent indifference to its populace, brighter moments appeared during the zenith of the Austrian baroque architectural style when the much-revered Maria Theresa presided for forty years over a multinational, centralized bureaucracy ruling over Austria, Slav Bohemia, and Magyar Hungary. Her son, Joseph II, ruling from 1780 to 1790, implemented a series of reforms, including the "Toleration Patent" (1781) that guaranteed substantial religious freedom throughout the realm. After Count Metternich's conservative policies in reaction to the French Revolution, Napoleon's ascent to power, and the social unrest of 1848, Francis Joseph came to power as emperor, a position he held sixty-eight years, until 1916.[13]

While Francis Joseph suffered major defeats in foreign relations at the hands of Russia in the Balkans, for instance, and of Prussia, insofar as Bismarck resisted any "chaining the trim seaworthy frigate of Prussia to the ancient worm-eaten galleon of Austria"—his major struggles had to do with internal governance. His empire encompassed the German sectors of Upper and Lower Austria, Salzburg and the Tyrol, and Carinthia and Styria in the east; the Czech and Slovakian populations of Bohemia, Moravia, and Silesia in the north; the Hungarian Magyars, Romanians, and Galician Poles to the east; and the Balkan nationalities of Slovenia, Croatia, Serbia, and Bosnia to the south. The internal unrest following Austria's defeat by Prussia in 1866 resulted in a new constitutional entity, the "Dual Monarchy," that granted autonomous rule to Hungary, with foreign affairs, defense, and the joint budget remaining the common responsibility of both Budapest and Vienna.[14]

This accord, though, by no means resolved all the tensions among the various nationalities. For example, the German-Austrians who made up 80 percent of the military officer corps frequently failed to understand their Hungarian and Slavic subordinates, and German-speaking opponents of pro-Czech language ordinances in Bohemia launched a filibuster with cowbells, sleigh bells, and snare drums that drove the Austrian prime minister, Count Badeni, from office. This German-Czech conflict, dating from a bloody suppression at Prague in 1848, eventually resulted in the German imposition of martial law. This further antagonized the Czechs, who boycotted German cultural events and were rumored to stick their fingers in their ears whenever Germans spoke to them. In some cases, cultural differences, instead of motivating a movement toward secession from the empire, prompted groups to secure advantages for themselves, as occurred in the 1905 Moravian Compromise, which permitted Moravia's different provinces to establish as official languages those of the ethnic majorities. Of course, the conflicts between the various Balkan populations, Austrian desires to curb Serb power, and the Russian strategic interests would finally explode into the First World War upon the occasion of the assassination of Archduke Francis Ferdinand on June 28, 1914. When Schutz wrote later on American race relations, he recalled these cultural struggles of national minorities in the Austro-Hungarian monarchy. He contrasted "real" equality, based on special rights (such as use of one's national language in schools), with the "formal" equality that those who resisted claims to special rights might be willing to grant.[15]

Because of the difficulties of governing this welter of diverse nationalities, Austro-Hungary built up an imperial bureaucracy of tens of thousands, whose efforts to restrain centrifugal nationalist pressures created a political climate of authoritarianism, replicated in the *Gymnasium* system in which this bureaucracy educated its sons. The struggles, frequently violent, between various Austro-Hungarian parties and national-racial groups reflected a lack of the kind of experience of democratic procedures that Schutz was delighted to find his own children having in the United States. As Gordon Brook-Shepherd described it:

> Like the Austrian Social Democratic party, which Viktor Adler created almost single-handedly in 1889, the Christian Socials never knew the tolerance and decencies of democratic Parliamentary life, with its respect for opposition as well as government. The Reichsrat

> of Shönerer, Lueger, Adler and the rest was essentially a public arena for the racial battles of the Monarchy; it saw much brawling, hurling of inkpots and banging of desks, but hardly any rational debate. This remained of little more importance than the antics of a circus so long as the Emperor stood over it, aloof and near omnipotent. It became another matter when the dynasty vanished, and real power and responsibility suddenly passed into the hands of deputies who had no experience of either.[16]

Because of this decrepit political atmosphere, many Viennese simply withdrew, and Sigmund Freud, who did not register to vote until age fifty-two, exemplified a political apathy and despair attacked by the cultural critic Karl Kraus.[17]

In spite of these intercultural tensions, the empire flourished economically. The population increased by two million to twenty-four million during the 1880s. Despite recessions, the empire's gross national product in the period 1895–13 nearly quadrupled that of 1872–95. Industrial production grew at an annual rate of 6.3 percent from 1903–07. In 1907 the government budget recorded its greatest surplus in history, and domestic prosperity exceeded anything that could be remembered. Unfortunately, the fruits of this economic expansion were not evenly distributed. While government reforms sought to correct seventy-hour workweeks and child labor abuses and to protect collective bargaining, the Social Democratic Party revived under Viktor Adler in 1888 and continued to press for reforms even after the First World War. The major cities of the empire were unprepared for the massive influx of population, including farm workers, seeking manufacturing jobs, as is demonstrated by the facts that in 1910 the average Viennese domicile housed 4.4 persons, 1.24 per room, and only 22 percent of homes were equipped with indoor toilets. Moreover, many people lived in caves and under bridges, and in 1905 some thirty-five persons were dwelling in trees in Vienna's public parks. Rather than coming to terms with these social problems, the Austro-Hungarian bureaucracy proved itself corrupt; it succumbed to blackmail and bribery, entangled itself in excessive red tape, and sacrificed impartiality for feudal etiquette codes. The Austrians coined the word *Schlamperei*, meaning "slovenliness," to refer to the way their government fell far short of neighboring Prussia in efficiency.[18]

Liberalism, whether the socially conscious *Alt-liberalismus* of Josephinism, the more militant "high liberalism" after 1867, or the turn-of-the-century enlightened absolutism and bureaucracy, demanded that cultural groups abstract from their particularity and group feeling to submit to impartial, universal legal processes—an abstraction with immense cultural repercussions. This rationalization of political processes, along with society's increasing economic rationalization, gave birth at the end of the nineteenth and early twentieth centuries to German-Austrian counteremphases by such figures as Freud, Nietzsche, and Arthur Schopenhauer. These authors focused on psychological analyses and feeling and on the recovery of the Dionysian dimensions of the psyche from the Apollonian. In music, for instance, Richard Wagner hailed Beethoven's work as a counter to rationalism and developed operas with mythic, mystical overtones, appealing to the whole person, as did Gustav Mahler, who also emphasized Schopenhauerian themes of world-will and resignation in such works as his Third Symphony. No doubt, Schutz recognized the value in some of these cultural trends insofar as he tempered his own rationalist leanings by integrating into his thought the concerns of Bergson and phenomenological psychology.[19]

The reaction to societal rationalization also appeared in versions of German nationalism in Austria, such as Georg Schoenerer's anti-Semitic Germanism, the Pernerstorfer Circle's cultural Germanism without anti-Semitism, or Adler's socialistically inclined German nationalism. Adler, along with other Jews, at this time even favored *Anschluss* with Germany, and he further resisted overrationalization by ritualizing the worker's movement (e.g., through the elegant processions of workers in May Day demonstrations) in ways that Hitler later came to admire. Moreover, the Pernerstorfer Circle, in reaction to liberal, bourgeois atomism, sought to communicate through art and literature the communitarian values learned from their Benedictine educators.[20]

The literature, architecture, painting, and music of the time developed in reaction to the cultural crisis brought on by societal rationalization. In opposition to such rationalization and in concurrence with Freud, the playwright Arthur Schnitzler emphasized much-maligned erotic longings, only to be countered by Hugo Hofmannthsal, whose dramas attempted to revivify sagging moral traditions. When liberalism was just beginning to become more predominant, the novelist Adalbert Stifter's *Der Nachsommer* (1857) presented a "garden" of the bourgeois virtues such as self-discipline and self-reliance. However, Leopold Andrian-Werburg's *The Garden of Knowledge* (1895) criticized high liberal culture for its negative qualities of self-preoccupation and the inability to love. Further, Robert Musil's *The Man Without Qualities* as well as works by Franz Kafka and Rainer Maria Rilke exposed the communication problems underlying widespread sexual licentiousness and depicted the disintegration of Austria's hierarchic society and its rational culture. The Ringstrasse, constructed in the second half of the nineteenth century, epitomized liberal modernity, contrasting with the nearby Gothic Votivkirche, joining unrelated buildings "in their lonely confrontation of the great circular artery," and drawing critical fire from art historians for its "heartless rationalism," "utility," and "lack of community." In painting, Gustav Klimt rebelled against classical realism and nineteenth century certainties in a series of university paintings that shocked bourgeois proprieties and faculty sensibilities, for instance, in a law school painting that depicted the Furies in power. Finally, the composer Arnold Schoenberg joined Mahler in his struggle for authenticity by developing atonality and "emancipating" dissonance, which in its dynamism challenged rationality, just as Bergsonian temporality, accessible only to intuition, defied intellectual dissection for Schutz. Schoenberg's music, like Freudian psychology, turned to the subjective, interior world, and emphasized the wilderness nature of life in contrast to the bourgeois pursuit of comfort.[21]

Instead of seeking to reform bourgeois liberalism, others simply drowned the harsh realities of everyday realities in the oblivion of Straussian waltzes or Viennese cafés. Cultural critics such as Johann Schnitzler attacked the self-centeredness and indecisiveness of aesthetes frequenting the coffeehouses. Similarly, Karl Kraus, whose work Schutz knew by heart, began publishing his *Die Fackel* in 1899, criticizing the feuilleton tradition of writing chatty essays that were breezy, superficial, and popular—the apotheosis of *Schlamperei*. Another way of fleeing the misery of Austrian liberal, bourgeois culture was to immerse oneself in currents of cynicism and nihilism. For example, Musil dubbed Habsburg Vienna "Kakania," a word referring by its initials (K.K.) to the "imperial" and "royal" and at the same time meaning "Excrementia" or "Shitland," as anyone familiar with German nursery language would have understood. Some proponents of a type of medical nihilism ended up dismissing the obstetrician Ignác Semmelweis, a pioneer in the use of antisceptic procedures, because they "deemed his concern for the patient unbecoming to a professional." This cynicism and nihilism took its toll at the turn of the century in frequent suicides, even among well-known public figures, including Mahler's brother, Wittgenstein's three elder brothers, Crown Prince Rudolf and his lover, and the neurologist Nathan Weiss, whose death initiated Freud's career in psychology. The widespread nature of suicide so attracted the attention of the Vienna Psychoanalytical Society that it scheduled a symposium on the topic in 1910.[22]

One can detect in Alfred Schutz traces of several of these cultural factors. There is the turn to the subjective interior experience that one might find in a Freud or Schoenberg, but also the commitment to rationality characteristic of political liberalism and economic rationalization, both of which Schutz the social scientist had studied. Schutz's liberal, rationalist leanings also appear in his frequent effort to preserve a pluralism of perspectives and in his avoidance of the field of ethics, which several of his mentors took to be inherently less rational than the sciences, as we shall see later in Schutz's tête-a-tête with Eric Voegelin. Schutz would have never embraced an extreme liberal individualism, however, since he showed himself acutely aware of the social, intersubjective dimensions of experience, something that would even require accommodations in the way he conducted phenomenology. One perhaps can detect in Schutz's interest in *Lebensphilosophie* (life-philosophy), such as Bergson's, and in the life-world itself an opposition to any totalizing rationalism and a desire to establish rationality's limits in the lived flux of *durée* and the richness of everyday life. Schutz also endorsed Bergson's idea of duration to counter logical positivism, which itself arose, no doubt, to counteract the irrationalism it had perceived in the intellectual atmosphere. One can even understand Schutz's temptations to suicide, of which Ilse Schutz spoke above, as emerging from the winds of nihilism sweeping the Austrian culture of his time.

Finally, in order to understand Schutz himself and the events that would eventually induce him to emigrate to the United States, it is important to understand the position of Jews within the Austro-Hungarian empire and the anti-Semitism poisoning the empire's atmosphere. Joseph II's Toleration Patents and the liberal measures adopted after the 1867 creation of Austro-Hungary granted Jews equal civil, political, and religious rights, removing medieval restrictions on Jewish occupation, political and civil rights, and residence, such as the prohibitions against owning homes or living in Vienna. Despite liberalization, centuries-old Austrian anti-Semitism continued appearing in laws forbidding intermarriage and requiring conversion to Christianity for certain positions, in demonstrations aimed at excluding Jews from the University of Vienna, and in the blame placed on Jews for everything from localized murders to the 1873 stock market collapse. Further, anti-Semitic demagogues exercised increasing influence, such as Georg von Schoenerer, who inspired Hitler and urged German unification (long before the *Anschluss*); Karl Lueger, who unified various anti-liberal groups and once claimed, "I decide who is a Jew"; and Eugen Dühring, whose writings justified racial anti-Semitism. Some authors, however, such as Johann Schnitzler and Hugo Bettauer, protested rising anti-Semitism; and Jewish reactions spread out on a continuum from Theodore Herzl's militant, antiassimilationist Zionism to assimilation to the point of conversion to Christianity (as in the cases of Adler, Hans Kelsen, Mahler, Schoenberg, and Otto Weinenger). Jews further inserted themselves within the surrounding culture by increasing their economic and social standing. At this time, they abandoned in large numbers trade occupations and swelled the ranks of salaried white-collar employees, such as those working in insurance and large businesses, a common source of employment for those living in Schutz's Mariahilf neighborhood. In brief, the Jews flourished even in the face of anti-Semitism, and so it is not surprising that the Viennese Jewish population grew to over 175,000 by 1910, 8.6 percent of the total population. Nor is it surprising that Steffy Browne, a member of Professor Mises's circle along with Schutz, estimated that 79 percent of the circle members were Jewish.[23]

On an identity/assimilation continuum, Schutz personally inclined toward the assimilation pole. Although he was quite capable of acknowledging his Jewishness in correspondence with colleagues such as Machlup and Gurwitsch or with Voegelin and Farber, he never associated with Zionist or nationalist movements. Nevertheless, he was fully aware of perils to Jews in the earlier twentieth century, as is shown when he resisted having children because, as Ilse Schutz recounted him saying, "It's not the right time to bring Jewish children into this world." In addition, he resented the anti-Semitism he encountered on a business trip to the United States and, as a result, at first opposed moving there. He sent his daughter and son to the Ethical Cultural Society for religious education, objected to naturalistic explanations of biblical events, and was thoroughly knowledgeable about Jewish ritual practices, though he never participated in them. Moreover, his assimilation was evident in the fact that from childhood on he composed Christmas poems for his parents, sent Christmas greetings to friends, and gave Christmas gifts, such as those to Maurice Natanson's children. Such actions also show that the adult Schutz was quite willing to enter generously into others' worldviews in their terms, even though those terms might not have been his own. Similarly, although he personally seemed somewhat indifferent to religious practice, it is a tribute to his breadth of mind and openness to viewpoints foreign to his own that he made a place for a religious province of meaning in his essays "On Multiple Realities" and "Symbol, Reality, and Society." Moreover, following Johnston's observation that "[e]ven the most secularized of Austrian thinkers imbibed during childhood Jewish or Christian attitudes that could not easily be shed," it can be shown that Schutz lived out the Jewish ethical values praised by Kraus and Schnitzler. Given his distance from the practices of institutional Judaism and the utter disruption of his life that he would suffer due to his Jewish origins during the *Anschluss*, the following comment in his essay on equality takes on a personal poignancy:

> What has been unquestioned so far looms now as highly questionable, while heretofore subjectively problem-irrelevant factors become vitally relevant to the now imposed problems. To cite just a few examples: persons who believed themselves to be good Germans and had severed all allegiance to Judaism found themselves declared Jews by Hitler's Nuremberg laws and treated as such on the grounds of a grandparent's origin, a fact up to that time entirely irrelevant.[24]

From War's End to the *Anschluss*

The years 1918–39 constituted a formative time in the life of Alfred Schutz. During this time he completed his education and formed important friendships that he would maintain for the rest of his life. In addition, he secured employment and proved himself a trusted employee in a company with which he would also be associated long after moving to America. Finally, and perhaps most importantly, he married Ilse Heim and they together began a family. Furthermore, in this setting Schutz developed his own philosophical perspective, undergoing rather fundamental transitions leading to his own critical acceptance of Husserlian phenomenology. Before addressing these many strands of this critical period in Schutz's life, we must consider in some detail the macropicture—the political, economic, and cultural conditions of Vienna from the end of World War I onward that finally led to the 1938 *Anschluss* that profoundly changed Schutz's life.

Before the war's end, the revered Francis Joseph had died on November 21, 1916, after having ruled for sixty-eight years. In the fall of 1918, after the humiliating defeat of four hundred thousand Austrian troops in Italy and with the Central Powers overwhelmed and exhausted by war, Charles, Francis Joseph's successor and great-nephew, and the German chancellor petitioned President Wilson for peace talks. Charles permitted six nation states to declare their independence from Austria, and on November 12, 1918, the democratic Austrian republic under the leadership of Karl Renner was established.[25]

The fledgling republic faced daunting problems. The wheat and rye crops fell to less than 50 percent of their prewar yields, and there were shortfalls in meat, potatoes, and fats. Eighty percent of the schoolchildren in Vienna were registered as undernourished, and an influenza epidemic, which in 1918–19 killed twenty million worldwide, more than all those who perished in the world war, took the lives of thousands of Austrians, including Freud's daughter, Sophie. The newly established Czechoslovakia refused to ship any coal to Austria that winter, paralyzing Vienna's blast furnaces and transportation system. Meanwhile, according to Ilse Schutz hordes of returning soldiers were spurned for participating in a war that many thought was fought in vain, in much the way that soldiers returning to the United States from the Vietnam War were treated. These soldiers, some of whom plundered civilians and were considered a most radical and dangerous element, also inundated already fragile labor markets, increasing unemployment. Such unemployment grew, too, due to the shutting down of war industries and the lack of available raw materials. While 45,675 Viennese were unemployed in December 1918, by May 1919 the number had risen to 185,235. Since large numbers of the population needed public assistance, deficit spending and inflation resulted. Even buildings were in shambles, since no repairs had been done in years. Thus the severe winter of 1921–22 shut down the University of Vienna because its roof had not been repaired since 1914. It is no wonder, then, that the two years following the war saw the dominance of the Austrian Social Democratic Workers' Party, although this party's dominance of Vienna exacerbated anti-socialist sentiment in rural Austria, which often withheld resources from the capital.[26]

In the political domain, Schutz's mentor Hans Kelsen drew up a new constitution, which favored the Parliament over the president and which contained a bill of rights that was eventually eliminated. The first elections of the republic gave a slight edge to Social Democrats over their conservative Christian Social opponents, with German-National groups trailing, though—ironically, in light of subsequent history—both the Social Democrats and German-Nationals favored, for different reasons, reunification (*Anschluss*) with Germany. Bitter rancor and the lack of constructive dialogue characterized the proceedings of the new congress, which focused now on class conflicts and governmental social policies instead of on the nationalistic divisions typical of the Hapsburg era. Although the Social Democrats passed some measures on unemployment and workers' insurance to alleviate the misery of the postwar era, in the 1920s the Christian Socials gained power. They would hold it for the next eighteen years, with the Social Democrats opposing them through generally obstructionist tactics.[27]

During the period 1922–1929, the Christian Social chancellor Ignaz Seipel secured a League of Nations loan to quell galloping inflation, but he failed to roll back earlier social legislation due to a severe depression from 1924–26 that so heightened tensions that right-wing *Heimwehr* paramilitaries, outnumbering the Austrian army, battled the socialist *Schutzband* in street warfare. One of several right-wing chancellors, Engelbert Dollfuss rose to power in 1932, and at the prompting of his *Heimwehr* allies implemented a version of martial law; but his rapprochement with Mussolini to block Hitler's designs on Austria resulted in increased Nazi activity in Austria and his eventual assassination in 1934. Kurt von Schuschnigg, who succeeded Dollfuss, integrated the *Heimwehr* within the more pacific Militia of the Fatherland Front; but after many efforts to appease Hitler, especially by conceding to his demands at Berchtesgaden in February 1938, he called for a national plebiscite on Austria's relationship with Germany. On March 11, 1938, Hitler postponed the plebiscite, Schuschnigg resigned, and German troops invaded Austria on March 12, annexing it without a shot being fired. When Hitler entered Vienna three days later, 250,000 Austrians turned out to welcome him, and the plebiscite conducted a month later favored *Anschluss* by 99.73 percent, with Jews not being allowed to vote. Anti-Jewish measures commenced immediately, including violence against Jewish property, ejection from schools, and the disbarment of Jewish lawyers. Under the supervision of the Central Office for Jewish Emigration under Adolf Eichmann, 79,000 Jews left Austria by the end of 1938, and this number increased until only 8,102 Jews remained in Austria by the end of 1942. In addition, Heinrich Himmler supervised the construction of thirty-one concentration camps in Austria, starting with Mauthausen in March of 1938. Dr. Simon Wiesenthal has speculated that because of this massive execution system, Austria may have been responsible for the deaths of half the six million Jews executed.[28]

Education and Employment

Schutz studied under the faculty of law and social sciences at the University of Vienna and at the Business School of the Institute for International Trade. He received his LL.D. from the University of Vienna in 1921 and continued postgraduate research in the fields of international law, sociology, economics, and philosophy. In later affidavits, he acknowledged that his mentors included Friedrich von Wieser and Ludwig von Mises in economics, Hans Kelsen and Alfred Verdross in international law, and Husserl in philosophy.[29]

Schutz, as Kelsen's student, first met Mises when he appeared as one of the examiners for the economics examination requisite for a law degree, much to the surprise and discomfort of those to be tested, who were well aware of Mises's reputation for rigor. Hearing Schutz claim that he had read a book by John Bates Clark, Mises asked if he had read it in the English original or in German translation, and when he replied that he had read it in English, Mises applauded him, since there had been no German translation. Subsequently, Schutz's friend, Fritz Machlup, invited him to attend the meetings of Mises's private seminar, and he did so reluctantly, since he considered himself more of a sociologist than an economist. However, once Mises (who, Schutz believed, had consulted Kelsen about his—Schutz's—ability beforehand), assigned him to present topics, he came to enjoy the seminar and attended it regularly. The seminar was thoroughly interdisciplinary in character, with seminar members regularly presenting in areas other than their own discipline.[30]

The Mises Circle was one of many Viennese "circles," another was the renowned "Vienna Circle" of Moritz Schlick, which counted among its participants Rudolf Carnap, Otto Nuerath, and Ludwig Wittgenstein. Mises had instituted his circle in 1922 to succeed one started by Carl Menger in the nineteenth century and carried on by Eugen von Bohm-Bäwerk from 1905 until 1914. In addition to this circle, Schutz was involved in the Geistkreis, an interdisciplinary group founded by Herbert Furth and Friedrich Hayek that numbered as participants several members of the Mises Circle (but not Mises himself). This circle had been criticized for not including women, in contrast to the Mises Circle, which reckoned several women among its members (e.g., Stephanie Braun-Browne, Mariann von Herzfeld, Helen Lieser-Berger, Gertrus Lovasy, and Ilse Mintz-Schüller). In the Geistkreis, which was predominately oriented to the humanities and social sciences, Schutz presented papers entitled "The Meaning of the Opera," "Theory of Music," "Theory of Language," "The Joke" (two lectures), and "Graphology."[31]

In the Mises Circle, he expounded on such topics as Max Weber's methodology, the economic thought of Wieser and Sombart, Scheler's approach to the social sciences, the I and the Thou, group soul and group spirit, and understanding and acting. Members of the seminar included the economists

Stephanie Braun-Browne, Walter Froehlich, Gottfried von Haberler (later to teach at Harvard), Friedrich A. von Hayek, Helene Lieser (secretary of the International Economic Association, Paris), Fritz Machlup, Ilse Mintz (later of Columbia University and the National Bureau of Economic Research in New York), and Oskar Morgenstern (a Princeton professor) who anticipated contemporary game theory; the philosopher Felix Kaufman; the political scientist Eric Voegelin; the historian Friedrich Engel von Janosi; the Viennese lawyer Emanuel Winternitz (eventually curator of the Musical Instrument Collection of the Metropolitan Museum of Art in New York); and Paul Rosenstein-Rodan from the International Monetary Fund. The group met every two weeks on Friday at 7 p.m.; and, when it had completed its formal meeting at about 9:30 p.m., the members adjourned to an Italian restaurant known as the Green Anchor until about 11 p.m. Conversations went on after dinner in a nearby coffeehouse frequented by artists and university students. Machlup and Schutz would proceed to accompany Mises (who never left before 1 a.m.) to his home and then talk together until three or four in the morning.[32]

The group was not all business, since in the Schutz archive one can find copies of various drinking songs that the group intoned with such regularity that the words were written down. The titles of such songs included "The Whole and the Parts," "Pure Theory," "Understanding (*Verstehen*) and Marginal Utility," "The Marginal Utility School," "Discussion Mises-Mayer," "The Mises-Circle Song," "Economics in Paradise," "Departure of Professor Mises," and "Lamentation Song of the Circle." An excerpt from the "The Mises-Circle Song" is illustrative:

> Dear Children
> since today is Friday
> There is a Mises-Private Seminar.
> One speaks never so beautifully in Vienna (*Wien*)
> about the economy, society, and meaning (*Sinn*). . .
>
> Is the spirit at about ten o'clock of wisdom full (*voll*)?
> And does the stomach feel itself sad and empty (*leer*)?
> Soon it will receive its import duty (*Einführungszoll*),
> Since we are going to the Green Anchor (*Anker*).
>
> There gaiety is our motto (*Motto*)
> Among spaghetti and risotto (*Risotto*).
> How time passes, no one would have thought (*gedacht*)
> Since all of a sudden it is already midnight (*Mitternacht*),
> And yet comes the most genial idea (*Idee*),
> One can now still go to the artists' cafe (*Künstlerkafee*).[33]

One cannot overestimate the importance of the relationships formed and sustained within the Mises seminar for the future professional and personal lives of those involved. For example, Schutz, Kaufmann, Machlup, and Voegelin repeatedly encouraged each other and read and criticized each other's works, and Schutz once acknowledged that without Kaufmann he would not have been able to produce his major work, *Der sinnhafte Aufbau der sozialen Welt*. Kaufmann, in a glowing review, described this book as constituting a significant advance in the theory of understanding the Other (*Fremdverstehens*), a foundational problem for the human (including social) sciences, and said that it went beyond the results achieved by Dilthey, Lipps, Spranger, Scheler, and many others. In addition, after the *Anschluss* and the forced emigration of several circle members to the United States, they managed to keep each apprised of each other's fate and to act on each other's behalf in whatever way possible. In their relationships, they also addressed mundane issues, inquiring, for instance, about stocks or the recovery of goods confiscated in Europe. Later, at Schutz's instigation, members of the circle would be able to come to the financial assistance of Walter Froehlich, whose wife's hospitalization after a fall had exhausted all his hospital insurance.[34]

Schutz's relationship with Mises, in particular, remained significant throughout his life. Mises, as secretary for the Banking and Financial Department of the Viennese Chamber of Commerce, recommended Schutz for his first employment as secretary of a small bankers' organization. Schutz and Mises cooperated in assisting Viktor Stadler to emigrate from Austria, and Ilse Schutz thanked Mises for having intervened so "vehemently" to persuade her husband not to return to Austria after the *Anschluss*. Despite their friendship, Mises remained a private person, who, visiting Schutz's home only a few hours before Schutz's son was born on February 23, 1938, never mentioned to Ilse that he was to marry in a few days, even though at that time the marriage must have been completely planned. For his part, Schutz helped Mises emigrate by arranging his passage from Lisbon to the United States in 1940, notifying other circle members of his pending arrival, personally meeting him when his ship docked, and eventually serving as the sponsor for his naturalization. The Schutz and Mises families visited each other regularly, and personally Schutz always found his mentor brilliant and full of wit in repartee and conversation, especially in German. In Schutz's view, Mises was one of the best speakers he had ever known and an excellent, enthusiastic teacher, who could spark the interest even of those resistant to economics. In the end, Schutz felt that Mises was fully justified in feeling hurt that he had remained a dozent and had never been made a full professor, since Austrian law even before Hitler denied to any Jew full professorship (though Kelsen had achieved that academic rank through baptism).[35]

Schutz's relationship with Hans Kelsen lacked the intensity of his connection with Mises. When asked by Marvin Farber to review an article touching on legal theory for *Philosophy and Phenomenological Research*, Schutz did reminisce fondly about vigorous discussions with Felix Kaufmann and others in Kelsen's apartment in the early 1920s. However, upon reading Roscoe Pound's criticisms of Kelsen's pure theory of law, Schutz admitted to Farber that, although under Kelsen's influence earlier, he would have now sided more with Pound. Nevertheless, Schutz and Kelsen exchanged cordial letters when Schutz invited his mentor to review Pound's *Law and Social Control* and when Kelsen later appealed to Schutz for testimony on behalf of his naturalization process.[36]

Another important friend at this time was the Japanese scholar Tomoo Otaka, who had worked with Hans Kelsen and Edmund Husserl and who regularly visited Schutz's Vienna home. According to Ilse Schutz, Alfred helped Otaka with difficulties with the German language, and Otaka returned the favor by helping finance the publication of *Der sinnhafte Aufbau der sozialen Welt*, which Springer printed in 1932 along with Otaka's *Grundlegung der Lehre vom sozialen Verband*. Otaka had been motivated to write this book by the desire to protect the rationality of the state from irrational movements, to criticize justifications of the divine nature of Japanese emperors, and to advocate for the democractic values that, as shall be seen later, were dear to Schutz's own heart.[37]

Although this discussion of Schutz's education has focused on the persons and practices involved in his theoretical development, he never abandoned the aesthetic interests of his youth, particularly literature, music, and poetry. In an interview, Ilse, commenting on his continuing interest in literature, claimed that he was capable of quoting by heart Goethe, Shakespeare, Johann Nepomuk Nestroy, and Karl Kraus, and she described his written studies on Goethe. She further recalled his love for music:

> He played piano every night until about ten-thirty, when it was not allowed any more in order not to disturb the neighbors. We had a lot of chamber music in our house. He studied with them [those who came to play at Schutz's house] for a half a year trios and quartets; he had his violinist coming every Saturday afternoon, when they played violin sonatas, for eighteen years. I think he could have been without food all week long, but he couldn't have been without his Saturday afternoon violin sonatas. There was a flutist joining [them], who didn't do anything else but play the flute; my husband knew more about the flute literature than the flutist. And that happened with the cellist and others. He went to the library and copied scores[,] which were not even published. And then, after having practiced for

> half a year, we invited a lot of friends as guests, and gave a wonderful concert afternoon, with all of them performing.[38]

He coached various singers throughout the 1920s, evaluating their interpretations of scores, and he himself would have been able to become a polished pianist—his son George speculated years later—if his other activities would have allowed him the time.[39]

Moreover, Schutz continued writing poetry. Among his personal papers, one can find a volume of plays and poems dated February 10, 1925, that contain poems such as "Quaker Religious Service" and a long poem entitled "To A Friend." A lovely poem entitled "Venedig" (Venice), dated November 28, 1922, captures a melancholy about opportunities passed by. While a child might know nothing of such a melancholy, a young man deepened by experiences of war and facing the self-limiting choices of career and future lifestyle (marriage) would be keenly aware of it. Schutz wrote:

> And so it is with all things
> Which meet us on our way:
> We think to grasp them, them to gain
> And yet they are still so far off . . . and everything is illusion
> And we, we glide by.
>
> And it is always: On our way
> One time someone comes, a man comes before us
> Perhaps he could be. . . . And yet we are sad.
> And we remain alone on our way
> And we glide and glide by.[40]

Schutz's lifelong familiarity with different forms of literature, poetry, drama, and the novel became evident years later when in 1955 he delivered a lecture entitled "Sociological Aspect of Literature," which addressed the sociological relations between reader and author in all these literary forms.[41]

Winternitz, in an essay in a memorial volume honoring Schutz, summarizes how important art was for him, beginning with their first encounter in the standing room section high up under the roof of the Vienna Opera House, each clutching his score of *The Abduction from the Seraglio*. In addition to possessing a comprehensive knowledge of French and German literature, Schutz, according to Winternitz, could become ecstatic before Giovanni Bellini's *Pietá* or Rembrandt's *Jewish Bride*. When it came to his deepest love, music, he was thoroughly familiar with the theory and history of music, and his interests extended from Pachelbel to Heinrich Schütz to Alban Berg's *Wozzeck*. Winternitz continues:

> He knew by heart J. S. Bach's Passions, most of his Cantatas and the Goldberg Variations; he was equally at home with Mozart's Masses and operas and the chamber music of Brahms. One of his special idols was Gluck; he knew every page of the standard treatises by Spitta, Schweizer, Chrysander, Jahn-Abert, and Thayer. He played the piano with little technique, but the form and emotional content were magically conjured up by his enthusiasm. We played four-hand music throughout all the years of our friendship, and though we often squabbled over Brahms's triplets or Bruckner's hemioles, his shining face and radiant pleasure and our ensuing arguments belong to my dearest memories. We often discussed the experience provided by music, and analyzed the nature of flow, succession and time and their relationship to Bergson's *durée*, and the musical structure as a model of the role and function of memory as creator of form and flux.[42]

While later discussions will examine how Schutz intellectually engaged his mentors, it is important to consider his employment. According to Ilse, two months before his final law examination he was hired, with Mises's intervention, as executive secretary in the Association of Austrian Middle Banks. Schutz himself recorded in his various curricula vitae that in this position at the service of thirty-seven Austrian banks between 1921 and 1927, he acquired a general knowledge of the legal, financial, economic, and tax problems in Austria and the Central European countries. In that same time period, as a member of several committees, he counseled the Austrian government on pending legislation. In addition, he participated in negotiations relating to the formation of the Austrian national bank, to currency reform in Austria, and to the League of Nations loan to Austria, secured by Seipel.[43]

In 1927, he was named executive officer of Reitler and Company, one of the leading Viennese private banking firms with international business relations. Reitler introduced Austrian shares at foreign stock exchanges; arranged and underwrote international loans for Austrian provinces, communities, and industries; financed exports and imports; and managed investments. At Reitler, Schutz supervised sixty people under Robert Lambert's supervision and gained a solid grasp of the legislation, economic situations, and industrial problems of Hungary, Czechoslovakia, Germany, France, Luxembourg, Switzerland, and Holland. Splitting his time from 1931 onward between Vienna and Paris, he served on boards of international corporations, including the Societé de Pétroles Silva Plana, S.A., and reorganized the international brewery interests of R. Gaston, Dreyfus & Cie, and Heineken of Amsterdam in French, British, and Dutch colonies and Egypt and Palestine. In 1937, he visited the United States and Canada on business for several months and left a diary to be considered later. After the *Anschluss*, he continued working in Paris for R. Gaston-Dreyfus &

Cie, S.A., and he later joined with Emil Reitler, Lambert, and Paul Jeral in the United States as they financially advised former clients, pursued real estate interests, and undertook new industrial ventures in the United States, Canada, and Mexico. After the war, Schutz frequently traveled to Europe to reestablish old contacts and to attend to business interests. He was not only constantly busy, but his work was of the highest quality, as Emil Reitler testified in an affidavit for his 1943 civil service application. Reitler wrote: "Schutz has been employed for over seventeen years in various organizations under my and my associates' control in Austria and France, and since 1939 in the United States. He has always held executive positions of responsibility and enjoyed the full confidence of my associates and myself."[44]

This account of Schutz's employment is from an objective viewpoint, based on public, official documents, but his subjective experience of this employment is revealed in his personal papers, especially letters to and from his wife. In the mid-1930s, Schutz found himself quite angry when, for instance, Robert Lambert demanded that he assume the company responsibilities at which others had failed. Lambert himself was a moody person, and Schutz dreaded business trips with him, often feeling discouraged in his dealings with him. Moreover, Lambert often sent him on unexpected trips, frustrating his expectations to spend time with his family or attend to academic duties. In addition, there were repeated conflicts with Lambert over salary, and Schutz often would prepare himself for salary discussions by poring over his figures with Ilse. When Lambert experienced difficulties arranging his passport and delayed his return to France in 1939, Schutz wrote Ilse, "I'm glad that at least in this respect we made ourselves independent of him." Ilse felt that Lambert took great advantage of her husband, and so she pressed Alfred to insist on his full vacation time so that they could plan vacations together. At one point, Paul Jeral confirmed for Ilse how Lambert mistreated Alfred. He admitted that time and time again he had cautioned Lambert about asking the impossible of Schutz; one day Lambert expected Schutz to use his own initiative and the next to be his mouthpiece. It comes as no surprise that Ilse in an interview much later would summarize in an understatement that Alfred "certainly did not love his other [nonacademic] profession." In spite of all these difficulties with Lambert, Schutz displayed great magnanimity in allowing Lambert to appoint him guardian of Lambert's illegitimate daughter, whom he would visit regularly.[45]

Marriage and the Founding of a Family

Ilse Heim was born February 10, 1902, to Leopold Heim of Zagreb, Yugoslavia, and Gisella Heim, born Frankl, in Vienna. Her father, who supplied the railway with lumber, moved his family to Sarajevo two years later, during the construction of the transcontinental railway system. Ilse's parents sent their daughter to a nunnery school and even hired a tutor so that she and her younger brother Eric would learn German. When Archduke Francis Ferdinand was assassinated in Sarajevo, the Heims returned to Vienna, where Ilse enrolled in a *Mädchen Realgymnasium,* since girls could not attend the boys' gymnasium. In spite of her shyness, she did well at school, took piano lessons at a private institute, and developed an interest in the history of art that she would later pursue at the University of Vienna. Ilse's memories of her youth included hunger demonstrations during wartime and summer vacations in resort towns, where boys and girls—about ten to a group at a time—played tennis, bicycled, or climbed mountains. She had even dreamed that she would meet her future husband on top of a mountain, with him ascending from one side and she from the other.[46]

In July 1920, she *did* meet her future husband on a mountain, when he, who had climbed the mountain—but on the same side as her group—joined her group to search for a lost wristwatch. Ilse was formally introduced to Alfred Schutz, who fell in love with her at first sight, but she feared that he might be too serious too soon and later confessed that "no fire was burning in me, even for years." Their courtship, though, continued for years, with them meeting infrequently. Ilse sometimes refused to meet with him until a week after he had asked to see her, and she often marveled at his patience, "because he usually was very spoiled." In Alfred's personal papers, there are signs of his persistence in numerous small envelopes containing his calling card with messages inscribed on the back. At times, though, Alfred grew weary of trying, and he expressed this weariness on an undated newspaper editorial that praised the greatness of a will committed to moral living beyond mere conventionality. He wrote, "I believe I won't marry Ilse. Why, were you not up to your ears in love? I was, but finally one gets fed up, hearing only 'no,' when one makes a proposal to her." However, in 1923, they met again with others on vacation in the Swiss Alps, and the following summer they met in Aussee; and from then on their letters took on a decidedly intimate tone. Alfred commented, "I begin to test all my relations to things and people, profession, books, my spiritual direction, art, friends, women, prospects, meanings, truths, half-truths, and I order them anew." He added, "I want to tidy up much rubble, to throw away much ballast, to free myself from superficial bonds of a personal and material type, in order to be free and light and ready for you." Not surprisingly, they were engaged in 1924.[47]

Ilse and Alfred finally married on March 28, 1926. For the occasion, Winternitz composed a romantic poem entitled "Poem with a Hyacinth Dedicated to the Schutz Married Couple." Alfred, too, partook of the romanticism of the moment, writing from his office to thank Ilse for their beautiful days at Aussee (on a delayed honeymoon or merely summer vacation) and to wonder what they had done to deserve such happiness. The intensity of their affection rendered the anonymity of everyday bourgeois life, criticized by the authors and artists of their time, all the more difficult to bear. To these sentiments, Alfred's letter gave voice: "And now I sit in this horrible (*grauslichen*) office in a horrible city and among horrible workers and I think of you, dear loved one, and the beautiful atmosphere that you know how to create."[48]

The honeymoon never seemed to end, since the couple was able to sustain a high level of expressiveness throughout their marriage. Ilse observed about Alfred:

> He could love so deeply as few other human beings could love. But not only in his heart and soul, he could also say it and express it in words, what [*sic*] I rarely could. There was rarely a day when he didn't tell me I was the only woman he ever could live with. For him I was high on a pedestal from the beginning to the end. His last words before he died were: "Even now you are wonderful."[49]

Every birthday and every wedding anniversary day, he sent flowers and a card on which he would write "Behalt mich lieb," the expression that was inscribed on her engagement ring and that she translated as "Keep loving me." Nine years later, after meeting a colleague cheating on his wife, he would write her, "I thank the dear God every day that it is so pure and clear among us, that we can allow ourselves [to be together] without boring each other and to love without hurting each other."[50]

After Ilse informed him that she was pregnant the first time, he wrote her a letter in which he deliberately embraced responsibility for his marriage and family, revealing clearly his own personal relevance-ranking:

> The only content, the only totally clear and fulfilled hope of my life is our relationship—our child I include in this concept "our marriage." I have experienced many illusions in life . . . I have never experienced people to be as superfluous or as unsatisfying as I do now. I do not like my profession, as you know. Voegelin's book, the last theory of Kaufmann, the difficult (*schlechte*) book of Mises, and the heavy tome of Otaka with which I am occupied—all this has convinced me of the disvalue of such activity. I once thought of being a poet, another time a musician. I recognized these as illusions. Today I see wholly clearly and even peacefully that my scientific talent (*Begabung*) is *no* illusion. But also, that it, under the prevailing circumstances—at least then, if not generally—is meaningless, that is, to want to work scientifically, be it through lectures or publications. When I have completed these [book] reviews, I will cease work on these areas. You and the child will no more regularly be

> confined to Sundays and holidays. I will study and think more systematically and intensively than before but without any goal orientation (e.g., publication). I want to divide up my week with a measured number of hours to be reserved for study—help me with this. I'd like to spend some measured time on music. You and the child will stand in the center; your needs will take precedence over mine, over all my projects under all circumstances. Help me to realize these plans.[51]

And give generously to their relationship Alfred did. They vacationed together to enjoy their mutual love of nature, mountains, and hiking; they regularly took excursions together on Sundays; and they socialized with the music group and members of the Mises Circle. Ilse showed herself continually appreciative of the fact that because of his responsibility for his family he continued working for the likes of Lambert and was unable to devote his life solely to philosophy and sociology.[52]

By the same token, Ilse proved herself utterly generous. She discontinued work on her own dissertation to help him with his work, and she took the dictation of all his papers, at least until the invention of tape recorders, one of the first of which she gave him as a birthday present. Over a period of twelve years, he dictated the entire *Der sinnhafte Aufbau der sozialen Welt* five or six times to her; she recorded it in shorthand, returned it to him for revisions, and retyped it. In addition, she patiently endured the many difficulties that any married couple face, such as, for instance, the fact that they had to live the first four years of their marriage with his parents until they obtained their first apartment in 1930. The *great* inconvenience in their marriage, though, had to do with his frequent absence from home because of business trips. On the basis of his letters, which indicate his absence from home, one can conclude that he was gone during (at least parts of) July 1929; October and November 1931; June and August 1932; September 1933; January and May 1934; and February, May, June, July, August, October, and November 1935. In 1936, he was on trips in April, June, July, August, September, and December; and in 1937 he took his already mentioned business trip to the United States from March 18 until May 12. In 1938, the year of the *Anschluss*, Schutz was apart from his wife, in what must have been an excruciating time, from early March (the *Anschluss* occurred on March 13) until June 12, when Ilse and the children arrived in Paris. He was also impelled to travel on business in July, August, September, and October 1938; and in May 1939, it was she who journeyed to the United States to prepare for their emigration there. In Alfred's absence, Ilse filled her life with various familial and cultural activities, from playing with the children to reading Dostoyevski. In brief, Ilse showed herself as generous as Alfred in taking responsibility for their marriage and in reacting with strength and creativity to its inescapable diminishments, absences, and dissatisfactions. It is not shocking then, that she could sum up her relationship with Alfred in an interview twenty-two years after his death: "Our personal relationship was always a wonderful one, I had a very wonderful marriage, from the first minute to the last . . . "[53]

Chapter 2

Social Science and Philosophy (1919–38): Weber and Bergson

Having discussed the personal details of Schutz's youth, education, employment, and marriage, we will now turn to the philosophy he developed from 1919 to 1938. This chapter will discuss the first phase of his philosophical development: his encounter with the thought of Max Weber, which he sought to found philosophically on the basis of Henri Bergson's philosophy, rather than on positivistic or Neo-Kantian alternatives. In the second phase, which began in 1928 and will be discussed in the next chapter, he replaced his Bergsonian base with Edmund Husserl's phenomenology, which equipped him to engage critically the thought of his Viennese mentors, Mises and Kelsen. Perhaps no problem is more significant for his philosophy than that of understanding the Other (*Fremdverstehens*), a thematic that lies at the basis of the social sciences and that Schutz's phenomenology significantly advanced, according to Kaufmann. His concern about understanding others and its limits is not surprising, given his interest in the social sciences and his wide experience. That experience allowed him to understand the misinterpretations characteristic of Austro-Hungarian ethnicities and of an employer indifferent to his family or academic life, as well as to the mutual attunement that typified his own marriage and friendships. At the same time, aware of the sometimes irreconcilable differences in group value-schemes and dedicated to the value-freedom of his social scientific mentors (Weber, Mises, Kelsen), Schutz avoided articulating a theoretical ethics, though he lived an exemplary moral life and though this omission would evoke criticism from Gurwitsch and Voegelin. These two themes, then, will be focal in the exposition of his thought: intersubjective understanding and ethics.

Schutz and Max Weber

In his autobiographical comments, "Husserl and His Influence on Me," Schutz admitted that from his early days at the University of Vienna he sought to provide philosophical foundations for the social sciences, particularly Max

Weber's sociology. Weber, who had lectured at the university in the summer of 1918, during which he befriended Mises, was so influential that Fritz Machlup acknowledged that he had read Weber's works over and over even before meeting Schutz. Schutz confessed that he too was "under the spell of Max Weber's work, especially of his methodological writings." Besides lecturing on Weber before the Mises Circle and defending him in book reviews against Mises and Otaka, Schutz effusively praised Weber in his *Phenomenology of the Social World* (henceforth *Phenomenology*) for having determined conclusively the proper starting point of the philosophy of the social sciences. He had done this by recognizing the importance of intended meaning and thereby taking a step beyond the Southwestern German Neo-Kantianism in which he had been educated. Near the end of his *Phenomenology*, Schutz reiterated that "the tremendous significance for all the social sciences of Weber's achievement cannot be sufficiently stressed." In a letter accompanying his book sent to Marianne Weber, Max's widow, on April 27, 1932, he informed her that he had spent twelve years intensively occupied with her husband's work and that he hoped that his book would promote the wider development of the much-misunderstood *verstehender* sociology. The book sought to show the convergence of Weber's basic thoughts with the sound results of the most recent epistemological criticism (no doubt, phenomenology). Schutz must have been delighted when Mrs. Weber immediately responded that she wished Max were still living to be able to thank him.[1]

In his "Preliminary Survey of the Problem" at the outset of the *Phenomenology*, the first thing that Schutz praises Weber for is his insistence that "the social sciences must abstain from value judgments." Weber himself warns that when historians, for instance, begin to evaluate, their causal analysis suffers; they "explain" an actor's action as the result of a "mistake" or "decline" when it results from an ideal simply different from their own, and thus they fail in their most important task, "understanding." Not only does the interjection of values in the social sciences lead to possible misunderstanding, it also confuses the sphere of empirical science with philosophy. Empirical science can never tell anyone what he or she *should* do, since the most such science can demonstrate is the indispensable means to achieve an end and the practical consequences of choosing one course of action over another. Philosophical disciplines, Weber mentions, may be able to lay bare the meaning of evaluations and indicate their place within a totality of possible evaluations; however, when it comes to what one "ought" to do, no rational or empirical scientific procedure can provide one with a decision. Weber, it appears, denies to philosophy the capacity even to justify ends, limiting its purpose to value-clarification. As he states it, "Only on the assumption of belief in the validity of values is the attempt to espouse value-judgments meaningful. However, to *judge* the *validity* of such values is a matter of *faith*." Weber does grant, however, that the problems selected from reality for investigation are "relevant to values" in the sense that values govern the selection and formulation of the objects of empirical inquiry.[2]

Weber's effort to exclude value-judgments from the empirical sciences derives from a conviction that plays a central role in much of his thought—namely, that various spheres of human activity and scientific knowledge are separate and autonomous. For example, in "Politics as a Vocation," Weber is fascinated with the dilemmas faced when *wertrationale* individuals, who attempt to realize an absolute value without any concern for foreseeable consequences, enter the political domain with its means-end, consequence-driven imperatives. Such persons can renounce political action (and fail to realize their values in the world), or embrace political processes, knowing that they can often achieve good ends "only at the price of morally dubious or at least dangerous means and the possibility, or even the probability[,] of evil side effects." Because of the autonomy of different spheres, Weber opposes simple reductionism and affirms, for instance, that religion and economics mutually influence each other. Weber's belief in distinctive spheres of activity also appears in his frequent discussion of the unpredictable consequences, as, for instance, when the Protestant ethic plays its role in the birth of capitalism, which in turn unleashes an acquisitiveness and competition that undermine religion. Similarly, Weber cautions economic theorists about venturing beyond the boundaries of their science to predict how people will act, since he never believed that "life is in fact dominated by rational considerations" or that the regions of science and real life are easily harmonized. Furthermore, when one moves out of the realm of ideas, one must always ask the question of what is practicable—whether liberalism could be realized in tsarist Russia, for example, or whether socialism could ever be implemented in the West.[3]

Schutz approved of Weber's methodological individualism that resisted Marxian ideal constructs of necessarily unrolling developmental sequences, which were subject to "an almost irresistible temptation to do violence to reality in order to prove the real validity of the construct." To concentrate on the intended meanings of individuals, the focus of his methodology, Weber developed his famous ideal type, described as a mental construct (*Gedankenbild*) formed by one-sided accentuation of one or more points of view and synthesizing a great many diffuse, concrete individual phenomena. Such types took account of the subjective viewpoint of actors, asking, for instance, "How *would* men act if they were being ideally rational in pursuit of purely economic goals?" And such constructs of rational action were able to illuminate how nonrational motivations functioned. As a consequence, Weber exclaimed, "The more sharply and clearly constructed the ideal types are—in other words, the more *unrealistic* they are in this sense—the better they perform their function, which is terminological and classificatory as well as heuristic."[4]

In addition to describing how types were formed, Weber also demanded that social scientists criticize their types, especially by distinguishing their objective or outsider view from the subjective or insider one of the actor, whose actions they were seeking to understand. For instance, in the essay "The Concept of 'Following a Rule,'" Weber described two people of different cultural backgrounds "exchanging" objects in the wilderness but cautioned against the sociologist stipulating "that the two men wanted to 'regulate' their reciprocal relationship in a manner conforming to the ideal 'concept' of 'exchange.'" Such an interpretation from the observer's point of view without evidence of the actors' subjective viewpoint would no more correspond to the meanings of the actors than if one were to say that the dogs barked because they wanted to realize the idea of protecting property. In addition, Weber developed methods for testing the adequacy of ideal types, utilizing examples from history and the study of comparative religion.[5]

In summary, the very method of ideal type construction of intended meanings distinguished the social sciences from the natural, since "we do not 'understand' the behavior of, say, cells." But, since the social sciences were required to validate their ideal-typical constructs by demonstrating their adequacy, the social scientists could remain "scientific." W. G. Runciman's recapitulation of Weber's approach to the social sciences converges with Schutz's in his "Concept and Theory Formation in the Social Sciences": "The distinctiveness of Weber's contribution lies chiefly in his reluctance to accept either that there is, after all, no difference between natural and social science or that the difference is such as seriously to undermine the unity of scientific method."[6]

Though positively assessing Weber's thought, Schutz repeatedly emphasized that it rested on unexamined philosophical presuppositions—a conclusion with which Mrs. Weber's biography of her husband concurred by acknowledging that he often lost interest in more fundamental, epistemological problems that seemed to afford no help in resolving his sociological problems. In his "Preliminary Survey of the Problem," the first section of the *Phenomenology*, Schutz faulted Weber for taking these problems for granted and for conflating the meaning structures of everyday, prescientific experience with those of social scientists observing and interpreting that social world. With few exceptions, sociologists, who selected aspects of this social world for investigating, neglected the basic structures of meaning-establishment and understanding that had to be clarified in terms of consciousness and intersubjective relationships. Schutz's own dismantling of higher-level meaning structures arrived at a fundament—inner time-consciousness, the deepest stratum of experience accessible to reflection and explicable through Bergson's account of *durée* and Husserl's of time-consciousness. As he commented pithily, "The problem of meaning is a problem of time."[7]

Schutz's critique of Weber unfolds in three separate areas of the *Phenomenology* and on three different sets of questions, all having to do with the problem of intersubjective understanding: (1) meaningful action and understanding the behavior of others, (2) social action and social relationship, and (3) problems in interpretive sociology.

After showing in chapter 1 of his *Phenomenology* how Weber selects rationally purposeful behavior as the archetype of meaningful action, instead of rationally value-oriented, emotional, and traditional alternatives, Schutz objects that Weber confuses the meaning of an action with its motive. He clarifies this terse comment by insisting that as soon as one identifies a behavior as purposive, value-oriented, emotional, or traditional, one has *already* isolated it from the flux of experience and, by this very turning of one's attention to it, one confers a meaning on it. After elucidating this basic level of meaning having to do with internal time-consciousness and reflection upon it—a basic level of meaning to which Weber does not attend—he separates experiences of nonmeaning-endowing, primordial *passivity* from meaning-endowing *active* behavior, which involves both spontaneous, reactive behavior (*Verhalten*) and planned action (*Handlung*).[8]

Schutz then shows how Weber misunderstands another's planned action through his distinction between observational understanding, by which one directly observes the subjective meaning of another's act, and motivational understanding, in which one grasps the motive of the actor by placing the act in an intelligible, more inclusive meaning-context. As an example of observational understanding, Weber points to the observational comprehension of the action of one who reaches for a doorknob to shut a door. But Schutz objects that the subjective meaning of the actor is not as easily given as Weber supposes. He wonders whether the man holding the doorknob is grasping it in order to shut the door or is merely holding it in order to repair it. In effect Weber is not merely observing what is given but already *interpreting* the action, and he introduces motivational understanding into his observational understanding insofar as he claims that the person grasps the doorknob *in order to* shut the door. Just as Weber overlooked the interpretive meaning-giving involved in selecting out an experience from the flux of consciousness, so here he fails to be cognizant of his own interpretive activity. Furthermore, insofar as Weber neglects his own interpreting activity, he also conflates his objective, observer's standpoint with that of the actor, who may not be reaching for the knob to shut the door as the observer supposes, even though Weber had admonished against just such a conflation elsewhere.[9]

To shore up the distinction between the objective, observer's meaning and the subjective, actor's meaning, Schutz turns to Husserl, who battled psychologism in his *Logical Investigations* precisely by disjoining objective meanings (propositional contents) from subjective meaning (acts grasping the contents). However, since intersubjective understanding involves not so much grasping propositional contents as the intended meaning of an actor, Schutz finds a more promising framework in Husserl's *Formal and Transcendental Logic*, which presents two possibilities for interpreting another's meanings, the first of which takes such meanings as complete and already constituted. In such an approach, however, one leaves out of awareness the second—that is, the intentional operations of the consciousness that constituted these meanings. Were one to turn to these operations, one would discover an emerging world (of meaning), now and ever being constituted anew in the stream of another's enduring ego. Objective meaning here would refer to phenomena indicating another consciousness but prescinding from the constituting processes within the living consciousness of another, i.e., the subjective meaning. As part of seeking out the subjective meaning of action, one would need to determine the other's overarching project, already phantasied in the future perfect tense and guiding its subactions. In brief, the present action cannot be understood apart from its more encompassing temporal dimensions, and temporality is once again of the essence for understanding the other's subjective meaning. However, since such encompassing temporal dimensions would include the whole of the other's flux of experience, never to be completely repeated or understood, one must settle for an understanding of the other's subjective meaning that would be only *adequate* for one's purposes.[10]

In chapter 4, Schutz returns to Weber to take up his depiction of social action and social relationship. Schutz criticizes Weber for including under social action either (a future-oriented) action affecting the other or an action that is affected by another's (past) action, each of which takes place within a different temporal framework. Also, as a result of speaking of future-oriented social action with reference to another's past action, Weber introduces the strange possibility that one could orient one's social action to the past action of another, which, as completed, one could never hope to affect. But there is a further problem, even if one emphasizes that one's social action is only *affected* by the other's past action. As Schutz puts it succinctly, "[S]urely what makes my action social is not that its *activating stimulus* was someone else's behavior as opposed to a natural event. What makes my behavior social is the fact that its intentional object is the expected behavior of another person." Further, Weber's conception of social relationships as consisting of two people reciprocally oriented toward each other breaks down into the subquestions of whether a relationship or a probability of interaction exists—questions that for Schutz will be answered differently depending on whether one adopts the viewpoint of observer or actor.[11]

In the final chapter of his *Phenomenology*, he tries to illustrate the payoff for his phenomenological reading of Weber in terms of the problems facing the *verstehenden* sociology. He explains how the types constructed by life-world actors to understand their Contemporaries, Predecessors, and Successors anticipate the social-scientific ideal types of the social scientists whose task is to construct an objective, observer's meaning-context out of the subjective meaning-contexts of everyday actors. While one can test a personal ideal type by seeing if the other defies one's predictions, one can also check social-scientific types for their causal or meaning adequacy, that is, ask if they are consistent with one's own past experience or with the sum of one's experience of the actor.[12]

In a penultimate section Schutz tries to mediate between Max Weber and his mentors Mises and Kelsen, with the focus on Mises. He argues, for instance, against Mises that Weber's later types in *Economy and Society* attain a level of formalization, generalization, and universal validity that could account for decisive elements motivating economic activity within a market economy in a way not all that different from Mises's own work. In fact, Mises's own examples of the economic principle, the basic laws of price formation, and so forth, could be conceived as ideal types in Schutz's and the later Weber's sense; indeed, one could conceive all the social sciences as type-constructing.[13]

In conclusion, Schutz shared Weber's notion of value-freedom in social science, based on the autonomy of the domains of science and philosophy; and, as we shall see later, he even concurred with Weber's denial that philosophical ethics could provide rational justifications for ends. In addition, Schutz approved of Weber's use of ideal types, his distinction between subjective and objective viewpoints, and the test of adequacy to ensure that the distinctive viewpoint of the actor, as opposed to that of the observer, was taken into account. However, Schutz also brought to Weber a philosophical heritage based on intentionality and time analyses, and he insisted that Weber be sufficiently attentive to his own hidden interpretive activity regarding his experience and understanding of others and that he articulate clearly the concepts of social action and relationship. For Schutz, his Weberian and philosophical inheritances became labile tools for coming to terms with the philosophical problems of the social sciences, particularly intersubjective understanding. Let us now turn to the first philosopher to whom he turned in his endeavor to find a philosophical foundation for Weberian sociology: Henri Bergson.

From Bergson to Husserl

In "Husserl and His Influence on Me," Schutz says he felt himself dissatisfied with Weber's understanding of "the subjective meaning a social action has for the actor" as well as with Kelsen's attempt to explain this subjective meaning philosophically via Neo-Kantian authors such as Cohen, Natorp, or Cassirer. Things changed, however, when, through Eric Voegelin's mediation, he encountered Bergson's philosophy, which

> impressed me, however, deeply. I was convinced that his analysis of the structure of consciousness and especially of inner time could be used as a starting point for an interpretation of the unclarified basic notions of the social sciences, such as meaning, action, expectation, and first of all intersubjectivity.[14]

Between 1925 and 1927, he worked out the Bergsonian philosophical foundations of the social sciences, principally in the essay "Lebensformen und Sinnstruktur," which Helmut Wagner translated, published, and adapted to an American audience as "Life Forms and Meaning Structure."[15]

From the beginning, Schutz is very clear about the purpose of his investigations, "the grounding of the social sciences in the Thou experience." He strives to delve beneath the social sciences, bent as they should be on conceptual-categorical comprehension, the "highest and most powerful life form," to a level of experience that precedes, conditions, and makes possible such comprehension. If, however, one "bows to the primacy of conceptual thinking," as did the positivists and Neo-Kantians, one cannot gain access to this prescientific sphere of experience and the unity of consciousness, which lose their particular character when subjected to conceptual formulation and which neither science challenges nor experience refutes. To pinpoint this prescientific level, Schutz contrasts "the feeling of life," given in lived experience, as one breathes in and out without reflecting on it, and higher-level empirical, conceptual explanations of the physiology, biology, or psychology of such lived experiences. Of course, in this endeavor to reach behind intellection to capture what precedes it, one must inevitably make use of a kind of philosophical intellection—a predicament of which Schutz was quite conscious, as we shall see.[16]

He begins describing the unity in this prescientific domain of the indivisible "I," experiencing its ongoing unfolding as a continuous and ever-changing awareness of quality experiences flowing inseparably and indivisibly into each other. This experience involves no reflective grasping of something having passed away, and one is, as it were, immersed in a continuing melody. However, even to grasp that one is carried along in a streaming consciousness, or duration, one must be looking backward from a "now" point to an earlier "before," which is held in memory; and, as a result, one is fixating a point in inner experience instead of flowing with it. To explain, he reverts again to a musical example, "I will have to have noticed the second-last tone of the melody in order to know whether the tone sounding now is higher, lower, stronger, weaker, or of different timbre—in short, whether it is different from its predecessor." Memory thus arrests duration's flow and turns its continuum into a manifold of distinct components, and, therefore, memory cannot be identified with pure duration. Rather it reveals a new stance toward the world (and the self), a new "life form," of I-consciousness. In fact, the memory image—e.g., of the second-to-last tone, which has already ceased sounding—differs from the apperceptive (or quality) image of that tone as it was lived. The memory image actually stands for that apperceptive image, as a symbol.[17]

The difficulty, of course, is that "the sphere of pure, simple, and symbol-free duration remains inaccessible to our symbol-conditioned thinking" of memory:

> This [the mutual founding of memory and duration] is not a fault because it merely contains the admission that *pure duration* can only be deduced with the help of the symbol system of the more complex life form (memory): it is impossible immediately to *experience* duration, even by intuition. . . . I do not intend to assert the impossibility of pure duration without memory (so, the duration of plants) but only the impossibility of experiencing *immediately* in the sense of "evidence." This merely means that evidence (as "Being-Thus" experience of a "Now and Thus") can only appear in a least complex symbol sphere which can occur in memory. Pure duration is a necessarily marginal concept, an unexecutable postulate, like its counterpart immortality. Thus in this investigation, I can only speak of a "relative approximation of duration." The reason for this is the necessity to assume the existence of a symbol-free life below memory combined with the impossibility to reach below memory.[18]

But this passage raises another question: how do we know *at all* that there even *is* a symbol-free duration, since any knowing of duration would seem to assume it already within the domain of memory, which betrays or conceals its true character?[19]

Before considering this paradox, it is important to spell out Schutz's overall position. Besides duration and memory, he separates out four other life-forms: the I as acting, Thou-related, speaking, and thinking. Although his delineation of these multiple life-forms improves upon the dualisms of Kant (sensibility and understanding) and Bergson (duration and memory), as Ilja Srubar has pointed out, Schutz refuses to claim that his enumeration of life-forms is exhaustive. Further, he repeatedly insists that, from within his own thinking life-form, he has only differentiated these ideal-types of life-forms by a process of artificial abstraction and reconstruction, since one lives in all life-forms simultaneously. It should be noted that the 1925–27 manuscript "Life-Forms and Meaning Structure" develops the life-forms of duration, memory, and the acting I, while the essay "Meaning Structures of Language," drafted earlier, in 1925, treats sketchily the other three life-forms.[20]

Schutz not only distills out these life-forms, but also reflects on their status, affirming that "inner duration," "memory," "somatic feeling," and "consociates" really amount to fundamental presuppositions of experience such that it would be impossible to conceive experience without them. One could neither imagine experience without temporality, a before preceding a now, nor conceive of grasping a thing as objective, without the idealization that a Thou would see that thing in the same way if the Thou were in one's position. Schutz thinks that he, like Scheler and Heidegger, has discovered "A priorities of experience" that constitute the conditions of cognition itself. He is also self-reflective when he recognizes the paradox of duration and concludes that his book is paradoxical, since it is "in conflict with its material" insofar as its language and concepts deal with experiences beyond language and concepts. Schutz, though, sees clearly that "we will never succeed in breaking through the cover of language and concept" and settles for trying to "irradiate" the symbolic cover, resorting to something like what he would later call "indirect communication." However, must not this irradiation still presuppose some access to pure duration in the light of which one would be able to understand how symbolism falls short of what it symbolizes? For this reason, Helmut Wagner is correct to claim that pure duration begins to appear like a kind of Kantian *Ding-an-sich*.[21]

In addition, Schutz keeps in reflective focus the artificially constructed nature of the ideal types of life-forms whose multiplicity, differentiated by philosophical reflection, ought not disturb the unity of the I that lives in all the life-forms simultaneously. Although later he never abandons this typically Bergsonian distinction between lived experience and reflection, he never again presents the I as a unity of life-forms differentiated through an ideal-typical methodology. According to Wagner, the problem was that Schutz attempted to describe duration, which is not given in empirical evidence, through a Weberian ideal-typical methodology, whose results would have to be empirically validated. Although a different methodology was called for, the real problem was that the ideal-typical methodology rigidly isolated duration from memory, neglecting how a string of retentions linked duration with reflective memory, as Husserlian phenomenology would disclose and as we shall see in the next chapter.[22]

Schutz never dispenses with the notion of Bergsonian duration in his *Phenomenology*, even though he opts for Husserl's more disciplined account of how one gains access to it. In order to elucidate his continuing attachment to this idea, it is important to appreciate its role in intersubjective understanding, since after all the entire purpose of his Bergson writings aims at "the grounding of the social sciences in the Thou experience." One easily loses sight of this overall purpose, since he only gets around to dealing with the

Thou relationship briefly in the second (actually earlier) essay of *Life Forms and Meaning Structure*, "Meaning Structures of Language." Moreover, in the Bergson essays, he does not touch much at all on the relationship between his foundation and the social sciences, even though he intended to eventually. Consciousness seems to be such a dominant theme that one can mistakenly characterize his position as an egology that attempts to deal with issues of consciousness without reference to spheres of interaction and intersubjectivity, as if such spheres were an afterthought (as Wagner at times suggests). In fact, however, it is possible to read his discussions of duration in the light of his accounts of intersubjective interpretation. In that light, it could well be that his concern for problems of intersubjective interpretation, in line with his overriding purpose to found the social sciences, influences his preference for the Bergsonian idea of duration, as much as duration informs his accounts of intersubjective interpretation. The fact that his earlier essay "Meaning Structures of Language" deals with the Thou relationship and language before he ever addresses conscious *durée* in the later "Life Forms and Meaning Structure" supports the position that he approaches subjectivity through the lens of intersubjectivity.[23]

This way of reading Schutz can be further substantiated if one turns to a crucial turning point in his *Phenomenology:* when he takes up in chapter 3 the question of the possibility of intersubjective understanding after the second chapter's treatment of the stream of consciousness. He writes:

> The postulate, therefore, that I can observe the subjective experience of another person precisely as he does is absurd. For it presupposes that I myself have lived through all the conscious states and intentional Acts wherein this experience has been constituted. But this could only happen within my own experience and in my own Acts of attention to my experience. And this experience of mine would then have to duplicate his experience down to the smallest details, including impressions, their surrounding areas of protention and retention, reflective Acts, phantasies, etc. But there is more to come: I should have to be able to remember all his experiences and therefore should have had to live through these experiences in the same order that he did; and finally I should have had to give them exactly the same degree of attention that he did. In short, my stream of consciousness would have to coincide with the other person's, which is the same as saying that I should have to *be* the other person. This point was made by Bergson in his *Time and Free Will.*[24]

Although moments of interpersonal interaction are underarticulated in the unfinished "Life Forms and Meaning Structures," the structure of his argumentation above suggests that one *first* experiences gaps and limits in interpersonal understanding, which one can *subsequently* explain through Bergson's duration. Similarly, in the earlier Bergson manuscripts, after introducing the Thou and language, Schutz describes how the understanding between two interlocutors, though they comprehend common meanings sufficiently for practical purposes, "remains an approximation between subjective and objective meaning, between intended and interpreted meaning." Here again, it would seem that Schutz starts with the moments of dissonance and strangeness in interpersonal relationships, often disregarded in the haste to achieve pragmatic ends that require one to bracket one's subjective meanings. It is perhaps to such moments that one can trace the origins of his affinity for Bergsonian duration.[25]

Even though in his order of presentation intricacies in *self*-understanding frequently serve as a prelude to discussing limits in *other*-understanding, he describes self-understanding at times as if it were a form of other-understanding. For instance, an act of recollection selects out an experience that has already been absorbed into uncounted other experiences of one's duration with the result that the earlier experience is seen from the perspective of the later moment, including its relevances. To illustrate this point, Schutz describes a childhood experience of anesthesia prior to an operation—a description itself already constructed out of later memory images. At different periods of one's later life, different aspects of that experience will emerge into prominence, depending on the interests prevailing at those later periods. Hence at one moment, the "man-in-white" will be most significant, later the memory of the smell of the liquid, and finally the counting of numbers as one drifted off to sleep. In interpreting one's own experience, the interpreter to a degree takes up a position *as if from outside that experience, as if he or she were a different person from the person undergoing the experience*. Self-understanding, then, always conditioned by one's own temporal perspective, limited, and never exhaustive, actually mirrors what takes place in other-understanding, and the constraints on self-understanding parallel those of other-understanding. In this light, the earlier paradox regarding the inaccessibility of pure duration to memory is more suggestive than is recognized by one who takes it for merely a contradictory *Ding-an-sich* to be overcome through Husserlian retention. The conundrum that memory only interprets *durée* through meaning-contexts that will never correspond exactly to the experience of *durée* reflects the quandary that anyone bringing interpretive meaning-contexts to bear on the living *durée* of others will never understand them exactly as they understand themselves. In postmodern parlance, contradictions can be interesting and instructive, if one looks for more than their logical flaws.[26]

In Schutz's earliest writings, one can find similar parallels between self- and other-interpretation by comparing the misunderstandings involved both when one interprets one's subjective process of free choice, as Bergson explains it, and when social scientists criticize unfairly economic actors' investment decisions. For Bergson, free choice involves deliberation regarding several contesting options, through which the ego runs, modifying one after another in a series of successive, different states, as its own sentiments, motives, and goals continuously expand and grow richer, until "the free act detaches itself . . . like an overripe fruit." But this subjective process through which one arrives at a choice is usually lost from sight when one reflects on it after the event, from an objective viewpoint outside that subjective process, and projects back an image of oneself standing before two simplified options. By positing two pathways or routes one might have taken before the event, this retrospective interpretation spatializes a much richer durational flow. This discussion might seem to be entirely concerned with internal psychological processes, were it not for important correlates with social relationships present already in papers on the philosophy of the social sciences written in the 1930s. In two 1936 essays, Schutz examines an example of hysteron-proteron in economics—for instance, when one judges an investment as mistaken or irrational after it fails to yield an anticipated profit. But this judgment, from a subsequent, after-the-event, objective point of view, may fail to do justice to the subjective viewpoint of the investor, who may have proceeded perfectly rationally but whose investment may have turned out badly because of intervening events that no one could have rationally foreseen. Just as one misinterprets one's own decision process after the event, oblivious to its own unfolding before the event, so one can misinterpret an investor's behavior as erroneous after the event, oblivious to its unfolding before the event. These symmetries suggest that it is at least as likely that Schutz's awareness of the perplexities of intersubjective interpretation (e.g., in economics) impelled him to examine conscious temporality as that he began with an egology and looked for social scientific situations to apply it to.[27]

With Bergsonian duration, then, Schutz secures for himself a foundation that spells out the limits of intersubjective understanding, but, as a foundation, it also explains how it is possible that one can understand others *better* than they understand themselves. For Schutz, the structure of *durée* gives one an access to the other that one does not have to oneself. This is so because one can observe the other's lived experiences in *durée* as they are actually unfolding in the present, whereas to grasp one's own experiences it is necessary to turn reflectively to experiences that have already passed. However, even though one experiences the other's experiences simultaneously with their unfolding and therefore has access to a segment of the other's duration, one inevitably lacks familiarity with the *entirety* of the other's experience, and so one's meaningful arrangement of that experience will never correspond completely with the other's. It is no wonder that Schutz early on in his *Phenomenology* claims that the problem of meaning is a problem of time, and, further, it is evident why Bergson and Husserl were of such importance to him for the riddles of meaning-establishment and interpretation.[28]

Schutz endorsed other aspects of Bergson's thought, such as attention to life, the various planes of consciousness, the body as the locus where outer space and inner *durée* converge, music as a model of *durée*, and multiple types of ordering. However, he disagreed with Bergson on his biological, evolutionary theory and his vitalistic belief in a suprapersonal élan vital, even as he rejected the views of Scheler, Husserl, and others on group souls, spirits, or forms of suprapersonal consciousness. As Wagner indicates, in 1958 he taught a seminar at the New School entitled "William James and Henri Bergson" in which he entertained secondary literature critical of Bergson's metaphysics, especially George Santayana's *Winds of Doctrine* and Horace Kallen's *William James and Henri Bergson: A Study in Contrasting Theories of Life*. While it is not exactly clear how he used these texts, he might have found Kallen appealing because he opposed Bergson's monism to the pluralism of being of William James, whom Kallen called a "democrat in metaphysics" and whose thought might have converged with Schutz's own democratic inclinations. Santayana, while tracing Bergson's theses to repeatedly and unfairly alleged psychological anxieties, rejected Bergson's one all-embracing world process, and—perhaps of interest for Schutz—criticized Bergson for projecting anthropomorphic qualities onto nature and thereby overstepping the canons to be observed in interpreting another.[29]

Besides their fruitfulness for intersubjective understanding, Schutz's Bergson manuscripts contain fleeting references to ethics—for instance, to the need not to act against the Thou, to the ethical dimensions of listening and sharing in communication, and to the ethical relevances operative in selective perceiving or remembering. However, his awareness of the uniqueness of each person's stream of experience and the consequent relativity of human experience left him skittish about endorsing any universal ethical principles and set him on a collision course with colleagues less relativistically inclined in their ethico-theoretical commitments, as we shall later see.[30]

Against this backdrop, it is striking that he asserts at one place that his manuscripts lead to the "self-liquidation of relativism." He claims this after recognizing his own work's a priori character and expressing a willingness to accept the charge that he does metaphysics, "provided one means by metaphysics that truly transcendental method which finds the precondition of cognition not in cognition but in experience." This self-liquidation, he adds, occurs "in a similar way as in Einstein's physics." A key to this comment can be found in Bergson's 1922 *Durée et simultanéité*, which, repeatedly cited in the *Phenomenology*, presents Bergson's confrontation with Einstein's thought. In that book, Bergson criticizes those who interpret another system, S', as in motion with respect to their own position, S, while assuming that S is at rest in a motionless ether. Actually their position, S, is not so privileged, but rather is in motion itself with respect to S', which, in turn, moves with respect to S. Nevertheless, the Einsteinian physicist assumes a position above the mutual relativity of positions, since the physicist "knows that the laws he formulates will be confirmed, no matter from what vantage point we view nature." The physicist then need not fear arbitrarily making himself the center of the world, by referring everything to his personal system of reference. If *Durée et simultanéité* affords a key for understanding Schutz's text, then he liquidates relativism by articulating a universal set of apriori structures of experience such as *durée*, the various life-forms, the temporal and interest conditionedness of all interpretation, and so on. Paradoxically, these apriori structures, universally and necessarily shared by all interpreters, ensure a maximal relativity, such that anyone's knowledge of another is always relative to one's own history and such that no one can ever understand another as that other understands him- or herself. Schutz's "transcendental" system resembles that of the Einsteinian physicist who establishes universally that every position is relative to every other.[31]

This universalization of relativity in Schutz's specific meaning of a "transcendental" sense specifies how persons *in fact* experience each other, but it does not yet establish the kind of ethical standpoint that his colleagues, such as Voegelin, would later plead for him to articulate. The next chapter will explore further reasons, beyond Weber's distinction among domains and insistence on value-freedom and Bergson's insights into temporal relativity, why Schutz avoids the region of ethics. Although his work lacks discussion of an ethical theory, ethical rationality, or first principles, one can discern certain ethical *dimensions* in his epistemic/metaphysical analyses, positing at the root of social scientific theory the unique duration of individuals and the limits it prescribes for any social-scientific understanding of another.

Chapter 3

Philosophy and Social Science (1919–38): Husserl and Mises and Kelsen

Following a summary of Schutz's autobiographical comments on his relation to Edmund Husserl, this chapter will show how he appropriated Husserl's thought in his *Phenomenology*, especially with reference to the problem of intersubjective understanding, one of the key foci of that book. In addition, his *Phenomenology* provided him with a philosophical fundament for the social sciences, enabling him to engage critically his own mentors, Mises and Kelsen. The issues of intersubjective understanding as well as the possibility of theoretical ethics and the relationship between ethics and economics and law become particularly prominent in this engagement.

Edmund Husserl's Phenomenology and *The Phenomenology of the Social World*

As Schutz tells us in his autobiographical musings in "Husserl and His Influence on Me," his way into Husserl was highly unusual. He turned to Husserl for philosophical foundations for Weberian sociology after finding unsatisfactory the resources provided by Bergson and by Neo-Kantian authors such as Cohen, Natorp, and Cassirer. In spite of his reading of Husserl's *Logische Untersuchungen* and the first volume of *Ideen*, at the recommendation of Felix Kaufmann, Schutz at first had not found Husserl helpful for his own problems. But then he read the 1928 *Vorlesungen zur Phänomenologie des inneren Zeitbewusstseins*, for which his work on Bergson had prepared him, and *Formale und transzendentale Logik*, which appeared in 1929 and which made focal the problem of intersubjectivity. Having seen the relevance of Husserl's thought "for all the questions which preoccupied me," Schutz informs us that he undertook a rereading of Husserl's earlier works—from the later philosophy of Husserl he rediscovered the earlier. Coming to Husserl from the social sciences, he approached phenomenology in an "unorthodox" manner, more interested in what Husserl's "Nachwort zu meinen 'Ideen' " called "phenomenology of the natural attitude" rather than transcendental phenomenology. Although he acknowledged "the importance of the phenomenological and the eidetic reductions for the foundation of a presuppositionless philosophy," he described social reality on the basis of the account of time-consciousness, discovered by Husserl within the transcendental sphere but still valid within the natural attitude. Three works—the *Vorlesungen*, *Logik*, and *Nachwort*—emphasized the corresponding themes of time, intersubjectivity, and the social world and were all oriented toward the basic problem of understanding another. They served as the three pillars on which Schutz built his *Phenomenology*, a copy of which he sent to Husserl.[1]

In a letter dated May 3, 1932, Husserl responded:

> I wanted to write you directly to tell you that I enjoyed very much your work on the meaningful construction of the social world, as well as the letter accompanying it. I hear that you are coming to Basel from Otaka, who has just left here[,] and that you would be inclined to take an excursion to Freiburg. That would be a great joy to me. I am interested in making the acquaintance of such an earnest and profound a phenomenologist (*einen so ernsten und gründlichen Phenomenologen kennen zu lernen*), one of the very few who have penetrated the deepest sense of my life's work, access to which is unfortunately so difficult. It is these few whom I, as the hope-filled founder, might be allowed to consider as themselves representatives of the authentic *philosophia perennis*, of the philosophy that alone is pregnant with a future. So do come, and I will make myself free for you. It should be a beautiful moment of philosophizing together (*symphilosophein*).[2]

Schutz hurried to visit Husserl, himself of Austrian origins but now living in Freiburg, and, until the end of 1937, he visited him three or four times yearly, whether at Freiburg, Vienna, or Prague. He recalled accompanying Husserl on "philosophical walks," in the company of Husserl's assistant Eugen Fink and the philosophers Dorion Cairns and Ludwig Landgrebe, and participating in evening discussions in which Husserl would at first entertain questions and then proceed to explain his own latest findings in a "long monologue." Schutz engaged in extensive correspondence with Eugen Fink, whom Husserl had delegated to respond to all criticisms, which included Schutz's reviews of *Formal and Transcendental Logic* and *Cartesian Meditations*. Husserl even invited Schutz to serve permanently as his assistant, but Schutz was unable to for personal reasons. In "Husserl and His Influence on Me," he reminisced about his final visit to Husserl, who, bedridden and near death in 1937, explained that his fully developed transcendental phenomenology made it indubitable that he, the mundane individual, would have to die, but that the transcendental Ego would not perish. Husserl was so deeply moved at that point that Mrs. Husserl had to end their meeting. Schutz concluded his reflections on Husserl by recollecting an ad hoc classroom lecture delivered around the time of his 1935 "Vienna Lecture." It left a lasting impression on the students and Schutz himself:

> I had never heard Husserl talk with such persuasion and deep feeling. His emotions swept over the fascinated young hearers who learned certainly for their whole lives what philosophy means and what a philosopher is. Husserl speaks somewhere in his writings of his endeavor to live a philosophical life in its full earnestness. By this statement he has revealed the innermost kernel of his personality. Everyone who met this astonishing man came immediately to the impression "*Ecce philosophicus.*"[3]

The very structure of Schutz's *Phenomenology* interweaves Husserlian phenomenology and Weberian sociology. Beginning with gaps in Weber's basic methodological concepts in chapter 1, Schutz sojourns briefly in the transcendental realm in chapter 2 before returning to the natural attitude to develop a phenomenology of the natural attitude from within the natural attitude. Hoping by such a phenomenological psychology to bypass a nest of problems with transcendental intersubjectivity that Husserl stated "but by no means solved" in the *Formal and Transcendental Logic*, Schutz describes phenomenologically intersubjective understanding and the structure of the social world in chapters 3 and 4. He then revisits and resolves several problems of Weberian interpretive sociology in the final chapter.[4]

As mentioned in his autobiographical comments, in writing his *Phenomenology* Schutz drew on Husserl's *Vorlesungen zur Phänomenologie des inneren Zeitbewusstseins* for an account of time that would be crucial for intersubjective understanding. Delving beneath the "objective time" of clocks, Husserl uncovered the "experienced now" in which a primal impression (of an object, for instance) immediately passed into a "retention" (or primary memory) of that impression as just having been. That retention, in turn, passed into another retention in such a way that the now-apprehension stood at the head of a "comet's tail of retentions," and this entire extension from the primal impression in an instant now through its retentions constituted a "specious present," encompassing both present and past intentionalities. In contrast to retention, recollection (or reproduction or secondary memory) involved a reflective activity that re-presented an object, establishing it as an enduring objectivity, selecting it out from the flow of experience, and distinguishing and throwing into relief discrete experiences that were previously phases, flowing one into another in *durée*.[5]

This analysis of time-consciousness enabled Schutz to resolve his quandary in *Life Forms and Meaning Structures* regarding how to bridge the gap between memory and *durée*. Through careful phenomenological descriptions, Husserl dissolved this dichotomy, also accepted by Franz Brentano and Alexis Meinong, by discovering that the (specious) present itself *already involved* memory—i.e, primary memory, or retention—of the immediate present in the flowing now. The string of retentions, "keeping in grip" the primal datum given in the present, conveyed that present up to the point at which a reflective looking back in recollection supervened, converting elapsed phases into an object. "We therefore owe it to retention that consciousness can be made into an object," Husserl commented, preserving the Bergsonian distinction between lived experience and reflection. Because Schutz's Bergson writings operated with a less differentiated notion of memory, he ended up isolating the present primal impression from secondary, (reflective) memory. Husserl's examination of the consciousness of internal time exemplified phenomenological method at its finest, defying the traditional prejudice that separated the lived present and memory, testing concepts (*durée* and memory) against lived experience, and recovering the dynamic activity of consciousness behind what seemed to be given as already established.[6]

Schutz, of course, developed Husserl's notions of temporality and intentionality in the direction of a theory of action and intersubjective understanding. Schutz began by distinguishing "experiences of primordial passivity" that did not confer meaning (e.g., a pain) and experiences that were meaning-endowing and included either spontaneous attitudes taken up toward experiences of passivity (e.g., I suppress my pain) or the adoption of reflectively designed projects issuing in actions. Further, Schutz embellished this account of action by including its temporal dimensions. For example, in devising one's project, one imagined the act to be realized as if it were already completed in the future, and hence in "future-perfect tense," before one even began the action. Then, one commenced a set of subactions aimed at realizing that project and continued in a future-orientation, anticipating the outcomes of these subactions with protentions or expectations that were either fulfilled or not as the action unfolded. While Schutz's account of a project was reiterated in his handling of "in-order-to motives," he also was aware of the change in temporal configurations that occurred when one sought to determine "because motives." To discover these motives, one turned to the past existing before one adopted or executed a project—and since this adoption or execution was itself already past, one would be looking in the past before the past, or pluperfect tense, for influences that led one to adopt one's project.[7]

In this entire discussion of action and temporality, Schutz never lost sight of his overriding goal of providing philosophical foundations for the social sciences, and in particular, for problems of intersubjective understanding. First of all, by rendering *durée* accessible through phenomenological methods, he was able to conserve all its implications for such understanding that he had discovered in the Bergson writings—for example, the limits to understanding insofar as one's stream of consciousness never overlaps with another's. In addition, the temporally articulated theory of motivation could illuminate social-scientific problems of understanding, such as one regularly discussed in the Bergson writings, namely, that sociohistorical actors often intended one action and another resulted. To avoid misunderstanding such actors, social scientists needed to "go behind" the finished action to understand the temporal processes through which an actor built up that action (or another intended one) in the first place. Schutz further showed the relevance of his phenomenology for other social scientific problems involving understanding, such as the subjective or objective probabilities of an action achieving its goal or the problematic of interpretive adequacy on meaning or causal levels.[8]

In addition to the lectures on inner time-consciousness, Schutz's autobiographical comments mention the 1929 *Formal and Transcendental Logic* as important for the development of his own *Phenomenology*. The *Logic* treated formal logic, including the formation and consistency of propositions and the essential conditions of truth, and transcendental logic, which considered the transcendental subjective processes correlative to the idealities they constituted. Although Schutz credited the *Logic* for focusing on the problem of intersubjectivity, as it did near the end, it was the earlier analyses of constitution that were significant for his own treatment of the social world. In section 5 of the *Phenomenology* in a discussion of "objective meaning," he denied that Husserl's distinction between ideal objectivities and (subjective) acts in his critique of psychologism in *Logical Investigations* was relevant for problems of intersubjectivity. Schutz, however, then proceeded to list three texts from the *Logic* on the problem of constitution. "Objective meaning," he commented, refers to those meaning-structures that abstract from or leave out the intentional operations of the consciousness of others or of the person who himself or herself constituted these meanings. However, it is possible to make focal these intentional operations, and the results are significant: "Then I no longer have before me a complete and constituted world but one which only now is being constituted and which is ever being constituted anew in the stream of my enduring Ego: not a world of being, but a world that is at every moment one of becoming and passing away—or better, an emerging world."[9]

Not surprisingly, Schutz immediately links this ever-merging constituting of what appear by themselves to be "inert" constituted meanings from *Formal and Transcendental Logic* with "the most basic fact of my conscious life," that is, with *durée* in Bergson or "internal time-consciousness" in Husserl. This synthesis of the problematics of inner-time and processes of constituting, which both stand over against the "inert" constituted meanings, can be correlated with the subjective and objective meanings in the social world that he had been discussing with reference to Max Weber:

> When we make the transition to the social sphere, there accrues, in fact, to the pair of concepts "objective and subjective meaning" a new and sociologically relevant significance. I can, on the one hand, attend to and interpret in themselves the phenomena of the external world present themselves to me as indications of the consciousness of other people. When I do this, I say of them that they have objective meaning. But I can, on the other hand, look over and through these external indications into the constituting process within the living consciousness of another rational being. What I am then concerned with is subjective meaning.[10]

This synthesis of constitution with internal time-consciousness enables Schutz to elucidate various phenomena. For example, his earlier discussion of freedom in Bergson, repeated in the *Phenomenology*, retrieves from behind a static, constituted decision between what appeared as two fixed options a constituting ego running through a series of psychic states, expanding, growing richer, and oscillating between several options, each modifying the others. Similarly, interpreters need to attend beyond the completed act to the conscious processes, especially the phantasying of a project and its subacts, that went into building up that act. Finally, one builds up a total content of life experience, including familiarity with ideal objects, but one can forget the series of conscious actions through which these schemes of experience in one's stock of knowledge were acquired. Thus, instead of conceiving the Pythagorean theorem as a monothetically completed meaning structure, one can recover the step-by-step processes by which one came polythetically to understand and appropriate the theorem in the first place. Schutz's effort to get behind constituted meanings to the temporal processes of constitution in which meanings were built up no doubt explains the German title of his magnum *opus:* the "meaningful buildup" (*sinnhafte Aufbau*) of the social world.[11]

This distinction between constituted meanings and constituting processes continues to prove its fruitfulness for understanding another in chapters 3 and 4 of the *Phenomenology*. For instance, Schutz stresses the limits to understanding insofar as another's subjective meanings appear within a *durée* and insofar as one would be able to understand those meanings exactly as the other does only if one had lived through all the other's experiences in their order and intensity. Because of such subjective, temporal processes, the "objective meanings" of any sign-system, invariant independently of any user and codified in dictionaries, are accompanied by a subjective meaning for someone, "having its origin in the unique quality of the experiences in which he once learned to use the sign." Thus, an objective meaning, such as that of "demonic" in German, acquires a subjective meaning for an author such as Goethe that one could only discover by considering his works as a whole. Moreover, for Schutz, partners to the simplest conversation in their convertible roles of speakers and listeners gradually constitute meanings that can be excerpted from the intricate processes of their buildup. Finally, one must approach those not physically but temporally present (Contemporaries) or those not even temporally present (Predecessors, Successors) through inferentially constructed types that leave out precisely the constitutive processes to which one would be privy in a face-to-face Consociate relationship.[12]

As if to remind the reader that his philosophical investigations seek to provide foundations for the social sciences, Schutz in his concluding "excursus" at the end of the third chapter applies the distinction between objective and subjective meaning to social scientific problems. It is one thing to concentrate on the objective theses of economic theory, such as Mises's principles of catallactics that describe with a sense of universal validity and the ideality of "I can do it again" how a universal "one" would act economically. It is quite another to focus on what is going on (subjectively) in the mind of particular historical individuals. Likewise, law students understand that legal propositions can be considered objectively, i.e., in accord with philological or juridical canons of interpretation, or subjectively, in terms of the "intention of the legislator."[13]

Although Schutz relies heavily on Husserl's accounts of temporality and constitution, there is evidence from the start of his disagreement with Husserl about the problems of transcendental intersubjectivity, a disagreement that would find its fullest expression in his paper presented in Royaumont in 1957. For instance, at the beginning of the third chapter of the *Phenomenology*, Schutz refuses to deal with the social world from the point of view of transcendental phenomenology, thereby bypassing a whole nest of problems whose significance and difficulty Husserl had pointed out without resolving them, Schutz thinks. Moreover, as early as June 12, 1940, Schutz informed Marvin Farber that he was thinking of writing a critical study of the Fifth Cartesian Meditation, and numerous criticisms of Husserl's transcendental treatment of intersubjectivity are scattered throughout the Gurwitsch correspondence.[14]

Finally, Schutz locates his own project with reference to Husserl's phenomenological architectonic when he mentions in autobiographical comments that from the very beginning he was interested in what Husserl called in his 1930 "Nachwort zu meinen 'Ideen' " a "phenomenology of the natural attitude" rather than in his transcendental phenomenology. Reiterating this interest in "Phenomenology and the Social Sciences," published in 1940 in a memorial collection for Husserl, Schutz affirms that the prescientific life-world, the cultural world of shared signification (*Cartesian Meditations* #58), is the meaning-basis of every science and that Husserl had no intention of rejecting it in transcendental phenomenology. In relevant passages in the *Nachwort*, Husserl delineates the task of a phenomenological psychology from the natural standpoint: to describe "inner experience" but in essential terms, "inquiring, that is, after the invariant, essentially characteristic structures of a soul, of a psychical life in general." For Husserl, the result will not be only "scanty, superficially classificatory descriptions, but a great self-supporting science." Schutz envisions his own work as realizing this task in "Phenomenology of the Social Sciences" and in his important methodological "Appended Note" at the end of chapter 1 in the *Phenomenology*. He conceives his "constitutive phenomenology of the natural attitude" as describing what precedes any theoretical stance taken toward everyday life, whether those of phenomenology or the of various social sciences. Schutz's *Phenomenology*, remedying the deficits of his Bergson era to provide a foundation for Weberian sociology, develops an approach to intersubjective understanding based on temporality that could support the social scientific achievements of his mentors Mises and Kelsen. These teachers no doubt influenced his own appreciation for the relativity of value-schemes—a relativity that would be a point of contention later with Eric Voegelin. However, his presentation of the theoretical viewpoint of economics as adopted with reference to the broader context of everyday life heads off any economic reductionism and makes possible at least an engagement between the value-spheres of economics and ethics.[15]

The Austrian Economic School, Value-Freedom, and the Context of Economic Science

Schutz's approach to intersubjective understanding both supported and was shaped by the so-called Austrian economic school, whose major proponents included Mises and Hayek and whose important features will be sketched in the section that follows. One of the distinguishing features of the Austrian school (and Weber and Kelsen) was an emphasis on value-freedom, and the Austrian endorsement of *theoretical* value-freedom correlated with certain ethical values that Austrian economists believed to be embodied in the *practical* economics of the free market for which they usually advocated. Given Schutz's exemplary ethical life and later theoretical confrontations and developments regarding the subject of ethics, this chapter will examine how Schutz appropriated the notion of "value-freedom" and how he conceived the interface between ethics and economics in ways that concurred with and differed from members of the Austrian school.

From the outset it is important to be clear about the meaning of value-freedom. Max Weber in his classical formulations recognized that the very selection of what should be a topic of scientific investigations depended inescapably upon some context of value-relevance (*Wert-Beziehung*). For instance, the values of social scientists' cultures induce them to single out for investigation only parts of the empirical reality surrounding them, such as law, religion, or economic activity; values are unavoidably involved in the selection of topics for study. However, once that direction of interest is adopted, the social scientists for the purposes of their empirical discipline undertake a "value-free (*wertfrei*)" investigation, that is, they seek to refrain from any value-judgments on the material to be described and try to produce propositions that are objective, verifiable, valid, and true. As Schutz put it:

> The scientific problem, once established, alone determines what is relevant for the scientist as well as the conceptual frame of reference to be used by him. This, and nothing else, it seems to me, is what Max Weber means when he postulates the objectivity of the social sciences, their detachment from the value patterns which govern or might govern the behavior of the actors on the social scene.[16]

The Austrian Economic School and Value-Freedom

Carl Menger, simultaneously with William Jevons and Leon Walras and in conjunction with his own colleagues Wieser and Eugen Bohm-Bäwerk, initiated what gradually came to be recognized as the "marginal revolution" in economics. This revolution extended over several generations, including a second generation of Mises and Joseph Schumpeter and a third of Haberler, Hayek, Machlup, Morgenstern, and M. Rothbard. Before Menger, classical economics had questioned why objects of greater utility (e.g., iron) were valued less than those of lesser utility (e.g., gold) and concluded that the price of objects depended not on use-value but on the *objective* processes conferring value on them (e.g., production costs, labor time invested). Menger, however, focused on the *subject,* who in different times, places, and conditions and in accord with what afforded greater or smaller satisfaction chooses to purchase them. For Menger "the goods-character is not a property inherent in the good themselves," but rather one finds "the causal source of market phenomenona in the actions of human participants in the market process."[17]

In the view of Mises, Menger's rediscovery of the subjectivity of the consumer (and producer) dispelled the ghost of the mechanistic market haunting classical economics:

> It is customary to speak metaphorically of the automatic and anonymous forces actuating the "mechanism" of the market. In employing

> such metaphors people are ready to disregard the fact that the only factors directing the market and the determination of prices are purposive acts of men. There is no automatism; there are only men consciously and deliberately aiming at ends chosen. There are no mysterious mechanical forces; there is only the human will to remove uneasiness. There is no anonymity; there is I and you and Bill and Joe and all the rest. And each of us is both a producer and consumer.[18]

Rejecting anthropological characteristics of human beings as passive hedonists interested only in maximizing pleasure, the Austrians generally considered the essence of humanity to reside in purposeful activity and thus preferred a cognitive psychology focused on choice and preference. Attunement to subjective, psychological processes led Menger further to recognize motivational complexity, since "along with self-interest, which at most can be recognized as the mainspring of human economy, also public spirit, love of one's fellow men, custom, feeling for justice, and other similar factors determine man's economic actions." He even included among these psychological factors *error*, that is, the fact that people can be mistaken about their economic interests or economic state of affairs. His appreciation for the complexity of motivations and the different intensities of preference for each person that complexity entails led logically to the law of marginal utility—which Mises claimed is already implied in the category of action. According to this law, consumers, aware of their subjective wants and the objective conditions for satisfying those wants, attribute to physical things particular degrees of importance. They end up choosing between two satisfactions (e.g., whether to pursue an increment to n-units or remain at $n\text{–}1$ units)—both of which they cannot have together. Stephen Kresge summarized the Austrian attunement to the complexity and differing intensities of motivations when he observed that "[o]nly the individual can know what one is prepared to give up or substitute to obtain the use—that is, the value—of something else."[19]

This Austrian "subjective turn" shook economics to its methodological roots. First of all, the endeavor to delve beneath market laws to the subjective activity of the consumer led Menger to reduce "the complex phenomena of human economic activity to the simplest elements that can still be subjected to accurate observation," and thus to pursue a methodological individualism. Echoing Schutz's own description of economic generalizations, Barry Smith explained such a methodological strategy through the principle that "all talk of nations, classes, firms, etc. is to be treated by the social theorists as an in principle eliminable shorthand for talk of individuals." Second, the complexity of subjective motivation of each individual and the disharmony of individuals' knowledge and intentions render the market and market equilibrium more fluid and less predictable, as Hayek emphasized in his 1936 essay "Economics and Knowledge"—originally a lecture attended by Schutz. Just as Schutz would later point to the unpredictability constitutive of everyday life in "The Problem of Rationality in the Social World," so Mises and Hayek concurred in conceiving economic human decision-making as grappling with an undetermined future fraught with uncertainty. Third, the inconstancy and unforeseeability of subjective human action prevented, according to Hayek and Mises, any easy reconciliation with positivistic, quantitative methodologies, such as E. Mach's. Furthermore, the difficulties of applying such methodologies suggested a distinction between the "objects" of economic science and those of the natural sciences—a matter of central importance to Schutz in his "Concept and Theory Formation in the Social Sciences."[20]

The Austrian incorporation of the subjectivity of economic agents, provoking the methodological accommodations of individualism, a disequilibrium approach to the market, and a hesitancy about quantitative positivism, in effect put in place dimensions of an economic foundation that future economic theories could not afford to overlook. This foundation addressed issues of consumption, demand, and the restoration of economic ends to their rightful place in the interpretation of economic behavior and its organization. Moreover, by acknowledging the subjectivity of economic agents at the foundation of economic science, Menger, Mises, and Hayek all found themselves becoming self-reflective about economic theory itself, about its limits, and in particular about the value-freedom appropriate to it. In addition, they became reflective about the values in the practical domain paralleling *theoretical* value-freedom.

Given the indeterminable factors motivating economic actors, from greed to altruism, Menger refrained from passing any ethical judgments on consumers, but studied instead how their preferences, whatever their motivation, evoked entrepreneurial creativity as a response. One could conceive such value freedom under the rubric of a "tolerance of motivations." Menger also explored on a more macrolevel, the connection between values and the economic system, starting with his own fascination about how out of an anarchy of subjective preferences behavioral regularities and even well functioning institutions could emerge. Although resisting the relativistic tendencies of the German Historical School, he found appealing its views regarding the "subconscious wisdom"—manifested in institutions, such as law, language, the state, markets, prices, interest rates—that had developed "organically," without intentional direction, high above "meddlesome human wisdom." Such an organicist account of economic institutions, flowing from the Austrian subjective turn, could imply a laissez-faire approach to the economy in which one refrained from meddlesome value-based interventions into it and bracketed one's values in *practical* relation to the economy as one had to do in the conduct of *empirico-theoretical* economic science. However, because Menger recognized the central importance of subjective, intelligent, purposive activity, he thought it possible to give intelligent direction to institutions through a common will expressed, for instance, by mutual agreements or legislation. Recognizing that this "pragmatic" approach to the economy would justify interventions into the economy that the organicist perspective would rule out, Menger decided to separate the noneconomic dimensions of human experience on which the pragmatic approach would draw from the autonomously functioning economic sphere of activity. He limited economic theory to describing this autonomous sphere by depicting how a strictly economically motivated *Homo oeconomicus* would behave, leaving open the possibility that noneconomic aspects of human existence might warrant value-guided interventions in the economic domain.[21]

Like Menger, Mises embraced "toleration of motives" value-freedom, insisting, for instance, that it was economically unimportant whether market demand for weapons originated from law-abiding citizens or from criminals and revolutionaries, since all that mattered economically was the existence of a demand in a definite volume. But for Mises value-freedom also entailed an instrumental approach to rationality insofar as rational action involved choosing between means to attaining one's most ardently desired goal, which the actor alone determined and which economic science had no business prescribing for an actor. Thus, bizarre actions (e.g., buying an expensive house so one could sip cocktails in a duke's neighborhood) or unhealthy choices (e.g., purchasing poisonous nicotine) ought to be conceived as "rational" insofar as they are directed to the purchaser's own satisfaction, and hence "notions of abnormality and perversity have no place in economics." Clearly the instrumental-rational interpretation of value-freedom here converged with a tolerance of motivations understanding. Since rationality only concerned choosing means to one's goal, any attempt to apply even the terms "rational" or "irrational" to ends would fail. Mises supported this value-freedom regarding ends by aligning himself with a long philosophical tradition that considered all value-judgments to be nonrational and arbitrary. Hence, "to call something fair or unfair is always a subjective value judgment and as such purely personal and not liable to any verification or falsification." In conclusion, for Mises every human action, beyond the mere reactive behavior of the organs of the human body, turned out to be rational, in contrast with Weber, who judged actions as rational or irrational according to his distinction between purposive-rational action and value-rational, affectional, habitual, and traditional action.[22]

Mises rejected Menger's idea of the *Homo oeconomicus* that limited economics to one aspect of human existence, whose other aspects, including the ethical, might call for policies constraining economics. This elimination of the *Homo oeconomicus* depended on Mises's theory of human action, which originated in discontent and led to a choice of means to one's "most ardently desired goal," namely satisfaction. In opposition to the relativizing tendencies of the German Historical School, Mises considered this conception of action to be a priori and not historically relative or merely empirical, as were Weber's ideal types. Hence, Mises detected this concept of action as operative even in the Middle Ages:

> Though the men of the Middle Ages would not have understood the law of marginal utility, they nevertheless did not and could not act otherwise than as the law of marginal utility describes. Even the man of the Middle Ages sought to apportion the means at his disposal in such a way that he attained the same level of satisfaction in every single kind of want. . . . Even in the Middle Ages no one voluntarily exchanged a horse for a cow unless he valued the cow more highly than the horse.[23]

This theory of the a priori features of choice and preference, underlying all action pertaining to all times and cultures, "goes far beyond the horizon which encompassed the scope of economic problems as circumscribed by the economists from Cantillon, Hume, and Adam Smith down to John Stuart Mill." This new a priori choice/preference theory, which Mises dubs "praxeology," emerges "out of the political economics of the classical school" even as it "enlarges the field of economic studies." In giving birth to a theory of choice and preference, economics "widens its horizon and turns into a general science of all and every human action." For Mises, the real problem now becomes how to distinguish from general praxeology the narrower study of specifically economic problems, or what he refers to as "catallactics," which focuses on the determination of money prices of goods and services exchanged on the market on the basis of monetary calculation.[24]

To distinguish economic action from other types, classical economics had selectively focused on the activities of the business person (as opposed to the consumer), whom it conceived as driven only by the economic motive of maximizing profit, with all other motives being consigned to the bin of noneconomic motives. Economists, including Menger, constructed the fictitious image of "a perfectly selfish and rationalistic being for whom nothing counts but profit": the *Homo oeconomicus*—although they were aware that other motives guided real persons. When Mises shifted the focus of economics to the subjectivity of the consumer, whose motives for entering the market could be as materialistic or idealistic as possible, any motives, from generosity to greed, were able to serve as economic motives. On a praxeological plane, all motives, aimed at removing uneasiness and improving satisfaction, resembled each other, but when agents pursued this aim as consumers exercising preferences within the catallactic sphere of the market, their actions became identifiably "economic," because of their sphere of activity rather than because of any specific "economic" motivations. Moreover, Weber's distinctions between purposive-rational, value-rational, traditional, affective, and habitual behaviors lost significance, since market preferences based on religious or traditional values would be as rational (in the sense of taking actions to remove uneasiness and improve one's satisfaction) as those of the most cunning trader.[25]

By doing away with the idea of the *Homo oeconomicus*, Mises took value-freedom to a new level. From now on, economists could no longer look down with evaluative scorn upon those whose motives were formerly considered "noneconomic" or irrational because they did not calculate as effectively as the *Homo oeconomicus*. Similarly, moralistic foes would no longer be able to denounce the entirety of economic activity as egocentric, as they could have when the *Homo oeconomicus* was paradigmatic, since behind many economic preferences lay the loftiest of motives. Finally, not even purposive-rationality would be normative, since value-directed, traditional, and habitual actors could equally demonstrate preference-rationality. All motives could be tolerated as legitimately economic insofar as they underlay market preferences, and all preferences could be (instrumentally) rational insofar as they sought to remove uneasiness and procure satisfaction. Moreover, Mises stressed that his unconditioned support of value-freedom in the theoretical sphere could be translated into increased respect for the freedom of choice of others within the practical domain. In that sphere, dictators, totalitarians, majoritarians oblivious to the rights of minorities, social engineers, monopolies, and labor unions often presumed to decide what was in the best interests of others. As a result, they ended up massacring others, running roughshod over their rights, excluding them, and treating them "in the same way in which the engineer treats the stuff out of which he builds bridges, roads, and machines."[26]

While Mises's a priori economics upheld the rationalistic dimensions of the Austrian tradition, Hayek from his earliest essay, "Economics and Knowledge," denied the belief of classical economics in quasi-omniscient market participants and emphasized organic economic processes, which resisted rationalistic or value-guided interventions from spheres beyond the economy. Agreeing with the organic approach that Menger never completely endorsed, Hayek emphasized that "most of the rules which do govern existing society are not the result of our deliberate making." Instead they represent the outcomes of a slow evolutionary process in which more experience and knowledge was precipitated than any one person could fully master. While opposing positivism for espousing a predictability in human affairs possible only in natural science, Hayek also took exception to Mises's a priori approach, which, with its excessive rationalism, could not adequately oppose the socialism belonging to the rationalistic tradition of classical economics from Adam Smith to the French Enlightenment. In addition, Hayek cemented his own take on value-freedom within economic science by highlighting with Mises the instrumental nature of rationality, which David Hume had restricted to the role of serving human ends by clarifying alternatives, value-conflicts, and means-ends relationships. Like Hume, Hayek claimed that, when it came to determining ultimate ends, reason could not serve as a judge, because "the rules of morality are not the conclusions of our reason."[27]

Like Mises, Hayek commented at length upon the values to be realized in the practical sphere if people refrained from imposing their values on others after the fashion of the value-freedom required within the theoretical realm. He did this most explicitly in *The Road to Serfdom*, a copy of which Schutz had personally presented as a gift to Adolf Lowe. In that book, Hayek warned against socialistic projects that appear to act "unselfishly" but in reality act at others' expense, and against the hurt that can be inflicted on others in the name of majoritarian politics or union and monopoly economic strategies. He cautioned against trying to control society as one might nature, criticized totalitarian systems for reducing human beings to mere means, and argued that free enterprise systems tended to be more sensitive to their weak and infirm. In addition, he characterized methodological individualism as "an attitude of humility before this social process and of tolerance to other opinions, . . . the exact opposite of that intellectual hubris which is at the root of the demand for comprehensive direction of the social process."[28]

Alfred Schutz: Value-Freedom and the Context of Economics

In his three essays "Basic Problems of Political Economy," "Political Economy: Human Conduct in Social Life," and "Choice and the Social Sciences," Schutz more explicitly than elsewhere presented his own views on economic theory and criticized Mises. From the very start, though, Schutz agreed with many of the basic premises of Mises and the Austrian economic school. Like them, he criticized the objective economic methods focused on statistics, price fluctuations, and formulas of market equilibrium, as if the knowledge of the economist about these interrelations were alone relevant. By contrast, the social scientist, in Schutz's view, unlike the natural scientist, was not the sole person to confer meaning on the world but had to determine the meanings that social agents gave to their world. As a result, in these writings Schutz called on economists to undertake the "Copernican turn" that the school of marginal utility had introduced: a "decisive, methodological step" toward the subjective mode of consideration. After this turn, one would no longer describe human behavior merely in terms of causes and effects as if one were describing purely physical phenomenon, but would inquire into the intentions, purposes, and meanings of actors. In "Choice and the Social Sciences," Schutz interpreted Mises's "feeling of uneasiness," the need to be satisfied, as a type of "because motive," provoking an in-order-to project. Also, agreeing with the marginalists, Schutz stated that any project originated in "a choice between the problematic possibilities accessible [to an economic actor] . . . each of these possibilities has for him its own weight, although this weight is not the same for his fellow-actor, to whom other possibilities—also problematic—are accessible."[29]

In "Basic Problems of Political Economy," Schutz affirmed Mises's general value-free stance as it appeared in his critique of Werner Sombart's introduction of value-judgments into empirical economic science. Concurring with Mises "toleration of motivation" value-freedom, Schutz cited favorably Mises's comment, "For the science of human action, the valuations and goals of the final order at which men aim constitute givens which it is unable to explain further." Schutz also subscribed to Mises's and Hayek's instrumental notion of rationality when he asserted that "Values are the irrational as such; the latter never can be an object of science."[30]

While in accord with value-freedom, Schutz retrieved the *Homo oeconomicus*, which Mises had eliminated in order to fend off possible interventions into the economy from noneconomic spheres, and this retrieval depended upon extensive adjustments in the understanding of economic theory and human action that Mises favored. Embracing Max Weber's thought in spite of Mises's opposition, Schutz understood the fictive *Homo oeconomicus* as an ideal type constructed by economists and equipped with conscious experiences sufficient for understanding human behavior with reference to economic problems. For Schutz, as for Menger, the *Homo oeconomicus* gave expression, as Schutz put it, to "merely *one* side of our being human." Schutz was quite clear that such conceptual models are formed in abstraction from the "actual world." In that "full existence," one deals with "you and me, with Peter and Paul, or finally with everyone who is a human being in daily life and as such is also producer and consumer, householder or economic leader or employed," who "plans, acts, expects, is disappointed in all his rational and nonrational thinking." Schutz here reflected in phenomenological style on the enterprise of economic theorizing and situated it with reference to its own nontheoretical horizon, namely, the life-world out of which it arises and from which it abstracts. Ironically, Mises, for all his reflection on the a priori epistemological status of his own economic claims, fell short of adequate self-reflection insofar as he neglected this life-world ground of economic theory.[31]

By marking off the life-world from theory, Schutz was also able to offer an alternative definition of economic theory that was to be constructed in accord with the regulative principle for building up its system of ideal types: the principle of marginal utility. Hence, the economist was to build ideal types *as if* all actors had oriented their life-plan and activities to the chief end of realizing the greatest utility with the minimum cost. Correlatively, only those actions became the focus of economic theory which were oriented according to this principle, whereas Mises, according to Schutz, thought that *all* action followed the principle of marginal utility and reduced *all* acting to economic acting "because it implicates preference and planning." By dispersing marginal utility throughout the life-world instead of limiting it to a defining principle of an economic theoretical approach toward the life-world, Mises had effectively conflated economic theory with the life-world.[32]

Schutz rebutted Mises's objections that Weberian types, such as the *Homo oeconomicus*, were merely historically relative, and he even suggested that Mises's categories—e.g., regarding basic laws of price formation—operated with types claiming universal validity, though the question of their status as "a priori" was philosophical rather than economic. A more central problem for the inquiry into the relationship between ethics and economics concerned the reduction of all action to economic action, a position Schutz summarized when stating, "no action is conceivable that does not occur following the principles of marginal utility: all acting is economic acting." For Schutz, the question whether all action was economical was ultimately "terminological," since Mises would have to explain why actions in psychology and philosophy were interpreted as noneconomic and why, if all action were already economic, people usually singled out some actions as specifically economic. Schutz concluded without much elaboration that "it seems purposeful to separate acting turned toward so-called economic goods from other acting," and to see choosing and preferring as subspecies of the classification "action." While Mises, too, distinguished a general understanding of action (praxeology) from a narrow sense of economics (catallactics), he had generated that general understanding of action out of an economics that "widens its horizon and turns into a general science of all and every human action (praxeology)." In contrast, Schutz in his *Phenomenology* first developed a more ample understanding of action, including noneconomic action, within which he situated economic action, just as he had located economic theory with reference to the life-world.[33]

Schutz elaborated his earlier cursory distinction between economic and noneconomic actions in "Choice and the Social Sciences," in which he first disputed Mises's collapsing of Weber's differentiation between rational and irrational action on the grounds that any action aimed at achieving most ardently desired goals was rational. Schutz began by appropriating Leibniz's complex, unreflected-upon "small perceptions" that determine many of our nondeliberated activities, which Schutz described as doing or thinking without a previously projected act and which Leibniz called "the class of empirical behavior." In addition, these small perceptions produced the states of uneasiness at the base of projected actions also, *but as their because motives* to be recovered via a retrospective reflection after completing the projecting or projected action. Schutz correlated Weber's irrational habitual, traditional, or affective action with the class of empirical behavior provoked by small perceptions. But, as Leibniz insisted, these activities could not serve as ultimate explanations of human activity, which *also* consisted in devising projects and in considering how those projects related to each other, which means might have best achieved those projected ends, and whether one project should be chosen over another. Schutz illustrated the difference between automatic and rationally, in-order-to, determined activities through the example of someone walking through a garden discussing a problem with a friend and then turning left or right because a chain of small unapperceived perceptions producing slight unease so prompted him. Schutz insisted that such semiautomatic activities, which Mises might consider to be economically rational, would fall short of rational economic action a la Schutz and Weber. Turning to the right or left involved no deliberate choice between alternatives, which required reflection, a comparison of alternatives, and volition—all leading to the purposive-rational action paramount for Weber. Economic science illuminated such rational economic activity by delineating how an actor would perform "if he had a clear and distinct scientific knowledge of all the elements relevant to his choice and the constant tendency to choose the most appropriate means for the realization of the most appropriate end." Perhaps to avoid judging any actor's preferences as less than rational, Mises deemphasized precisely this deliberative activity, which both consumer and entrepreneur perform and whose scope and predictability scientific economics could enhance.[34]

In addition to upholding Weberian purposive-rational action, Schutz also delineated a realm of human activity and action beyond economic action. First all, by upgrading economic action beyond mere "selection" or "singling out without comparison" to a "conscious choice between alternatives which presupposes reflection, volition, and preference," he identified a field of activity (e.g., making a turn in the garden walk) beneath the threshold of economic preference. Furthermore, by construing economic preference as "rational-purposive action," Schutz made it possible to distinguish economic purposeful actions from others, since economic theorists treated *only* those rational-purposive actions as "economic" which were oriented toward the principle of marginal utility definitive of economic science, that is, which sought to realize the greatest utility with minimum cost. Via his theory of action and his understanding of economic theory, Schutz was thus able to isolate economic action from a more encompassing noneconomic life-world.[35]

Finally, to offset Mises's reductionistic approach to human action, Schutz turned to his favorite theme of temporality in "Choice and the Social Sciences." He started by asserting diversity of regions of action, since one may have to choose between God and Caesar, ethics and law, life and science, and he concluded, "All attempts at bringing these systems under one single denominator must fail, whatever this denominator is." Utilitarianism, though, often homogenized this diversity of realms by *retrospectively* interpreting completed acts in its own terms. Schutz summerized the utilitarian argument as follows: "Everybody seeks pleasure; there are, however, ascetics who refrain from seeking pleasure; consequently their asceticism brings them more pleasure than the pleasures from which they refrain." One could extend this same critique to Mises's view also, insofar as he assumed that all rationality consisted in seeking to remove uneasiness and achieve satisfaction. Thus, if someone acted in a way resulting in increased ease and satisfaction, Mises would read his truncated notion of rationality into the actor from a retrospective perspective by claiming after the event that the actor only "aimed at removing uneasiness and at improving . . . [his or her] state of satisfaction." In so doing, he would fail to pay sufficient attention to the actual in-order-to motives of the actor and the actor's deliberation about them and the means to be taken to realize them.[36]

To conclude, Schutz clearly agreed with Mises on the subjective turn and the need for a value-free economics (in opposition to Sombart) under the auspices of both the tolerance of motivations and instrumental rationality. Indeed, Schutz's elaboration of an account of rationality by which actors deliberated about their "in-order-to motives" beyond merely seeking means to their satisfaction continued to maintain a value-free epistemology. After all, the economist pronounced no value-judgment on those projects but only inquired into how well coordinated projects were with each other and with the means taken to bring them about. However, in contradistinction to Mises, who tended to subsume all action under economic action, Schutz through the revitalization of Weber's *Homo oeconomicus* signaled his intent to place economic action and theory within a broader context. He achieved this intent by delimiting economic theory as a reflective stance governed by the principle of marginal utility, directed toward a more encompassing life-world. In addition, Schutz resisted Mises's reduction of all action to economic action by accommodating Mises's account of action within a more comprehensive theory. That theory included the adoption of and deliberation about in-order-to projects to be coordinated with each other and their means; only some of these projects were susceptible to an analysis by an economic science defined according to the principle of marginal utility.

To be sure, circumscribing the domain of economic action and theory does little to indicate what noneconomic domains and values might play a role in relation to the economic sphere or whether they should do so. Nevertheless, Mises's reduction of all action to economic action has the curious effect of eliminating a distinctive noneconomic sphere capable of interacting with the economic domain. As a result, for Mises, the only manner of introducing ethical values into the economic sphere would seem to be by registering one's values through market preferences (e.g., not purchasing from companies engaging in pollution). Furthermore, given the reduction of all rationality to instrumental rationality and the consequent impossibility of any rational assessment of ends, this preference would be no more rational than another (e.g., purchasing from that company because its prices were lower). But if a distinction could be drawn between noneconomic and economic spheres, then it would be possible that values originating in the noneconomic spheres (e.g. ethics, politics) could be brought to bear on the economic sphere. Of course, in order to introduce such noneconomic values into the economic area, one, along with Menger, could not believe in a totally organicist understanding of the economy that would prohibit any value-directed interference with economic processes.

Schutz was fully aware that individuals, at the intersection of various roles and relevances, faced difficult problems of reconciling conflicting relevances, economic and noneconomic. He had observed that "the interests I have in the same situation as a father, a citizen, a member of my church or of my profession, may not only be different but even incompatible with one another." The problem, however, becomes more complex when a whole society seeks to determine how different spheres (e.g., the economic and political) ought to interact. Mises and Hayek, of course, were highly suspicious of any attempt to provide ethical or political direction for the economic sphere, since they believed that such direction would deprive agents of their autonomy at a practical level. A society better protected this autonomy by bracketing rather than interjecting values into the economy, just as bracketing values on the theoretical level led to better economic science. For Mises and Hayek, intervention was the first step toward tyranny. Schutz never recommended any value-guided interventions in the economy, and he had difficulties articulating his own ethical commitments at all, as later correspondence with Eric Voegelin and others will show. Only in the 1956 Ethics Institute in the aftermath of *Brown* v. *Board of Education* did Schutz acknowledge an ethical value of ultimacy that could be developed into an ethical principle emphasizing citizens' needs to be recognized and to participate actively in decision-making. Whatever ethical imperatives for the economic sphere might have followed from this principle, the totalitarian imposition of such imperatives obviously would have run contrary to its spirit.[37]

Hans Kelsen, the Pure Theory of Law, and Alfred Schutz

Hans Kelsen drafted the 1920 Austrian constitution, served on the Constitutional Court until removed by the conservative Christian Social party, then taught in Cologne until expelled to Geneva by the Nazis, and finally immigrated to the United States in 1938. His legal theory passed through phases: critical constructivism, conceiving legal concepts as normative in a Neo-Kantian tradition; the pure theory of law, taking law for normative and continually self-regenerating; and a skeptical phase (in the 1960s), construing law as a voluntaristic product of will. In his pure theory of law phase, when he knew Schutz, Kelsen stressed the normative character of law, emphasizing that it made no causal predictions about how people would act, that norm violations did not "cause" punishments, and that natural law, deriving norms from facts, had committed the naturalistic fallacy. Furthermore, the law created the state, rights, and the legal person rather than the other way around, and, in opposition to Otto von Gierke's idea of collective persons, also opposed by Schutz, Kelsen insisted that the state was not a person, but a mere conjuncture of rights and obligations. In addition, Kelsen described how a "ground norm," such as a constitution, prescribed procedures and authority for creating new laws, and he ruled out any inquiry behind ground-norms in search of some ethico-jurisprudential justification of legal systems, which he considered to be positive in nature. Kelsen resisted any moral justification of legal systems not only because of their self-containedness, but also because moral beliefs widely varied, because rationality could not establish first principles in ethics as it could obtain objectivity in science, and because rational cognition was basically instrumental, as Weber, Mises, and Hayek thought. Justice was "at bottom alien to logic," but the lack of conclusiveness and relativity of views about justice promoted tolerance and a self-responsibility that was often missing among those who, in flight from their responsibility, submitted to a moral order beyond themselves.[38]

Without attacking Kelsen publicly, Schutz praised Felix Kaufmann for supplementing Kelsen's thought by showing phenomenologically how norms emerged from the will's stance toward an emotively experienced object or state of affairs, how norms and sanctions were experienced conjointly, and how in everyday life a person experienced the is/ought distinction. By founding law upon phenomenologically clarified experience, Kaufmann improved upon Kelsen, who posited a strange, ontically originary normative meaning sphere, "containing in itself a cosmos of values" and knowable to a special experience-transcendent knowledge based on oppositions between being and validity, being and meaning, or real and ideal objects. Schutz also revealed his opinions on Kelsen's work in a letter to Marvin Farber in which he agreed with Roscoe Pound's criticisms of Kelsen's 1942 *Social Control through Law* in spite of Kelsen's early influence upon him. Although Pound advanced many criticisms without mentioning Kelsen's name, perhaps Schutz, given his endorsement of Kaufmann's work, would have agreed with Pound's view that Kelsen had detached his theory from the lived, practical necessities of everyday life. Pound, linked to American legal realism and critical legal studies, had leveled a similar criticism against the U.S. Supreme Court for its frequent rulings that New Deal legislation, important for the relief of massive suffering, was unconstitutional.[39]

Interestingly, though, the principal reason for Pound's objections to Kelsen had less to do with the tensions between lived experience and theory and much more to do with Kelsen's relativism. Pound found a kind of skeptical realism resulting from Neo-Kantian relativism in jurisprudence and politics. Since for Kelsen the Constitution did not guarantee any preexisting rights and since there were no values with which to weigh competing rights claims, all that mattered was whether rulers could back up their threats with force. However, even Oliver Wendell Holmes, who considered the legal order as an order of force, recognized morality as "a check on the ultimate domination of force." Although Pound acknowledged that there might not be any consensus on a universal legal measure of values, there were certain commonly accepted postulates of practical activity that had proven their worth in the tradition and that could regulate a legal order. Kelsen's relativism also drew fire from the legal theorist Luis Recasens Siches and the political scientist Eric Voegelin, but Schutz himself never mentioned this specific critique of Kelsen's theory, even though he knew of this criticism from reading Pound and corresponding with Recasens Siches and Voegelin. Part of the problem, at it appears in correspondence with Voegelin, is that Schutz himself shared Kelsen's value-relativism.[40]

What becomes apparent in this chapter is that literally every one of Schutz's mentors espoused a kind of skepticism about moral-practical rationality, with the possible exception of Bergson or Husserl, both of whom, however, never made ethical theory the centerpiece of their philosophical reflections. Mises, Kelsen, and Weber refused to articulate any first ethical principles, did not believe that most people would ever agree to such principles, and denied or deemphasized any rationality other than that of the natural sciences that could instruct agents on the means for achieving their ends. Moreover, Schutz's mentors believed that epistemological value-freedom resulted in positive ethical consequences, such as promoting tolerance and self-responsibility. It is no wonder, then, that Alfred Schutz himself remained rather silent about his own ethical commitments and refused to elaborate them theoretically. This silence and an accompanying tendency to relativism, however, irked intellectual interlocutors such as Gurwitsch and Voegelin. Further, such silence on theoretical ethical matters seems somewhat at odds with the life of a man who showed himself to be a model of ethical living.

Chapter 4

Matters Unpublished

The Problem of Personality in the Social World

After critically synthesizing the work of Husserl and Weber in *Der sinnhafte Aufbau der sozialen Welt* and engaging the views of his mentors, particularly Mises's economic theory, Schutz spent the summers of 1936 and 1937 deepening his own philosophical position in manuscripts entitled "The Problem of Personality in the Social World." Due to the political upheavals in Germany and Austria that led to his immigration to the United States, only in the mid-1940s would he have the time and energy to publish an edited version of these manuscripts as "On Multiple Realities" in *Philosophy and Phenomenological Research.* According to Ilse, her husband produced some of these manuscripts during vacation, writing "half of the night" after hiking with her during the day in the mountains around Kanzelhöhe in Carinthia, and he wrote others at Iselsberg, where he had vacationed with the Machlups, prior to Hitler's "poisoning" of their lives. Four manuscripts make up the set entitled "The Problem of Personality in the Social World," in The Papers of Alfred Schutz. Schutz identified the first as being produced at Weitlaubrunn, from July 28 to August 22, 1936, and he designated the titles, places, and dates of the next three as follows: "The Unity of the Body" ("Die Einheit des Leibes"), Iselsberg, July 31, 1937; "The Temporalities of the Ego" ("Die Tempora des Ich"), Iselsberg, August 13, 1937; "The Constitution of the World of Working and its Modifications" ("Die Konstitution der Wirkwelt und ihrer Modifikationen"), Kanzelhöhe, from August 22 to August 27, 1937.[1]

Schutz interjects a pragmatic slant into his earlier views in the first manuscript by emphasizing the general thesis of the "acting ego," the origin of the "pure pragma," i.e., a working (*wirken*) upon the world, and by establishing the ego's unity on pragmatic bases, since every *cogitare* is an *agere.* He turns critically to his own work, mentioning how in the very consideration of a project one witnesses "the inbreaking of the great category of 'fiat,' which even *Der sinnhafte Aufbau* has evaded, as has all of phenomenology," though Max Scheler and William James made reference to the term. Philosophers err, according to Schutz, in neglecting the *ego agens* engaging the world from the start, in isolating a *durée*-immanent stratum of consciousness free from any working in the world, and then in appending the *ego agens* to *durée*. Schutz proceeds to describe how a pragmatically conditioned act of reflection singles out a *me ipsum* (e.g., oneself as a symphony-goer) as an object appearing in one's field, and this *me ipsum*, already past, represents one of the several partial personalities of one's self (e.g., one is also a teacher). Insofar as this self-reflectivity effectively splits the unified self into a plurality, the normal self experiences on a regular basis a kind of schizophrenia. Although the civic time (*bürgerliche Zeit*) of days, months, and years is pragmatically constructed to accord with world-rhythms, such as hunger or sleep, the subjective experience of time involves the temporal modifications: now (*Jetzt*), past (*Früher*), future (*Fortran*). Past experiences can either be still living in the (specious) present, capable of being reawakened in the present, or "dead" if they will never return and be effectual again, and this last continual "killing off" of earlier egos reveals the process of aging and the irreversibility of time. In action, one continually changes from *hic* to *illic*, exchanging near for far in the physically present surrounding *Umwelt* or exchanging the *Umwelt* itself for the contemporary *Mitwelt*. Such modifications suggest other potentialities: the interpersonal possibility to implement actions observed in others and the potentiality to enter into the differing "worlds" of phantasy, dreams, or theory. Schutz concludes this first manuscript by distinguishing strata of the personality and locating in the intersection between one's pragmatically conditioned attention to life and hierarchy of plans a site that any serious doctrine of ethics must take into account.[2]

In "The Unity of the Body," a year later, reiterating the importance of pragmatic motivation that even permits possibilities for choice to arise, Schutz highlights how one's partial self-typifications, as roles, may conflict, to the point of schizophrenia. His comments take on an autobiographical ring when he adds: "I in my workplace may take advantage only with difficulty of opportunities with my family, but in my home or on vacation I wish to know nothing of myself as a person with an occupation, and to do this is required a great overcoming—in a certain measure, to keep one's housecoat on and one's business suit off." In addition, insofar as one's personal center includes essentially actual experiences of which one is often only barely aware or has difficulty speaking, one's reflection can never be exhaustive. Returning to the themes of ethics and intersubjectivity, he remarks that one of the personalities in conflict with others is the ethical person, and he insists that the conception of an ego isolated from social reality is only an arbitrary abstraction.[3]

"The Temporalities of the Ego and Their Perspectival Division" reiterates the opaqueness to reflection of one's "now," which, as the thick center of an *ego agens* rather than an isolated point, "encompasses an endless mix of elements, attitudes, actions, [and] experiences which are regulated in accord with my present interest and attention." Such pragmatic interests lead and direct any reflective turning to one's own experience, and such reflection converts the civic time of hours and days, which pertains to the working ego in the now, into (dead) "world time." Reverting to the previous year's discussion of the past as living, able to be reawakened, or "dead," Schutz provides examples of the last: one's childhood, one's being a soldier on the front, or the Neo-Kantian philosophical phase through which one passed. In a passage that is lengthy but worth quoting, he develops this last point into an interesting piece of what could be called phenomenological *philosophy*, discussing the issue of immortality in conjunction with his own favorite topic of temporality:

> We have denominated this last group of phenomena of the past ego with the metaphorical terms "the deceased partial egos." But it is more than simply a metaphor, when we bring into connection with the ur-phenomenon of death these life forms of our past ego that have sunk into the past and will never again see the light of day. We will leave to the side the metaphysical result that death is no life-transcending phenomenon but rather a life-immanent one, a result that makes immediately visible in complete earnestness the problem of immortality. We will limit ourselves to this point, namely that precisely the continuing killing off (*Abtötung*) of earlier life-forms is that which produces that essential grounding fact of human existence that we call "aging." And, further, that the therein included irreversibility of that time—of *durée*, of the world-time, of civic time—is identical with the inescapability of death. We cannot avoid that death, which constantly threatens our total ego in the now, our ego itself. In addition, we cannot elude those partial deaths, which concern the basic attitudes of the most intimate layers of our personality, as well as the ego itself, which, however, will survive the death of these partial egos due to its ability to be always newly present as *ego agens*. In this experience of one's own partial deaths lies a significance to be found within every death, which must befall this *ego agens*, the ego, my ego. Upon this certainty rests Kierkegaard's problem of anxiety and Heidegger's problem of "thrownness in the world." But upon the daily experience that we survive our partial deaths, upon this experience that we are only changed, rests all our hope in immortality, which takes from death its horrors and shows it to us as something to be trusted. It is on this experience that Plato bases his doctrine of the wandering soul with all its consequences (including the theory of *anamnesis*); on this experience rests the

> Christian basic attitude of hope as well as Nietzsche's doctrine of the eternal return.[4]

For Schutz, the future does not simply follow chronologically on the present, but rather penetrates it, and, for that matter, the present relevance system, on which one bases uncertain decisions about the future, will change and no longer exist in the future as in the present when one decides. From these discussions of temporality, he draws out implications for the social sciences, since in order to understand the subjective chance that actors attribute to their action, it is important to return to the relevances and stock of knowledge they had at hand when they adopted their in-order-to projects. He even situates his analyses with reference to ethics, since

> [e]very true ethics, which will be able to appear as science or to remain as one, must take for an object of its investigation the phenomenon of fundamental anxiety and the typical reactions to it. But it will be able to do this only if it engages the doctrine of the temporalities of the ego in their different manner and if it makes for its own the truth of Leibniz's comment that the past is pregnant with the future.[5]

In other words, he conceives himself as laying out certain fundamental structures of a philosophical anthropology, with which any theoretical ethics must come to terms.[6]

He claims that his final manuscript, "The Constitution of the World of Working and Its Modifications," surpasses his *Phenomenology* in taking as its focus *Wirken* rather than *Handeln*. In that manuscript, he clarifies previous terminology (e.g., "pragma" as a spontaneous experience aimed at the volitive act of fiat), reasserts that all perceiving and apperceiving are pragmatically conditioned, and affirms that the act of working seeks to become secure about the unity and coherence of the world within reach. This essay then takes up the modifications of the *Wirkwelt* effected when one experiences "shocks" or "leaps," in Kierkegaard's sense, that catapult one into the worlds or provinces of meaning (*Sinngebieten*) of phantasy, dreams, and theoretical contemplation. Each possesses its own regulative principles, compossibilities, meaning-lawfulness, and specific accent of reality that close it off from the others, without any transformation formulae assisting facile movement between them. This treatment, closely resembling that of "On Multiple Realities," differs in using the vocabulary of pragma, in stating forthrightly that the analyses of phantasy and dream worlds were aimed at developing the notion of theory, and in neglecting to develop more fully the basic features of a "finite province of meaning."

Further, this earlier work draws interesting comparisons and contrasts between rational action as Weber depicts it and scientific rationality (since both, for instance, strive for distinctness and clarity of concepts and proceed step by step in pursuing goals that lead to other goals). Nevertheless, as he would do later on the basis of the phenomenological paradoxes of Fink and Farber, he reflects extensively on the indirect communication involved in articulating scientifically domains quite distinct from science, such as those of fantasies, dream, and the world of working prior to its theoretical description.[7]

These manuscripts show us a restless Schutz, criticizing his earlier work, setting out in new directions, and emphasizing pragmatic dimensions that will later equip him for engaging the American pragmatists, often cited in his later writings—clearly he made a pragmatic turn before ever arriving in the United States. The *ego agens* here emerges into prominence even over *durée*, resting upon layers of personality of which it is barely conscious and placing at the base of cognition and reflection themselves a selecting, assessing, and attending. At the same time, he does not abandon his past work, for it is clear that these manuscripts display the concern for the irreducible pluralism of spheres (whether temporalities or multiple realities) and dissonance of roles (e.g., family member and business person), both of which preoccupied Max Weber. Indeed, the ethical personality constitutes one of those roles to be reconciled with the others for Schutz, as it did for Weber in his wrestling with an ethics of responsibility. A concern for the domain of ethics is never absent from these manuscripts, whether at the intersection of the attention to life and one's hierarchy of plans or in the entire effort to articulate a philosophical anthropology that no ethics could afford to neglect. One can further wonder whether Schutz's interest in autonomous and irreducible spheres of activity and the conflicts possible between them may not reflect his own life, in which he sought to juggle often to the point of exhaustion the worlds of business, philosophy, music, and family. Likewise, these manuscripts manifest an ever-present recognition of temporality with its uncertainties, incongruities, and permutations that one needs to take into account to avoid intersubjective misunderstanding and to address the profoundly ethico-practical questions of aging, death, and immortality. The tumultuous events of Germany and Austria in the 1930s were about to bring about changes in his life that he never could have totally foreseen and that would put to death life as he knew it, and from the ashes of that death Schutz's *ego agens* would rise.

Diary of a 1937 Visit to the United States

From March 18 to May 12, 1937, Schutz visited the United States with business associates and recorded his impressions in an unpublished diary clearly revealing his biographical situation, i.e., his typifications and relevances, which become evident whenever a Stranger adjusts to a very new set of circumstances. Not all the experiences on this trip were pleasant, and Schutz in a letter to Raoul Rabinerson written on December 15, 1939, after a few months of permanent residency had changed his negative attitudes toward the United States, referred to the "unhappy impressions" earlier communicated to Rabinerson immediately after this first visit. Ilse Schutz, too, in her interview with Anne Schwabacher, mentioned that her husband had misgivings about moving to the United States in 1939 because of experiences on this earlier trip. Although he may have hesitated about the move because he was a Francophile and "didn't like anything English," Ilse recalled that on this trip "he learned for the first time the meaning of 'restricted.' Jews were never invited together with Gentile people; the hotels were restricted, the houses you could buy were restricted." She affirmed that he had said "he'd rather bring up his children in France, during the war, than move to the United States," but she eventually convinced him otherwise.[8]

At several points in his diary, he referred to American anti-Semitism. For instance, the March 23 entry mentioned a conversation with the head of a brokerage firm, himself Jewish, who mentioned that the United States had always been anti-Semitic, denying Jews access to hotels, better clubs, professorships at key universities, such as Harvard, or employment positions—for instance, at General Electric. Even though Jews had been active in politics and even held cabinet positions, this executive reported that a friend had refused to invite him out alone or with others because insults against Jews were as normal a part of the conversations as talk of the weather or stocks. Schutz lunched on April 1 with a vice-president of the Chase National Bank and observed that the latter was the only Jew working in the bank. These experiences of anti-Semitism affected him, and, when the Haberlers came from Boston, he recorded that Mrs. Haberler had become more prejudiced (*nachteilig*) and that he experienced difficulties communicating with an Aryan like Haberler, even though he knew him to be of good disposition. Two days later, while attending a boring movie and stepping outside with Haberler to smoke, Schutz recalled how Voegelin had said that Haberler sometimes felt that he was the measure of all things, implicitly substituting himself for "man," when he said that "Man was the measure of all things." Their parting of ways was "cool," and Schutz decided not to visit him at Harvard. Schutz rarely referred to anti-Semitism in his public writings or other correspondence, but one can see here the intense feeling and souring of relationships that the worldwide anti-Semitism of the 1930s produced, even though the full force of its virulence was yet to be felt.[9]

Schutz was also extremely alert to anti-black prejudice, much like Simone de Beauvoir, another European philosopher, whose diary of a visit to the

United States showed her repeatedly attentive to unfair discrepancies in the treatment of the races. After attending a black nightclub and commenting on the elegantly dressed black women patrons and the songs and dances of the performers, Schutz confessed his surprise upon hearing that in some states in the South marriage between blacks and whites was prohibited. He noticed that the cook preparing a meal served in an apartment was black, that it was "natural" in the United States for blacks to polish shoes, and that mostly black men worked in the horrible setting of the Swift packing plant in Chicago. Beyond this sensitivity to the racial composition of difficult workplaces, he also pointed out that all personnel preparing packages under the dehumanizing conditions of the Sears Roebuck mail order industry were women.[10]

His sensitivity to the plight of outsiders, such as Jews, blacks, or women, also reached to European intellectuals in the United States. For instance, he found a lunch with Gerhard Husserl and his sister a sad affair, since neither of them had succeeded, their futures were highly uncertain, they were separated from their families, and Gerhard received a paltry stipend of $150 a month. Schutz sensed the solitude of Machlup and Farber when he visited them in Buffalo, since "each has few people to talk to," in spite of the fact that Machlup had formed a philosophical discussion group there that had included Farber and Richard Hays Williams. Dorion Cairns, with whom Schutz repeatedly dined, admitted to having only one person with whom he spoke. Cairns, whom Schutz considered to be perhaps the most gifted Husserl scholar, had not been able to attract enough students, had not published anything of his own in twelve years, and relied entirely on the salary of his wife, who taught in a Montessori school.[11]

Landscapes and cityscapes in the United States moved Schutz positively and negatively. For example, looking out over New York from the eighty-sixth floor of a large building, he observed the whole city growing organically in a discrete and suitable fashion; New York appeared there in all its magnificence—the opposite of his idea of what Americanism was about. Forty-second Street in Times Square, however, appeared as one of the more tiring and tasteless streets he had ever seen. Houses in Brooklyn struck him as ugly, and Robert Lambert informed him that such houses were typical in places outside well-known metropolitan areas. The trip between New York and Washington bored him, with its monotonous landscapes dotted by run-down houses all along the route—one of the saddest tableaux he had even seen. Lambert again considered such landscapes typical, and another business colleague could not cease speaking about the depressing effect of such countryside. It amazed Schutz that a self-service convenience store was located on the site of Niagara Falls, and when the New York City subway stopped at 107th Street, he perceived a "counter-New York," dirty and unkempt, filled with children playing in the streets. On the other hand, he seemed to enjoy the multicultural side of New York, in which every time one turned a corner, one ended up in a different world. Washington impressed him as resembling a beautiful European garden city, and he visited the various monuments there as well as Mt. Vernon. Even though far from his family on his birthday, April 13, and filled with melancholy thoughts on account of his absence, he felt consoled by the hilly vistas along the Hudson River. In Chicago, he was impressed with Michigan Avenue and with a massive hailstorm that stalled his tour.[12]

He not only exercised his aesthetic sensibilities on landscapes and cityscapes, but he also regularly visited museums and attended plays and movies, evaluating what he saw. Within three days of his arrival, he visited the Metropolitan Museum of Art and stated that the quality of its works was uneven. Several days later, he attended a play entitled *The Women,* which he judged to be deficient in its acting and wholly predictable in its dialogue, even though the settings were well done. On a later visit to the Metropolitan, he discovered the Altman collection of Chinese porcelains and delighted in paintings by Rembrandt, Hals, Vermeer, and Velázquez. Mia, a friend of one of his acquaintances, Lacy L. Kux, a partner of Byfield and Company, a New York Stock Exchange firm, guided him on a tour of Greenwich Village, and together they watched a performance of George Bernard Shaw's *Candida.* The play evoked a comment from him to the effect that whereas earlier he had stood on the side of the young revolutionary, Marchbanks, critical of repressive Victorian social mores, he more and more concurred with the pastor, Morrell, who maintained his marital commitments while striving for societal reforms. The next afternoon, Schutz attended with Mia a performance of the New York Philharmonic, about which he remarked that the wind instruments far surpassed those of the Vienna orchestra, that each individual performer was wonderful, and that the orchestra as a whole was excellent. He detected in the director, Arthur Rodzwiski, the influence of Arturo Toscanini, and he concluded his assessment by noting that the production was well studied, generally precise, and attentive to all the necessary details. The only problem with the concert was the dance suite by Copland that Schutz thought was dreadful (*fürchterlich*). That evening he returned to the Metropolitan to examine once again the Altman collection and to see other works, particularly those by Rembrandt, one of his favorite painters, as Winternitz had observed. During a short trip to Chicago, he acquainted himself with the Chicago Institute of Art and discovered its sizeable modern French painting section, with Renoir well represented. He finished off his day at a tasteless, Midwest show in the Parisian style. Throughout his visit to the United States, he showed himself a critical, well-experienced observer of all the arts.[13]

Despite this mixed review of the state of the arts in the United States, he found the country quite advanced in technology. Although the stock exchange seemed hellish, the high quality of those working there stood out for him, since in their operative style he detected no English stiffness, French roundaboutness, or German pedantry. The efficiency and volume of work both astonished and "scared" him, reminding him of the threshing scene of *Die Meistersinger*. After having directed some queries to a New York lawyer who had granted his group an interview, he was awestruck when he received a ten-page note citing previous cases—all compiled within the space of two minutes. More was accomplished in that law firm in a half hour than would be in a week in Paris. Although more bored and uncomfortable during his trip from New York to Chicago on the *20th Century Limited* than he had been on European express trains, he marveled at huge weather map at the Chicago Board of Trade, the largest grain stock market in the world. It was one of the few things that Americans claimed to be the "biggest," the "largest," or the "tallest" that actually was so. Even little technical devices caught his attention, such as the beautiful machine that made orange juice in the apartment of one of his hosts.[14]

When it came to his economic and political observations, he usually simply reported people's comments, reserving his own judgment, as if he were a social scientist describing other's thoughts. For instance, he merely asserted that a group of bankers with whom he met in New York approved of Roosevelt's New Deal as a way of stimulating the economy. Although these bankers felt that the intervention of government had warded off a catastrophe, they continued to have their questions about the constitutionality of the Wagner Act. He also marked the fact that a New York lawyer with whom they met was one of Roosevelt's advisors. Even though his friend Fritz Machlup opposed government intervention, Schutz recalled that Machlup had agreed with Roosevelt's effort to restrain the flight of capital from the United States. Roosevelt had his opponents, though, such as the vice-president of the Chase National Bank, who, at a luncheon accused Roosevelt of acting irresponsibly; the banker was a Republican, as, Schutz claimed, all the leading bankers were. This banker desired a return to gold-backed currency, and it amused Schutz that his critique of the American economy paralleled Mises's. Finally, Schutz mentioned how quickly a train of events had turned against labor, particularly with the Supreme Court's testing of the Wagner Act and criticisms of the strike movement by the Canadian prime minister.[15]

On two occasions Schutz's compassion clearly shone through, though he refrained from spelling out any thorough political or economic position. While in Chicago, he had visited a Sears Roebuck Company catalog mail office. He began by tabulating the benefits of such a catalog mail business for those who lived in rural areas and experienced difficulty traveling to large cities to make purchases. He then indicated that all orders were to be sent to the packaging room within an hour of their reception, that all the personnel in the packaging room were women, and that they were required to wrap ten packages every fifteen minutes. If they failed to do so, they were penalized fifteen cents on an hour's salary—a large amount, given their meager salaries. This entire arrangement evoked the following comment from Schutz:

> In a pure economic sense, this enterprise is in a great manner completely rationalized. However, when one sees the poor women pursuing their work at this murderous (*mörderischen*) pace for only $20 per week wage, then one understands that neither this ultimate form of the division of labor nor generally the economic point of view is the goal to be desired.[16]

This compassionate comment suggests why he believed that economic science, valid with its own domain, belonged within the wider context of the life world, whose values might curb the excesses to which a rationality only economic in character might be prone.[17]

Also in Chicago, he had visited the Swift packing plant. Noticing that mostly black men worked in the setting, he dramatically depicted the series of events taking place when one large black man entered a small room, into which pigs had been crammed. The black man grabbed their hind legs and hung them with a hook on a chain passing by him; the animals would scream, and then their throats were cut. The chain proceeded to carry the convulsing corpses through boiling water, and the white cadavers emerged three minutes later without any bristles. The next set of workers awaited the chain, one to cut off the pigs ears, another to open their stomachs, a third to take out their intestines, and a fourth to saw the animals in two. Each carried out his "sorry job" so efficiently, Schutz said, that twenty-nine minutes after entering the plant, the pieces of meat lay in a smokehouse. He added, "I must say that the conveyor belt that in record time transforms a mother sow from a living organism to a cadaver and to a delicacy, appeared to me, in spite of all the hardness known to be part of these things, as something wholly horrible (*ganz abscheulich*)." He then watched the process for sheep, which did not know what awaited them and which gave him an occasion for all kinds of reflections on politics. These reactions to the infliction of cruelty on human beings and animals in the name of economic efficiency, as well as his constant attunement to the plight of Jews, African Americans, and women, reveal ethical sensitivities and commitments that, I will argue later, are implicit throughout his philosophical writings.[18]

Chapter 5

Anschluss

The *Anschluss*, the conjoining of Austria and the Third Reich, was, as mentioned, formally promulgated on March 13, 1938. Under the pretext that Artur Seyss-Inquart, a Nazi who had been appointed minister of the Interior and Security as a result of Hitler's Berchtesgaden meeting with Schuschnigg, had sent a telegram requesting the aid of German troops to restore law and order in Austria, Hitler's troops seized Austria. Hermann Göring informed Sir Neville Hendersen that Hitler, entering with his troops and traveling to Linz and later Vienna, was merely visiting the grave of his mother in Austria. As mentioned previously, Hitler was warmly welcomed by large crowds and by officials such as Cardinal Innitzer, the Catholic primate, who met with him in his hotel suite even before he arrived in Vienna and promised that Austria's Catholics would become "the truest sons of the great Reich into whose arms they had been brought back on this momentous day." After the 99 percent plebiscite vote in favor of the *Anschluss*, which even Karl Renner, the former first chancellor of the "German-Austrian Republic" of 1918 had endorsed, the persecution of the Jews described earlier began in earnest.[1]

The Emigration of the Immediate Family, March 13, 1938–June 12, 1938

The impact of the *Anschluss* upon Alfred Schutz and his family was catastrophic, as Ilse recounted. Five years after the birth of Evelyn Elizabeth Schutz, born May 22, 1933, George, their son, had been born on February 23, 1938. After Alfred had ascertained that his wife and newborn son were of sound health, he had left on a business trip to Paris for two weeks. During his stay in Paris, with his family still in Vienna, Hitler invaded Austria. Since the Nazis would have suspected Alfred as an international banker and businessman of moving monies out of Austria, it was perilous for him to return to Austria, but he was tormented by the thought that the family he loved remained in Vienna. He stayed in Paris as the result of very strong recommendations from Max Mintz and his wife and Ludwig von Mises, the latter of whom Ilse later thanked profusely because he had vehemently insisted that Alfred not return. Years later, and sometimes in her sleep, Ilse remembered the *Anschluss*'s haunting sounds: four hundred planes roaring over Vienna and tanks rumbling into town and stopping at a Nazi center that seemed to be located directly across the street from their home.[2]

Insofar as all mail entering and leaving Austria was censored, the *Anschluss* exacerbated the painfulness of the separation between Alfred and his family, since Ilse felt reluctant to express any honest feelings other than to say in repeated correspondence, "All is well." The frequency of her letters indicated that she was quite aware of how concerned Alfred must have been about even the continued existence of his family; she obviously hoped that a regular flow of letters, even though lacking in expressiveness, might allay such a concern. Alfred complained to Fritz Machlup about these lifeless letters:

> All that I hear are warnings "for God's sake to write more cautiously," as I do anyhow and regularly, and these letters [from them] are written in the style of summerhouse idylls which in their untruthfulness (*Verlogenheit*) are doubly wounding. I have never received such letters from my people until now.[3]

In addition to the many letters warning him to be careful, he fortunately received several others from those who had seen Ilse and the children and reported that they were in good health.[4]

Schutz's parents, nicknamed Hansi and Peter, inundated him with tokens of their loving concern. They wrote regularly, sent birthday flowers, related anecdotes about his children, told him how proud they were of him, kept Alfred posted on Ilse's changing immigration status, and informed him finally of her departure on the *Orient Express* for Paris. Letters from various friends no doubt both consoled him and heightened his anxieties. For example, Hayek promised to do everything possible to help and invited him to visit Zurich. In correspondence with Machlup, now at the University of Buffalo, Schutz inquired about the possibility of finding employment in London and requested a letter promising to support him for some months in another land until he found employment. Referring to "the fearful events in Vienna," he mentioned that the Mintzes had fled to Zurich and Froehlich to Paris, that Karl Schlesinger had killed himself, and that Winternitz and Kaufmann, for all he knew, were still in Vienna. He described refugees arriving in Paris with anxiety flashing out madly from their eyes and narrating the most obscene details—all of which produced in him the most heartfelt (*brustester*) anxiety over his family.

Machlup, who had received eleven requests for immigration affidavits as of April 5, 1938, responded immediately with a guarantee of support for six months and reported that Kaufmann had found a job at the New School, as had Morgenstern at Princeton. Machlup was also assisting Voegelin, Schiff, and Winternitz to immigrate, and he hoped that Schutz still had time for his scientific work. He urged him to go to a quiet bench in the forest and bracket his *Mitwelt* for a while. Vilma Thierry, Emanuel Wintnernitz's cousin, kept Schutz abreast of the visa status of his friend, who was intent on leaving Austria before the *Reinmacherie* (the purification of Germany from Jews). On departing the Third Reich, Walter Froehlich expressed a desire to visit Schutz en route to London, and later notified Schutz that Fritz Unger and Marianne Low-Hamburger were both in custody and that Mises and Kelsen were suffering bouts of depression. Fleeing Austria, Felix Kaufmann met Schutz in Paris for a hurried two-hour dinner en route to the United States, and showed him his invitation from Alvin Johnson to teach at the New School. Later, by mail, he implored Schutz to secure a French entry permit for a friend. It was no wonder that Schutz informed Machlup that he could not even think of scientific work, adding ruefully, "I never would have thought that the beautiful weeks which we experienced with each other last summer would form the end of the whole period."[5]

Other friends wrote about their arrests, incarcerations, and property confiscations, and one friend saw his writing career interrupted completely because a Nazi physician had refused to treat the arterio-atrophy in his leg. In spite of all this bad news, Schutz pressed on, engaging in numerous services on behalf of others: arranging immigration details, answering immigration queries, pursuing passport inquiries, transferring bank accounts, recovering lost funds, providing investment information, advising (Fritz Machlup) regarding stock accounts, referring people to American contacts, writing letters of recommendation, and explaining France's Aryan/Jewish marriage laws. Frequently, those petitioning his assistance expressed gratitude, because they recognized how overburdened he already was.[6]

In addition to all these difficulties, Reitler and Company informed him that his services would terminate on August 31, 1938. He responded by thanking Mr. Reitler for the privilege of working eleven years with him, mentioned his interests in international law or academic work, and entreated him to send his severance pay to Paris and to transfer his funds out of Austria. No doubt the upheaval the company experienced required even more efforts beyond those necessary for its day-to-day functioning, and at one point he was working thirteen hours a day, from early in the morning until 9:30 at night.[7]

In spite of his huge expenditure of energy for work and on behalf of others, the central issue of concern was, of course, the safety of his family back in Vienna. While Ilse was familiarizing herself with all the details of immigrating, Alfred, having learned that his employment would be discontinued, proposed to her in a letter of May 8, 1938, some decisive measures. He would have to find employment in Paris, London, or the United States, but he also pointed to friendships to which they could always appeal for help: the families Rougier, Beaufils, Monteux, Robbins, Goldschmidt (who offered to welcome Ilse as a semipermanent house guest) in Amsterdam, and Machlup in the United States. He observed, "Darling Ilse, if one has friends like that, one doesn't have to fear the future," and, anticipating hard times ahead, added, "This opens up a life of doing without and living a humble existence, but, Ilse, you are brave and clever, and we will get through this together." In addition, so that she might complete various forms and applications in Vienna, he provided information about his political neutrality, military record, and business comportment—all of which benefited the "fatherland"; and, expecting that her visa would be ready in a few days, he urged her to obtain a reliable, first-class lawyer. The letters between Ilse and Alfred subsequent to that decisive letter of May 8 were filled with expressions of affection and mutual support, and Ilse informed him that Husserl had congratulated him on George's birth, urged him to relax by playing music, and recounted anecdotes about the children. Among these many letters was a stark document, stamped with a swastika. It affirmed that Alfred Schutz and Ilse Heim were emigrating from the Third Reich and that they promised that neither they nor their children would ever set foot in the Reich again.[8]

Ilse provided the details of the final passage to freedom in her interview with Anne Schwabacher. She did not know where to put George, three and a half months old at that time, and dreaded trying to hold on to Evelyn and carry George while Nazi soldiers interrogated her at the frontier. However, Evelyn had received for her birthday on May 22 a beautiful doll's carriage, which she did not want to leave behind. So Ilse put George in the doll's carriage, and they traveled safely by train without meeting any Nazi officers and without running short of money, even though they had only been allowed to carry ten marks. Ilse gave the money as a gift to the conductor at the border. Upon meeting the family at the train station, Alfred asked anxiously where his son was, only to find him asleep in the doll carriage.[9]

Arranging the Emigration of Schutz's Parents from Vienna to Paris, June 12, 1938–April 6, 1939 (and Ilse's Mother, Gisela Heim, June 4, 1939)

Many tasks confronted the family immediately. Hansi and Peter cleaned the apartment and supervised the packing and shipping of goods (and forbade the movers to use books as hammers!). It was also extremely important that workers for the family were satisfied, since if they were not Jewish and disgruntled they might go to the Nazis, but Ilse, before leaving Vienna, had arranged severance pay with the cleaning woman, and Alfred, from Paris, assisted the maintenance man regarding employment opportunities for a relative. In addition, Alfred's studio apartment in Paris was overcrowded with the arrival of the rest of the family, the children's crying (which Hansi said that she longed to hear) disturbed other tenants, and the landlord threatened to raise the rent. As a result, the family took up summer quarters by the ocean in Normandy, while Alfred found a new apartment with a three-year lease, which they occupied on October 3, 1938. During this time, he wrote officials, legal experts, and friends on behalf of his friend, Wintnernitz. The latter, on the edge of despair, was overjoyed when he finally received an entry permit for Switzerland and a visa for the United States. Machlup, who arranged for a teaching position for Wintnernitz, found the prospect of him teaching economics in Kalamazoo humorous, but unfortunately the position fell through, and Winternitz, having moved to the United States, found himself forced "to capture the shabby remains of my existence and glue them together anew."[10]

Schutz, as was usual, was impelled to come to the assistance of many others beside Winternitz. He assisted people regarding employment, job applications, letters of recommendation, money deposits outside Germany, communication links, exit papers and transit visas, bank account transfers, currency exchanges, loans, curricula vitae preparation, stock dividends, balance appraisals, the cashing and crediting of checks, recovery of confiscated properties or moneys, affidavit writing, the search for lawyers, finding temporary housing, making contacts for refugees, locating needed expertise or lost heirs, or even the placement of Jewish children in homes in England. He showed himself an understanding reader and listener in letter exchanges with friends such as Renée Hiemasch, Anna Kaff, Erich Stadler, Marcel Friedmann, Alice Gerstl, Walter Froehlich, Viktor Stadler, Max Mintz, Eric Voegelin, Felix Kaufmann, Oskar Schutz, and Amy Emödi. For instance, Paul Landsberg, a French student of Max Scheler communicated to Schutz his grief over his mother's suicide, and Felix Kaufmann reported the arrest and confinement of relatives in Dachau. Except for attending an occasional colloquium (e.g., with Walter Lippmann), Schutz was simply unable to find the time or leisure for scientific work.[11]

In spite of these many involvements, again Schutz's principal concern during this period from June to April was rescuing his parents, Hansi and Peter, and Ilse's mother, Gisa, who had been widowed in 1936. Since Gisa owned a house that had to be sold to obtain an exit permit and to pay her emigration costs, and since no buyers were forthcoming, she had to submit her applications (*Demandes*) for an exit permit a second time; then she had to submit it a third time when the Nazis "lost" her second application. Meanwhile, Alfred, Ilse, and her brother Erich, who had moved to Prague, explored the possibility of moving Hansi and Peter to Czechoslovakia to live with Otto Weissberger, the uncle with whom the young Alfred had vacationed. However, all the efforts to prepare the legal documentation collapsed when the Munich Agreement of September 20, 1938, permitted Hitler to enter Czechoslovakia to seize the Sudetenland. Everything began moving at an accelerated pace when in early November Nazis invaded the parents' apartment at gunpoint, seized the 8,500 marks that Peter needed to pay an excise tax, and ordered them to vacate the property within three days. Peter and Hansi moved from one relative's house to another, and this enormous stress resulted in Peter taking nitroglycerin for heart problems and in Hansi developing severe sciatic and hip pains and needing to use a cane.[12]

Alfred wrote letters explaining the documentation his parents would need, and they finally managed to secure entry permits for Luxembourg and Cuba, but then Hansi, after a five-hour conversation with someone "well versed" in immigration matters, figured out a way to emigrate to France. On December 31, 1938, having presented thirty-five documents to the Jewish Kultusgemeinde, assisting Jewish immigration, they were told they would depart by mid-January 1939. The Nazis recalled their files, but then later reinstated them, due to Peter's persistence, and they left Austria at last on April 6, bound for Paris. Navigating this Nazi bureaucratic maze was no mean feat for such elderly people as Peter, with his angina and rheumatism, and Hansi, with her hip inflammations, so Peter conferred the power of attorney on a substitute who waited in line for him, but only after he had certified his health maladies to Nazi officials. Similarly, when the Nazis continually required new and unanticipated documentation and when Hansi's health would not permit her to walk long distances to offices in the depth of the Austrian winter, she hired taxis. But hiring substitutes and using taxis even only occasionally were expensive, and they felt quite anxious about spending money before they knew accurately the continuously changing fees that the Nazis would charge anyone who intended to leave the country. Subjecting the elderly to this bureaucratic torture was a form of physical cruelty to be matched only by the psychological cruelty of continually postponing the departure dates. The letters at this time indicate that the anticipated departure dates were postponed nine different times, and one can imagine the tensions Alfred and his family must also have felt when their hopes were regularly built up and then dashed.[13]

Despite these physical and psychological pressures, Hansi rose to the occasion even more than Peter or Gisa, running to government offices, waiting in lines, and even taking formal courses in French. She admitted to Alfred and Ilse, "I am amazed at my energy and composure," and said, "I cannot even recognize myself with my calm and demeanor, and Peter will verify that

I'm also being a strong support for him and Mama." Sustained by letter exchanges and telephone conversations with the family in Paris and by her religious faith, she called to mind the separation she experienced in sending her son off to World War I and thinking that after this parting she would not have to sacrifice any more. Recalling on January 6, 1939, the exact date when he had gone to the front—namely, January 7, 1918—she expressed hope that this same time of the year would now bring them together. Alfred mirrored his mother's strength, assuming responsibility for so many people while working long hours for the Reitler company and the disagreeable Lambert, often not taking lunch breaks and not being able to write his parents until two a.m. For Alfred, it was particularly painful to have to go on business trips after June 12 and to separate again from his family, who had just rejoined him after months of absence. His parents, aware that he was exhausted, suffering from insomnia, and deprived of the tranquility needed for scientific work, worried about the grief on his and Ilse's faces and his weight loss, both of which they detected in the photographs he sent them.[14]

When his parents finally arrived in Paris, a great burden was lifted, though. At about this same time, Schutz received a letter from Edward Rebhan, Ilse's cousin by marriage, who himself had just fled Austria and who gave voice to the mixed feelings of horror, anger, uncertainty, and elation that refugees such as Schutz's parents (and Schutz and his family) must have felt. The eloquence and poignancy of Rebhan's letter bears extensive quoting:

> What a relief to communicate openly, person to person, without having to disguise, feign, and couch things and how marvelous it is to be able to live here as a free person again among equals instead of as a leper kept by vicious, underhanded animals who are out to kill. . . .
>
> One forgets that one has only been here a few weeks and is a refugee without a home, without work, and without a penny in one's pocket after having spent thirty years saving and getting established in order to provide security for one's old age and one's loved ones. . . .
>
> The thieves removed from our apartment all of our jewelry, cash, and my saving account books, and they took me into the party headquarters during the night of November 11 and beat me for two hours and put me through a punishment routine (*strafexercieren*), twelve men against one. I then engaged an Aryan lawyer. Considering that the plundering took place at the official local party headquarters and since I had known a number of those people there by name, I had counted on a return of a few of those things. The lawyer was pessimistic from the start and said one cannot really speak of justice in these circumstances, since Berlin protects and orders the *Aktion*, as the plundering is called. Three nights later, I was visited

> by the Gestapo for a night inquiry about my bank safe-deposit box and key. The Gestapo told me that I would get back the assets after my taxes were paid. I never saw a thing even though my tax payments were totally in order. The Gestapo official in charge denied everything and no lawyer could intervene on behalf of a Jew or he would be blacklisted. We were driven out of our apartment with ten days' notice. We couldn't sell securities until our departure was assured. This was difficult because officially Jews were not allowed to own anything and accounts could be liquidated only for the benefit of Aryan firms. One is frightened to death because every day ten new regulations are issued and all clerks are confused.
>
> The entire existence of this country of 90,000,000 people only revolves around and culminates in its 600,000 Jews. One sees nothing in the street, the newspapers, the offices, except J . . . J . . . J, as the purpose and focus of the civilization; and all the rules and regulations, as impossible to fulfill as they are, are designed only to set traps for Jews in which they can be caught. Unfortunately, they succeed all too often and when they do, they scream like wild Indians [*sic!*], "[We] caught Jewish criminals again." And the entire population believes them and is angered that there is still a place where this scum of the earth exists. The saddest part of the whole thing is that this is impossible to fathom if one hasn't lived in the midst of it oneself, as a chased animal. It is impossible to understand a situation such as this hunting down of human beings because it has never existed in the history of mankind. And one cannot explain it to anyone. One can imagine defaming a political or ethnographic minority in order to draw life-juices for the other, the beloved party. But no one understands when the only goal for organizations is focused on the Jews because of historical propaganda.[15]

The Departure of the Schutz Family from Paris for the United States, April 7, 1939–July 14, 1939

No sooner did Schutz's parents arrive in Paris than the French government required that foreigners (including those enjoying a right of asylum) between the ages of eighteen and forty-eight (Schutz would have been about forty at this time) register for military service. On April 18, 1939, Schutz wrote Lambert in the United States, explaining this new predicament and warning that if he were drafted, Reitler's business interests would be interrupted. Realizing that he would have to emigrate by July 28 when his French *Titre de voyage* expired, and, fearful to leave his family behind again, he obtained the last three available quota numbers but would have to wait for a year for new numbers to become available. As a result, Ilse would have to prepare her papers by the end of April and travel to the United States to apply for preference quota numbers for the children. In a worst-case scenario, if he were forced to leave France before she returned, he would leave his children in an English children's home "and put their fate in God's hands because my parents cannot physically care for them." He concluded by assuring Lambert of his desire to protect the company's interests. He cautioned that the present European unrest would last a long time, although he did not think it would result in war. The day he had spent setting up this plan was as "horrendous" as one could imagine.[16]

Continuing to attend to his business clients and personal friends, he enjoyed cordial relationships with several of the world-famous scholars living in Paris. He had already met Aron Gurwitsch in 1935 on a business trip to Paris, to which Gurwitsch and his wife Alice (Raja) had emigrated from Germany on April 1, 1933. This meeting occurred because Husserl had recommended Schutz "as a young man in Vienna who spends his days at the bank and is a phenomenologist by night," according to Alice's recollection. In Paris, Gurwitsch moved among circles including communists, socialists, those (such as his wife) associated with the League for Human Rights, and a group of Jewish emigrants. This latter group consisted of Gurwitsch and his wife, the Schönberg student pianist Erich Kahn and his wife and parents, Hannah Arendt and Gunter Stern, Siegfried and Lilli Kracauer, and, when they arrived, the Schutzes. Schutz also was familiar with Lucien Goldman, Gaston Berger, Alexandre Koyré, Gabriel Marcel, Hélène Metzger (niece of Lévy-Bruhl the anthropologist), Jacques Maritain, Maurice Merleau-Ponty, Jean Wahl, and Raymond Aron and Louis Rougier, the last two of whom were particularly close to Schutz. After Schutz's emigration to the United States, the Gurwitsch, Kahn, and Kracauer familes fled to a Paris suburb. Kahn and Kracauer, because they had German passports, were later interned, as Schutz worked from New York to assist their immigration to the United States.[17]

Since Gisa was still stranded in Vienna, Alfred sought legal advice on her behalf, kept Ilse informed of her mother's situation while Ilse traveled to the United States, and allowed Gisa access to one of his escrow accounts. Her son, Erich, persuaded his employers at Marks and Spencer in London to assume financial responsibility for her and arranged for her entry permit. She obtained a visa and flew to London on June 1, 1939.[18]

During Ilse's preparation for her trip to the United States, Alfred inquired into possible schools in London to which the children might be sent should her mission fail, transferred funds to a New York bank, and repeatedly visited the American Consulate in Paris, often up to three times a week. On May 3, 1939, Ilse departed on the *Queen Mary* for New York, and Alfred and she traded several letters, expressing affection and care for each other, with Alfred signing one message with "BML" ("Behalt mich lieb"), the letters inscribed in her wedding ring. In one of her letters, Ilse urged that they not succumb to anxiety and fear, since that would be to cede to Hitler the ultimate victory, the victimization of their spirits:

> Don't believe that Hitler is ruining our lives and contaminating our home because we are the ones permitting him to do that and calling to him from all sides and allowing him to spread out everywhere. He must be thrown out of our environment, not taken notice of and not taken into consideration . . .
>
> It all depends on the first step that we have to take. Then neither Hitler, nor Lambert, nor the problem with the parents will pull the floor out from under us. We will instead pick ourselves up from within with renewed strength to face our new, rich and fulfilling lives, for each other, with each other, for and with our children and for everything that is good and profound. Just one step is necessary.[19]

By three p.m. on May 9, within twenty-four hours of docking in New York and thanks to an immigration official sensitive to the plight of European Jews, Ilse had arranged that their application for preference numbers and a reentry permit be dispatched to Washington for the price of $3.00. While waiting for the preference numbers to be sent to Paris, she held a rendezvous with Lambert and Jeral, in which she defended her husband. She also discovered that Jeral and Reitler had participated in the Luxembourg guaranty for Alfred's parents and recommended that Alfred send Jeral "an unrestrained thank-you letter." Although Alfred urged her to remain in New York for a while after she found out that the preferences had been sent, news of an assassinated German in Poland and the threat of an immediate outbreak of war prompted her to return, satisfied with what she had achieved:

> I get a kick out of the fact that I was able to get things on their way all by myself without help from strangers and especially without lawyers. . . . All of that without having had to spend any money and without help or support from Lambert and Jeral, who still can't even fathom how it is possible that I came to New York without knowing my way around and quite simply took care of things without standing there helplessly and coming to them begging for advice.[20]

Only one somewhat painful incident marked Ilse's journey. After Felix Kaufmann and Max Mintz had visited with Ilse, they each wrote Schutz on May 11 to say that she appeared happy and confident despite the strain and that they looked forward to his arrival. Kaufmann, however, sent an "unofficial" letter the next day depicting how "incredibly hard you are making life for both your wife and yourself." Attributing this fact to Schutz's neurosis, he laid out four useful, if unsolicited, points: that Ilse verged on severe psychological damage, that Alfred needed to control himself as well at home as at work, that he needed regular conversation with a friend who would challenge him, and that he would lessen anxiety if he worked less. Ironically, Ilse mentioned in a letter after the meeting that she did not have as good an impression of the Kaufmanns as she did of the Mintzes, who seemed relatively happy. She noticed that Felix's hearing was very poor, that his wife was nervous about upcoming language examinations, and that both were quite worried about their relatives still in Germany. Alfred responded to Felix in a letter dated May 25, 1939, acknowledging the concern evident in his May 12 letter, but grieved that he had spoken of their relationship in past tense. Utilizing his own philosophical categories, Schutz challenged Kaufmann's type construction of him as a Contemporary, which imputed to him a kind of neurasthenia that had prevented him from making the transitions through the crises of the last fourteen months with the ease that Kaufmann himself had exhibited. Schutz attributed his lack of academic productivity to weighty business obligations from which Kaufmann was fortunate enough to have been spared and to what he had earlier called "unending exhausting attempts" to help friends and acquaintances. Because Schutz's life-sustaining work had never coincided with his academic work, as it had for Kaufmann, he had never dared to compare himself with Kaufmann. After Alfred immigrated, there was tension in their relationship, particularly with regard to the phenomenological society, and a kind of competitiveness between them, but they resumed friendly scholarly exchanges in the mid-1940s. Perhaps the most that can be said regarding this incident is that the enormous turmoil that Hitler introduced even took its toll on the long-lasting relationships between intimate friends.[71]

When the time came for the family's departure, they planned to take a train to the boat, but to reach the train they had to cross the Champs-Elysées; however, that day, July 14, Bastille Day, the entire English army had come to France to parade along the avenue. With the cooperation of a tank crew who paused for their passage, they reached the train station on time. Fortunately, Ilse had rejected a proposal by Hansi and Peter that the children go to the train station in one taxicab with the grandparents, while Alfred and Ilse would take another cab—a stroke of luck because the grandparents' taxi never arrived in time to see them off. The Schutzes boarded the *Nieuw Amsterdam* on July 14, and one can find the souvenir menu for dinner that evening among Alfred's personal papers. Nevertheless, as the family headed westward, the disruption that the *Anschluss* introduced into Alfred's life was not finished, since he would not be able to leave his parents and Ilse's mother in Europe much longer.[22]

In the light of the immense weight of responsibility shouldered by Alfred Schutz during the fifteen months from March 13, 1938 until July 14, 1939—responsibility for wife, children, parents, mother-in-law, and many friends—one can only be impressed by his generosity to the point of exhaustion. Precisely because Schutz was a lawyer with extensive experience in international banking and with many important business connections and because he had the good fortune to be "caught" at the time of the *Anschluss* outside of Austria, he was able to do so much for his family and so many others. Emmanuel Levinas, another Jew who endured grievous affliction under Hitlerian barbarity, has articulated philosophically how assuming ethical responsibility for others can establish a sense of personal identity. His words, which flesh out what an ethical identity is, could as well summarize the life of Alfred Schutz in the cauldron of the *Anschluss*: "To utter 'I,' to affirm the irreducible singularity in which the apology is pursued, means to possess a privileged place with regard to responsibilities for which no one can replace me and from which no one can release me. To be unable to shirk; this is the I."[23]

Chapter 6

Reestablishing

Life in the United States and Its Insecurities

After the trip on the *Nieuw Amsterdam,* during which both Schutz children fell ill and George took his first steps, the family arrived on July 22, 1939, in New York. They resided in the Hotel Anderson until September 1941, when they moved to 25 West Eighty-first Street. Because they were unaccustomed to the intense heat and humidity, after a few weeks they decided to vacation in a boardinghouse by the sea at Larchmont, New York, within commuting distance to Alfred's New York office.[1]

In spite of these difficult initial living conditions, Schutz's attitude toward his new country was not entirely pessimistic, as is evident in a letter to Raoul Rabinerson on December 15, 1939. Although he complained about high New York rents, the harsh climate, and the frequent sicknesses that befell his children, he contrasted his present upbeat morale with the negative feelings prevalent after his 1937 American visit, of which he had written Rabinerson earlier. In the 1939 letter, he admitted that earlier he had entirely accepted the views regarding the United States of Georges Duhamel and André Maurois, both of whom had led him to expect the worst.[2]

Schutz's diary of his 1937 visit recorded many of the kinds of things these authors found typical in Anglo-American culture. Duhamel, writing after the First World War and explicitly under the influence of Bergson, whose thought was also attractive to Schutz, opposed a society built on the possession of goods instead of the capacity to enter empathetically into the wonders of nature and the experience of other persons. Favoring intuitive surrender to the world instead of imperious efforts to master it intellectually, Duhamel explicitly characterized Anglo-Americans as identifying well-being with comfortable luxury, succumbing to the corruption of money, and implementing automation to shorten the time of work, with the result that they evacuated work of any joy. In a diary of his travels to America in 1927 and 1931 and published in 1936, Maurois showed himself no less critical of

American society, considering it still a nation of pioneers, unable to appreciate leisure or to be skeptical about the purposes of its frenetic agitation and labor. The country for him lacked a critical sense and a tradition of culture; he pointed out, for example, that a recent American book on the history of philosophy had devoted sixty pages to Voltaire and three to Descartes; such cultural deficits engendered a kind of national boredom. Schutz's confidence in these authors may have derived in part from his Francophile tendencies, which, according to Ilse, led him to dislike anything English—just the opposite of her, who stated, "I loved everything English and I loved America and New York from the very first moment I arrived."[3]

Schutz wondered in his letter to Rabinerson whether his newfound positive attitude toward the United States had resulted from the European catastrophe that had diminished his nostalgia for Europe or from the fact that he had just met better Americans this time around. He went on to praise the New York Public Library, in which he found books on Leibniz that were published in Paris in 1938 and that were unknown to him while he was living there. He also mentioned his enjoyment of a nine-day Beethoven festival under Toscanini's direction, Saturday transmissions of the Metropolitan Opera, Sunday musical chamber concerts, and Sunday evening performances of Bach's cantatas. He found the scientific life "quite remarkable," with European scholars receiving an extraordinary appreciation, and he was enthused about the prospects of an international phenomenological society founded at the University of Buffalo, about which more will be said later.[4]

Schutz's immigrant situation was always highly fluid. Even before immigrating, he had informed Machlup that he was reading rural and urban sociology to be able to take advantage of whatever academic opportunities presented themselves, and he entertained the possibility of returning to Paris by himself if war did not break out. In the United States, he anticipated the European situation being clarified within a year or two, but he became demoralized because he was forty, had depleted his savings, and could not easily find an academic job, which might allow him to stay beyond the one year permitted by his entry permit. Machlup, to whom Schutz had grown closer after their vacation in Isselsberg, beyond the formal "Herr Colleague" relationship of their student days, and whom he had visited twice during his 1937 trip, sought to calm his friend's anxieties. One simply could not calculate the chance of war, he thought, and it would be difficult for Schutz to obtain a teaching post, since he lacked teaching experience, did not fit in the disciplines departmentalized in American universities, and lacked the personality of the "popular" undergraduate teacher sought by American universities. Machlup did, however, believe that he might secure a research position with an institution like the Harvard Committee for Social Research, and he suggested contacts and offered to write letters of recommendation. A few weeks later, Schutz, reassured because Voegelin and Haberler had been assisting him in pursuit of a more extended reentry permit, humorously suggested that Machlup would do better to find him a position in urban rather than rural sociology, since he had at least read Lynd's *Middletown*. Of course, the outbreak of war in Europe placed any return out of the question, and, though Schutz's employers thought that the war would be over in four months and Ilse anticipated reclaiming their Paris apartment, Alfred by this time was not nearly so confident that the war would rapidly terminate.[5]

The process of adjusting to the new culture had its continuing difficulties. For instance, around the middle of February 1940 his daughter Evelyn developed a mastoid ear infection that lasted seven weeks and that required antibiotics and painful surgery in an age without developed anesthetics. In addition, Alfred took courses in English and speech at Columbia University in order to adjust and enrolled in a course on American legal terminology. He complained to Gurwitsch about the difficulties and jested to Machlup about not yet being acclimatized, since in November he did not know what Thanksgiving meant, except that it was important to thank one's friends, and so he concluded that he loved very dearly Fritz and his wife and children.[6]

Helping Others Emigrate

Alfred and Ilse remained preoccupied with the situation of their parents, and Peter and Hansi sent letters on the average every other day, offering them encouragement in their new and strange surroundings. The parents moved from Paris to Périgueux to Vichy to Clermont Ferrand, Nice, and Montpellier, and when they were finally placed on the American Consulate's waiting list, Alfred transferred funds, arranged visas, secured affidavits, prepared them for consulate interviews, coordinated their departure with his Aunt Putzi's, and booked their passage. When matters became complicated in April 1941, he lamented to Gurwitsch, "I have hardly any hopes left of seeing my parents, if ever, before the end of the war," but by May he seemed to have things back on track by enlisting the service of an American lawyer. But then, as was typical in such immigration matters, the entire process was suspended when it was discovered that Otto had a brother in Vienna and when the U.S. Department of State took over from individual consulates the administration of visa procedures. Schutz's parents finally departed from Lisbon on October 27, 1941, to reunite with their son, who had willingly depleted his savings on their behalf even though he himself was far from being securely established.[7]

Schutz assisted many others to escape the catastrophe in Europe. He aided Dr. Oswald Glasberg, nicknamed Waldja, his cousin by marriage, by advising him on his visa, loaning him transportation money, and even gathering information about how the medical profession was practiced within various states within the United States. In addition, he did everything possible to arrange for the immigration of his uncle, Oskar Schutz, whose steamer tickets sent by a Catholic committee for German refugees never arrived, with the result that Oskar's visa affidavits expired and he was eventually executed. Because of his mastery of the maze of immigration procedures, which Gurwitsch called "passology" or "emigrantology," Schutz counseled many old friends, including Husserl's wife, the musician Erich Kahn, and the philosopher Jean Wilde, on immigration and financial matters. In addition, he continually supported intellectuals, such as French political theorist Raymond Aron and his wife Suzanne, who remained in Europe. On behalf of Gurwitsch, he convinced a donor to finance a two-year teaching fellowship, negotiated with colleges and universities where that fellowship might be applied, and offered advice on job opportunities.[8]

Business as Usual and a New Academic World

Schutz continued working with Reitler, now transplanted in the United States. In 1940 missives to Ilse, written while on a business trip to California, he lamented the ineptness of the company leadership, who resented his criticisms and whose shenanigans even caused him physical sickness. He also reported a lengthy private conversation at the Palmer House in Chicago in which he asked to be paid in dollars rather than in the devalued currency he was receiving. Despite his gratitude for the company's help in escaping Europe, he was outraged when Robert stated that he was of little use in the United States and would be of greater value in Europe. He protested to Lambert that he would have ended up either drafted into the French army or confined within a concentration camp if he had remained in Europe. In response to a request for greater pay, Lambert recommended that he leave New York, where things were more costly, and Schutz retorted that he needed the New York libraries for his studies.[9]

Despite this unhappiness, he made several initial sorties into American academia by: (1) cooperating with Marvin Farber on various editorial and organizational projects aimed at advancing phenomenology, (2) participating in academic conferences, (3) publishing various articles in his own right, and (4) pursuing an intellectual exchange with the Harvard sociologist Talcott Parsons.

Marvin Farber, a student of Husserl's whom Schutz had met at the University of Buffalo during his visit to the United States in 1937, was planning a memorial volume for Husserl and invited Schutz's contribution, the article "Phenomenology and the Social Sciences." Farber also named him a board member of the International Phenomenology Society, founded in December 1939, and requested that he join the editorial committee of *Phi-*

losophy and Phenomenological Research (henceforth *PPR*), the society's publishing organ. Schutz helped draft the constitution of the society, solicited Gurwitsch's help in securing the cooperation of French philosophers, and reviewed manuscripts. However, when Farber complained that his responses had not been timely enough, he responded forcefully:

> Objectively I merit your blame because of my tardiness in answering your letters. Subjectively, I must ask your indulgence. You may have hopefully gotten the conviction that I am not the sort of person to leave a letter unanswered or not to fulfill tasks that I have accepted. I ask you to reflect, though, on the fact that I do not lead a contemplative philosophical existence and that I do not have the good fortune of having a regular academic post. My workload, which I have to carry, depends unfortunately upon events in the world and surely you can understand that the extraordinary events of the last weeks demand extraordinary measures in business life. As long as I must earn my bread in this way, I cannot avoid having [my] other interests pressed into the background. In order to avoid any misunderstanding between us both, I must ask you to give me your trust that I am doing what I can. To me it is painful when I cannot discharge the things that need to be done quickly enough. On the other side, I make it my business to read the manuscripts set before me conscientiously and to take seriously everything that has to do with the Society.[10]

Because the journal did not receive enough manuscripts of quality, Schutz edited and prefaced for the first volume of *PPR* Husserl's manuscript "Notizen zur Raumkonstitution: Fortsetzung der Untersuchungen zur phänomenologischen Interpretation der kopernikanischen Lehre." Schutz and Farber worried together about everything from printer charges to the fate of European professors/phenomenologists such as the imprisoned Eugen Fink and Ludwig Landgrebe, and the jobless Paul Landsberg and Jean Héring. Meanwhile, Farber attempted to rescue as many of the manuscripts from the Husserl Archive in Louvain as possible in cooperation with Rev. H. L. Van Breda, the director of the archive. He also consulted with Schutz on editorial decisions, such as whether to allow Wild to publish in French while requiring an English translation from Maritain, or on the possible destructive consequences of Felix Kaufmann's battle with John Wild over phenomenology's relationship to metaphysics and logical positivism. Both Schutz and Farber bemoaned the many responsibilities that prevented them from attending to their own philosophical work. Schutz encouraged Farber's work on his 1943 *The Foundation of Phenomenology*, which would further phenomenology as much as a year of the journal, and invited him to visit his family in Larchmont.[11]

While Schutz as an editor maintained the same honesty and integrity evident in the rest of his life, he showed himself particularly broad-minded and tolerant in the case of the Thomist philosopher Jacques Maritain, a Roman Catholic. Schutz, who befriended Maritain in Paris, explored the possibility of soliciting an article from him for *PPR*, but when Farber proposed this article to the editorial board, he encountered opposition from, among others, Dorion Cairns, who expressed his "doubt concerning Maritain's affiliation, while not objecting to Maritain himself." Feeling deflated by such opposition and yet encouraged by Farber, Schutz pressed on, requesting a paper from Maritain, with whom he was at this time working on visa matters and communicating information relayed from the New School about the Russian philosopher Nicholas Berdaieff and Paul Landsberg. After some hesitancy, Maritain considered writing on the conflict of methods in medieval philosophy, and Schutz encouraged him, noting Husserl's treatment of the difference between the natural scientific and mathematical methods. When Maritain concluded that his paper might be better placed in the *Thomist*, Schutz replied that he understood his reasons but asked that he keep *PPR* in mind in the future. Throughout this entire incident, Schutz appeared free of anti-Catholic bias, magnanimous enough to bridge divisions that others in the phenomenological movement could not (a trait he would show repeatedly in the future), and interested in exploring linkages between phenomenology and divergent philosophical traditions, such as Neo-Thomism.[12]

Not all Schutz's relationships in the United States turned out so felicitously. In the previous chapter, we saw how his relationship with Felix Kaufmann deteriorated, and in the United States, their correspondence was limited to formal exchanges, often about the immigration of members of Husserl's family, except for an involved scholarly exchange in 1944–45. Marvin Farber informed Helmut Wagner that both were saddened by the breach, but unable to do anything to repair it. However, by the time Schutz delivered his eulogy in honor of Kaufmann at the New School on January 4, 1950, many of his wounds must have been healed, since Schutz referred to him repeatedly as a friend and the address breathed of Schutz's admiration for Kaufmann's work.[13]

Schutz integrated himself into the American scene by participating in various conferences, such as a Unity of Science Conference at Harvard in 1939, the annual meeting of the American Sociological Society in Boston in 1939, and a conference on methods in philosophy and science in New York in 1941. In addition, he resumed the publishing that so many cataclysmic events had interrupted. Having received his invitation to publish in the Husserl memorial volume in December 1938, he had his paper "Phenomenology and the Social Sciences" ready for its publication in 1940. The first section situated phenomenological reduction with respect to the pregiven natural attitude and summarized Husserl's views on the constitution of the alter ego. Schutz conceived of the life-world as the foundation of the natural sciences and proposed a constitutive phenomenology of the natural attitude as a foundation for the cultural and social sciences. In the second section, he spelled out structural features of this life-world and exposited the peculiar reflective stance that social and cultural scientists adopt to study it. In sum, he made it clear how phenomenology could be of aid to the social sciences and elucidated his own particular appropriation of phenomenology for this purpose—a perfectly appropriate topic for a volume dedicated to Husserl's memory.[14]

On April 13, 1940, he presented his paper "The Problem of Rationality in the Social World" at the Harvard Faculty Club at the invitation of Talcott Parsons and Joseph Schumpeter. This presentation at the Harvard Faculty Club, a version of which was published in *Economica* in 1943, repeated earlier themes, distinguishing the social world as lived and as studied through scientific observation and clarifying the pervasive "cookbook knowledge" of everyday life, that is, pragmatically necessary habits and unquestioned platitudes. After analyzing six possible meanings of "rational action"—"reasonable," "deliberate," "planned or projected" (not merely reactive), "predictable," "logical," and "selective of the most appropriate means to ends,"—he insisted that "the ideal of rationality [clearly and distinctly grasping the elements involved in action] was not a particular feature of everyday thinking." He listed all the elements one would have to know to make a rational choice and commented on how this complexity increased when a social action had to occur in relation to another actor. To conclude, he examined how social scientists proceed and demanded that they be able to convert their generalizations and idealizations into descriptions of the activities of individual actors and that they comply with the postulates of subjective interpretation, logical consistency, and adequacy.[15]

At the suggestion of the philosophy professor Maurice Mandelbaum, Schutz presented "William James's Concept of the Stream of Thought Phenomenologically Interpreted" at the end of December 1940 at the Eastern Division meeting of the American Philosophical Association in Philadelphia. It should come as no surprise that Schutz selected as his topic his strong suit—namely, something in the area of temporality and consciousness—and that, bridge-builder as he was, he sought to relate Husserl's thought to that of a prominent American philosopher. After he had submitted his paper to Mandelbaum on October 31, 1940, he asked for criticism from the revered American philosopher and student of James, Horace Kallen, who felt that in spite of resemblances, the central visions of Husserl and James differed, though he had not read enough Husserl. Schutz may have sought Kallen's opinion because of trepidation about his new intellectual context; he had written Gurwitsch that "there is surely hardly any chance that it will be accepted."[16]

The essay, published in *PPR* in 1941, irenically indicated "where the ideas of great masters coalesce," while preserving the distinctiveness of each viewpoint—an intellectual task parallel to Schutz's effort to adapt culturally, that is, to understand his new culture without distorting it through the categories of the old one. After detailing the differences between Husserl and James he turned to two areas of convergence: the stream of thought and the theory of fringes. Both thinkers compared personal consciousness to a stream, through and through connected, such that consciousness does not consist in a multiplicity of elements needing to be reunited, but rather a unity from which one separates out components. Husserl's view of a noematic kernel persisting through modifications of a thing could serve as a bridge to James's belief that kernels or topics of thought have their "fringes." Furthermore, each thought contained its fringe, or horizons (in Husserlian terms), linking it to every other one; hence when we hear thunder, it is not thunder pure, but thunder-breaking-in-upon-silence-and-contrasting-with-it. James, in a like fashion, had highlighted the broader topic forming the context for thinking an object. Just as James allowed that one could maintain an abiding belief even after the steps leading to its derivation had faded, so Husserl described how a monothetic act could grasp as a unity what had been polythetically built up. The depth of Schutz's discussion of James and his continued reflection, on the relationships between James, Bergson, and Santayana until the end of his career illustrated that he was interested in James's thought in itself and not merely a means for linking phenomenology with American philosophy.[17]

One of the few books Schutz had brought from his apartment in Paris was Max Scheler's *Wissensformen und die Gesellschaft*, and so when Farber began planning a Scheler volume of *PPR*, he thought of preparing something, even though it would mean facing the momentous task of crystallizing Scheler's scattered thoughts in a single article. He kept Gurwitsch posted on the article's progress; and, when it was published, he informed Machlup that it was the best paper that he had published thus far. The first half of "Scheler's Theory of Intersubjectivity and the General Thesis of the Alter Ego" describes the levels of psychical existence in Scheler's philosophical anthropology; his philosophy of the person, whose acts are nonobjectifiable; and his treatment of problems of intersubjectivity. Regarding this last problem, Scheler had opposed inference and empathy approaches to proving others' existence, since one's own self was not the first thing given us (as is illustrated by the fact that we often think others' thoughts in such a way as to be unable to distinguish their thought from our own). Furthermore, according to Scheler's perceptional theory of the alter ego, one grasps another's experiences as a whole (another's joy in his or her smile) instead of isolated bodily components from which one has to infer what the other thinks or feels. Finally, since the acts of the person are not objectifiable, in the end they can be seized only by coperforming or reperforming them.[18]

In the critical second half, Schutz resists explaining the existence of other egos on the transcendental level and situates the whole discussion in the natural attitude, in which one does not doubt the datum of others' existence. In that natural attitude, while living in one's acts, one does not clearly distinguish one's own thoughts from others' and the "We" is pregiven to the sphere of the "I," as Scheler believes. However, as soon as one adopts a reflective attitude toward one's stream, one becomes aware that the experiences *are* one's own. Scheler, however, mistakenly precludes any such reflection on one's acts because of certain ethical commitments to the nonobjectifiability of the person. While criticizing Scheler's argument for the priority of the We to the I on the basis of the empirical psychology of primitives and children, who only gradually separate an I from their We, Schutz upholds the priority of a We through his own theory of temporality. That is, before reflecting we live in each other's present unfolding experience as we "grow older together," though our individual experience is given only to a past retrospective glance. To accommodate Scheler's idea of an inner (indubitable) perception of the other, Schutz argues that in vivid simultaneity the *existence* of the other is indubitable (and hence given to something like inner perception). Since, though, we can be mistaken about specific thoughts of the other, these are given as something transcendent and therefore dubitable.[19]

Schutz was engaged in another intense activity that became visible only subsequently, namely his letter exchange with Talcott Parsons in late 1940 and early 1941. When Parsons's *The Structure of Social Action* appeared in 1937, Schutz undertook a careful study of it early in 1938 because of Parsons's own insights and excellent discussion of Max Weber, and he proposed to Frederick Hayek to write a review for *Economica*. After Schutz finally met Parsons at his presentation on rationality at Harvard, they agreed that Schutz should write down some "questions in the form of critical remarks" for future discussion; and Schutz spent the summer of 1940 producing a "monster paper" of 25,000 words that he eventually sent to Parsons. Schutz was enthused about the possibility of an exchange with Parsons, and before sending his monster paper, he had asked the philosophy professor Richard Hays Williams at Buffalo to correct his English and to keep the entire paper confidential so as not to offend Parsons. Before their discussion of the monster paper commenced, Parsons had sent Schutz another manuscript for review, and, as Richard Grathoff notes, there was "a considerable misunderstanding on both sides as to which of their papers each of them meant when referring to each other."[20]

After an introduction highly laudatory of Parsons's work, Schutz's essay spends the first thirteen of roughly fifty pages presenting Parsons's theory, which distills from analyses of Marshall, Pareto, Durkheim, and Weber—the best analysis available in English, according to Schutz—an action system. "Unit acts" consist of an actor (whose subjective viewpoint is distinct from the observer's objective viewpoint), an end, conditions (over which the actor has no control), means (over which there is control), and a normative (in neither an ethical nor a legal sense) orientation of action. Although for utilitarians actors operate atomistically, their ends interacting with each other randomly and their choice of mean-ends based merely on efficiency, positivists explain choices of ends from an objective perspective, focused on hereditary and environmental conditions that disregard actors' subjective viewpoints. Parsons opts for a voluntaristic system of action, admitting conditional, nonnormative elements as well as normative components, and he separates a concrete level referring to unit acts from an analytic level including elements (properties) of action systems such as rationality that are not embodied in a concrete act.[21]

Schutz's critique of Parsons focuses on four principal areas. First, he finds confusions between the unit and element levels, asserts that element analyses must always be able to refer to the subjective viewpoint of the actor (given in unit analysis), and accuses Parsons of misunderstanding "subjective" as referring to an actor's causal mental processes. Second, Parsons takes scientific and formal logic as paradigmatic instead of seeing that the thought and logic of everyday life differ from that of the social scientific observer. Third, Schutz believes that normative values would be better understood in terms of the in-order-to motives informing the subjective viewpoint of an individual actor as opposed to society-wide norms accessible to an objective viewpoint. Fourthly, the definition of a unit act varies if determined by an actor or observer, since one can only determine the meaning of a subact in light of the actor's temporally overarching project, which he or she alone knows, and even distinguishing means from conditions depends on the actor's viewpoint.[22]

A common thread running through these criticisms is Schutz's intent to preserve the subjective view of the actor, which Parsons recognized as important but of which he did not take sufficient cognizance, perhaps because he considered such concerns distracting from more important social scientific tasks, as Schutz suggests:

> The reader might already impatiently ask why the subjective point of view is defended here with such stubbornness. Apparently, it does not seem to lead to a system which is of practical use to social scientists, but which obviously ends in an impasse of solipsism and psychologistic subtleties, both outside the scope of social science. We must ask him for a little more patience.[23]

For Schutz, on the contrary, "Safeguarding the subjective point of view is the only, but a sufficient, guarantee that social reality will not be replaced by a fictional non-existing world constructed by some scientific observer."[24]

The deficiency in Parsons's response to Schutz's critique that he did not take sufficiently into account the subjective meaning of the actor is striking. He answers that the determination of a unit act is "operationally relevant to the problems in hand" and depends on what "proves operationally convenient to treat as a unit for the purposes in hand," but Parsons here is still construing the unit act solely from the observer's point of view. Parsons's objections that taking account of the subjective point of view would not "automatically decide" an act's definition, that Schutz seems to consider the actor as "absolutely rational," or that he is propounding an "ontological" reality of what an actor "really" experiences seem to hit targets other than Schutz. By asserting the significance of subjective categories for any description that does not reduce phenomena to "biological or physical" terms, Parsons equates "subjective" with "mental" or "psychological" in contrast to Schutz's description of it as "taking account of the actor's perspective as opposed to [that of] the observer." These responses indicate that Parsons failed to appreciate one of Schutz's key beliefs—namely, that careful attention to the subjective viewpoint of the actor enabled scientific observers to become critical of their own perspective. For this precise purpose Schutz had developed his own analyses of action and temporality, the usefulness of which Parsons admitted that he did not appreciate.[25]

Anyone reading the Schutz/Parsons correspondence can detect a mutual sense of woundedness and hurt beneath the surface of their repeated assurances to each other that they appreciate each other's work and intend no offense. This sense explains why their correspondence broke off after Schutz's April 21, 1941 letter and why in May, 1941, Schutz sent the entire correspondence and an anxious letter to Haberler, at Harvard with Parsons, inquiring about Parsons's feelings. Voegelin, who corresponded with Parsons briefly after the exchange, reassured Schutz that the controversy had been as unpleasant for Parsons as for his friend. Whatever Schutz's responsibility may have been for this rupture, however he may have failed to take account of how the words he used might have been interpreted by his interlocutor, it is also true that he exerted himself mightily to understand Parsons's work. As he stated, he studied it continuously, personally questioning Parsons about it, spending a summer examining it, rewriting three times his exposition of it, and trying to rely as heavily as possible on Parsons's own language.[26]

This very effort on Schutz's part to be self-critical and to understand the other's perspective characterized his concurrent endeavor to set aside his preconceptions and come to appreciate the American culture he had joined. In addition, he showed a deep comprehension of the anguish of those endangered by warfare or Nazi persecution, whether parents or relatives or European scholars, and was able to sympathize with outlooks that others found difficult to fathom, whether that of the irritable Farber or the Catholic Maritain.

He displayed magnanimity and fairness to thinkers from diverse standpoints, such as James and Scheler, and thereby exemplified precisely the qualities of character that he proclaimed toward Parsons when trying to heal the breach opening between them:

> I hope sincerely that you are convinced, if not of the relevance of my statements, then at least of the loyalty and fairness of my attitude toward you personally and toward your ideas. By nature and temperament I am always inclined to search in daily and scientific life for common bases of mutual understanding rather than merely to criticize.[27]

Speculating on the because motives of Schutz's capacity to enter others' perspectives empathetically, one thinks of his parents, who in France's turmoil and terrors set aside their own worries, and wrote their son every other day for months to make his adjustment to his new cultural setting easier.

Chapter 7

World War II Years

Editing, Teaching, War Research, Business

Throughout the war years Schutz's involvement with Farber, the journal, and the phenomenology society continued strong. He arranged for book reviews and evaluated manuscripts, and at times the latter process landed him in delicate situations, as when C. J. Ducasse—rightly, in Schutz's view—criticized the excessive length of a Gurwitsch paper that he had originally approved. Since Gurwitsch at that time seemed angry with him for some unknown reason and since he feared that Gurwitsch might suspect that he had scuttled the paper's publication, he asked Farber to inform Gurwitsch that he had recommended acceptance and that the objections had come from another quarter. There were other difficulties, too. The cost of printing compelled Schutz and Farber to look for less expensive printers; and when Richard Hays Williams, treasurer of *PPR* and the phenomenological society, innocently mixed these institution's funds with his own, Schutz had to straighten out the bookkeeping procedures. Not everything involved crises, though. The connection with the journal afforded him opportunities to meet other scholars, such as Albert Salomon, of the New School, who approached Schutz when *PPR* had failed to take up his offer to contribute to the Scheler issue. In addition, after Mises recommended that Schutz forward an issue of *PPR* to the Mexican political philosopher Luis Recasens Siches, the latter sent Schutz a list of possible Latin American subscribers and thereby commenced a friendship that would last for the rest of Schutz's life.[1]

Schutz, Farber, and the board of the phenomenological society were continually generating new and interesting projects. For instance, Schutz, enthused about Farber's *The Foundation of Phenomenology*, urged that it be issued as the first volume in a series under the society's sponsorship; meanwhile, Farber maneuvered to publish the proceedings of the Yale Inter-American Conference of Philosophy. In June 1943, in order to acquaint Anglo-American philosophy with phenomenology, Schutz and Herbert

Spiegelberg conceived the idea of a phenomenological source book, modeled on Wlliam Ellis's "A Sourcebook of Gestalt Psychology," though Cairns opposed chopping up Husserl's texts for such a purpose. Further, Schutz and Farber edited and wrote introductions for Husserl's manuscripts, included one too hastily edited by Cairns at a time when his enlistment in the military was imminent, and they published memorial notes, some of which were composed by invited guest philosophers acquainted with the deceased.[2]

Because Farber had dedicated himself to improving the reputation of phenomenology in the United States, he was outraged upon hearing that the philosophers Ernst Nagel and Irwin Erdman had commented that phenomenology had no influence in the United States. He wrote sarcastically to Schutz, "I am informing you, of course, so that you will not want to waste any more time on phenomenology, after hearing the opinion of these two great experts." Moreover, when some suggested that existentialism held the key to phenomenology's future, Farber insisted on injecting strict phenomenological procedure into the general stream of philosophy. Otherwise both phenomenology and existentialism would be swept away, he said, by the growing tidal wave of logical analysis. Schutz, usually more irenic than Farber, did not agree with Farber's disdain for existentialism, since he believed that it would be easier for phenomenologists to reach some understanding with existentialists than with neo-positivists. When Jean Wahl suggested that the "blooming, buzzing confusion [of William James]" might offer the only refuge from positivism, the sardonic Farber, though liking Wahl, told Schutz that he hoped to tempt him away from that "confusion" to the clarity that one would expect of a French scholar.[3]

The relationship between Schutz and Farber went beyond business insofar as Schutz enlisted Farber's help in finding a job for Aron Gurwitsch and regularly invited Farber to comment on his writings. They further exchanged nonphilosophical books and discussed them, such as a Hitler book, probably *Mein Kampf*, published in 1943. Farber expressed immediate concern when Schutz's son suffered from a certain vision impairment, and Schutz sympathized with Farber whenever the work of the journal and the society overwhelmed him. After Schutz's citizenship ceremony on November 29, 1944, Farber expressed most eloquently his affection, writing, "I trust that this letter will greet you as an American citizen. That means that you will be with us always. All of us (and I in particular) are very much indebted to you, and feel happy in the thought of your permanent status as an American. I look forward to many years of fruitful collaboration with you."[4]

Schutz's contacts with the New School for Social Research began with his cooperation with Else Staudinger and Alvin Johnson in their efforts to recruit for U.S. institutions faculty endangered in Europe. According to Ilse, Albert Salomon also invited Schutz to participate in the "General Seminar," the "nucleus of academic life of the Graduate Faculty," in which faculty members, colleagues from other universities, and students shared. After these informal contacts, on December 22, 1942, Alvin Johnson invited Schutz to teach as lecturer in the department of sociology; and in the spring of 1943, he taught his first course, an introduction to sociological theory, covering Cooley, Park, Thomas, Znaniecki, and Young and acquainting students with concepts such as in-group and out-group, situation, crisis, maladjustment, social self, and social causation. Since the New School for Social Research was a graduate school, many of whose students worked during the day and attended classes at night, Schutz, who also worked days, taught in the evenings, often from 8:20 to 10:10 p.m. He remarked to philosopher Helmut Kuhn that in this first teaching job he found himself dedicating all his free time to preparing.[5]

In the fall of 1943, he taught a course on the theory of social action, focusing on George Herbert Mead, Parsons, Znaniecki, Pareto, and Weber and taking up the structure of the social world and scientific reflection on it. In the spring of 1944, Salomon and he taught a course on Mead. In the fall of 1944 (and 1945), he taught social groups and the problems of adjustment that touched on major authors, including American sociologists such as MacIver, Cooley, and W. I. Thomas, and that dealt with cultural patterns, gangs, brothers in crime, the ghetto, the marginal man, strangers, and homecomers. Also that fall, Schutz taught a course in the problems of the sociology of knowledge that fused the continental tradition of Durkheim, Scheler, and Mannheim with the American pragmatists. In the fall of 1945, he repeated his course on social groups. Besides teaching, he circulated a memorandum proposing that the graduate faculty edit a set of Anglo-American books on the social sciences in German in hopes of promoting the democratic ideals that permeated the Amercian masters' approach to society, economics, and politics. He regretted that German-speaking countries had been underexposed to Anglo Saxon literature due to the underfunding prevalent since World War I, Nazi censorship, and a false sense of German superiority that looked down upon the intellectual products of others nations as "unphilosophical, materialistic, dilettante."[6]

While he seemed to have modified earlier beliefs about Anglo-American culture that had been shaped by the French authors Maurois and Duhamel, he nevertheless retained a critical attitude toward the Western democracies, as he showed in endorsing his colleague Eduard Heimann's article "The Just War of Unjust Nations." Heimann opposed any self-righteousness on the part of democracies that had contributed to the rise and continued popularity of fascism by allowing rising unemployment, by failing to promote cooperation among the post-Habsburg states, by promoting isolationism and appeasement, by exhibiting racial arrogance in the Japanese internment camps, and by avoiding the reforms necessary to stop communism. Heimann, however, rejected any argument that might conclude from these injustices that the Western powers ought to withdraw from the war and submit to the punishment they deserved at the hands of the Germans and Japanese. Schutz thanked Heimann, stating, "I read this essay with the greatest pleasure and I find it very important and to the point," and asked if he might send a copy to Voegelin.[7]

During the war, Irene Opton of the Foreign Economic Administration and Richard Tirana of the Reoccupation Division of the Board of Economic Warfare requested Schutz to provide analyses useful for the occupation of Germany and Austria at the end of the war. Schutz immediately agreed to do all he could, sent a curriculum vitae, and in April 1943 met in Washington with Tirana, who appointed him a senior consultant of the Board of Economic Warfare and assigned him a salary and secretarial assistance. Six months later, Irene Opton thanked him for his splendid report, in which he discussed German credit cooperatives, the system of short-term agricultural credits, and the Central Agricultural Bank, and recommended that the occupational forces govern rather than commissaries and accelerate seasonal credits to farmers to avoid food shortages. Opton further arranged for Schutz and Fritz Unger to produce a study of Austrian banking. Completed in April 1944, it drew the attention of Herbert Furth of the board of governors of the Federal Reserve System, who consulted him about banking developments in Austria. Schutz conveyed to Gurwitsch what all this work cost: "This work takes a lot of time, more than I had expected, since I have to write a series of memoranda for Washington, which require painstaking researches in libraries. Thus, my really scholarly work has been reduced to the short vacation period of seventeen days which I passed most pleasantly in Lake Placid." In spite of the cost in time, he was quite pleased to contribute to the war effort and felt pride that his new homeland had invited him into a deeper relationship with it.[8]

Schutz undertook these many activities while working full time for the Reitler Company, which, having lost much of its business in Europe, was searching for new clients. For this purpose, he traveled to Mexico early in 1942, but he grew impatient, since contacts with American firms were scarce. As a result, he began to consider the possibility of looking for new work, and Ilse, as usual, urged upon him frank conversations with Lambert.[9]

Family and Friends

Peter Schutz, who had arrived in the United States only six months earlier, died on May 18, 1942, after a period of sickness, and several of Alfred's friends sent their condolences, knowing how close the relationship between son and father had been and regretting that Peter had not had more time to enjoy the freedom for which he had longed. Ilse recalled that in the middle of the night Alfred spontaneously moved his mother into their apartment; there she lived the next seven years. Gisa, Ilse's mother, eventually emigrated from London to the United States on April 10, 1945 and stayed with Alfred and Ilse in their apartment as well. Except for having to deal with George's eye problems, the family lived a rather regular existence. Alfred sought the most expansive education possible for his children. For example, he sent his daughter Evelyn to Camp Sheldrake, "a unique experiment in international relations," with ninety-three children who hailed from various consulates and embassies and who represented thirteen foreign countries. Pondering the fate of his friend Paul Villard's mother, who had unsuccessfully attempted suicide while being deported by the Nazis to Poland, Alfred reflected in a letter to his mother, "All in all, our nuclear family has had the greatest fortune." In that same letter, however, he betrayed some despondence about the future: "I am generally mistrustful of the future, personally, economically, and politically—and I scarcely believe that in my whole life I will have just one day without cares."[10]

Schutz kept up extensive correspondence with friends. Marcel Friedmann discussed with him law, the continuing plight of African Americans in Texas, and his own divorce, which had occurred a year earlier. In addition, Schutz advised Mises about how to ship his goods across the Atlantic, encouraged Robert Horecki's business undertakings, uplifted Walter Froelich when his teaching contract was not renewed, organized a group of Austrians to purchase a wristwatch for Hayek, explained international financial laws to Haberler, and testified in behalf of Kelsen's naturalization.[11]

Schutz continued sharpening his own philosophical positions through exchanges with academic colleagues, as when he and Machlup informed each other of important articles, such as Frank H. Knight's "What is Truth in Economics?" which Schutz found "ingenious" and considered answering. Knight criticized positivist approaches to the social sciences, addressed problems of other minds and motivation, insisted that economic theory be placed within the broader context of everyday life and political decisions, and stressed the importance of the temporality of economic actors—all favorite themes of Schutz. Machlup praised Schutz's principle of "for whom?" by which he frequently questioned whether an interpretation pertained to the objective viewpoint of the observer or the subjective point of view of the actor. Because of his reliance on Schutz's principle, Machlup had become a troublemaker. As he said, "I have made of the nicest and clearest theories of the governing doctrines a complete chaos, without having the power to create a new world (in seven days or in seven chapters, for that matter)." Machlup admitted to having learned from Schutz previously that varying degrees of anonymity characterized ideal-types and that one could ascribe different degrees of certainty to diverse economic claims. However, he resisted what he took to be Schutz's complete separation of subjective and objective meaning systems, since there were certain features that any subjective viewpoint would have to acknowledge, such as the existence of the economic system itself. He did concur, however, with Schutz insofar as he posited an objective meaning over and beyond a meaning's subjective dimensions.[12]

Of course, Machlup and Schutz tended to discuss many other issues besides intellectual ones, such as final wills and testaments, investment portfolios, exchange rates, appropriate candidates for business or government positions, copyright laws in post-*Anschluss* Austria, and employment opportunities of which they should take advantage. In a moment of humor between them, Schutz reported that his secretary had mistakenly written *Der sühnhafte* (that which makes atonement) *Aufbau der sozialen Welt* instead of *Der sinnhafte* (meaningful) *Aufbau*, and then Schutz added, "[S]he has no inkling of how right she is." Similarly, Schutz recommended that Machlup ask Farber to show him his paper on William James, and Schutz observed, "As you can see, I am going the American Way."[13]

Schutz also reconnected with Eric Voegelin, who expressed fears about being drafted and frustrations with teaching, and portrayed for his friend the courses that he was offering and that the War Department had solicited. Once, he reported speaking before Jewish people in Baton Rouge on Deutero-Isaiah, about which Schutz knew nothing; however, unlike his Jewish brothers and sisters who prayed before Voegelin's talk, Schutz claimed that he would have first begun to pray after it. The two friends consulted about job opportunities, shared information about missing European scholars, expressed concerns about Winternitz, and commented on recent books, such as Hayek's *Road to Serfdom*, which elicited from Voegelin a doubt about whether Lord Acton's view of liberalism could do adequate justice to present-day problems.[14]

Confident in Voegelin's insightfulness, Schutz solicited for *PPR* his paper on Siger of Brabant, whose intellectual work reflected a compromise between Christianity, awaiting a salvation yet to come, and worldviews that attributed to history an immanent meaning, such as the political synthesis of Joachim of Flora. Schutz requested that Louis Rougier review the article, but Voegelin found Rougier's review an example of a "mandarin-philology" that lacked understanding of the problems of the history of the spirit. For Voegelin, one could not understand the political theory of the Middle Ages without reading Alois Dempf, whose *Sacrum Imperium: Geschichts- und Staatsphilosophie des Mittelalters und der politischen Renaissance* first interpreted the medieval period from the viewpoint of a history of political ideas. For Dempf, modernity was born out of political and philosophical medieval currents that turned away from transcendent Christianity toward the "this-worldliness," exemplified in Siger of Brabant's naturalism or Joachim of Flora's struggle to realize the Spirit's reign on earth. In his *New Science of Politics*, Voegelin concluded that this effort to realize the kingdom of heaven on earth resulted in various forms of "gnosticism," among which Voegelin included scientism, totalitarianism, and "pusillanimous" liberalism, all of which abandoned transcendence for immanence. This early discussion in their correspondence initiated a discussion that would last over decades.[15]

After Schutz presented his paper on the Stranger, which dealt with the adaptations necessary for a new society, some New School faculty reacted with hostility. Voegelin attributed this to their isolation from the American society they had lived in for years. In the same letter in which he offered support after the Stranger presentation, Voegelin also questioned Weber's (and Schutz's) interpretation of all behavior as derivative from rational behavior and traced Weber's exaltation of the rational over charismatic behavior to his being ill at ease with sentiments or values. In contrast to Weber, Voegelin, like Pareto, conceived the rational sphere as penetrated with feeling, and since he believed that theoretical objects depended on a pretheoretical constitution at the level of the sentiments, he wondered how Schutz's conception of rationality would come to bear on sentiments and the institutions shaping one's life-plans.[16]

To appreciate Voegelin's criticisms, a brief recapitulation of his theory is called for. Voegelin attended to the concrete, existential consciousness of theorists, participating in the reality they articulate instead of standing over against it as an external object. This human consciousness experiences itself within Plato's *metaxy*, that is, between a human pole, stretching toward the eternal, and a divine pole, experienced as a call and the interruption of grace. This experience of the *metaxy* precedes any mythical or philosophical symbolization, which, in its turn, always runs the risk of becoming detached from the experience from which it emerges and thus appearing a lifeless dogma or rationalistic scheme, divorced from an underlying experience of participation. Modern rationalism, for example, detached from its existential, ontological, ethical, and religious origins, culminates in the isolated Archimedean observer outside the movement of Being, the *res cogitans* of Descartes, Sartre's *moi*, or the "monster of Hegel's Consciousness which has brought forth a God, man, and history of its own." The ambiguity of the *metaxy*, with which various forms of gnosticism become impatient, appears in Christian descriptions of the uncertainty of "openness toward God, the waiting, the periods of aridity and dullness, guilt and despondency, contrition and repentance, forsakenness and hope against hope, the silent stirrings of love and grace." Since the gnostic "lusts for massively possessive experience," he or she immanentizes eschatological symbols, interpreting his or her political, social, or religious movement as bringing to realization the *eschaton* on earth.

Voegelin's own philosophical recovery of these origins of thought, which he describes as anamnesis, functions self-critically insofar as it is a limited symbolization arising from the metaxy and is thus itself inadequate to express the full reality of knowing participation.[17]

After Felix Kaufmann sent Voegelin a copy of the first two parts of Husserl's *Crisis of the European Sciences* on September 17, 1943, Voegelin mailed Schutz a "cathartic," fifteen-page letter accusing Husserl of manifesting gnostic tendencies. In the previous correspondence, Voegelin had been critical of Husserl from as early as Schutz's edition of Husserl's manuscript on space constitution, which had left him with an impression of agoraphobia, since Husserl had spiritualized time by reducing it to a phenomena within consciousness. The 1943 letter began by praising Husserl's text as "the most significant epistemological performance of our time," but then attacked Husserl's view of history as Victorian, due to its omission of reference to Hellenism, Christianity, and the Middle Ages, and his historical method, which pretended to understand past philosophers better than they did themselves. Voegelin then raised two central objections: that Husserl's effort to determine the objectivity of knowledge of the world did not advance the basic problems of philosophy and that he depreciated earlier generations by viewing them as stepping-stones to his own "apodictic beginning." For Husserl, the Greeks and Descartes served as the "historical manure" in which the Husserlian final foundation bloomed; and he was without the scruples that Kant felt about such scorn for predecessors and had neglected to consult the testimonies of such predecessors. Voegelin concluded by assailing Husserl's lack of understanding of the meditative context of Descartes's *Meditations*. He attributed to a lack of experience of transcendence Husserl's other problems, such as taking the humiliation of his predecessors for a goal, much the way that advocates of the Marxian final reign or the Hitlerian millennium did.[18]

Responding two months later, Schutz admitted that he admired Husserl's *Crisis* at whose intellectual incubation he had been present, and then he listed the issues addressed, stating that they were philosophically fundamental and that the denomination of them as detachedly "epistemological" seemed arbitrary. Schutz then criticized Voegelin for faulting Husserl for producing a cultural history that interpreted everyone as a stage en route to himself, since Husserl had never intended to write a cultural history in the first place. Rather, he was seeking to appropriate a philosophical tradition in which he already stood, and, not smugly self-satisfied but filled with wonder, he produced a text both autobiographical, in that it selected historical elements alive in his own thinking, and "eidetic," in that it grasped those features that defined his present philosophical situation and its tasks. In this sense, Husserl was performing an act of anamnesis similar to Voegelin's. Further, he did not come up with the "final foundation of the entelechistic movement," but rather an inescapable (apodictic) beginning point, namely the life-world to which philosophical reflection attends. Finally, he did not espouse the idea of a "world soul" unfolding through history (and climaxing in himself), and he did not treat Descartes's meditative context simply because it was not of relevance to him.[19]

Voegelin replied with another lengthy letter, the third and last in this series on Husserl's *Crisis*. He contended that what Husserl took to be "his" tradition he also took erroneously to be the "objective," "European," even "human" tradition, contrary to Schutz's interpretation that his *Crisis* was merely autobiographical. Furthermore, while Voegelin accused Husserl of assuming that his interpretation trumped all others, he also objected to a kind of "relevance-relativism" on Schutz's part. Against Schutz's offhand comment in the previous letter that "it is a matter of personal evaluation whether one will refuse philosophical rank to an 'epistemological achievement,' " Voegelin insisted that one could give rational arguments and arrive at an objective decision regarding what were important philosophical problems. Finally, in a postscript, Voegelin jokingly remarked that it was not nice of Schutz to compare Husserl's self-interpretation to "anamnesis."[20]

Schutz had based his interpretation of Husserl's purposes in the *Crisis* on a better knowledge of Husserl than Voegelin possessed, as the latter admitted; and by reading Husserl as a totalitarian trampling on others whom he failed to interpret fairly, Voegelin did to Husserl what he claimed Husserl did to others. To answer Voegelin's final objections, Schutz could have returned to his interpretation of the *Crisis* as both autobiographical and eidetic; that is, he could have maintained that Husserl's personal appropriation of the history of philosophy involved the conviction that the problems raised by selected figures were essential, i.e., fundamental, ultimate, and inescapably needing an answer. While Voegelin and Husserl (and Schutz) might have differed about whether these problems were in fact essential, as Voegelin mentioned, reasons could have been given, since the decision about the basic problems of philosophy did not depend simply on uncriticized taste. Schutz's statement about the choice of problems being "a matter of personal evaluation" was unfortunate, and it hinted at a kind of relativism that Voegelin found objectionable here and in the correspondence to come. However, after this comment, Schutz listed a series of problems that Husserl had addressed, and Schutz affirmed that they "touch upon fundamental problems." Presumably, Schutz would have been able to give the reasons Voegelin asked for as to why such problems were fundamental, even though he did not do so in his letter to Voegelin. In other words, Voegelin was asking for justifications that Schutz did not offer but might have, and his criticisms have less to do with Husserl's dogmatism or Schutz's relativism.

Upon receiving a copy of Schutz's "On Multiple Realities," Voegelin lauded Schutz for breaking through the usual restriction of philosophy to epistemology, focusing on a plurality of meaning realms, and overcoming Husserlian solipsism. However, Schutz neglected the body as a condition of life-sustenance, the interconnection of animal and higher layers of human experience, and questions about birth, survival, bodily movement, and sexual functions. In other words, while Schutz may have broken out of an epistemological paradigm, he did not go quite far enough. Voegelin also objected to Schutz's claim that one was not responsible for thoughts, but only actions, and he proceeded to raise several questions to which Schutz's multiple realities might have afforded answers, such as regarding the transition from experimental magic to experimental science.[21]

Aside from an important discussion of Schutz's essay "The Stranger," Gurwitsch and he exchanged letters on William James, the advantages of trying to communicate phenomenology to nonphenomenologists, and the irreconcilable spheres of existence (since Schutz was preparing "On Multiple Realities"). Further, they weighed options regarding the Schutz family belongings that Gurwitsch had consolidated in Paris and shipped, but that had been detained in Casablanca and were about to be auctioned off. (Schutz concluded that it would be easier to go to Macy's and purchase new things.) Mindful of the increasing savagery of the European war, Gurwitsch observed, "At times I begin to believe that you are right when you say that science, music, and so forth are a flight into realms in which a sense and order that have completely disappeared in our world still reign." Schutz, bemused that Gurwitsch made his living by teaching physics at Harvard rather than the philosophy he loved, noticed the parallel in his own life: "I have always drawn a sharp line separating that from which one lives and that for which one lives."[22]

In October 1944 and September 1945, Felix Kaufmann and Schutz examined their philosophical differences in a letter exchange that indicated that their relationship had not been definitively ruptured. At the end of October 1944, Kaufmann commented on his own interests in the logical structure of science, which were prominent in his 1944 book from Oxford Press, *The Methodology of the Social Sciences*, an almost complete revision of his 1936 *Methodenlehre*. Though no longer interested in science's *umweltliche* underlayers, he praised Husserl's work on prepredicative thinking and his critique of transcendental psychologism. The publication of "On Multiple Realities" stimulated a new interchange, with Schutz emphasizing the life-world as science's substrate, unquestioned unless there were some motivation for questioning it, and admitting that his idea of the "epoché of the natural attitude" surpassed Husserl's work without being incompatible with it. Schutz insisted that his distinction of *Wirkwelt* from science was a matter not of ontological limits, but of different meanings, since the pragmatic motive prevailed in the *Wirkwelt* in contrast with science, which was characterized by freedom from fundamental anxiety and removed from the reachable world and time-dimensions of the we-relationship. The ground attitude (*Grundhaltung*) of seeking to change the world through action (in the *Wirkwelt*) differed significantly from that of striving to solve a theoretical problem (e.g., in science).[23]

This exchange in the 1940s culminated a philosophical relationship between Kaufmann and Schutz that had endured many years in spite of their personal differences. Machlup remarked that from as early as the Mises seminar, Kaufmann and Schutz were the most influential "philosophers of social science," with Kaufmann being a phenomenologist inclined toward logical positivism and Schutz a phenomenologist leaning toward Weber. Although Machlup, along with Haberler and others, had originally leaned toward Kaufmann's position, Machlup admitted that Schutz had gradually convinced him to become a "faithful disciple" the rest of his life. Kaufmann had assisted Schutz's production of his *Phenomenology*, and in his 1936 *Methodenlehre*, Kaufmann frequently acknowledged the influence of Schutz. For example, Schutz made possible controlled affirmations about others' meanings, developed a complete account of the structure of the social world, and clarified the distinction between objective and subjective meaning (better than Weber had) as well as the function of scarcity as a "because motive" in economic science.[24]

The influence was by no means one way. The *Methodenlehre* addressed a topic Schutz took up in depth later—namely, the empirical controllability of natural and social scientific claims—and it raised issues that Schutz developed immediately, such as the possibility of shifting research from scientific generalizations to individual activity and the epistemic status of the principle of marginal utility. Schutz considered these issues in his 1936 essay "Political Economy," specifically citing *Methodenlehre der Sozialwissenschaften* and presenting the principle of marginal utility as a nonanalytic statement about the world that delimited a realm of knowledge, though he did not think that social scientists needed to explain its epistemic status. Moreover, in reaction to the *Methodenlehre*'s questions about the range of data upon which social-scientific laws, particularly statistical laws, depended, he illustrated how different subjective attitudes (e.g., of economic actors or economists) and temporal locations determined what counted as data. Furthermore, he criticized deductive models that might take general propositions (such as the principle of marginal utility) as major premises, and data claims as minor premises since types had to be retested at each level of discussion and since, as Kaufmann noted, each proposition within a deduction required empirical validation. Both Kaufmann and he opted for a diversity of methods as opposed to the purity of methods of the Neo-Kantians, who broke up comprehensive bodies of knowledge into smaller pieces, each requiring its own methods, and assigned those pieces not fitting their Procrustean beds to the sociology of history. Schutz, by contrast, believed that social scientists needed to find out for themselves what methods worked for specific areas, demarcating a path that philosophers might follow rather than prescribe in the first place.[25]

Kaufmann's 1944 English work appears not to have significantly influenced Schutz's essay "On Multiple Realities." To be sure, Schutz cited Kaufmann's work in his essay, agreeing that problems emerging within a field partake of the style of the field and must be compatible with preconstituted problems and solutions, though one could freely object to the way those problems had been preconstituted. Kaufmann's insight that one could object to a problem's preconstitution modified only slightly the idea of preconstitution already found in Schutz's 1937 manuscripts, which laid the groundwork for his 1945 essay on multiple realities. No doubt Kaufmann's 1944 book made little impact on Schutz, because his reading of Dewey and his desire to address a North American public had refocused his attention away from the *Umwelt* problematic and toward the logical structure of scientific investigation. To show Kaufmann's influence on Schutz's account of theory in the 1945 "On Multiple Realities," one would have to show his influence on the 1937 manuscript "Die theoretische Welt der kontemplativen Betrachtung," which the 1945 article follows very closely. But Schutz's manuscript concentrates on different problems (e.g., about action, relation of theoretic action to *Wirkwelt*, etc.) than those focal in Kaufmann's 1936 *Methodenlehre* (e.g., marginal utility, data, role of deduction, plurality of methods, etc.), although Schutz's essays at the time (e.g., "Political Economy") did address issues raised by Kaufmann's book.[26]

Although Schutz corresponded very little with Emanuel Winternitz (because he lived in New York), there was frequent contact between them. This, as George Schutz recalled, Winternitz visited the Schutz household every Tuesday at six p.m. to give George lessons (often in the form of games). He would then stay on, to dine with the family, to play music with Alfred until eleven p.m., when building codes forbade the playing of music, and to engage in conversation. He had worked in art museums in Buffalo and Hartford before ending up as a curator of rare instruments for the Metropolitan Museum of Art, thereby following a career that Schutz had urged as more fitting with his deepest interests, as opposed to law, for which he had been trained. One can find signs of his affection for Schutz in his dedication to his own book, *Musical Instruments and Their Symbolism in Western Art,* which reads: "In memory of Alfred Schutz, thinker, musician, and noblest of friends."[27]

Publications

After his talk on rationality before the Faculty Club of Harvard, Schutz submitted a copy to Frederick Hayek, who published it in *Economica*, even though Hayek had his doubts about whether ideal types could escape historicism. The published version reproduced the basic structure of the talk, except that it omitted the list of problems raised in the second section and distinguished between actor and social scientist in terms of attitudes rather than rationality, a category that pertained to scientific observation.[28]

In addition to "The Stranger," to be considered in the next chapter, Schutz published a partner essay, which appeared in 1945 in the *American Journal of Sociology* under the title "The Homecomer." It considered the timely subject of the soldier soon to return from the front. This essay, exemplifying Weberian type analysis of an actor's subjective viewpoint, describes how homecomers expect to return to an environment of which they always had and—so they think—still have intimate knowledge. "Home" involves face-to-face relationships, sharing the same space and time, intermittently disconnected and reestablished, and not necessarily entailing personal closeness. The essay reveals how those at home and the homecomer, by having related as distant contemporaries via inferential types, fail to take account of each other's ongoing temporality. Schutz describes pointedly how easily one can overlook the irreversible flow of time, as did the economists who committed *hysteron proteron* when blaming actors for not knowing what could have been available to them only after acting:

> The mere fact that we grow older, that novel experiences emerge continuously within our stream of thought, that previous experiences are permanently receiving additional interpretative meanings in the light of these supervenient experiences, which have, more or less, changed our state of mind—all these basic features of our mental life bar a recurrence of the same. Repetition might be aimed at and longed for: what belongs to the past can never be reinstated in another present exactly as it was. When it emerged, it carried along empty anticipations, horizons of future development, reference to chances and possibilities; now, in hindsight, these anticipations prove to have been or not to have been fulfilled; the perspectives have changed. . . .[29]

This entire discussion of temporality illuminates the subjective meanings of the homecoming soldiers, which also include an unwillingness to assume former roles, an astonishment at the anomie of civil society, and a sense of lost prestige when one no longer dons a uniform. The entire essay actually aims at improving intersubjective understanding between the homecomer and those at home, by urging the latter to commence a process of becoming self-critical by striving "to destroy the pseudotype of the combatant's life and the soldier's life in general and to replace it by the truth."[30]

In "Some Leading Concepts of Phenomenology," originally presented before a group of New York philosophers, whom Schutz identified only as being unacquainted with phenomenology, he explains basic phenomenological concepts, outlines Husserl's general project, contrasts it with Descartes's, and explains phenomenological reduction as opening the field of intentionality. He describes the formation of ideal objects, shows how phenomenology can found logic, discusses eidetic methodology, and hints at phenomenology's foundational role for the social sciences. Leo Strauss, editor of *Social Research*, in which the paper was published, found the manuscript the best introductory statement on phenomenology that he had ever read.[31]

Having begun "On Multiple Realities" in his 1936–37 manuscripts and published it in *PPR* in June 1945, Schutz informed Gurwitsch that he had devoted seven (lean) years to it. Its structure, dealing with the world of daily life and then its modifications, paralleled that of "The Constitution of the World of Working and Its Modifications." He omitted or refashioned many details in the manuscripts concerning temporality, the body, aging, and immortality, and some of these reflections were included in an early draft of an essay entitled "Tiresias," the final draft of which would be published in 1960.[32]

The discussion of the reality of everyday life focuses on the natural attitude, understood by Schutz as practical, in contrast to Husserl who conceived it as involving practical and theoretical dimensions and emphasized the latter. Within this practical world, Schutz distinguishes three levels of experience (essentially actual experiences, conduct, and action), as he had in his *Phenomenology* and the 1936–37 manuscripts. He also singles out "working," the overt performance of a project through bodily movements (as opposed to the covert performances of thinking), and examines tensions of consciousness, temporality (including how reflection dissolves the unified, living self into partial, role-taking selves), and the social world's structure (e.g., consociates, successors). Beginning with one's body as the center, one inhabits the world within reach (including Mead's manipulatory sphere) and the world within potential reach, which includes the temporal worlds within restorable reach (the past) and within attainable reach (the future). Schutz concludes by characterizing the world of working as the paramount reality, organized in its relevances around the fundamental anxiety arising from the inevitability of one's death.[33]

In the second part of this essay, Schutz treats the various finite provinces of meaning, modifications of the world of working, which stand over against a consciousness that confers an accent of reality on them, in contrast with James's "psychologistic" subuniverses of reality. While conferring this accent and participating in the cognitive style of a particular province of meaning, one is able to determine what exists depending on whether it is compatible with the other elements within the province. Schutz then develops the logical, temporal, corporal, and social dimensions of the worlds of phantasms, dreams, and scientific theory, and finishes by highlighting a dialectic between the theoretical sphere and the world of working. He inquires, for instance, how the solitary theorist can find access to the social world of working—a question related to that of how one might give an account of dreams, which are not amenable to reflection while one lives in them. The social theorist constructs in theory artificial ideal types of preexperiences of others in the world of working, accentuating aspects (and not the full humanity) of life-world actors and ensuring that these types are self-consistent and adequate. A second problem concerns how one would be able to communicate one's theoretical findings that are discoverable only in solitude. Comparing this problem to the paradox that phenomenologists face in attempting to communicate their findings to those who have not implemented the reduction, Schutz criticizes the presuppositions fueling the paradox. The paradox exists insofar as one mistakenly construes finite provinces as ontological static entities between which one moves, like a soul transmigrating to another world, instead of conceiving them as varied tensions of one and the same consciousness, in and out of which one passes throughout a day. Because the boundaries between provinces are permeable, working acts can become the "contents" of dreams or theories, just as working acts can communicate the experiences of dreams or theorizing, and, furthermore, enclaves of theory or phantasy can crop up within the world of working. It was on the occasion of reading this essay that Gurwitsch, perhaps as a gesture of reconciliation after their dispute over the Stranger essay, deployed his famous metaphor of himself as the digger of a tunnel who could hear the knocking that announced the other worker from the other side.[34]

In a week in July 1944, Schutz developed the manuscript "Fragments toward a Phenomenology of Music"—clearly a first draft, according to the editor's preface to it in *Collected Papers 4*. The essay begins by arguing that music differs from language in being nonrepresentative and that a phenomenological approach to music would emphasize the meaning of music (beyond its physical nature as sound waves), its character as an ideal object, and its necessarily polythetic constitution. Phenomenology clarifies the functioning of music, independently of space and intimately in connection with inner temporality, and discusses the identification of a thematic sequence of tones by explaining continuance, the subtle differences that context introduces, and the experience of recurrent likeness. The grasping of a theme, as opposed to living in the flow of music the first time one hears a piece, requires reflection and emerges from an interplay between elements in the music inviting and inciting the listener and the listener's attention and interest.[35]

In a particularly insightful preface to "Fragments," Fred Kersten has elucidated how this manuscript anticipates Schutz's later essays "Making Music Together" (1951) and "Mozart and the Philosophers"(1956) by showing how musical experience exemplifies the face-to-face relationship, the fundamental social interaction, as a matter of shared time. Both music and inner time unfold polythetically and cannot be grasped monothetically, and, since only polythetic constitutings that are grasped monothetically can be conceptualized, certain dimensions of consciousness elude conceptualization and thus demarcate limits of rationalization. This conclusion—if it is Schutz's and if it is his final one—would iterate, in a musical key, the paradox explored theoretically from the Bergsonian period onward, and would give music as central a place in Schutz's philosophy of inner time. Schutz, in Kersten's opinion, also differentiates the passive associative syntheses of sight from those of listening, the latter of which involve no identification of numerically distinct items but only an illusion of identification. By showing that sameness in music consists not in numerical unity but recurrent likeness, Schutz challenges a fundamental Husserlian thesis, namely, that the synthesis of identification in passivity is universal, lying at the world's constitutive origins. Kersten's essay portrays Schutz digging beneath *even the usual phenomenological conceptions* to recover the phenomenona that those conceptions anonymize, as he did with conceptions about temporal consciousness, the social world, and strangers. And in criticizing phenomenological conceptions, he proved himself *more* astutely and paradoxically phenomenological.[36]

In conclusion, Schutz allowed the war to impinge upon him, devoting himself to writing reports for the Office of Economic Warfare at the cost of research time and applying his insights into temporality and the subjective interpretation of meaning to improve the likelihood that returning soldiers would be understood. In addition, Schutz displayed in his writing an admirable inclination to foster pluralism, to bring ever so delicately to light the differences (e.g., in temporality) that frustrate mutual understanding, and to exercise self-critique with reference to himself as theorizer. These qualities in his writing appeared in his everyday activities, in his responsiveness to friends, and in his ability to soothe a regularly militant Marvin Farber and to approach irenically positions at odds with his own, such as existentialism or Thomism. Furthermore, when Voegelin's passion to attack the evils of modernity and gnosticism led him to run interpretive roughshod over Husserl, Schutz's depth of character, e.g., his painstaking devotion to understand others in their terms (in this case, Husserl *Crisis*), emerged all the more plainly. Although Schutz's life and writings reveal admirable ethical dimensions, including a deep, continual concern for intersubjective understanding, the next chapter will explore objections raised by Voegelin, Gurwitsch, and others to what they took to be his inability to espouse and articulate ethical principles theoretically.

A Son's Illness

Letters throughout the summer of 1944 refer to a "serious illness" befalling Schutz's son, George. To understand the impact of this illness, which I have previously mentioned in passing one must be aware that by age three George knew by heart Mozart's *Magic Flute* and Bach's *Mass in B Minor* and that at age six he was able to sight read classical music and play duets with Alfred. One day, while playing in the park with Hansi he collided with another boy on a bicycle, and a subsequent eye examination revealed that he suffered from detached retinas in both eyes, a highly unusual condition that baffled the fifty doctors who examined him. All they could do was recommend further observation. When the boy reported seeing half black and half white in 1946, he was rushed into surgery. Today the procedure would be handled with lasers; back then, it required three weeks of immobilization. It left him unable to read with his left eye and still possibly needing surgery on the right.[37]

In letters to friends, Alfred described this experience as living with an "open wound," and, although at that time he continued collecting funds for Walter Froehlich's ill wife, he canceled all meetings and avoided socializing with friends. In addition, he was forced to travel to Europe in August on a two-month business trip to reestablish postwar business contacts, and he resorted to trans-Atlantic mail to keep apprised of his son's condition—a situation illustrating a tragic conflict between the roles of businessman and father. Lengthy letters to Ilse revealed further the subjective meaning of these events for Alfred and his greatness of character in the face of a horrible situation. He worried whether his son's vision would still be blurred if the use of eyeglasses made surgery unnecessary, whether the boy would lose his right eye and the capacity to read at all through another surgery, and when and how George should be informed if surgery were necessary. When Ilse and the doctors began to favor surgery to save George's sight even at the expense of his reading ability—they claimed "Reading is not the most important thing in life"—one can imagine what Alfred the scholar must have felt. Finally, the doctors arrived at a consensus to operate on the right eye, though they were willing to wait until later October, when Alfred would return.[38]

After that decision, Alfred oscillated between hope and depression, at one time confident in the rationality of scientific medicine, preferable to Christian Science, and at another imagining the hubris of the physicians, proud that they enabled a young child to see, while he worried about his ability to read. Hearing that the doctors thought it remotely possible that the operation might even result in diminished sight in his son's right eye, Alfred wrote Ilse that there was no need for doubt or hopelessness, since these would not change the outcome. To Ilse's tormented thoughts about how their children could be such a source of suffering for her husband, Alfred replied, "You know that you and the children are the only true meaning of my life." He added that if his son's fate would be to end up visually disabled, he would still love him and do his best to bring the greatest possible good out of the situation. Alluding to the *Anschluss*, he mentioned that they were passing through the dark tunnel again, hoping for the best, but not with an intensity that would produce disillusionment. Corresponding with her daily in October, he urged her to proceed with the operation if TWA labor problems delayed his arrival.[39]

The results of the operation were disappointing—a *Misserfolg*, as Schutz wrote Machlup—since his son lost all vision in his right eye. Schutz was not even permitted to mourn the loss with his son, since early in 1947 he had to leave on a business trip to California and Mexico. Returning from another trip to Montreal, he learned that another operation was necessary on George's right eye, though it had little chance of success, and Schutz wondered "if there were anything to hope for." But strangely, George's left eye began progressing, and during business travel that summer Alfred communicated constantly with Ilse and his son and rejoiced that George had been listening to sonatas, that his vision had become satisfactory, and that he had not fallen behind in school. Years later, eyeglasses were developed with great magnifying power, and they enabled George to read three letters at a time, if he kept the page he was reading near his eyes. One poignant trace of this four-year period of agony can be found in a folder in Schutz's papers entitled "Clippings," which contained several excerpts from different sources about children with blindness and doctors who were able to effect their cures. It is evident that Schutz never read a newspaper without his attention being directed by a matter dear to his heart, namely, his desire that someday a remedy might be found for his son.[40]

Ilse summarizes this entire episode, highlighting her husband's great generosity:

> [M]y husband, in addition to all his other activities, found time to sit down with him [George] and help learn everything by heart, because he couldn't read music any more, he who had been so fantastic a sight reader. Once, when he went to the piano after the operation, he couldn't play as he had before. He had never before played note by note, he always saw the entire phrase. Now suddenly it sounded like

the playing of a child. The first and only time he spoke about it, he said: "What has happened to me? Oh, it is because I can't see it." And he never wanted to go back to the piano. And that was one of the many, many great deeds of my husband, that he tried to help him learn everything by heart. And when he knew the music by heart, he could then start to practice. . . . He was really one of the finest human beings I have ever met in my life. He was a friend to so many. He, who had so many things to attend to, so many obligations, when a friend needed him, he just dropped everything and was there to help.[41]

Chapter 8

Schutz, a Nihilist?

This chapter will focus exclusively on Schutz's philosophy, critically assessing its strengths and weaknesses by examining those junctures where it evoked particularly strong opposition or where its astute critics show a certain convergence. One such juncture appeared in Gurwitsch's forceful reaction against "The Stranger," and Voegelin, in correspondence with Schutz, concurred with several of Gurwitsch's criticisms, even though neither Voegelin nor Gurwitsch were aware of the other's criticisms. The criticisms center on tendencies in Schutz's thought that might be characterized under the umbrella term "nihilistic," as Gurwitsch meant the term, and it is paradoxical that someone whose life was ethically exemplary should find his theoretical endeavors criticized as nihilistic.

Gurwitsch and Schutz on "The Stranger"

On November 9, 1942, Schutz informed Gurwitsch that he had completed "The Stranger." It was published in *the American Journal of Sociology* in May 1944, and, in July 1944, Gurwitsch acknowledged receipt of an offprint and apologized for not having responded sooner. Schutz, though, may have sent him a draft well before July 1944, perhaps accompanying the November 1942 letter, because, as Schutz remarked to Marvin Farber late in 1942, he felt that Gurwitsch's attitude toward him had changed. At that point, he attributed the change possibly to a reception Helmut Kuhn had given to Gurwitsch after he had introduced them. Something, though, had obviously gone awry in their relationship. They had exchanged twenty or more letters per year until 1943, but then they sent only two letters; and in 1944, the only letter was Gurwitsch's critical reaction to "The Stranger." After that reaction, they did not correspond for almost another year. The editor of *Philosophers in Exile* acknowledges a problem, directing attention to Schutz's salutation of his friend as *Mr.* Gurwitsch in a June 1945 letter, but he then hastens to reassure the reader, "Whatever coolness might have developed, it is gone by the time of Gurwitsch's letter of September 3, 1945." It is important, though, not to pass over too quickly this strain in their relationship in a rush to reconciliation, since Gurwitsch had earlier drafted a French paper in opposition to what he took to be nihilistic philosophical currents, traces of which he, in his critical letter, detected in Schutz's essay. Gurwitsch published his criticisms of nihilism in English in "On Contemporary Nihilism" in the *Review of Politics* in 1945.[1]

"The Stranger" constructs a type whose outstanding example was the immigrant. Schutz describes the stranger's relevances and knowledge, which is incoherent, partially clear, and not free from contradiction. It relies upon taken-for-granted recipes, useful "for interpreting and handling things and men" for the best results with a minimum of effort. Without sharing the history of the in-group, strangers approach it with cultural patterns that prove inadequate, since their home group formed such patterns as disinterested observers with no intention of interacting with the foreign group. Schutz explains how strangers express themselves clumsily due to their lack of acquaintance with the in-group's connotations, idioms, or literature, how they take typical traits for individual ones (and vice versa), and how they confuse the remoteness and intimacy appropriate to situations. Taking in-group patterns as a field of adventure rather than a matter of course, strangers recognize the limits of "thinking as usual" and exhibit doubtful loyalty toward the in-group—attitudes that generate a complex looking-glass relationship between themselves and in-group members. For Schutz these experiences of familiarity and strangeness pertain to our general interpretation of the social world, and just as we convert what is strange into warranted knowledge, so the stranger often adapts to the in-group, ceasing to be a stranger.[2]

Gurwitsch's critical letter recognizes the formal sociological level of Schutz's analysis in the essay, but objects that the present immigrants from Nazi Europe face crises "incommensurable with those fundamentally harmless problems of adapting." Appealing to Schutz "the philosopher," Gurwitsch argues that, for immigrants such as Schutz and himself, it is more important to be responsible for the world and to give an account of it, according to Husserl and Plato, than to learn recipes for dealing with things. The philosopher's task is not to conform to conventions, the *consensus communis*, but to challenge them, even if by such challenging he or she ends up a complete failure in the public eye, as happened to Socrates and Thales. Gurwitsch bridles at any social-psychological reduction of humanity to trainable animals and at Schutz's concentration on the "average" person, and he links his analysis to events on the continent, since "it is precisely those things that no one wants to hear about here that hell has revolted against in Europe."[3]

Gurwitsch's "On Contemporary Nihilism" never names specific opponents, though his 1944 letter resounds within it. In an initial section against naturalism, Gurwitsch deplores the emphasis in the social sciences on "adjusting" to one's environment. Further, when one reduces ideas to corporeal reactions, *episteme* to *doxa*, validity to usefulness, abstractions (e.g., truth, justice) to concrete success, and conformity with truth to conformism, one undermines any idea of a universal truth. Such subversions open the door to a conflict of opinions (*doxae*) of diverse social groups in which the opinion of each is as good as the other's, each learns to "tolerate" others by being indifferent to them, and dialogue across groups becomes difficult. Such relativism spells the death of discussion "undertaken by rational beings for the purpose of corroborating and correcting each other." A second section attacks psychological naturalism—in particular, biological or vitalistic reductionism—and contrasts contemporary psychological naturalism with that of the seventeenth-century rationalists, who preserved rationality by assigning psychology a place within a comprehensive system of sciences. In a third section, Gurwitsch contends that various pragmatic tendencies emphasizing adaptation, toleration in the form of indifference, the subordination of truth and rightness to usefulness, and the replacement of *bon sens* by *sens commun* all culminate in nihilism. He detects a similar nihilism in totalitarianism, which redefines truth as what is satisfactory or useful for one group as opposed to another. Human salvation, however, rests with a rationality that resists allowing what is the case to dictate what ought to be and that is freely capable of transforming reality instead of succumbing to its inertia.[4]

Gurwitsch's reactions to Schutz grew out of an earlier, never published manuscript entitled "Some Philosophical Roots of Nazism" that was produced in tandem with a letter exchange with Dorion Cairns in the late thirties and early forties. In that manuscript, Gurwitsch criticized the romantic nationalism of German idealism, particularly Hegel's and Fichte's versions, according to which an individual emerged out of sociohistorical processes of which he or she was merely the instrument. This emergence, "not conceived under the light of knowledge or truth to be attained," ultimately resulted from naturalistic and materialistic processes, however much Hegel might have spoken a spiritualistic language. Dialectical materialism construed these processes in terms of economic productive forces and the Nazis in terms of "pseudo-biological" factors, such that the philosopher was expected to express the peculiarity of the race-conditioned German soul and such that there would be no universal human truth but only several race-conditioned truths.[5]

In all fairness, Schutz never espoused psychological naturalism or reductionism, since the ideal-type methodology, originating with Max Weber and utilized in "The Stranger," was predicated on the idea of a free subjectivity that was no mere product of causal biological, psychological, or sociological forces. As a result, it is not surprising that Schutz, in a letter written almost one year after Gurwitsch's critique of "The Stranger," agreed "heartily and unrestrictedly" with everything Gurwitsch had said in his nihilism article. But he also claimed a legitimate place for sociology as long as it did not overstep its bounds by attempting to "explain the riddle of the world" and thereby "fall prey to the nihilistic devil." Schutz's point here—and it seems valid—was that "The Stranger" offered a kind of empirical, sociological description of everyday life and one of its types, but it by no means provided answers to philosophical questions. One needed to keep distinct the boundaries between disciplines and recognize the limits of what Schutz was attempting in an essay that he explicitly designated as piece of social psychology and not philosophy. Furthermore one could not draw any necessary conclusions about his philosophy from his social psychology, in the same way that one could not conclude from a description portraying the pragmatic motivations dominating a life-world that the phenomenology describing those motivations partook of them. As Schutz put it, "[F]or the most part, pragmatism is, therefore, just a common-sense description of the attitude of man within the world of working in daily life, but not a philosophy investigating the presuppositions of such a situation." Furthermore, to Gurwitsch's critique that he conflated different types of immigrant experience, Schutz might have responded that that he was describing on a very general level the stranger's experience and that one ought not expect that this description would do full justice to every immigrant experience. There were indeed highly significant details that differentiated 1930s' and 1940s' European immigrants from others and that might therefore require a subtype, but in many ways these immigrants still had to adapt to everyday life in their new setting in the ways Schutz portrayed. Finally, Schutz may well have placed too much emphasis on "adaptation," but he also entertained the possibility that immigrants might criticize the in-group they joined, since their different relevance-orderings and critical abilities enabled them to see through "thinking as usual."[6]

Gurwitsch suspected Schutz of nihilistic tendencies because his paper on the stranger failed to situate its sociological analyses with reference to a broader philosophical framework, as did the seventeenth-century rationalists. However, Schutz had carefully located his phenomenology of the social world in relation to the overarching Husserlian scheme, and had he done something similar with his article on the stranger, Gurwitsch probably would not have reacted as he did, since he resumed their relationship after Schutz endorsed his nihilism paper. By contrast, Eric Voegelin, who recognized immediately that an article like "The Homecomer" applied Schutz's overall philosophical outlook, had no problems with it. Over the years of his engagement with Schutz's overall philosophical position, he too came to have doubts about the worm of nihilism in Schutz's thought. It was precisely *because* of his abstract-descriptive phenomenology, though, and not because it had not been spelled out.[7]

The Voegelin/Schutz Debate

Voegelin and Schutz both realized that they could coexist peacefully, with each working on a different kind of theory. For example, Voegelin, after receiving Schutz's twenty-seven page letter in November 1952 on his *The New Science of Politics* and criticisms of his chapter drafts of his book on Israel and Revelation, claimed that he concentrated on a theory of politics while Schutz was working out a general theory. Similarly, Schutz acknowledged the validity of their different theoretical purposes and even the greater importance of Voegelin's:

> Likewise I know that it is far more important to point out that social and political existence has something to do with the order of the soul as well as that there exists besides the anthropological principle a theological one. Nonetheless, I am asking myself whether it is not necessary for a philosophy of history as well as for a theoretical social science to take into account the self-interpretation of this existential order by the concrete society itself and in representations of this order given by other concrete societies. Would this too not be theory even if not in the sense intended by you? Such a theory may not be theory in the sense of Aristotle. In any case, I believe that this scientific task, regardless of what one may call it, can be carried out without recourse to concepts like sophon, kalon, agathon, and the like.[8]

Whereas Voegelin aimed at a philosophical/theological anthropology at the base of political existence, Schutz was interested in the *verstehenden Soziologie*, in grasping the subjective meaning—for instance, a society's self-interpretation and other societies' interpretation of that society.[9]

But this mutual rapprochement did not prevent Voegelin from detecting in Schutz's work and correspondence traces of the nihilism that Gurwitsch described, although Voegelin did not have access to the Schutz/Gurwitsch correspondence and did not frame the debate in quite these terms. For instance, although Voegelin commended Schutz's "The Homecomer" for applying well his conceptual apparatus to a concrete problem and for translating his thoughts so well into "American," Voegelin raised questions similar to Gurwitsch's:

> Also the customary social-psychological categorization of "adjustment," "adaptation," etc., appears to me not only theoretically insufficient, but above all as a perfidious immorality, which proceeds on the supposition that the "environment" is something within which one has to fit. The question is not even raised whether the Homecomers might not do better if they attempted to adjust the environment to themselves, etc.[10]

Voegelin correctly detected Schutz's emphasis on adaptation, but Schutz at least envisioned the possibility that Homecomers would criticize the society to which they returned when he suggested that soldiers, having discovered their own gifts in war, would feel dissatisfied with the opportunities available at home.[11]

Another trace of nihilism appeared in the friends' discussion of Husserl's *Crisis* recounted in the previous chapter. Schutz had asserted that it would be merely a matter of (unargued) personal evaluation if one considered an "epistemological achievement" less important than other philosophical accomplishments. Voegelin's comments on this statement converged with Gurwitsch's concern about the relativistic undermining of rational discourse and philosophy itself, which requires discussants to open themselves to corroboration or correction from interlocutors:

> When you absolutize the idea of relevance in such a way that one is not permitted to ask about the relevances of A or B, then you abolish the community of philosophizing. Obviously every philosophizing person must hold something for relevant, otherwise he or she never would have begun to philosophize. But can such a person not make a mistake? Can he or she not hold something for relevant which in fact is objectively irrelevant? Is there no rule for choosing? Is a relevance-scheme an irrational fact, which cannot be rationally criticized and discussed? Is every philosophizer a relevance-monad? I cannot believe that this is the purpose of your argument. When one is permitted to criticize another's choice of relevances, what shall become of the argument of "personal" evaluation? Naturally my evaluation is personal, insofar as the points of view about the relevance of one or another philosophical problem must be the points of view of a person, in this case, mine. But what follows from that? Is there no hierarchy of philosophical problems? Is the problem of such a hierarchy not able to be discussed in rational arguments? Would it not be fundamentally thinkable that epistemological problems are surely philosophical ones, but secondary when compared with the catalogue of problems in Scheler's *Man's Place in*

> *Nature*? . . . I do not intend with these questions to have said anything in this moment about the correctness of a relevance judgment in the concrete. I only ask to point out that here is in fact a realm of discussion that would be destroyed [if] one retreated to the position that what one holds for relevant is a matter of personal evaluation and not something for rational argument.[12]

Schutz's comment was unfortunate, as mentioned above, but his subsequent listing of the fundamental problems Husserl addressed suggests that he had arguments he could have given as to why these problems were fundamental.[13]

Several of Schutz's comments above indicate a pattern with which Voegelin took exception, namely, a reluctance on his part to commit himself on questions of ethics and values. In September 1952, after reading Schutz's 1951 publications, including "Choosing among Projects of Action," Voegelin questioned why Schutz, in spite of excellent analyses and lucid exposition, refrained from adopting any substantive ethical position and from asking ultimate ethical questions, much as Gurwitsch had censured him for neglecting ultimate epistemic questions.

> Why should a theory of action exclude that which is most important for action, namely, a doctrine of goods and virtues? Why should ethics be truncated and reduced to a theory of goal-rational (*zweckrationalen*) action without any substance? When a positivist decides upon such limits because he or she holds problems of ethics and metaphysics for only an "apparent" problem, I can understand it, even though I do not approve. But why do you do this? Your return to the argument that everyone has his or her interests appears unsatisfying to me, since this argument is not rational. . . .[14]

Three weeks after Voegelin's September 1952 letter, Schutz responded that far from denying a doctrine of goods and virtues, he relied upon Leibniz's account of them to develop a general structure of action applicable to all goal-directed (*zweckhafte*) action and not just goal-rational (*zweckrationale*) action. He also granted that, for Voegelin, whose interests centered on a generalized theory of ethics or happiness, a doctrine of virtues would be of utmost importance; however, his own work headed in another direction. He sought instead to explain the prescientific interest-constellation that, as given without question, set in motion all action. Indeed, it was to explain such interest-constellations that he had just completed his manuscript on relevances, on which he had worked from 1947 to 1951. Schutz's defense here against Voegelin seems plausible: it is not that he forbids any discussion of goods or virtues, as Voegelin accuses him of doing, since they can find a place within the general structure of action that he defines. However, the problem remains that Schutz refrains from committing himself to any ethical stance.[15]

This lack of commitment becomes clearer in a letter of Voegelin to Schutz in January 1953 in which Voegelin challenged Schutz's statement that dogmatism pertained not just to gnosticism but to any historical position engaged by a counterposition:

> Formally Socrates is in conflict with Athens; you can take up one or other side of a question, and then the other side emerges as a counterposition. But this appears to me to lead to historical relativism. Here one must arrive at the decision: Socrates was right and Athens wrong (Or that found by modern liberals: democracy is right and Socrates was a fascist). . . . It is not a matter of indifference whether Plato thinks beyond a declining Athens or whether the national socialists and communists want to destroy the Greco-Christian tradition. A general relevance theory (always presupposed that I have correctly understood it) would be accompanied by the danger that it would explain this more concrete problematic as irrelevant; and therefore it would come in conflict with philosophy, which has arisen by becoming aware that these problems are centrally relevant.[16]

Here Voegelin suggests that Schutz's very process of abstraction involves stepping back from the conflicting positions presenting themselves before him in order to describe the universal structures they presuppose. In effect, this very abstractive procedure exempts Schutz from having to commit himself to any of these positions appealing for his assent. The process of abstraction has the effect of making two concrete conflicting positions appear as equally legitimate manifestations of a common overarching structure, thereby relativizing each (since one is no better than the other) and perhaps dissipating any commitment on the part of its adherents. Voegelin is arguing, in brief, that the very process of abstraction itself, undertaken within a project of describing general structures, has the capacity to undermine ethical normativity and hence harbors within itself a kind of nihilism.

Voegelin's critique of ethical "nihilism" paralleled but differed from Gurwitsch's antipathy toward epistemic nihilism, which undermined rationality by refusing to live up to its ultimate standards. Voegelin's entire theory served ethical purposes insofar as he located all human activity within the *metaxy,* in which one grew toward a never-reached divine pole, all the while patiently accepting one's limitations in a manner of which gnostics, forgetful of their origins and driven by ideological schemes, were incapable. The task of ethical theory was to demarcate the anthropological, religious, and ethical limits, which gnostics such as Joachim of Flora, Hitler, or Stalin continually violated in pursuit of totalitarian projects; these totalitarians, in Gurwitsch's view, always forsook in some way the standards of rationality. For Voegelin, Max Weber, Schutz's mentor, exemplified gnostic theory insofar as his notion of rationality, shaped by natural science and the French Revolution's opposition to tradition, forbade any adjudication among values that might end up proscribing certain actions. Weber's analysis stood in stark contrast to ancient and medieval theories of practical rationality that he never considered in depth and that developed natural law, marking out the boundaries action had to observe. Likewise, Husserl proved himself a gnostic theoretician insofar as he established epistemology as first philosophy, founded knowledge in the constituting subjectivity, and, as a result, conceived the history of philosophy as passing through a few great historical figures en route to himself. For Voegelin, it must have seemed that Schutz was repeating Weber's and Husserl's errors by developing an account of relevances without any accompanying ethics or ethically oriented philosophical anthropology, both necessary for Voegelin to establish critical limits for the pursuit of goals and interests. Moreover, for Voegelin, Schutz's relativism and stress upon uncritical adaptation to group norms, both of which Gurwitsch also criticized, not only undermined rationality but also and perhaps more importantly ruled out any prospects for justifying such critical limits. Schutz, it seemed, would not even take the first step of committing himself practically to some ethical stance, let alone developing a consequent theory that might justify constraints on gnostic endeavors to realize utopia on earth.

Although no *conscious* nihilism motivated Schutz, he admitted to Voegelin that for years he had consciously accustomed himself not to speak the language of values or even to think in these categories (which he claimed parenthetically have become nearly unusable because of a Babel of linguisitic confusion). He refrained from such language not because he did not understand the meaning of these terms and not because he was a positivist seeking to exclude them from scientific investigation. Rather, he believed that the category of relevance was the widest possible, within which value-schemes defined in terms of virtues or happiness could also find their place. Moreover, when Voegelin confessed that Gurwitsch's work lacked relevance for his problems, Schutz detected the presence of Voegelin's his own relevance scheme, which, as one of many such schemes, testified precisely to the pluralism of relevance schemes that Schutz's theory accommodated.[17]

Correlative to Schutz's claim that his relevance theory encompassed diverse concrete value-stances, he questioned in his lengthy letter of November 1952 the potential insularity of Voegelin's position, particularly in his *New Science of Politics*. Schutz wondered, for instance, whether Voegelin was claiming that any falling away from Christian faith involved gnosis, that every great metaphysician in history was a gnostic, that anyone who rejected

Christian eschatology would be involved in closing the soul, and that reason itself involved a fall from grace. Referring to his account of relevance-structures and interests, which exceeded (even as it included) doctrines of virtue and happiness, Schutz concluded:

> Methodologically it seems to me that a theory that will explain more (or seek to explain it) involves a narrower option. You know how much I admire your work. It stands too high even to have to be justified. But why, why, why do you adopt such a monopolistic, imperialistic attitude? In life as in science each works within the limits within which he or his daemon puts him. But when one oversteps these limits, one courts danger. And it is also dangerous to forget that in the house of our father there are many dwellings.[18]

Voegelin defended himself against this charge of narrowness by explaining more fully his own work, denying that it was an apologetics for Christianity and affirming that it allowed for experiences of transcendence independent of Christianity, apart from which one could philosophize. For example, Voegelin affirmed that when Plato's metaphor of the cave spoke of the prisoners being forced to turn toward light en route to liberation, Plato was describing the experience of the irruption of the Transcendent in human life, which the Christian symbol system would identify as revelation or grace.[19]

In the end, Voegelin reverted to his earlier point of contention that Schutz's generalized descriptions effectively evaded any decision about which concrete positions were right. Granted that people were oriented toward their respective preferences "relatively naturally" in everyday action, they were ultimately guided by one or some of a variety of preferences (*Präferenzen*), for glory, power, or truth, as Aristotle observed, or for religious, aesthetic, hedonistic, utilitarian, and moral values, as Voegelin added. But Schutz would still face Aristotle's problem in the beginning of the *Nicomachean Ethics*: must one simply remain with a classification of relevance types or is it possible to rank them and to ground these differences in a philosophical anthropology? Aristotle affirmed this latter possibility, and Voegelin was ready to follow him even if he should fall prey to an "imperialistic monopolism." If this Aristotelian "next step" beyond Schutz's description of relevances were possible, then a "scientific ethics" such as Aristotle's would not just be one further example of a relevance ordering, but rather *the* relevance theory.[20]

Voegelin's use of the word "preferences" here may obliquely refer to Schutz's background in the Austrian economic tradition in which the subjective preferences of diverse economic participants were beyond question, as in Mises's theory. In addition, the stance maintaining the undecidability of values calls to mind the opinion of Max Weber that capitalism had resulted in a conflict between a polytheism of gods that no scientific knowledge could resolve. One thinks also of Hans Kelsen's notion of law as a positive, self-contained system, immune to critique by moral systems, which cannot secure unanimous assent. Indeed, here we can only speculate—and perhaps Voegelin is doing so, too—about the "because motives" in Schutz's theoretical background shaping this position so at odds with Voegelin's.[21]

Assessment of the Debate: The Need for a Participant Stance in Ethics

Is Schutz, then, a nihilist? The philosophers P. F. Strawson and Jürgen Habermas have developed a distinction useful for answering this question—namely, that between a participant point of view, in which one commits oneself to a position, and the observer stance, which catalogs various competing positions without supporting any. Voegelin continually presses Schutz to commit himself to some first-person, participant ethical position, whereas Schutz repeatedly adopts the objectivating attitude of the nonparticipant, third-person observer, describing various commitments and endorsing none. If one construes the Schutz/Voegelin debate this way, it becomes evident why Voegelin would be dissatisfied with merely distinguishing levels of analyses and differing theoretical relevances, as when one claims that Schutz works out a general theory of relevance for a *verstehende Soziologie* and Voegelin a philosophical/theological anthropology foundational for politics. This mapping out of their different positions itself resorts to a third-person descriptive account, without deciding on the questions that Voegelin poses to Schutz, and thereby favors Schutz's objectivating attitude. One can even wonder if my descriptive parceling out of their positions in the category of participant and observer is itself an objectivating evasion of the participant perspective to which Voegelin invites Schutz (and this author!).[22]

However, when one considers Schutz's engagement with Gurwitsch through the lens of this participant/observer distinction, he appears to adopt not an observer's but a participant's stance. For he commits himself in "The Stranger" to his *own* account of everyday actors' relevance-structures, takes *this* account to be more accurate than any competitors, and would never reduce his differences with alternative views to a mere conflict between *doxae*, each as good as the other. As Plato, Husserl, and Gurwitsch demand, Schutz is assuming responsibility for the world and giving an account of it, open to corroboration or correction by other discussants. Insofar as he refuses to take for granted structures that conventional actors and the *consensus communis* presuppose without examining, his analysis could be located on a trajectory toward fuller self-reflection, compatible and continuous with Gurwitsch's critique of naturalism for failing to ask ultimate epistemic questions about itself. Gurwitsch would not have been satisfied with merely a more reflective stance toward common sense, which even the naturalists could claim; nevertheless, he could have seen Schutz as more allied with himself than with the naturalists had he paid greater attention to the critical, committed position of "The Stranger." Had he read Schutz this way, he would not have been surprised that Schutz "heartily and unrestrictedly" endorsed his nihilism essay, and he would have understood that Schutz refrained from criticizing naturalism because of the spatial and thematic limits of "The Stranger" and not because of latent nihilistic tendencies.

Schutz appears less the participant when it comes to ethics, the domain in which Voegelin pushes him. When Voegelin solicits a doctrine of goods and virtues, Schutz replies not by presenting his own doctrine on ethics but by showing how his descriptive theory, drawing on Leibniz, is sufficiently comprehensive to include any such doctrine. Moreover, by understanding Voegelin's own relevance scheme, which strives to spell out the limits for projects regardless of their relevance scheme, as one more relevance scheme among others, Schutz in effect neutralizes the whole enterprise of adjudicating between values and specifying limits for their pursuit. That Schutz repeatedly offers abstract descriptions when Voegelin requests commitment to an ethical stance permitting evaluation of other relevance-schemes shows how the exchanges with Voegelin differ from those with Gurwitsch, in which Schutz agrees almost immediately with Gurwitsch's critique of nihilism. In the ethical domain, in which a commitment to some "ought" is called for, Schutz seems unable to do more than provide descriptions of structures pertaining to the realm of fact, the "is," with the nihilistic consequence that he cannot justify any ethical constraints upon gnostic undertakings.

It is possible, though, to argue that Schutz, in spite of himself, actually embraces an ethical position. For instance, one might claim that he adopts a participant (though not theoretically elaborated) ethical perspective merely by adopting an epistemic position at all. Merely by "giving an account" one has already heeded the ethical summons of others to respond and has already made oneself vulnerable to their corroboration or correction. Gurwitsch himself hints at such a convergence of ethical and intellectual responsibility when he states explicitly, "[T]he opposition to the *consensus communis* becomes precisely one's intellectual and therefore moral duty." In addition, Schutz gives expression to his *own* ethical leanings insofar as he accuses Voegelin of holding a "monopolistic, imperialist attitude," appeals to the many dwellings in "our father's house," and questions the exclusivity implied in *The New Science of Politics*. Such comments indicate that ethical values of tolerance and respect for pluralism stand higher than others in his own relevance-ranking, though he never clearly acknowledges his commitment to them or positively justifies them, and Voegelin, who could have used these statements to his own advantage, never does so.[23]

One might further point out that Voegelin himself is an observer. Though Voegelin repeatedly recommends a participative stance, he himself is also *theorizing* about the participant attitude, as he does throughout his correspondence with Schutz, and thus stands at one remove from actually occupying such an attitude. As such, he is already on the same plane at the far end of which stands Schutz's abstract, formalized revelance theory. Schutz suggests as much when he points out the generalizing and descriptive character of Voegelin's concepts in *The New Science of Politics*:

> In my opinion, all of these questions are amenable to theoretical and philosophical treatment without recourse to a theory of the good, to a doctrine of goods, or to concrete problems of an empirical order. After all, in your book you proceed in a similar fashion. Your analysis of representation per se, of its elementary and its existential meaning, of its relation to social articulation, obviously is equally valid for all soteriological and all Gnostic types of self-understanding. Of course, I am quite aware that all these formal analyses can be carried out only on the basis of a philosophical anthropology in the widest sense; in fact, they themselves are part of such an anthropology.[24]

Moreover, precisely because Voegelin theorizes about the participation he recommends, precisely because he takes a theoretical distance from it, he is able to rescue it from its tendency to parochialism, as his defense of *The New Science of Politics* in his letter in January 1953 illustrates. The central difference, though, remains that Voegelin's theorizing explicitly serves an ethical purpose, namely, of recommending a participative ethical commitment (in his case, on behalf of individuals, irreducible to pawns in a gnostic historical process), while Schutz's theory generally avoids being explicit about his ethical commitments.

In conclusion, in "The Stranger" Schutz adopts a philosophical position that is compatible and continuous with the critique of nihilism that Gurwitsch develops more fully, although Gurwitsch does not notice this. Furthermore, since Schutz was unable to develop a full critique of nihilism due to the spatial and thematic limitations of his essay, I do not think his position is nihilistic in Gurwitsch's sense. While the abstract description of relevance systems constitutes a legitimate moment in describing the life-world, Schutz's repeated recourse to an abstract, descriptive account of relevances in the face of Voegelin's repeated requests that he commit himself to a participant stance in ethics *does* fall prey to Voegelin's version of nihilism. By the refusal to adopt an ethical standpoint at all, Schutz would have been contributing to a relativism that in Voegelin's view would have allowed the pursuit of gnostic projects without being able to mark out the ethical limits they overstepped. However, even if he had adopted a particular philosophical position—if he had, for instance, endorsed the pluralistic approach that he deploys offhandedly to criticize Voegelin—further effort would have been needed to justify philosophically this approach.[25]

Only at the Institute of Ethics in 1956, did Schutz acknowledge an ethical value of ultimacy from which to assess majoritarian democracy, namely, that citizens deserve to have their point of view, whatever it may be, recognized (but not necessarily endorsed) and that this recognition is best achieved within small publics. This view forthrightly espouses the kind of ethical commitment for which Voegelin had called, in this case an ethical insistence on the worthiness of individual participant citizens to be recognized, while it also upholds by its formality the pluralism and tolerance whose absence in Voegelin's statements had elicited Schutz's objections.[26]

Chapter 9

Peace and Productivity after the War (1945–51)

Working with Reitler and Company after the War

Schutz had depleted all his savings during the war in support of his parents, mother-in-law, and aunt and in helping friends escape Europe. Furthermore, he was burdened with deep financial worries about his son's medical condition and about the maintenance of the rest of the family, whom he alone was supporting. Twice in this six-year period, he explored with Machlup the possibility of leaving Reitler to work elsewhere, such as for the International Monetary Fund, some international bank, or the New School (as a professor). Though Machlup pushed for the less lucrative professorship, Schutz decided to stay with Reitler. In addition, he traveled on business extensively, to Europe in summers and early fall and to Mexico over semester breaks. He found painful the growing European anti-Semitism and the decadence and hopelessness of France, and barely endured Robert Lambert. The stress he experienced in trying to sustain the "doublesidedness" of writing philosophy and doing business became clear when he declined Farber's invitation to write for a new series of books:

> The only reason why I hesitate to accept your offer is the fact that I, unfortunately, have not your capacity for work. With a rather strenuous full-time business job and three evenings of teaching, to which has to be added the supervision of several doctors' theses, I find it humanly impossible to do any sensible writing during the school year. . . . Ilse implores me, pleased as she is with your invitation, not to add something to my work.[1]

The New School for Social Research

At the New School, he served as Visiting Professor in Sociology from 1944 to 1951; presented papers on the well-informed citizen, T. S. Eliot, and

Santayana before the General Seminar; and engaged in a variety of intellectual exchanges with Felix Kaufmann, Carl Mayer, and Maurice Natanson, a graduate student. Albert Salomon felt that only Schutz among the faculty treated him as if he were not a "dope." Horace Kallen felt himself "moved" by Schutz's memorial to Felix Kaufmann, and, at Hans Staudinger's request, Schutz assisted Else Kaufmann in disposing of her husband's pension.[2]

Schutz sought to have some of his personal friends hired by the New School and dissuaded others. For instance, in November 1948, Schutz forwarded to Kurt Riezler, head of a hiring committee, a curriculum vitae of Gurwitsch, whose forthcoming work on the field of consciousness he recommended as a genuine achievement in phenomenology that continued Husserl's work. Felix Kaufmann warned Voegelin that he might feel uncomfortable at the New School, and Schutz, agreeing that he would not be happy there, urged him to move from Louisiana State University to some larger, more prestigious university, which, given his achievements, would soon come courting.[3]

During this period Schutz repeated on and off his courses on social group, social action, and the sociology of knowledge, and offered in 1946–47 a new course, "Situations of Everyday Life and Current Events," which applied sociological technique to problems selected by the class. In the fall of 1949, he presented "Self and Society," covering phenomenologists and various pragmatists, such as G. H. Mead, and in the fall of 1950 he taught a course on social role, which treated various philosophers and such themes as the professions, family, stranger, and marginal man. In the spring of 1951 he devised a new course on the methodology of the social sciences dealing with the relationship between the natural and social sciences, objectivity in social sciences, social causation, rationality, constructs, and typologies. Whenever he repeated a course, he devoted extensive time and attention to updating it.[4]

The *PPR* Editorial Board and the International Phenomenological Society

Serving on the boards of *PPR* and the International Phenomenological Society brought Schutz a whole raft of extra responsibilities. He edited Husserl's "Die Welt der lebendigen Gegenwart und die Konstitution der äusserleiblichen Umwelt" for volume 6 (1946) of *PPR* and reviewed manuscripts regularly. In addition, Farber consulted him about whether to publish other submissions in French and German besides Husserl's manuscripts, whom to appoint to the editorial board (e.g., Ingarden), and how to lower printing costs. In 1946, Farber and Schutz gathered funds to provide regular care packages for the Europeans Eugen Fink and Ludwig Landgrebe, who were so underfed that they had to avoid all physical exertion in order to have energy to teach. Farber and Schutz also shared their personal lives and projects, with Farber keeping Schutz abreast of a cooperative volume on French and American philosophy he was editing and Schutz purchasing a violin bow for Farber in Europe.[5]

Farber had a caustic side that he often revealed only to his friend. For example, he wrote in 1950 that Fink would likely himself become a *Geheimrat* (the reverential word used of Husserl), since he had fallen under Heidegger's sway, and he commented on Helmut Kuhn who opposed one of his editorial policies, "Oh what a God Helmut would be!" After Hermann Leo van Breda, director of the Husserl archives, asked Farber to write UNESCO for financial support, Farber recalled his alleged anti-Semitic slur against Mrs. Husserl and speculated that Van Breda would try to convert even the dead Husserl and make himself a second St. Thomas, a St. Hermann. Such sarcasm rarely if ever appears in the letters of Schutz, who never shared with Farber's enemies comments made about them and who, by contrast, often mediated between Farber and them, displaying a patience and magnanimity that Farber often lacked.[6]

Kuhn's opposition to Farber's editorial policy is highly instructive in this regard. Farber had decided to publish papers by famous Russian philosophers, presenting one in every issue of *PPR* from 1946 until 1948. Since few board members knew Russian, V. J. McGill, a philosophy professor at Buffalo, and Farber, both of whom knew Russian, chose and translated the best available articles. Such a policy defied cultural trends that had begun after the war when politicians and authors began linking the New Deal with Communism, especially after the Yalta concessions to Stalin, whose insolent behavior in Eastern Europe and in the new United Nations made Soviet designs for world domination appear plausible. This was the era of Churchill's "iron curtain" speech, the "cold war," the launching in 1948 of the Marshall Plan to prevent the Soviets from taking advantage of European devastation, the trial of suspected spy Alger Hiss, China's fall to Communism, and the rise of Joseph McCarthy in 1950.[7]

In December 1947, Kuhn, who also opposed the publication of positivistic articles in *PPR*, believed that the Soviet Embassy had handpicked the Russian articles and accused *PPR* of assisting Soviet cultural propaganda in the United States. Since these articles did not deal with philosophical problems in the strict sense and were of inferior quality, Kuhn felt that the journal had compromised the principles on which Western civilization had been built! Though Farber may have been personally inclined to print these articles because of his widely documented sympathies for the thought of Marx, Engels, and Lenin, he insisted to Schutz that the *real* issue was whether he would let himself be pushed around in an indecent way by Kuhn. Meanwhile, Cornelius Krusé, member of the editorial board of *PPR* and the American Council of Learned Societies, explained to Kuhn that the purpose of the articles was to let American readers see how Russian authors thought while addressing their own countrymen, not the outside world. Nevertheless, Kuhn expanded his campaign against Farber by sending several members of the editorial board enclosed cards by which they could register disagreement with *PPR*'s editorial policy. He argued that neither the editor nor the editorial board had the right to make the official organ of the International Phenomenological Society serviceable to any other than philosophical purposes. One card was sent to Schutz, who had privately confessed to Gurwitsch that he had some difficulty about placing such articles in *PPR*.[8]

Although Farber took Kuhn up on an earlier offer to resign from the editorial board of *PPR*, Schutz, who had corresponded already with Kuhn for several years, proved himself more subtle and diplomatic. He wrote a formal letter, possibly for circulation among editorial board members, disagreeing with Kuhn's politicization of the issue by sending mailings to board members. The editorial policy of a learned journal, he said, ought to be free from "high politics." He urged Kuhn not to address the members of the International Society for Phenomenology, since such a widening of the battle would arouse dissension in a learned body that ought to be "above such quarrels, especially in a period like the present one." In a private letter, however, written to Kuhn that same day, Schutz began by affirming their close relationship. He said that on account of it he had attempted to weaken Farber's strong reaction against him, but that he also regretted that Kuhn had written the board without first consulting with him. He further assured him that he did not concur with Herr Popov's reading of Aristotle, although the article was of especially high quality when measured against Russian standards. Nevertheless, he favored publishing the article because the journal readers were quite competent to assess such things and because "publication is the best critique." In the present circumstances it was important to understand Russia and the tragedy of the contemporary situation, of which he was aware through his own study of Russian philosophy. One could challenge Farber's policies, but he hastened to remind Kuhn that the journal depended heavily on Farber's "unheard-of dedication" and that efforts to expand its base had resulted in accepting South American articles not of the quality of *Kantstudien*. Schutz's relationship with Kuhn survived this incident, and hence he could write him after a 1958 conference, "It was a joy to see you at Venice and to see that nothing has changed in our relationship."[9]

Schutz's capacity to distance himself from any definitive commitment had been criticized by Voegelin, but it functioned in the Kuhn/Farber dispute as a strength, permitting an appreciation for diverse viewpoints that he might not have had if he had aligned himself too quickly with any. Furthermore, he displays in this clash a concrete practical example of the kind of intersubjective understanding that had always been a central preoccupation of his theoretical writings. This ability to entertain divergent positions *personally* finds its *political* counterpart in his preference for a liberal, democratic pluralism that would allow participating citizens to reach their own well-formed judgments. One hears echoes of just this political position when he expresses trust that *PPR*'s readers were mature enough to evaluate published articles and encourages the publication of Russian articles as "the best critique." Further, he demonstrates the virtues requisite for such political practice by entering sympathetically into Farber's and Kuhn's views, sparing each of them public embarrassment (e.g., by writing Kuhn a private letter), looking for common ground, and presenting forthrightly his reasons for disagreeing with them.

A similar crisis among the editorial board of *PPR* erupted when Marvin Farber presented the De Laguna Memorial Lecture at Bryn Mawr College in 1950 and then published it as "Experience and Transcendence: A Chapter in Recent Phenomenology and Existentialism" in *PPR*. Favoring naturalism over the antinaturalism engendered by loose usage of the term "experience" in phenomenology, Farber hoped to replace the view, which he attributed to the later Husserl, of an isolated self idealistically producing the world and ignoring the natural, cultural, and historical conditions of inquiry. Although shocked at first, Schutz tried to convince Herbert Spiegelberg, who had drawn his attention to the article, that this naturalistic article should not be taken to indicate new editorial guidelines for the journal; after all, Farber had just published in *PPR* his own "Choosing among Projects of Action." While Schutz, with his usual forthrightness and confidence in rational, democratic procedures, suggested a counterpaper as an appropriate response, Spiegelberg pondered whether the article betrayed biases that had led Farber to reject some of his earlier articles and opined that Farber was no longer suitable to run the International Phenomenological Society. Gurwitsch, also fearful of a changed editorial policy, authored a defense of Husserl that he sent to Farber and that Schutz found convincing. Schutz dismissed psychological interpretations that explained Farber's article as resulting from unhappiness in Buffalo (Fritz Kaufmann's theory) or from resentment against phenomenology because Van Breda's success in Europe far exceeded his own in America (Husserl's daughter's theory). In spite of his disagreements with Farber, Schutz never mentioned Farber's paper in any correspondence with him, and their correspondence continued until Schutz's death in 1959. Clearly, for the survival of certain friendships and for coexistence in pluralistic societies, it is crucial to know that what one may disclose in one relationship one may not or need not disclose in another, without necessarily being duplicitous.[10]

A Family Tragedy and Friends

Ilse had once commented about Schutz that "when a friend needed him, he just dropped everything," and the case of Steffi Froehlich proves that true. Schutz had been regularly in contact with Walter, her husband, since the

Mises Circle days, and she, who suffered repeatedly from bad health, fell in the street in 1946, breaking both hips and developing a spinal infection that required multiple blood transfusions. Because her intensive treatment, including nursing care, went on month after month, Froehlich exhausted his insurance, and Schutz solicited $1,200 from former circle members.[11]

With his family, Alfred showed himself an exemplary father. He never missed an opportunity to attend parent-teacher conferences, summer camp visiting days, or father-daughter events at Evelyn's school. When on business trips, he constantly inquired of Ilse about his children's schooling, and even tutored Evelyn in Latin for an entire semester so she could meet a language requirement. When it came time to choose her college, he thoroughly respected her choice. He accompanied George to Yankee baseball games, and even memorized scores and players' names to be conversant on topics important to his son. In letters to Ilse from Europe, he recounted the anguish experienced at the hands of the Nazis by friends with whom he reconnected, and, passing by the old Paris apartment, reflected that things had not gone so badly for their family, George's vision problems excepted. Citing Goethe, on whom he would produce a lengthy manuscript the following year, he concluded, "The highest personal things belong in the realm of individual fate, which one can bear (*ertragen*) but not direct (*lenken*)."[12]

In the summer of 1948, a tragedy befell Dr. Oswald (Waldja) Glasberg, whom Schutz had helped immigrate to the United States. Waldja's late first wife had been the daughter of Schutz's Aunt Putzi. Alfred had been very close to her, as he had to his aunt also, and, as a result, Alfred and Waldja were like brothers to each other. What took place was that Waldja was accused of referring a well-known socialite to a Dr. Singer for an abortion, and, when the woman died during the operation, the highly publicized case against Singer and Waldja was brought to trial. On July 18, 1948, Ilse informed Alfred, traveling on business, that both Waldja and Dr. Singer had been found guilty of manslaughter by a 7-5 jury verdict, and the verdict had led Waldja to commit suicide in his cell by taking a capsule of cyanide. He had left a letter for Alfred that complained bitterly about American justice, provided instructions about his insurance and the liquidation of his holdings, and affirmed, "I have done the right thing and go peacefully to my death." The next day Ilse sent a telegram with the news that Putzi had then overdosed on sleeping tablets but still lived. Later Susi, Waldja's second wife, suffered a major mental breakdown. She required shock treatments, and never fully recovered. Alfred assumed responsibility for her as well as for Putzi, as Waldja had requested. In his fullest statement on the events, he wrote Ilse:

> Of course I will carry out Waldja's last wishes. I believe that one wishes Putzi no good if one will "save" her. Save her? O Death, how

> sweet you are. I am concerned that you get sufficient rest and that you not have any bad conscience, should you decide to stay at Lake Placid. I cannot predict the reaction of my mother, since she has experienced so many surprises, such as Peter's death. What Waldja wrote me in his last letter has touched me. The letter presents his whole person, with his whole approach to life and reality. He asked me to believe that he has done the right thing. I do not doubt that this is the case. I doubt not that he never did more than arrange an abortion without having any knowledge of the detailed circumstances. Why did he go to his death? This has to do with the rules of play of a corrupt civilization that converts morality into immorality by a law of punishment. Why has he suffered? That has to do with his threefold passion to stand up, to overcome, and always again to win. But all this happened so that he would end up in the freest land in the world sacrificed to a hypocritical Sunday-school justice that qualifies the arranging of abortion as a death stroke but does not dare to think of a 7–5 jury judgment as being an acquittal.[13]

It must have seemed like a terrible tragedy that Waldja had escaped the cauldron of Europe only to die in this way.[14]

Schutz maintained contacts with longtime European friends such as Aron and Beaufils, as well as with Fritz Machlup. He regularly exchanged publications with Machlup, and kept him informed about recent developments in economics, such as the newly devised concept of the "basing point," which determined how market competitors established regularized prices. Schutz had planned to visit one of Machlup's classes in Baltimore at Johns Hopkins, but an unforeseen business trip interrupted his plans. In 1951 Machlup sent his manuscript of a 566-page book, *The Economics of Sellers' Competition: Model Analysis of Sellers' Conduct*, and Schutz returned reactions within a month and a half, even though he was reviewing at the same time the manuscript for Gurwitsch's 570-page *The Field of Consciousness*. Eric Voegelin and Schutz discussed many mundane matters, mutual acquaintances, UNESCO organizations of economists and social scientists, and criticisms of Voegelin's chapter on character that appeared later in *The World of the Polis*. Voegelin commended Schutz's commentary on Goethe's *Wilhelm Meisters Wanderjahre* by stating that it grasped the central structure of the novel, and Schutz agreed with Voegelin's critique that Santayana's naturalism prevented him from understanding spirit and *Seele*. Schutz paid great tribute to Voegelin in recommending him for a Guggenheim fellowship: "As to his character I can safely testify that hardly another Austrian scholar will be found who fought the oncoming wave of Nazism with so great courage and disdain of personal risks."[15]

Schutz's correspondence with Aron Gurwitsch increased after years of near silence and covered many nonphilosophical topics, including the furniture finally delivered from Casablanca. Schutz commented, "I don't know anyone else who is so close to me in this double respect: philosophically *and* humanly." Another major concern during this period was finding employment for Gurwitsch, who had changed academic positions repeatedly; he could not feel at home at any of them, he said, because he was Jewish, not born in the United States, too old, and too good. After serving as a visiting professor at Johns Hopkins and Harvard, he considered teaching in France and at a nascent New York Jewish university, but Schutz, upon advice from French colleagues, urged against the French option since it was not secure, was underpaid, and was perilous due to omnipresent dangers of Communism and anti-Semitism. When the plan for the Jewish university collapsed, Gurwitsch reconsidered the French option and a prospect in Mexico before taking a temporary post at Wheaton College and finally a more permanent one at Brandeis beginning in 1948. That very year, Schutz explored the possibility of a position at the New School for him, but nothing materialized, because the Graduate Faculty felt that Kaufmann and Schutz already adequately represented phenomenology. As a result, Karl Löwith was hired instead. When Felix Kaufmann died in 1949, Schutz proposed Gurwitsch as a replacement, but Horace Kallen, then departmental chair, informed him that nothing would be possible at least until the 1952–53 school year. Ironically, Gurwitsch would finally be hired at the New School as Schutz's replacement after the latter's death in 1959.[16]

Schutz, who preferred to keep his philosophy politically neutral, found contemporary French philosophy too *engagé*, and commented with reference to Sartre that "politics smothers philosophy too." Gurwitsch reacted positively to Schutz's article on Sartre, but thought that he might have pressed Sartre more for imposing a theory of the subject-object dialectic on intersubjective relationships. Though Gurwitsch objected to Sartre's and Merleau-Ponty's displacement of consciousness onto the body by asserting that "I am my hand," he took pride that Merleau-Ponty attended his lectures in Paris in the 1930s and mourned the fact that "here I will never have such a fine influence."[17]

In "Présuppositions philosophiques de la logique," Gurwitsch had argued that one's experience of the everyday world limited the terms that could be substituted for formalized symbols, such that one could not meaningfully assert "The sum of the angles in a triangle is equal to the color red." Alexandre Koyré, the editor of the journal to which Gurwitsch submitted his manuscript, piqued Schutz's interest by asking how it could be that the sentence "The sum of the angles in a triangle is not equal to the color red" was true. To respond, Schutz affirmed certain strange life-world poetic meanings, such as "virtuous triangles (e.g., the Trinity)," "gray theories," or a statement such as "the golden trees of life are still green." Rather than the life-world constraining what could be substituted for formalized symbols, as Gurwitsch thought, it was logic, which, by ruling out such poetic meanings, unduly restricted life-world possibilities. To preserve a pluralism of meanings, Schutz, in his unpublished study of Goethe's *Wilhelm Meisters Wanderjahre*, distinguished three irreducible logics: those of poetic meaning, everyday practical life, and formal logic. He also suggested that in the life-world there could be functional dependencies between quantities and colors, that neat formal-logical distinctions (e.g., a cord is not a snake) appear more ambiguous to one facing problematic possibilities, and that negative judgments are generally formulated in reaction to a positive proposition requiring negation.[18]

Upon discovering that Lithuanians used one word for gray when speaking about wool and geese, another for gray in horses, and another for gray human hair, Schutz concluded that color names were actually "tied to situations" and thus explanable through a sociology of knowledge. To Schutz's argument, which ended by exclaiming "Oh, holy Mannheim!" Gurwitsch responded that this evidence showed only that colors were originally bound to objects in everyday language, but when one adopted a categorial attitude toward colors, one would find an eidetic order among them. One final topic discussed by them was Schutz's review of Gurwitsch's manuscript *The Field of Consciousness*, chapters of which first reached Schutz in May 1951. Schutz recommended stylistic changes, a larger introduction to the third part (on constitutive phenomenology), and greater clarity distinguishing Gurwitsch's position from that of the Gestaltists presented in section 2; and he criticized the Gestaltists for neglecting auditory, and, in particular, musical phenomena.[19]

Research and Publications

Schutz's article "The Well-Informed Citizen: An Essay on the Social Distribution of Knowledge" appeared in *Social Research* in 1946. He associated his idea of the distribution of knowledge with the work of economists and developed the ideal types of expert, man on the street, and well-informed citizen, assigning to the last the role of deciding "who is a competent expert." He then distinguished zones of relevance—reachable, mediately connected with those within reach, unconnected for the time being, and absolutely irrelevant—and he stressed the changing character of relevances, the topography of their interpenetration, and the difference between relevances intrinsic to a chosen theme and those imposed. Imposed relevances, which we experience as "the mere passive recipient of events beyond our control," suggest the many tragic conditions with which Schutz had to come to terms: Nazism, his son's visual impairment, and the economic constraints that prevented full devotion to academic work. Although he addressed the question of fate more fully in his unpublished writings on Goethe, he examined in this essay how interactors share intrinsic relevances and encounter unchangeable imposed relevances in each other, as he knew practically from negotiating the perilous shoals of the International Phenomenology Society. After considering how knowledge is socially derived from eyewitnesses, insiders, analysts, and commentators, he concluded his treatment of intersubjectivity by pointing to a dangerous paradox at the heart of modernity—namely, that its rationalization processes, which create greater anonymity, also produce the technology bringing everyone within immediate reach. Hence, "very soon every place in this world will be the potential target of destructive weapons released at any other place." To resolve this modernist dilemma, he suggested in his final two sections a solution that required citizens to surpass the self-enclosure within in-groups typical of the man in the street or within cliques of expertise by becoming well-informed citizens and by restricting more and more the zone of the irrelevant. Usually reticent on value-questions, he at this point endorsed a normative notion of democracy, in which the opinion of the well-informed citizen as opposed to that of the uninformed man on the street ought to prevail, although this notion remains formal, identifying neither any concrete well-informed citizen nor any opinion that should prevail. One could imagine, though, how Schutz might have utilized this essay to reply to Kuhn's objection to Russian articles in *PPR*: to offset the dangers of nuclear war, Americans ought not ensconce themselves in their in-group and allow the Russians to become increasingly anonymous.[20]

This essay reveals a Schutz acutely aware of the political events after the war and willing to address these events in research, writing, and correspondence. Thus, Gurwitsch and he fretted about the outbreak of the Korean War. Another significant sign of Schutz's concern about world events, particularly linked to this essay on the well-informed citizen, was to be found in folder 449 in his papers marked "Clippings." In addition to the numerous clippings about blindness and doctors curing the blindness of children, the folder contained several pieces referring to nuclear physics and the atomic bomb, including a statement by Albert Einstein, himself a pacifist, that the bomb was a mistake. A separate folder contained atom bomb clippings, among which, as an example of Schutz's sense of humor, one advertised that the atom bomb dancers would be performing at the Burbank Burlesque Theater. But most of the clippings in that folder are deadly serious in nature, depicting, for instance, the sufferings of those who were in Hiroshima when the bomb dropped. In addition, there were statements from Churchill on the bomb, a Vatican commentary deploring its use, and an explanation of Leonardo da Vinci's refusal to publish plans for a submarine as an example of past restraint in weapon design. Schutz wrote his mother on August 9, 1945, the day of the bombing of Nagasaki, about new details of what had happened to some of his relatives under the Nazis and concluded, "The world is becoming ever more horrible, unable to be understood, and evil. The atom bomb should call for less inspiration and more doubt."[21]

In 1948, Schutz published "Sartre's Theory of the Alter Ego" in *PPR*. Sartre avoided the extremes between empiricism (beginning with the other as a body), and idealism (reducing the other to presentations), and between the Hegelian outsider perspective and Heideggerian *Mitsein*, which construed the other as a constituent of the Self. For Sartre, the other was given as a subject through his or her Look, and the "I" could in turn objectify the other by returning the Look. Although Sartre originally intended to depict how one's body was given to the other, he described how the other's body was given to oneself, nonchalantly assuming the reversibility of these problems. In critical remarks, Schutz insisted that by conceiving the other as an autonomous center of activity, Sartre was more indebted to Husserl than he believed. Nevertheless, he concurred with Sartre's opposition to transcendental intersubjectivity, since the "I" of the Fifth Cartesian Meditation was only a modification of the mundane I. Still, Schutz criticized Sartre's Cartesian starting point in the cogito, reducible to an object by the other's look and leading to the result that no relationship between I-subject and other-subject would ever be possible. However, if the other's subjectivity always eluded my own, how, Schutz asked, could I assume that the other's body was given to me in the same way as my body to the other? While acknowledging that the other's relevances were imposed upon me, that is, that they did not coincide with my own, Schutz denied that such a fact implied that either of us belonged to the other as a utensil. Rather, Schutz pointed to the mutual tuning-in of relationships, to be more fully developed in "Making Music Together" of this same period, and the activity of speech as proof that we interact as "coperforming subjectivities" and that mutual interaction in freedom better describes intersubjectivity than Sartre's practical solipsism. How fitting a conclusion for Schutz, the diplomat who proved himself so adept at overcoming conflictual relationships, the devotee of reciprocal economic exchange and critical, interactive, democratic politics, and the musician who delighted in making music together.[22]

Schutz's essay "Language, Language-Disturbances, and the Texture of Consciousness," which appeared in *Social Research* in 1950 and had been developed in frequent interaction with Gurwitsch, showed philosophical parallels (in Bergson, Cassirer, and Merleau-Ponty) to Kurt Goldstein's distinction between concrete and abstract attitudes, relying on speech automatisms and propositional and rational language, respectively. He argued further that this distinction best mirrored Husserl's prepredicative/predicative levels, identified "empirical general concepts" with the abstract attitude, and elaborated Goldstein's distinction through relevances. Thus, the aphasic patient lacked an incentive to give the concrete "pencil sharpener" and "apple parer" the abstract name of "knife."[23]

Schutz's "Felix Kaufmann: 1895–1949," a memorial address delivered before the Graduate Faculty on January 4, 1950 and published in *Social Research*, highlighted Kaufmann's passion for deductive logic and clear thinking. Schutz praised his openness to other philosophical currents, and mentioned his various mathematical and legal contributions. Contrasting his own biographical situation with Kaufmann's, Schutz noted how Alvin Johnson's giving Kaufmann an academic position had liberated his energy "from the yoke of a disliked business activity." Though Kaufmann and Schutz differed on many issues, Schutz remarked, paraphrasing a comment to Voegelin, "there are many dwellings in the mansion of phenomenology." Such tolerance, a hallmark of Schutz's character, was particularly evident in this magnanimous and laudatory eulogy for a person with whom Schutz had been a close friend until a rivalry separated them and with whom Schutz had achieved a degree of reconciliation.[24]

In 1951, he published in *PPR* "Choosing among Projects of Action," in which he retrieved the language of the "fiat," utilized in the 1936–37 manuscripts, to distinguish a merely phantasied project from a decided purpose (which depends on one's in-order-to motive). He further differentiated the in-order-to motive lying in the future of an ongoing action from that same project considered retrospectively as an already adopted project containing an act anticipated as completed in future perfect tense. Moreover, he observed how one had to believe that a projected action was feasible at least as to its type in order to endorse it as a purpose, and such feasibility depended on the world taken for granted, filled with its open possibilities (for which nothing as yet speaks). One's biographical situation, which compelled one to choose one project over another, converted those open possibilities into problematic ones. Schutz contrasted choosing among objects within reach, which already exist and are well defined, with choosing among projects, which do not yet exist and which the chooser generates and considers in succession within inner *durée*. Schutz repeated as his own Bergson's sketch of the process of choosing by running through a series of several (as opposed to two clearly defined in retrospect) phantasied projects in their various versions and modifications, each possessing a quasiexistence. For Leibniz, deliberation involved positive inclinations constituting an antecedent will (*volonté antécédente*) before negative counterarguments enter at the stage of the intermediate will (*volonté moyenne*) and launch the deliberation, which reaches its termination when the decretory and decisive consequent will (*volonté conséquente*) intervenes. Such deliberation depended, as did all choice, on the conversion of open possibilities into problematic ones, and the positive or negative weighting of the devised projects (at the intersection of *volonté antécédente* and *volonté moyenne*) proceeded according to one's relevances. Of course, Schutz's formalized approach to this problem exempted him from venturing into any discussion of "absolute values," to which Voegelin might have invited him. Further, the reflective, retrospective, relevance-laden recovery of motivations (which have already done their motivating) and the constant fluctuation of one's biographical situation made impossible any complete comprehension of all the elements involved in choosing and thus any perfectly rational action.[25]

Schutz bills his essay "Choice and the Social Sciences," discussed above, as a paralipomenon, or social-scientific (especially economic) specification of "Choosing among Projects of Action," whose fuller portrayal of full human action recedes to the horizon of the paralipomenon's concentration on the type *Homo oeconomicus*. For the economist, all possibilities are comparable, scarcity establishes the limits of projects (e.g., not everyone has unlimited funds), and all action is perfectly rational, not subject to the contingency affecting the daily life actor.[26]

In the last of his published works of this period, "Making Music Together: A Study in Social Relationship," which appeared in 1951 in *Social Research*, Schutz begins by criticizing the musical theorist Maurice Halbwachs, who places musical notation at the basis of musical social relationships. Instead, he develops how beholders of a musical performance participate in quasisimultaneity in the composer's stream of consciousness and how musical coperformers mutually orient themselves toward each other, as well as toward the composer and the audience, sharing in each other's time and mutually anticipating each other's execution. Schutz concludes that a mutual tuning-in relationship, established by the reciprocal sharing of the other's flux of experiences in inner time, lies at the basis of all communication and all expression, even the unwilled expression that happens through bodily movement without expressive intent.[27]

Besides these published works, which focus on his favorite themes of intersubjective understanding and the limits of economic science, Schutz worked on several projects that have never been published. For instance, in a 154-page manuscript on Goethe's *Wilhelm Meisters Wanderjahre*, written in 1948 during one of the transatlantic voyages that gave Schutz time for his thinking, he resists critics, including Goethe's own secretary, who characterized the *Wanderjahre* as a "hastily pasted together work of old-age, full of editing errors." On Goethe's behalf, he points to deliberate, subtle changes introduced in the final version of the book and illustrates how the smaller stories, or *Novellen* (e.g., "The New Melusina"), shift person and tense to signal entrances into and exits from different spheres of reality. In addition, Schutz makes the case that "questions about rational-causal motivation are meaningless in the reality-sphere [of the novel]," and he raises the possibility of different logics, utilizing phrases and examples (e.g., the logic of poetic events, "virtuous triangle") identical with those to appear two years later in correspondence with Gurwitsch.[28]

Schutz's interpretation of the *Wanderjahre*, which for Voegelin captured its essence, explains how the three reverences—concerning that which is over us (God), under us (goods of the earth), and like us (human beings)—structure the three books of the novel. Thus the first book of the novel discusses Janos's chthonic universe and Makariens's cosmic planetarium, the second involves eating and drinking on a lake in a lovely natural setting and mountain festival, and the third deals with Wilhelm's choice to be a doctor, the saving of human lives, the effects of industrialization, love relationships, human solidarity, and the conflict between emigrating and patriotism. Throughout, Schutz touches repeatedly on the theme of fate, the mysterious course of one's life beyond reckoning, the impossibility of escaping life's limitations, the production of each wanderer through a particular historicity, and the inability to master life-plans without stumbling upon unforeseen "stones."[29]

This theme of fate recurs in Schutz's manuscript *Wilhelm Meisters Lehrjahre,* which he completed in typescript form on June 3, 1948 and which was farther along than the handwritten *Wanderjahre* manuscript. In this paper, Schutz selects key passages on fate and freedom, starting with the sad discovery by Wilhelm of his lover Marianne's supposed infidelity, which launches him on the long journey that yields great happiness. In book 2, he meets a stranger who expounds how the past limits possibilities, such that, for instance, a youth passed in sooty huts and barns might prevent one from becoming a great painter. In books 4 and 5, Wilhelm passes through a series of reversals of fortune (e.g., embracing a loved countess whose broach pierces her skin and ends up producing cancer), and these twists of fate justify Wilhelm's comparison of life with Shakespeare's drama, particularly *Hamlet,* in which "The hero has no plan, but it is the play that is fully-planned." In the final two books, the stranger reappears, cautioning Wilhelm against dismissing the value of life's earlier stages:

> Therein you err. All that we encounter leaves its trace. Everything contributes unnoticeably to our formation; but it is dangerous to wish to give an account of all this. For in doing so, we become either proud or negligent, or depressed or dispirited, and one is as much a hindrance in its consequences as the other. The surest thing that always remains is to do what lies before us and this is now to hasten to our quarters.[30]

These reversals of fortune continue throughout the last books, with Wilhelm discovering that his early love, Marianne, died, but that he is the father of her son, Felix, and that Nathalie is his true love though he had sought another, Theresa. The novel mirrors life, and life follows the pattern of the novel, which "must grant chance some play, though it [the novel] must be led and guided through the sentiments of the persons involved," because of whose nobility chance, while bringing forward pathetic situations, can never produce tragic ones.[31]

Readers of Schutz often overlook his immense interest in these Goethe novels, which is unfortunate, since it builds a bridge from his philosophical and sociological writings to his everyday life. Indeed, his theoretical writings of this time stressed the limits of rationality with respect to everyday life that compel scientists to construct artificial but illuminative types and puppets well-shielded against the contingency and unpredictability of everyday life. Further, he warned against the tragic possibility that, unless we were well-informed, anonymous powers could overtake us and impose their relevances, converting what was absolutely irrelevant into something of extreme importance. Nevertheless, the world of everyday life does not conform to the demands for scientific clarity or a well-informed management of events, and in that world a son can lose sight, a doctor can be driven to suicide, and a family can struggle for its very life because of a centuries-old powder keg of anti-Semitism that a megalomaniac ignites. Goethe's art illuminated these events for Schutz, for whom "the highest personal things belong in the realm of individual fate which one can bear (*ertragen*) but not guide (*lenken*)," and the "logic of poetic events" provided another rubric beyond the logic of everyday life and science for viewing the tragedies and irrationalities of everyday life. This logic could teach that in the opacity of tragedy rational or simple solutions weren't to be found and that only by nobility of character could one keep pathetic situations from turning completely tragic. In the midst of the sad circumstances of life, we could still "do what lies before us," that is, satisfy the "demand of the day" (*Forderung der Tages*) and leave to history the formation of our selves beyond our conscious reckoning.[32]

Finally, Schutz wrote Gurwitsch that during the summer vacation of 1947 he began a systematic investigation of relevances, a theme present in his 1937 manuscripts and increasingly prominent in his correspondence with Voegelin from 1943 onward and in "On Multiple Realities" and "The Well-Informed Citizen." By 1950 he mentioned to Gurwitsch that he was "with book," having dealt with types of relevances through a discussion of Carneades (Sextus Empiricus). At this early stage, Schutz was working on manuscripts, parts of which would be posthumously published in 1970 as *Reflections on the Problem of Relevance* and other parts in 1973 as *The Structures of the Life-World*.[33]

The first two chapters of the latter work contain the bulk of Schutz's work on the natural attitude. Presenting the natural attitude in the first chapter as taken for unquestionable and yet surrounded by uncertainty, Schutz develops in the second chapter the spatiotemporal arrangement of the everyday life-world. He displays an awareness of the finitude and constraints of human existence side by side with that existence's ability to change its place, to reach into various dimensions of time, and to live a *durée* that cannot be captured in terms of uniform, homogeneous spatiotemporal elements.[34]

Schutz produced the manuscript of *Reflections on the Problem of Relevance* during summer vacations between August 1947 and August 1951. Ilse described the modus operandi as follows:

> When we were in Colorado he went every morning on a long walk which led to a beautiful spot surrounded by mountains and meadows. It was a kind of outdoor Lutheran Church and meeting-ground for its members and there were tables and benches. He loved this place dearly and it provided an ideal place for meditating and writing. And there it was where the *Reflections on Relevance* came into being. It certainly wasn't intended to be published in this form. It was a first draft. Every paper he published had been written and rewritten many times. And all the papers were destined to be part of his planned book. And the Relevance-manuscript even more so.[35]

These manuscripts were to form part 1 of a five-part study on the world as taken for granted, a phenomenology of the natural attitude—a project that Schutz never completed, although the manuscripts of *The Structures of the Life-World* make repeated reference to this *Grosses Relevanzmanuskript*. Given that this manuscript was in extremely rough form, Richard Zaner chose "to tamper as little as possible with it" and only to bring it into linguistically acceptable shape.[36]

Admitting a debt to Gurwitsch and the pragmatic tradition, Schutz analyzes the motives that single a theme out of a horizon before he presents the various provinces of meaning, straddled by the contrapuntal structure of personality so useful for explaining the process of listening to music and psychoanalytic theory. The second chapter of *Reflections on the Problem of Relevance* presents motivational, interpretive, and topical relevances; the topical relevances are elucidated through Carneades' skepticism, which reveals how several configurations compete for interpretive assent. Schutz stresses that the autobiographical, situational conditioning of the thematizer and the systematic interconnections between themes constrain one's freedom to thematize in ways that Sartre overlooked, just as interpretive relevances, subsuming an experience under typical prior experiences, depend upon the interpreter's stock of knowledge and features of the object. The third chapter highlights the interdepdencies of these revelance-systems, showing how, for instance, experiences taken as topically and interpretationally relevant build up easily activated motivational relevances (e.g., a fear of snakes), and it develops a dialectic between habitual types and the atypical properties of an object. Refusing to privilege one relevance type over another, Schutz depicts how topical relevances clarify problems of values; intepretational relevances, questions of methodology and verification; and motivational relevances, issues of personality structure and intersubjective understanding.[37]

In chapter 4, Schutz examines the various factors involved in the genesis of a stock of knowledge: unquestioned inheritances, processes of questioning leading to doubt (*periodosis*) or well-founded assent (*diexodos*), and polythetic stages leading to monothetic acquisitions. The genesis of a stock of knowledge confirms both Gurwitsch's point that there are no isolated experiences, since they always occur within a context, and Bergson's insight into the importance of the sequence in which one acquires elements in one's stock. The fifth chapter continues this genetic analysis by exploring how disturbances can affect the process of sedimentation—for instance, when some topics are consigned to dormancy until reactivated or when other persons intervene in our lives, "hindering the unhampered flux of our activities," as Schutz's life experience had taught him. Of course, interpretational relevances can dominate their data, as when operationalism methodologically "creates" its object of inquiry, but the data can compel a revolution, as when one tailors the methodology to the data, as Schutz demands in writings on the social sciences. The tentativeness of all interpretational relevances reflects the ontological condition of the person and indicates that "the totality of this world in all its diversity remains to him fundamentally incomprehensible, that his own finitude bars him from grasping the infinity of the universe."[38]

In chapter 6, Schutz, pursuing a static analysis of the stock of knowledge, delineates structural features of the "life-world": spatiotemporal openness, provinces of meaning, routine recipes of action, assorted realms within reach, and "in hand" knowledge of one's body, the outer world, and others. Construing "knowledge" in the broadest possible sense, Schutz distinguishes its varied degrees and diverse types of "unknowing" (e.g., unquestioned, restorable, lost knowledge, knowledge of the atypical). He considers negation, occurring against the backdrop of what was taken for granted and striking it out, exploding expectations, and suggesting a theory of "vacancies" that intersubjective communication can fill in but never completely eliminate. A final chapter addresses the biographical situation, including history, relevances, typifications, the intentional objects of the various provinces of meaning, the prescientific relationship with nature, and one's lived body with its accompanying experiences of lived space and ontological temporal and spatial constraints. When

Schutz pictures these limits, the inability to be at two places simultaneously, the need for travel plans to take account of distances to be traveled and the time required, and the experience of imposed relevances that constitute "waiting," the connections with his life are indirect, but unmistakable.[39]

Schutz presented "T. S. Eliot's Concept of Culture" before the Graduate Faculty but refused to publish it, according to Alvin Johnson, because its defects could not be remedied by simple changes, though some have speculated that he regretted his critical stance toward a poet he respected. Criticizing Eliot's *Notes towards the Definition of Culture*, Schutz stresses inconsistencies between his putative sociological method and his dogmatic, unclarified suppositions, particularly his reliance on Mannheim. Schutz questions from whose perspective (*für wemenen?*) culture was defined as "that which makes life worth living." For the culture observed? For the observer? Assuming Eliot to speak from the perspective of the West when arguing that religion gives birth to culture and that culture unconsciously "incarnates" religion, Schutz accuses Eliot of abandoning a sociological viewpoint when he insists that one can only understand these truths from a religious outlook. Moreover, Eliot attributes without justification inordinate influential power to religion over other cultural factors, and he would have done better not to describe the person in everyday life as absorbing religious and other cultural belief systems "unconsciously" but rather as taking them for granted until further notice. When Eliot supports the view that an aristocratic elite stands atop a society divided into distinct cultural levels regardless of class structure, Schutz charges him with snobbery and cites a critic who characterizes his position as being "the most reasonable defense of social inequality that I remember reading." In this paper, Schutz manifests continual attention to the framework within which problems are considered and calls for a self-reflective luminosity, typical of a phenomenologist, about the viewpoint one adopts toward a problem, especially since Eliot seems to oscillate back and forth between in-group and out-group perspectives. Finally, dedicated to democratic processes that pay heed to every citizen, he opposes elitist hierarchies and recognizes a greater role than Eliot for class in enabling or inhibiting cultural achievement, just as he will later recognize how subjective obstacles (e.g., poverty) inhibit one from realizing society's "objective equality of opportunity."[40]

Chapter 10

The Years 1952 to 1956: Responsible Life at its Fullest

The Final Years of Full Business Life

Since Schutz officially relinquished his business work only at the end of this period, in the fall of 1956, these five years were the busiest of his life, so much so that it is no longer possible to deal with his activities and his writings in a single chapter. His work for Reitler and Company wreaked havoc on his life, for instance, when a summer trip in 1953 prevented him from arriving on time for his opening lectures at the New School. From mid-October until early November of that same year, in midsemester, he traveled to Europe, and on August 30, 1954, Lambert cabled him to come to Europe for the entire month of September to work on a business contract, whose negotiation he characterized as "strenuous." In addition to traveling, he regularly had to entertain guests in New York.[1]

These inconveniences and hard toil were magnified by the difficulty of getting along with Lambert. While visiting Mayan temples in Mexico, Schutz expressed his desire to distance himself from business personnel who could not enjoy such monuments, particularly "R. L." He resented Lambert's interrupting his academic work, and when he was running short of money during a Mexico trip, Robert condescendingly commented that he was not accustomed to the luxurious life of their Mexican hosts. Alfred told Ilse that he was going to provide for the "economy of his nerves" by investing no more psychological or nervous energy in dealing with Lambert. He did, however, take pleasure in the fact that Heineken, one of their clients in Europe, demanded that he, and not just Lambert alone, remain on the board of administrators of Cobra, one of their subsidiary companies.[2]

Family Life: Caring for Older and Younger Generations

Alfred continued to show himself the affectionate son, spouse, and father that he had always been. Whether on trips for business or pleasure, he regularly corresponded with his mother, showing concern for her health, sending birthday gifts, and thanking her for all she had done for him. In addition, George Schutz recalled that when she had moved out of the house with Putzi, Alfred visited her every Monday afternoon after work. He was in contact with her doctors until she, who had been a pillar of strength for her children and her husband during the Nazi era, died on February 28, 1955. He also saw to it that after Hansi's death Putzi was properly cared for and received a proper burial.[3]

Alfred and Ilse, as they had for over twenty years, regularly exchanged letters during his travels, conveying affection, tending to articles in process of publication, and discussing the activities of their son and daughter. The children at this time were emerging into adulthood. Evelyn purchased her first car, graduated from college at the University of Rochester, worked in England, toured Europe, and embarked upon an executive training program at the Abraham and Straus department store. In order to pursue musical studies at the Eastman School of Music, George, who had been accepted into Amherst, enrolled in the fall of 1955 at the University of Rochester, which would recognize his Eastman piano courses for credit. Schutz later thanked the Amherst director of admissions for admitting George, but he added that George would have to prove himself in his first year and would strive to live up to academic expectations without requiring too much of the help Amherst generously offered. Alfred always encouraged the maximal independence of his son and expected of him his best effort.[4]

Alfred had fostered his son's musical ability from the time when the young boy sat on his father's lap reading opera scores as they listened together. When George's sight deteriorated, his father would sit with him in the eye-doctor's waiting room, tapping out pieces on his hand and then asking him what piece he had been playing. His father was pleased with his musical ability and marveled at his son's perfect pitch and synesthesia, that is, his ability to see colors when listening to note scales—a capacity his father totally lacked. When George began developing an interest in jazz and more popular music, he concealed it from his father, because his father never had much interest in composers later than Debussy and Ravel, although he knew Schoenberg well. When Alfred found out about this developing interest, he assured his son that it was perfectly alright, purchased jazz records as gifts for him, and would even accompany him to jazz clubs. According to George, this ability to set aside his own interests, and to be open to learning from whatever quarter was typical of his father, who, as previously mentioned, memorized the names of Yankee players because of his son's love for baseball.[5]

Alfred loved music apart from his relationship with his son, however. He was adept at analyzing the structure of musical works, delighted in comparing how various conductors or performers interpreted great pieces, and regularly recorded radio performances, particularly those by Bruno Walter or Arturo

Toscanini. Fritz Machlup recalled how after listening to two singers performing the same piece, Schutz had pointed out the differences in the breathing pauses they had taken. As a young man he had copied music manuscripts at the Vienna Library, but later he built up his own personal library containing the scores of all Mozart and Wagner operas, an extensive collection of chamber music and sonatas, significant commentaries on major composers, and books on music history. He was a close friend of various musicians and performers, such as Erich Itor Kahn of the Albineri Trio or Alice (Gerstl) Duschak, whom he would accompany on the piano and who eventually served as a coach to the world-renowned operatic singer Jessey Norman. George Schutz recounted how in his own work on the Mostly Mozart musical festivals that he had founded in New York, he drew upon his father's knowledge of obscure works, such as the scatological canons or the concerto for a glass harmonica. Furthermore, his father had pointed out to him many of the European performers whom George later contracted for performances.[6]

George said that Alfred combined paternal concern, a love for music, and a sense of humor. George recalled his father laughing uproariously late one night because he had discovered that Haydn in a composition on the Ten Commandments had plagiarized the music for the seventh commandment, "Thou shalt not steal." Humor often stirred Schutz out of states of tiredness, depression, or pessimism, and he could laugh to the point of tears, provoking uncontrollable laughter in others not only by the jokes but by his own delighted reaction to them.[7]

Some of the personal letters sent from Europe at this time recounted memories of Vienna, including experiences of the vestiges of the suffering inflicted by the Nazis, and commented on the beauty of opera or concert performances. Other personal letters revealed how contact with nature revitalized him, as for example, when he commented to his mother on how the combination of mountain and sea in Bar Harbor, Maine, was wonderful, making that vacation the best one since Colorado. The picture that emerges is that of a sensitive man, in touch with his past and his memories, and continually open to the experience of beauty, whether in art or in nature.[8]

The International Phenomenological Society and Editorial Duties

Farber at this time was annoyed with Herbert Spiegelberg, who had requested the membership list of the Phenomenological Society and raised questions about its principles and board of directors, even though Spiegelberg had shown little interest throughout the years. When Spiegelberg began inquiring about access to Husserl's Louvain manuscripts, Farber asked him not to discuss the issue of manuscripts and to leave that matter to Van Breda and himself, snidely asking Schutz why Spiegelberg after years of disinterest suddenly wanted to carry the "white man's burden." To Farber's dismay, Spiegelberg also asked that Farber make regular reports to the *PPR* staff, and he suggested a reconstruction of the editorial board—a proposal that Farber attributed to his anger because *PPR* had rejected some of his papers. Farber rejected as unifiers for the phenomenological movement "any pretenders such as a recently motivated Mohammed [Spiegelberg], or, indeed a neo-phenomenological displacement of St. Thomas [Van Breda]," and, recalling Spiegelberg's offer to withdraw from the editorial board, he thought he should do so "before he assumed the status of a 'savior.'" Schutz, though, tried to make a little peace by mentioning that Spiegelberg had praised Farber's chairmanship of the Phenomenological Society's meeting in Rochester over the semester break of 1953–54. It is no wonder that Farber could praise Schutz, saying, "I liked the tolerant pluralism your remarks connoted when you mentioned that there is room for endless projects and activities." One thing was evident: the tolerant pluralism that Schutz so frequently promoted played a central role in keeping the Phenomenological Society from falling to pieces.[9]

Schutz and Farber shared other concerns, such as Cairns's translation of *Formal and Transcendental Logic* and Walter Biemel's new edition of the *Crisis* (including part 3, in addition to the two parts published in 1936), and the upcoming trial of of Jerry McGill for withholding names during the anti-Communist hysteria of the 1950s. However, just as Spiegelberg had been the focus of Farber's suspicions in 1953, so Van Breda became the target in 1954. Farber was fearful that Van Breda wished to establish Louvain as the center of world phenomenology and install a new "Holy Roman Empire of Phenomenology" in the interest of expanding Catholicism and securing his future beatification. When Schutz speculated that Van Breda might have been more interested in power than in the expansion of Catholicism, Farber felt that such a judgment would be even more damning, since prior to this Farber had been attributing to Van Breda at least *some* religious motivation. Farber, however, did reach an informal agreement with Van Breda that Schutz wholeheartedly endorsed, since it allowed each of them the "full freedom of action" appropriate to coperforming subjectivities. After their speculation about Van Breda's true motives, Schutz reminded Farber that "there is a 'coexistence' possible without any cold war."[10]

Schutz's mail contacts with Rev. Hermann Leo van Breda reached back to December 7, 1946, when Van Breda had drawn up a contract between the International Phenomenological Society and the Husserl Archives of Louvain. In 1949 Schutz's recommendation for funding for the archives to a committee of UNESCO netted Van Breda $2,000 and enabled Schutz to pen these words in tribute to Husserl: "As a philosopher and a man Husserl was deeply convinced that it is the eternal mission of the true philosopher to fight tyranny and in a deeper than merely political sense his interpretation of the social world has to be considered as the most cogent refutation of Nazi ideologies."[11]

Schutz, of course, made no mention of any of Farber's comments about Van Breda, but rather managed to carry on a cordial relationship with him to the practical benefit of both parties. Schutz's "neutrality," criticized in some contexts, enabled him to glide with ease between warring factions of the international phenomenology movement, to be a peacemaker between enemies who had difficulty speaking with each other, and to realize practical goals beyond the reach of ideological rigidities.[12]

Teaching and Administrating at the New School

Schutz's activity level at the New School for Social Research grew exponentially in the years 1952–56. Formerly a visiting professor in the department of sociology, in the summer of 1952 he was appointed by President Hans Simons a full professor in both the departments of sociology and philosophy at a salary of $3,000 per year. When invited to serve as chair of the department of philosophy, he mentioned that he already sat on a dozen committees for thesis work and had agreed to serve as principal thesis advisor to Maurice Natanson. Schutz may have had other misgivings about being chair, since the school was in a process of retrenchment, canceling contracts, losing faculty (Löwith moved to Heidelberg), and anticipating retirements (Kallen and Riezler were nearing 70)—and for these very reasons he urged Gurwitsch not to come. When Kallen invited him to switch to philosophy entirely, he refused, because he had just worked up a three-year program of twelve sociology courses, there were only four people in sociology, and he preferred teaching sociology. In spite of his objections, Schutz finally agreed to serve as chair during the school year 1952–53. His salary was increased to $3,500 in 1955–56, and in 1956–57, when he resigned the chairmanship and stopped outside work, he was receiving $8,500 per year.[13]

As far as teaching was concerned, in the spring of 1952, he developed a new course, "Man and His Tools," examining the psychological, epistemological, and sociological implications of utensil-using, the sociology of inventions, and the influence of machinery on individual and social behavior. In 1952–53, he repeated courses on the sociology of language, social role, and methodology, and in 1953–54 he presented a philosophy course on other minds, treating contemporary approaches to intersubjectivity from Russell to Heidegger and addressing problems of communication, the commonality of objects, and the genesis of different perspectives. In 1955–56, he worked up a new philosophy course on signs and symbols in which he evaluated the theories on sign and symbolism of Mead, Morris, Cassirer, Langer, Whitehead, Jaspers, and Husserl and showed the significance of the sign-symbol relationship for everyday life, science, art, and religion. In the fall of 1956 he taught "Equality, Prejudice, and Discrimination," which looked at varied concepts of equality and the sociological roots of discrimination and prejudice, with a particular focus on actual problems in American society. In addition to teaching, Schutz delivered lectures in the General Seminar of the Graduate Faculty on Don Quixote and Mozart.[14]

On February 5, 1955, Schutz spoke on a panel with Albert Salomon and Howard White concerning the topic "Aspects of the Social Role of Literature" before the alumni association, and Schutz's outline indicates that he examined the author/beholder relationship across three literary forms: poetry, drama, and the novel. He considered each form under various auspices—for instance, in relation to the author the listener to poetry witnesses the poet's self expression, while the drama spectator assumes an omniscience regarding actors, and the novel reader depends heavily on the author's intermediary, the narrator. As concerns the types of reality, Schutz described poetry as an entrance into the world of the poet, in inner time, and drama involves a "pretending to be real" in an imaginary present time, with the playwright disappearing behind the play, unlike the poet. The time of the novel focuses on the past, in which "because motives" are prominent, and the writer, who often uses the third person, interferes with the story by digressions and alters time arrangements by inserting flashbacks.[15]

Schutz coordinated his teaching with his research. For example, his first course in the fall of 1943, on social action, followed several years of study of Parsons's work and an interchange between the two, that had taken place two years before. In the fall of 1944 a course dealt with social groups and problems of adjustment and touched on the stranger, homecomer, and marginal persons, at precisely the time in which he was publishing his paper on the stranger and working on the homecomer. In 1944, he was also teaching a course on sociology of knowledge, dealing with pragmatists, and he published his pragmatically oriented "On Multiple Realities" one year later. In 1946, while he was teaching a class aimed at leading students to theoretical insight into everyday life situations, his article "The Well-Informed Citizen" appeared. In the spring of 1950, when he presented his course on sociology of language, "Language, Language Disturbances, and the Texture of Consciousness" appeared. He presented for the first time in the spring of 1951 a methodology course that examined questions of the relationships between the natural and social sciences, objectivity in the social sciences, and constructs and typologies. This course, repeated in 1952, played a role in his essays "Common-Sense and Scientific Interpretation of Human Action" and "Concept and Theory Formation in the Social Sciences," published in 1953 and

1954, respectively. His course on other minds and intersubjectivity, first available in 1953–54, drew on his earlier work on Sartre and Scheler on intersubjectivity, as well as set the stage for his 1957 work "The Problem of Transcendental Intersubjectivity in Husserl." The courses on symbols and equality in 1956 were the fruit of his articles "Symbol, Reality, and Society" and "Equality and the Meaning Structure of the Social World," published in 1955 and 1956, respectively.

The chair's position involved him in the usual day-to-day administrative duties, scheduling courses, collecting faculty records, planning for summer school, and defending the department against administrators' attempts to reduce the number of course offerings. In spite of the latter function, Schutz's correspondence with administrators in the New School is replete with kind and encouraging words on his side and theirs. One administrator in particular with whom Schutz warmly related was Alvin Johnson, school founder, president, and president emeritus after 1945. As editor of *Social Research*, Johnson solicited several of Schutz's articles, frequently encouraged his writing, and finally invited him to join the editorial board. For his part, Schutz put Johnson in contact with Lady Davis, a wealthy philanthropist, in 1955 when the school was seeking to double its space. Upon reading a copy of Jaspers's *The Origin and Goal of History*, which Schutz sent him, Johnson contrasted the author's focus with his own, saying, "To him the process of civilization is the ups and downs of the cultivated elite. To me it is the stubborn bent for survival of the common man." Schutz's life-world focus, his critique of Eliot, and his approach to questions of equality, would have converged with Johnson's philosophical populism. Despite this convergence, Johnson lacked sympathy with phenomenology and remarked once to Schutz, "Don't try to teach my children phenomenology. They do not swallow this stuff."[16]

The many diminishments in the philosophy department made it difficult to accept the chairmanship in 1952–53, but Schutz responded proactively, authoring a memorandum on the scope and function of the department, which began by highlighting the unique contribution that the entire Graduate Faculty could make to teaching the social sciences. Unable to compete with large, well-endowed departments, it possessed advantages in its flexible study program, its faculty's tutorial style, its interdisciplinary linkages between departments, and its theoretical rather than applied orientation. The student body, more mature and often pursuing studies at considerable sacrifice, frequently in addition to a full-time job, benefited by faculty expertise insofar as they came wanting philosophical enlightenment and a theoretical life, although at times their preparation was uneven. Furthermore, according to Schutz, one could only integrate the social sciences by basing them in some underlying philosophy, particularly a philosophical anthropology such as the one articulated in Kurt Riezler's *Man, Mutable and Immutable*. Schutz, respectful of student autonomy, insisted that students had to decide intelligently upon the appropriate philosophy and that the role of the faculty was only to expose choices and their implications. For Schutz, philosophy itself was part of the social sciences, understood in the European sense as "human sciences" (*Geisteswissenschaften*), and the various specialties of the Graduate Faculty formed branches of a common philosophical tree. Schutz believed that just as philosophy integrated the social sciences, "philosophical anthropology" could afford a unifying focus for the teaching of philosophy in the department, especially if that focus were examined systematically and historically. This memorandum served as the basis for the rebuilding process that went on during the 1953–54 school year, including the hiring of new faculty in the fall and faculty meetings in the spring to discuss the reconstruction of the department and its programs.[17]

Schutz faced a difficult situation in 1954–55 with Werner Marx, who had studied under Karl Löwith and Kurt Riezler; lectured at the New School on Aristotle, Heidegger, and philosophical anthropology; and was seeking a promotion (to visiting professor), against the New School's policy of not hiring its own students. In March 1954, he expressed surprise to Schutz that such an issue would arise, since Hans Staudinger had given him to believe that nothing would prevent his being appointed upon completion of his Ph.D. examination. Schutz proceeded quite astutely in this situation, sounding out his colleagues and reporting to Marx that faculty members were sympathetic to his plight. At the same time, Schutz opposed bringing Marx's specific case to the fore, since his promotion might have struck some faculty, particularly those whose friends had not been promoted, as unfair. Instead, Schutz urged Marx to be patient while he would launch a discussion in December or January (of 1955) about the general basis on which promotions could be made, without mentioning any specific case. In spite of this support for Marx, Schutz insisted that there was nothing shameful in the American system about the position of lecturer, which corresponded with the German *Privatdozent*. Upon completion of his examination, Marx was appointed a teaching fellow on the Graduate Faculty.[18]

In 1953–54, the department had decided to hire Hans Jonas, though the administration had turned Schutz down on the second position he had requested. On January 27, 1954, Schutz wrote Jonas to explain the present state of the department and to send him a copy of his own memorandum. In order to prepare the catalog for the 1954–55 school year, he inquired what Jonas would like to teach and informed him of what other faculty members were doing. However, the question of what Jonas might teach took second place to concerns about whether he would be able to immigrate at all, since he was on the verge of securing for himself and his family Canadian citizenship—an obstacle for U.S. immigration. As a result, Staudinger proposed that Schutz solicit the advice of his Canadian lawyer-friend, Louis Bloomfield, and that he request syllabi from Jonas and line up Cairns to teach, should Jonas not be able to come. Jonas, however, considered it "outright chimerical" to list his courses for the fall of 1954. He proposed that his first term be the spring one and that his fall courses, such as "The Systems of Philosophy Historically" be transferred to the spring and his spring courses to the fall. In response, Schutz, argued that such changes would damage the integrated program of the department, and hence he proposed that other faculty cover Jonas's fall courses; then Jonas could deliver the second parts of those courses in the spring. Staudinger determined that the catalog would list Jonas as a visiting professor so as not to place in peril his Canadian citizenship, as Bloomfield suggested, and he informed Jonas that he would probably start on January 1, 1955, the first professor in school history to receive tenure upon his appointment. While Jonas had his misgivings about Schutz's proposal, he did forward the necessary syllabi, and Schutz arranged for him to move into the apartment that Recasens Siches, who had been teaching at the New School, had vacated. Further immigration delays took place and it became doubtful whether Jonas would be able to arrive on time for classes in the fall of 1955.[19]

Responsibilities were quite pressing in the 1955–56 school year. Schutz developed a sequence of graduate courses and assigned teachers, and, in response to Hans Staudinger's request, he evaluated the Graduate Faculty in the light of a national approach in "The Graduate School Today and Tomorrow." The major weakness of the school's program lay in the fact that its students lacked an opportunity to gain teaching experience, since most earned their livelihood in nonacademic professions. Schutz also alerted Staudinger to health insurance opportunities for the faculty, and he suggested to President Hans Simons several possibilities for providing the New York area with dignified publicity about the New School's programs.[20]

One of the nastiest problems Schutz had to handle came in this fourth and last year, and it had to do with the relationship between Marx and the newly arrived Jonas. In January 1956, Jonas protested Schutz's scheduling of a course by Marx entitled "Problems of Fundamental Ontology," since Jonas would then have to change the title of his own course on Heidegger, which also contained the words "fundamental ontology." But he had further problems with Marx even teaching the course at all, since he believed that Marx was an "uncritical devotee" of Heidegger, as could be seen in one of Marx's articles that he had rejected for *Social Research*. After one department meeting, according to Jonas, Marx had in effect claimed precedence over him in lecturing on Heidegger, and Jonas felt that Marx had deviously persuaded Schutz to entitle the course as he had, even though Schutz had not been present at that postmeeting encounter. When Jonas discovered that Schutz was completely ignorant of these antecedents, it took the sting out of his dissatisfaction with Schutz's handling of these matters over the past months. Although a response to Jonas's letter detailing his complaints could not be found, Schutz had written on Jonas's letter to him, "So geht das nicht, Dr. Jonas."[21]

A second dispute arose when Jonas disputed the value of a book by Marx on Aristotle and charged that the book proved that Marx was unfit to teach on the graduate level. Schutz wrote a lengthy, courageous, forthright letter to Jonas, informing him that he had been on the committee for the dissertation from which the book had been produced. Although Schutz disagreed with Marx's reading of Aristotle and felt that he should have made use of more of Aristotle's texts and the secondary literature, he had deferred to Löwith and Riezler, better Aristotle scholars. In addition, Marx had received accolades from Hans-Georg Gadamer, the world-renowned professor at Heidelberg, who had suggested it for publication at Nijhoff; from the University of Freiburg, which had invited him to give a summer seminar; and from members of the Graduate Faculty, who had approved him as a teaching fellow. Schutz further acknowledged Jonas's grasp of Aristotle, but argued that even if he were completely right on Marx's scholarship, discussion of the merits or demerits of a published book should take place in the review section of leading journals and not within the author's department. Further, it would disserve the philosophy department to ask faculty from other universities to comment on whether someone voted assistant professor by the New School was competent to teach its graduate students. On grounds of principle, Schutz simply refused to participate in any action to revoke Marx's right to teach at the graduate level, but he added that he did think more highly of Marx than Jonas did and that many students spoke highly of his seminars. To show that Schutz's investment in the matter was a matter of principle only, he acknowledged the possibility that Jonas would be named chair next year and would then be able to make any further recommendation he saw fit with regard to Marx or his courses.[22]

Schutz carried on multifaceted relationships with many people associated with the New School. He was perhaps philosophically closest to Dorion Cairns, who had come as visiting professor in 1954, was promoted to full professor in 1960, and retired in 1969. Cairns studied with Husserl in Freiburg, received his doctorate from Harvard in 1933, found employment shortly afterward at Rockford College in Rockford, Illinois, where he stayed, except for military service in World War II, until 1950, when he took a deep salary cut and Schutz invited him to the East. The dearth of correspondence between them is no doubt inversely proportional to the amount of regular contact they must have had at the New School. Cairns offered courses at the New School on intentionality in Husserl, the phenomenology of thinking, general theory of value, and advanced theoretical ethics, as well as courses on the British empiricists, the Scottish School and Hamilton, nineteenth-century history of philosophy, and Kant.[23]

Schutz carried on a long-standing and affectionate friendship with Salomon, who shared with him teaching frustrations and intellectual topics such as Goethe, the I-Thou relationship as the basis of human bonding in speech, theological topics from eschatological thinking to the "religion of progress" of Lubac, and Dilthey's works. Salomon deeply admired Schutz, writing in 1954, "I wanted to thank you for your friendship from the bottom of my heart. . . . But I do not believe that I deserve it. You are a profound and enlightening thinker. . . . I really think you harm yourself when you tell other people that I complement your theoretical work. I am just a Heidelberg Café Intellectual: in that being Messianic, yours, Albert." Schutz, in turn, praised Salomon's presentation at a conference on symbolism held at Harvard in 1954 and the outline of his book *The Tyranny of Progress: Reflections on the Origins of Sociology*. Just as Schutz could write so sensitively about the viewpoint of the stranger, so he was able to enter empathetically into the life of Salomon, whose comments at times showed that he felt himself being on the fringes.[24]

The Schutz/Adolf Lowe intellectual exchange commenced when Schutz gave Lowe a copy of Hayek's *Road to Serfdom*, for which Lowe thanked him, adding that Hayek and he had been "friendly enemies" for twenty years. Lowe subsequently invited Schutz onto a dissertation committee on emigration because of his interest in the stranger and "other queer human beings." Sparks flew, however, when Lowe read Schutz's essay on equality and objected to the final sentence in the essay, about an individual's right to pursue "the maximum of self-realization which his situation in social reality permits." To Lowe, this sounded like "Enjoy what God allots to you," and he further opposed the suggestion that only under collectivism could the present prevailing stratification be altered. The last thirty years, he said, had exposed a large middle ground between laissez-faire and collectivism and whatever hope there might be for Western civilization depended on tilling this middle ground.[25]

A month later, however, Lowe had read Schutz's "Choosing among Projects of Action," and he inquired whether the social scientist referred to the same reality of the social world that appeared to the actor, expecting that Schutz would answer "no" in contrast to his "yes." Although Schutz felt that his original paper was a "mongrel," because philosophers had little interest in economics and economists little in philosophy, his answer to Lowe's question about whether actors and social scientists referred to the same reality was both yes and no. The social reality studied by social scientists, including motives, actions, and results, is the same as that of actors; however, social scientists employ different constructs than actors do, and they strive to maintain the attitude of disinterested observers, aiming to live up to ideals of clarity, distinctness, and consistency. Schutz attempted to show how the problems Lowe formulated, such as the ratio between consumer goods and capital goods output, referred to the typical motives of typical sellers and so could lend themselves to ideal-typical analyses that would refer to the motives of individual actors. Of course, no one would ever develop a law that everyone buys at the highest prices and sells at the lowest ones, since such a law would patently violate the principle of adequacy. For Schutz, one could engage in economics by simply presenting actors as behaving in accord with general validated ratios and devising incentives to alter such ratios, without speaking of functional-structural conceptualizations or discussion of wholes and subsystems. Schutz concluded that methodologists were only humble learners from the social scientists themselves.[26]

Schutz exchanged articles with Horace Kallen and thanked him for his "private lesson in English style" after they coauthored the memorial to Kurt Riezler that appeared in the American Philosophical Association *Proceedings* in 1957. In addition, Leo Strauss, editor of *Social Research* and professor of political science at the University of Chicago, to which he came via Hamburg and the New School, mentioned to Schutz that he had cited him in one of his articles as a "philosophically sophisticated sociologist." Thinking that Strauss's description of him as a sociologist was merely tongue-in-cheek, Schutz replied that he preferred to be dubbed a "sociologically sophisticated philosopher," and Strauss rejoined that Schutz was a "Janus-faced individual," whom he had denominated a sociologist because he needed a king's witness against sociologists.[27]

In all these relationships Schutz showed himself a participating citizen in the New School community, responding with concern and integrity to everyone he met. However reluctant he may have been to venture into ethical theory, as Voegelin has pointed out, there is no question that he was a model of ethical life. One could further discuss Schutz's relationships with Arvid Brodersen, who served as chair of the department of sociology, or with graduate students such as Helmut Wagner or Thomas Luckmann, who later distinguished themselves as sociologists. However, Schutz revealed himself most fully in relationship with that graduate student with whom he exchanged the largest correspondence and with whom he was most deeply involved, namely Maurice Natanson. In this relationship, Schutz showed his humor, his sense of responsibility, his love for children, and above all his love for a student, a friend, and an intellectual companion.[28]

Schutz, the Mentor

The very first letter in the Natanson file in The Papers of Alfred Schutz is strikingly comical, with Schutz portraying himself as a social scientist constructing Natanson, his student, as an ideal type. The letter commenced with "Dear Ideal Type" and continued, "If your destiny is to be a model of *Homo oeconomicus* you have no right to have a preference in music, or in philosophy, whatever this preference might be. That's not what your creator made you for." He gibed at Natanson's attraction for Sartre's thought, "If you were a human being in a similar situation, you would probably develop an existential philosophy. And you should praise your maker, if you could, that he has withheld from you two curses: hope and fear." Finally, he signed the letter, "Your affectionate observer in the secondary world and always your obedient servant, The social scientist."[29]

The Schutz-Natanson correspondence frequently touched on the progress of the student's career. At the end of his first semester, in December 1951, Natanson wrote to Schutz "the human being" and not "the professor at the New School," to indicate that he had not made progress as rapidly as he had hoped. But he added, "[T]he one thing which has really meant something to me has been my meetings with you." In this first semester, Natanson began exploring job possibilities, sending out five hundred applications within a two-year period and comparing job-hunting at philosophy meetings to the days in which the insect Gregor Samsor of Franz Kafka's *The Metamorphosis* was let out of his room only to be pelted with fruit. He regularly requested letters of recommendation from Schutz for universities that might hire him, for a summer school teaching spot at the New School, and for grant applications, though he dreaded "becoming a leech and scampering for aid on every matter." Although he preferred to study with Schutz rather than move elsewhere, he, existentialist as he was, affirmed that were he to leave the New School for the security of employment it would be his choice, not to be blamed in bad faith on the family he had to support financially. In the fall of 1953, he accepted a position at the University of Houston, a tenth-rate place, he thought, which negated the point of his last two years—namely that after studies he would *not* have to go to such a place. While there, he explored other opportunities.[30]

Schutz found Natanson's stories about teaching philosophy in Houston hilarious. Natanson claimed that 40 percent of the fifteen thousand students at the university were illiterate. Teaching in the department of philosophy and religious studies to mostly ministerial students or fundamentalists, who enrolled thinking that philosophy courses were Bible courses, Natanson described how he was perceived in class:

> For example, I mentioned something in one of my classes about the *problem* of immortality and one of the students said, "Do you mean the *fact* of immortality?" When I suggested that philosophy does not begin by presupposing the dogmas of religion, a sudden chill spread

> over the class and people drew back as if I were going to lure them into a life of dishonor.[31]

Reporting on other students, he mentioned a fifth-grade teacher who had taught children so long that she was on their intellectual level and a student who believed it would take *months* to figure out the deep articles in *Harper's* or *Atlantic Monthly*. When the head of the philosophy department mentioned the existence of "higher criticism" of the Bible, a minister in his class hurled his briefcase at the teacher, rushed to his desk, and screamed, "You son of a bitch, I'm going to stomp you through the floor." Natanson concluded the letter, "By the time you read this letter, I may have met my maker." Such a premonition might not have been far off the mark, since one of his students affixed to a final term-paper a clipping about a student who shot his teacher in Palermo, Sicily. When C. D. Broad visited the university, the faculty members sat around after the reception-dinner to discuss world politics with him, "the central question being 'What the hell did Britain mean by being anti-American?'" When Natanson discussed Darwin in his class, one student became hysterical and screamed again and again, "Prove the earth is that old! Prove it! Go ahead and prove it!" In spite of his frustrations, he did organize a faculty seminar and gave the first paper, on the experience of death, and Schutz encouraged him on his successes.[32]

Natanson's sense of humor could rob the saddest of circumstances of their sting. After MIT neglected even to send him a rejection notice regarding his book on Mead, Natanson wrote, "I'm becoming, despite my jolly intentions, the Underground Man of the academic world." He went on to describe his newfound special sneer, his particular way of thumbing his nose, the diary of slights and hurts he was starting, and the account book of revenges he was compiling, as well has his file for hate letters. Schutz joined in the fun after the Natansons' second son was born by congratulating Maurice on his continual preparation of baby formula, saying "This is most certainly the best spent effort you made for years." Natanson affirmed that the shift in his relevance structures was evident in that he now awaited a good burp from the baby with greater anticipation and interest than the answer from the editor of a periodical reporting on an article he had submitted. Moreover, when elected to the executive committee of the Southwestern Philosophical Conference, Natanson commented, "I suppose the reverberations of this election have already been felt throughout the nation. What a wonderful feeling it is to know that academic and philosophical destinies are now dependent on my decisions, that philosophers everywhere must tremble in anticipation of my wrath or gifts, that lifelong ambitions may come to shipwreck or to fulfillment as a result of a word from me." Even Natanson's lamentations over his own financial plight were humorous:

> As for myself I have entered at long last a euphoric state: I no longer have any financial worries! My situation is by now so clearly disastrous that bills and financial demands make no impression on me at all. In fact, I have entered what might be termed the "aesthetic" of finance: my interest in bills and monetary letters is with respect to the quality of printing, the type of paper, the various systems of book-keeping, the different creditors used, etc. I am like the financier who has been wiped out on the market and then continues to watch the ticker tape machine, lost in fascination of the intricate machinery that announces disaster. As both Father Divine and William Saroyan used to say: "Peace, it's wonderful."[33]

Both Schutz and Natanson delighted in the behavior of Charlie, Natanson's eldest son. For instance, when Dr. Garrison, senior member of the religion sector of Natanson's department, visited their home and began discussing his trip across the Bosporus, Charlie called out from his bed upstairs, "Once upon a time there were three bears." When the laughter died down, Garrison began again and Charlie yelled, "A mamma bear, a daddy bear, and little baby bear." Natanson speculated that Garrison would not visit again. In another letter, Natanson listed examples of Charlie's statements proving that he was well on his way into philosophy: "1. Who cuts the barber's hair? 2. You can't see part of yourself. 3. When you're sleeping you don't know you're sleeping." In one letter, Natanson cited Charlie's latest insight, "When there aren't any big noises you can hear little noises," and added to his mentor, "I like that very much." One senses Schutz's affection for the little child when he signed one of his letters, "With love to all of you and especially to invincible Charlie."[34]

The two friends exchanged much more than humor, sharing personal concerns and academic plans, and Natanson was willing to express his frustrations with New School faculty who were no doubt friends of Schutz. Natanson disclosed to his friend his deepest family anguish, narrating, for example, how the two miscarriages suffered by Lois Natanson prior to the birth of their second son had produced frequent melancholy and anxiety every time she became pregnant and had resulted in her stomach ulcer. Schutz showed himself completely sympathetic, understanding full well how much she had wanted a second child and why she was heartbroken. When the time for the birth of their third child approached, Schutz conveyed his concern and wished the best, and after Natanson had called to announce the child's birth, he sent a gift certificate and expressed great happiness over the birth. This son, Nick, was given the middle name "Alfred," and "with that name he will have a fine future," wrote Lois. Schutz replied that he was "deeply moved," though he confessed that the social role of a godfather was entirely new to him. Unfortunately, the child had problems with his feet. They were placed in casts whose effectiveness would determine whether surgery would be necessary in the future—a kind of situation with which Schutz was familiar. That Christmas, the Schutzes sent Charlie a music book and a magazine subscription, building toys; a lovely robe for Kathy, the Natansons' daughter; and music for the baby, Nick. Maurice wrote to thank Alfred, and Lois hoped that someday their children could meet these "mysterious and wonderful benefactors," now assuming the "mythical status of Mr. and Mrs. Santa Claus." The relationship between mentor and student was so close that Natanson experienced unrest whenever there was a lapse in correspondence, thinking that he might have offended Schutz, although such lapses usually resulted simply from Schutz being too busy to write. Of the many expressions of deep gratitude, Natanson was most eloquent when he reflected on wondering before meeting Schutz "how in the world could I be sure in advance that you would not turn out to be a stinker instead of the warm and gracious human being you are?"[35]

Both Schutz and Natanson took a strong interest in each other's writing projects. For example, Natanson edited Schutz's "Symbol, Reality, and Society," going through it line by line twice, the second time with his wife, Lois Natanson; checking all the quotations; and refusing any financial remuneration for such work. He commended it as the finest article of Schutz's he had ever read, with the possible exception of "On Multiple Realities," and he also proposed an English translation of *Der sinnhafte Aufbau*. Both Schutz and he consulted regularly about where to publish his book on Mead, especially since such a publication would have been a ticket out of Houston to a more serious academic setting. Natanson tried various university presses and Schutz made inquiries on his behalf. Finally, and probably only after Schutz's own importance had risen in the academic world, Nijhoff republished *The Social Dynamics of George H. Mead*, a book dedicated "to my wife Lois and to my midwife, Dr. Alfred Schutz."[36]

The friends frequently discussed philosophical issues. For instance, after a discussion of solipsism in Schutz's class, Natanson referred him to the comment of the American philosopher Charles Sanders Peirce, "Let us not pretend to doubt in philosophy what we do not doubt in our hearts." One detects Schutz's influence, in turn, in Natanson's Mead book when he criticized Mead for presenting the self as emergent from society but without providing the epistemological wherewithal to show the self's distinctness from the body, the constitution of intersubjective relationships in experience, and the foundational concepts of intersubjectivity. Epistemological distinctions were necessary, as was evident in Natanson's reply to Buber's fear that philosophizing about the "I-Thou" relationship reduced it to an "I-It." One needed to distinguish between relations as structures of social reality to be described and interpreted (as Schutz had done) and relations as lived engagements capable of transforming the social world. Natanson elaborated three levels of reflectivity: naïve, commonsense intersubjectivity lived as a fact; the placing in question of this naïve attitude by the philosopher or person in the street; and the transcendental question of intersubjectivity, namely, how one world could be valid for all.[37]

Early in his graduate school career, Natanson challenged Schutz's understanding of Sartre, stating that Sartre did not deny the *Lebenswelt* of the *pour soi* and *pour sois*, but was more interested in showing the failure and defeat of communicative situations. Concrete relations (even love) turned out for Sartre to be ultimate frustrations and experiential fractures in a way that a philosophical optimist, prepared to accept common sense reality as essentially successful, might overlook. Natanson granted that there was communication, that there were others, and that there was a real world of real things, but thought perhaps there was not so much cause for optimism. Natanson, who related to his mentor with a sense of his own independence and autonomy, even pointed to a specific passage in "Phenomenology and the Social Sciences" that exhibited the optimism Sartre was criticizing. According to that passage, "I assume that everything which has meaning for me also has meaning for the Other or Others with whom I share this, my life-world, as an associate, contemporary, predecessor, or successor." Although Natanson admitted possible problems in Sartre's use of phenomenological method, Schutz, it would seem, did provide a richer, more adequate phenomenological account of intersubjectivity, one that could accommodate the dissonances in understanding, to which Sartre points and of which Schutz was aware, as well as the successes. In some ways, though, the relationship between Schutz and his protégé models, as few relationships do, how coperforming subjectivities can make the sweetest of music together.[38]

Chapter 11

The Years 1952 to 1956: Philosophical Midwifery; Correspondence and Research

Collegiality in Correspondence

Schutz shared with Machlup his "Common Sense and Scientific Interpretation of Human Action" presented at the Princeton conference on March 15–16, 1952, entitled "Organizational Behavior Project Conference on 'Problems of Model Construction in the Social Sciences.'" They discussed the conference as well as questions in the methodology of the social sciences and the epistemology of economics, with Machlup favoring a chastened, fallible, evergrowing economic science over skepticism. Schutz, in a letter treating verification in economics, argued that all observational data in economics were theoretically saturated insofar as the economist took them as problem-relevant in the first place. Late in 1953, Machlup, teaching at Johns Hopkins, headed a committee to hire senior- and junior-level professors for the philosophy department, and, mystified by the pluralism in American philosophy, which exceeded that in economics, he frequently consulted Schutz, who recommended Natanson for the junior opening. They also considered the reclamation of pre- and postwar stocks and George's application to college, and Machlup, after a 1955 visit to Japan, relayed Otaka's greetings to Schutz.[1]

Although Schutz traded information with Eric Voegelin in 1952 about the dangers from neo-Nazis and powerful clerics in Munich, where Voegelin was thinking of accepting an Americanist position, most of their discussion focussed on *The New Science of Politics*. Schutz praised Voegelin's book for developing a phenomenology of how historically active societies constitute themselves; inquired how different groups, theoreticians, and commonsense actors might intepret this process differently; and challenged Voegelin's rejection of any *eidos* of history and his claim that gnostics "redivinized" society instead of reproducing Greek polytheism. Voegelin accepted most of Schutz's suggestions as friendly emendations, but reaffirmed that the gnostics misapplied the transcendent symbolism of the Christian *eschaton* to innerworldly history. Further, their redivinization of society involved no exact return to Greek polytheism, since this redivinization had to be understood as following on hundreds of years of Christianity that had de-devinized the political realm (as Weber thought), something of which Greek polytheism had no prior experience. Finally, Schutz recommended that Voegelin consider his account of gnosticism not in essentialist terms, but as merely a *historical* fact—namely, that the turn to gnosticism had its *historical* beginning with the immanentization of the Christian *eschaton*. The two friends mailed their other publications to each other and offered criticisms, and Schutz recommended Voegelin for a Guggenheim fellowship and commended his six-volume *Order and History* to Louisiana State University Press.[2]

Schutz engaged in a serious intellectual exchange with the literary critic Kenneth Burke, whom he met at the 1952 Princeton conference and who published a reworked version of his paper under the title "On Human Behavior Considered 'Dramatistically.'" In that paper, he observed that several of the conference papers approached the problem of models in the social sciences in "mathematical or technological ways," but he favored "the retaining of ethical or psychological terminology." Schutz thanked him for his wonderful paper and sent "Making Music Together." Burke thought that Schutz's intersubjective approach to music would be "medicinal" for the tensions resulting from the individual ownership of property. For Burke, human beings described "dramatistically," in terms of action rather than knowledge, deployed symbols promoting social cohesion in a manner that transcended what was possible for animals. Schutz responded that his paper on music developed the possibility of a nonbehavioristic prelinguistic and preconceptual communication, a "dramatistic" occurrence, and, considering how mutual expectations and typifications between actors could be upset, he evolved an entire theory of the negative, which always supervened on previous belief. While they concurred in locating the origins of the negative in actional rather than theoretical settings, Burke emphasized the hortatory, prohibitive negative proceeding from the Decalogue, and Schutz, the pragmatic negative (e.g., determining that the coiled rope was *not* a snake). Schutz illustrated the prelinguistic ontological category of the negative that supervened upon a previous belief by describing lie detector experiments in psychology in which testers asked a mental patient if he were Napoleon; when he then responded "No," the lie detector indicated that he was lying.[3]

By far, the largest volume of Schutz's correspondence in the period 1952–56 took place with Aron Gurwitsch. Having commented on part 3 of Gurwitsch's *The Field of Consciousness*, Schutz had worked his way carefully through part 5, on the thematic field; and, in his letter of January 19,

1952, he lauded highly the quality of his friend's work. In fifteen comments, Schutz contrasted his richer view of relevances, laid out in his relevance-manuscript completed in 1951 and including topical, interpretational, and motivational relevances, with Gurwitsch's, which contained only thematic (in Schutz's terms "topical") relevances. Furthermore, this letter surfaced the fundamental points of contention between Schutz and Gurwitsch: egology vs. nonegology; action vs. perception; noesis vs. noema; and intersubjectivity vs. individual consciousness. Heartfelt esteem characterized Schutz's next letter, of January 15, 1952, which he opened by calling *The Field of Consciousness* "the finest achievement in phenomenology since Husserl's *Experience and Judgment*" before discussing part 6, on ontological problems like those he had addressed under the rubric of finite provinces of meaning. Gurwitsch thanked Schutz for his enormous labor on parts 3, 5, and 6; acknowledged his need to explain the modifications and transitions between thematic fields; and admitted that his concluding coda had much to do with some 150 pages on marginal consciousness, which he had excised and which was eventually published posthumously. The one final installment of Schutz's reactions to part 4, on perception, reflected his interests in the noetic and intersubjective dimensions of experience, but he also stressed the disruptive and nonfulfilling dimensions of experience that Gurwitsch, by his noematic focus, threatened to submerge beneath a law of "good continuation."[4]

In April 1952, Gurwitsch called Schutz's "Common-Sense and Scientific Interpretation of Human Action" "an achievement of the first rank in the theory of science" itself (and not just social science). Nevertheless, he was puzzled how an ideal-typical homunculus created by social scientists would grasp another homunculus's knowledge, since social scientists conferred knowledge on each one. Gurwitsch also found problematic Schutz's use of the term "constructs" in everyday life, since it seemed to imply that the commonsense actor first grasped sense data and then overlaid them with a layer of constructed meaning. In answer to his friend, Schutz found no problem with the social scientists fitting out homunculi with knowledge of each other as was the custom in the social sciences, but he did agree that "constructs" was misleading insofar as it implied the adding of a level of meaning upon a "meaning-free" sensation of an object. In October of that year, Gurwitsch and Schutz traded observations about Schutz's essay on Husserl's *Ideas 2*, with Schutz finding Husserl's theory of subjectivity and intersubjectivity to be a desperate attempt to save transcendental phenomenology. In addition, Gurwitsch had claimed that reflection on oneself uncovers no ego but only ego-states, but Schutz accused him of overlooking the ego consciously focusing on those ego-states, the I constituting the Me.[5]

Gurwitsch appreciated Voegelin's phenomenological strategy in *The New Science of Politics* of going behind a society's present status to grasp its self-constituting processes; however, he objected that anytime one believed in a Messiah or presumed to be bringing God's action to fruition, one would fall prey to attempting to realize the *eschaton* on earth. Schutz thought that it might be possible to search for an essential meaning of history without necessarily seeking to make immanent the *eschaton,* and yet he commiserated with Gurwitsch, "Dear old co-gnostic and co-paraclete, do we two understand absolutely nothing *de anima*?" Gurwitsch informed Schutz that, because of such things as Voegelin's comments on Mariology and Christology, which seemed to attribute to the world ontological features with which Gurwitsch disagreed, he resisted Schutz's "ontologizing tendencies." Schutz, however, replied that his ontologizing was "pretty far removed from Christology." He simply thought that certain factors were imposed upon us in a way that we could not reject them at will, such as "Our place as human beings in the cosmos. I mean no more than that this is simply ontologically there, in its incomprehensibility and that it is only this primal foundation—as life-world—that makes all understanding possible."[6]

Upset at Ernest Nagel's review of Hayek's *The Counter-Revolution of Science* and Nagel's and Carl Hempel's positivistic approach to the social sciences, Schutz delivered "Concept and Theory Formation in the Social Sciences" in a New York University series on methods in philosophy and the social sciences. Though he invited Gurwitsch to be there "when your old friend Schutz is thrown to the lions," neither Nagel nor Hempel appeared, and the audience received the paper well. Schutz hesitated to publish it in *PPR* or *Social Research* for fear of becoming the "house poet" of these journals. Gurwitsch loved the article, particularly its systematic connection to "Common-Sense and Scientific Interpretation of Human Action" and its transition between everyday ideal types and those of social science, and he observed that Nagel and company only wanted to recognize "because motives." The most exciting discovery in the paper, for Gurwitsch, was that Schutz conceived the process of verification in the natural and social processes as *social* action; the very possibility of science presupposes certain structures of "human working-with-one-another."[7]

After a European journey in 1953, Gurwitsch let Schutz know that Paul Ricoeur's circle were waiting for something that only Schutz could give them, and the two friends discussed at length where to publish *The Field of Consciousness* after Harvard had called for unwelcome revisions. Beacon Press, for whom Cairns had been the reviewer, also rejected it, though Schutz suspected Beacon Press as the culprit; but finally Duquesne University Press published it in 1964, seven years after the French version by Désclée de Brouwer.[8]

Gurwitsch presented "The Kantian and Husserlian Conceptions of Consciousness" before the Graduate Faculty, since they were interested in hiring him as part of the rebuilding that Schutz directed as chair. Schutz, who could not advocate strongly on his friend's behalf, felt that the most difficult obstacle was that Schutz and Cairns already covered the area of phenomenology. In the end, Jonas, with the support of Leo Strauss's "clique," was given the position.[9]

Gurwitsch studied Schutz's essay on symbolism, presented in August 1954 at Harvard; and he denied, as he had before, that there could be a level of "pure experience" independent of sociocultural meanings and that only theorists could separate a physical sign from its meaning. Schutz, however, claimed to be focusing on the experience of transcendence discoverable only in the very being-with-things, which phenomenological reduction tended to put out of play and so concealed, and he held that the black marks of a sign were *seen* while they were *interpreted* simultaneously as letters. Gurwitsch was accurate, though, in distinguishing how social scientists and religious believers approach symbols differently.[10]

Beginning in the fall of 1954, both Schutz and Gurwitsch took interest in the publication of volume 6 of the Husserliana series, *Die Krisis der europäischen Wissenschaften und die transzendentale Phänomenologie*. Though Cairns thought the *Crisis* to be Husserl's weakest book, Schutz thought it magnificent and highly valuable for the social sciences, even though he did not think it could solve the problem of transcendental intersubjectivity. In reaction to Gurwitsch's review of the work in "The Last Work of Edmund Husserl," Schutz stated that Gurwitsch's "superb" exposition illuminated the weaknesses of the general position, the references of which to intersubjectivity proved to be a "jumble" and "beneath the dignity of the phenomenological method." Schutz particularly appreciated Gurwitsch's footnote suggesting that Aristotelian science could be taken as a general science of the *Lebenswelt*—an idea that Schutz felt was worth being expanded into a book. The friends speculated about the future of phenomenology, as Gurwitsch resisted existentialism's neglect of ultimate questions of knowledge, truth, and episteme, and bemoaned the abandonment of Husserl's project, even though Schutz thought that he was proclaiming its demise in his essay "The Last Work." Schutz, far less nostalgic, wondered whether there had ever been a phenomenological *school* and reaffirmed his intention to concentrate on the life-world, which phenomenologists were converting into a sphere of monads without windows and thereby dragging the *lumen naturale* in sacks into the solipsistic Holy of Holies.[11]

The friends exchanged information on matters other than philosophy, such as health concerns, grant possibilities, upcoming conferences, employment opportunities (for Gurwitsch), and the deaths of family members or friends, such as Erich Kahn or Salomon's wife. Schutz, upon reviewing his deceased mother's correspondence, observed how frequently the names of

Gurwitsch and his wife appeared in Hansi's letters from the bleak days in France, and, when newly developed glasses enabled George to read and do his schoolwork without any help, Schutz reported this "most important event" to his friend. Given their closeness, it was somewhat surprising that the Schutzes during their time in the United States only visited the Gurwitsches once, in Boston in June 1953. The two friends usually met in connection with attending a philosophy conference held in the city of one or the other.[12]

Schutz also corresponded with L. M. Lachmann, a professor of economics at the University of Witwatersrand in Johannesburg, who had dubbed Schutz's philosophy an "active subjectivism"—an apt title also for Schutz's political philosophy. Schutz exchanged letters with the philosopher Lewis White Beck and with the sociologists Howard Becker and Lewis Coser. Tomoo Otaka, Schutz's dear friend from his Vienna days, had written Schutz upon meeting Dr. Ronall, part of an Israeli delegation in Tokyo, who knew Schutz and praised his noble personality, the sincerity of his scientific research, and the enthusiastic but also logical manner of his teaching. Otaka declared that the memories of their friendship had lived vividly in his soul during the long blank period caused by "unhappy worldly events." The war had taken its toll on him, but he had recovered, writing numerous books in Japanese, attending UNESCO meetings regularly in Paris, and serving as acting dean of the law school at Tokyo University. He concluded his letter with the beautiful German words: "Es ist die Wissenschaft, die alle wieder bindet, die die weltlichen Angelegenheiten so herzenlos getrennt heben" (It is science, which binds everything back together that worldly matters have so heartlessly torn asunder).[13]

Schutz served as a kind of academic consultant for Richard C. Snyder, the director of the Foreign Policy Analysis Project at Princeton, who had authored a monograph entitled "Decision-Making as an Approach to the Study of International Politics." At Snyder's request, Schutz offered critical comments, correcting the view that multiple realities entailed the elimination of any objective situation common to all participants. Schutz argued, instead, that the paramount reality of everyday life was common to all, "although experienced in individual (subjective) perspectives and adumbrations by each of us. This is sufficient in order to explain why the same situation is differently defined and interpreted by the State Department and the Department of Defense." As opposed to Snyder's statement that the state was a decision-maker, Schutz, ever opposed to personalities of a higher order, contended that the political organization called "the state" had designated certain decision-makers, with whose decisions not every citizen would be in accord. Furthermore, Schutz understood the author's assumption that no private citizen could be a party to the state's decisions without having held some governmental office at least temporarily, but Schutz reminded Snyder that private citizens often devised alternatives of which decision-makers had not dreamed (e.g., pay-as-you-go plans). It is interesting in this regard how Schutz's opposition to personalities of a higher order and his preference for methodological individualism tended to support greater democratic participation and at least a consultative role for citizens in governmental affairs.[14]

Not all encounters in academia were pleasant, though. At the instigation of the sociologist Edward Shils, Jeremiah Kaplan of The Free Press suggested in a letter to Schutz that he publish a collection of his articles, and so he forwarded several reprints, many the last in his possession, insisting, in this era before photocopying, that they be handled carefully. Over the three years from 1954 to 1957, Schutz repeatedly sent inquiries about the status of the collection; Kaplan would respond that things were progressing, and then months of silence would elapse, with the result that Schutz had to bypass requests to publish his work from other presses or miss opportunities to subsidize their publication. The final piece in this unfortunate correspondence was a Western Union telegram from Schutz to Kaplan, stating:

> Am refraining from any comment on this manner of dealing with an invited author or on discourtesy in leaving correspondence unanswered which is against simplest rules of business practice. Have instructed my lawyer to examine legal aspect of the situation. Request your returning to me immediately material submitted to you in 1954 among which several copies are sole copies I have. You may be assured that I shall give wide publicity [to] our correspondence including present telegram among my scientific friends and other interested persons.[15]

This entire exchange shows how Schutz comported himself with integrity, refraining from publication in order to avoid violating his implicit commitments with Kaplan and The Free Press, in spite of the latter's lack of integrity in dealing with him. One can understand his fury about the lack of response to his letters, since he himself always showed himself most responsible in his correspondence to others. The entire incident makes manifest the ethical dimensions involved in correspondence between two persons, especially when one person runs the risk of costly losses while waiting and trusting in the reliability of another.[16]

Publishing on Wide-Ranging Relevances

In the introduction to "Santayana on Society and Government," published in *Social Research* in 1952, Schutz commented on the uniqueness of *Dominations and Powers*, a work written in Santayana's old age. He admired the author's aphoristic style, wisdom, and sovereign disdain for mere information, and his attempt to base politics on a philosophical anthropology—Schutz's own chosen philosophical focus for unifying the philosophy department. Schutz proceeded to discuss Santayana's ideal typical methodology in *Dominations and Powers*, his account of how circumstances release human instincts and powers (as did *Realfaktoren* for Scheler), and his naturalism, which resembled Husserl's rooting of thought in the life-world. He then described Santayana's three orders: the generative order, in which nature (including agriculture) and circumstances shape the psyche and produce liberty or servitude; the militant, in which a passion to dominate leads to the expression of hostility toward dissenting forms of existence; and the rational, which attempts to harmonize and control powerful forces. Santayana also explored the meaning of representative governments, "the people," compromise, and the limits of government. In a critical conclusion, Schutz opposed his reduction of economics to domination and his directing democracy toward the generative order to solve its problems, and he attributed Santayana's pessimism to his emphasis on the generative order and his naturalist/materialist founding of spiritual life upon the physical order. Perhaps Mises's positive account of capitalism as entrepreneurial service of the consumer influenced Schutz's optimism about economics, and Schutz hoped for more from democracy, as shall be seen in the next chapter, and believed in reason's power to criticize the very social origins that he stressed in other settings.[17]

According to Fred Kersten, "Santayana's discussions of James and Bergson formed the fulcrum around which Schutz read James and Bergson in ways amenable to a phenomenologist." As we have seen in chapter 2, Schutz may have relied on Kallen's work and Santayana's *Winds of Doctrine* to oppose Bergson's organic, monistic metaphysics, even though he never abandoned basic doctrines about temporality and consciousness. Santayana, as might be expected, opposed on naturalistic grounds James's positive approach to religion and his pragmatism insofar as it endorsed whatever might be "edifying" or "useful," whatever permitted humanity "to be boosted by an illusion," even if it were not scientificially verifiable. Insofar as James, in Santayana's view, romantically found the visions of philosophers more important than their arguments, Schutz may have striven to be more disciplined, systematic, and argument-focused than James. However, in Schutz's development of the theory of multiple realities, he concurred with James's belief that there were nonnaturalistic meanings and, as a phenomenologist, he would not have endorsed Santayana's metaphysical naturalism. Santayana, though, almost portrayed James as a phenomenologist, imposing upon himself a "suspense of judgment" in his dedication to describing accurately various depictions of the world—not that far from Schutz's view of social science.

> A psychologist who was not an agnostic would have indicated, as far as possible, whether the beliefs and experiences he was describing were instances of delusion or of rare and fine perception, or in what measure they were a mixture of both. But James—and this is what gives such romantic warmth to these writings of his—disclaims all antecedent or superior knowledge, listens to the testimony of each witness in turn, and only by accident allows us to feel that he is swayed by the eloquence and vehemence of some rather than of others.[18]

It is as if Schutz used Santayana as a critical counterpoint to keep him honest, rigorous, and critical of metaphysics in dealing with the nonnaturalistic positions of James and Bergson, with which he felt sympathetic.[19]

In the fall of 1952, Schutz had completed reviews of Husserl's *Ideas 2* and *Ideas 3* and published them in *PPR* in March and June 1953, respectively, and at the same time Natanson and he had been developing a rough paraphrasing of these works, though it was never published. In his *PPR* review of *Ideas 2*, Schutz illustrated the roots of *Ideas 2* in *Ideas 1* and explained that Husserl never published *Ideas 2* because, according to Schutz's recollections of conversations with Husserl, he had not yet found a satisfactory solution for the problem of intersubjectivity. The review rehearsed Husserl's main argument as it progressed from inanimate objects to the region of animalia to the psyche to the spiritual domain, accessible only to a personalistic attitude and characterized in terms of intentional-motivational processes rather than the causal ones on which the naturalistic attitude focused. Within the personalistic attitude, consciousness established a communicative environment and built up personalities of a higher order, such as nations, churches, and so on. In a final critical section, Schutz disputed whether one could determine solipsistically the "normal" presentation of a thing, questioned how the other's consciousness could be appresented through one's own consciousness, and objected that "motivation" covered very heterogeneous elements. He found problematic the transfer of localizations, since one's own body was given differently to oneself than another's and especially so if the other were of a different sex. Rather than found relationships upon communication, he argued that the "tuning-in" to others that he discussed in "Making Music Together" was the condition of communication, and he dismissed personalities of a higher order as inconsistent with the spirit of phenomenology. Schutz's *PPR* account of *Ideas 3* explained Husserl's depiction of how phenomenology can give an eidetic account of the differing realms of reality (things, animated body, psyche) that empirical sciences, including psychology, examine without reflecting on. Distinguishing the ontologist's search for essences from the phenomenologist's, which relies on the reduction, Schutz also contrasted the mere explication (*Verdeutlichung*) of verbal meanings with clarification (*Klärung*), by which one brings objects as meant to perfect self-givenness, lucidity, and vividness.[20]

These two essays on Husserl's *Ideas* in *PPR* indicate that Schutz felt a rather consistent responsibility throughout his scholarly life to disseminate Husserl's ideas, and not merely to present them but to examine them critically. Hence, he produced the earlier essays on phenomenology and edited German manuscripts published in *PPR*, and in the next period he would produce his famous essay on transcendental intersubjectivity. These essays on *Ideas* when brought into relationship with their contemporary, the essay on Santayana, illuminate Schutz's own stance on rationality. For he opposed Santayana's debilitation of rationality's power to criticize its own social origins, even as he objected precisely to Husserl's transcendental deployment of rationality without sufficient attention to the constraints its social origins imposed.

The next two papers, "Common-sense and Scientific Interpretation of Human Action" and "Concept and Theory Formation in the Social Sciences," together formed a theory of science and not just of social science, as Gurwitsch had noted. Having described his dissertation to Schutz in 1949, Harold Garfinkel invited Schutz on behalf of the Organizational Behavior Project at Princeton to participate in a seminar in March 1952 on the topic "Problems of Model Construction in the Social Sciences." Schutz sent a final draft of "Common-sense and Scientific Interpretation" to Gurwitsch, mentioning that from September to the end of February he had spent sixteen hours every weekend working on this paper. Schutz found several papers at the conference inferior in quality; observed that Parsons, who attended, was surprised to find no major differences with him; and enjoyed the opportunity to link up with Oskar Morgenstern, G. S. Brunner, and Kenneth Burke.[21]

"Common-Sense and Scientific Interpretation of Human Action" explores the commonsense thinking at the base of science: its typification and relevance systems, intersubjective dimensions, ways of coming to grips with the structures of the social world, and the structures of action, motivation, and interaction. Distinguishing degrees of intelligent behavior, such as sensible (conventionally appropriate), reasonable (springing from a judicious choice), and rational (with clear and distinct insight into means, ends, secondary results), he spells out all that is involved in rational action, concluding that only graduated degrees of rationality exist in everyday life. He then turns to rationality in the social sciences, the postulate of subjective interpretation, validity, the peculiarity of social science constructs, and other postulates (adequacy, logical consistency). While the social scientist's constructs must be scientifically rational, they need not focus on rational action only, although economics develops models of rational behavior to ascertain deviant behaviors, to compare such models with each other, and to gain insight by varying the conditions of their application.[22]

The title "Concept and Theory Formation in the Social Sciences" referred to the title of an American Philosophical Association symposium in which Ernest Nagel and Carl Hempel had presented papers. Schutz asserted that "one simply has to do something" in response. The final version of eight drafts presented diverse views on whether the social sciences should be conducted as the natural sciences, endorsed controlled inferences in social science, and recapitulated Nagel's position that social science depended on causal explanation based on observable behavior, since talk about the existence of inner states was unverifiable. For Schutz, Nagel was correct in stating that the social sciences need to develop and validate theory, that their lack of predictability did not disqualify their scientific character, and that Weber would have been wrong if his emphasis on the subjective viewpoint implied empathy with unobservable, introspective states. However, by limiting social scientific data to empirically observable behavior (behavioristically construed) and ruling out statements about inner states as unverifiable—that is, by pitting observable behavior against nonobservable inner states—the positivists played on a Cartesian map hundreds of years old. Instead, Schutz returned to everyday life experience in which intersubjective understanding took place without any bifurcation between observable behavior and inner states. Schutz's account of the life-world established first the *eidos* social reality that ought to dictate the methods for its investigation, in contrast with the positivists, who assumed the appropriateness of the methods of the natural sciences without first considering the object to which those methods were to apply. Since in social reality actors gave meaning to their world, in contrast to physical reality, whose entities (e.g., electrons, molecules) did not interpret their world, social scientists had to construct everyday actors' constructs, grasping their subjective meaning, by which Weber meant *their* meaning as opposed to an observer's. Such constructs, relying on ideal types that took account of actors' subjective meanings, could escape arbitrariness if social scientists adopted the scientific attitude and observed postulates of consistency and adequacy. In suggestive concluding comments, Schutz proposed that social science might actually form the basis for understanding the activity of natural scientists, who must interact socially to carry on science.[23]

"Don Quixote and the Problem of Reality" was first published in Spanish in the Mexican journal *Dianoia* after it had been translated by Mrs. Luis Recasens Siches and edited by her husband, who had taught law and philosophy as a visiting professor at the New School in 1953–54. In thanking them both for their exquisite prose translation, Schutz interpreted his article as an act of homage to that classical work and to the culture that produced it. Recasens Siches, in response, expressed gratitude to Schutz for all he had done for his family in the United States. The paper applied creatively the ideas of "On Multiple Realities" to Cervantes's great work, depicting Quixote's "world of chivalry" as one such reality, containing its own arguments for reality, its stock of knowledge, and its legal and economic system, and views of space, time, and causal functions, which frequently depended on enchanters. Although intersubjectivity was key in sustaining or challenging a subuniverse of reality, Quixote regularly managed to interpret any counter-evidence to his world of chivalry as the work of enchanters, at least until his own belief in Dulcinea was shaken. That belief was shaken when he began to wonder whether her transformation into nobility in the vision in the cave of Montesinos was only a dream or pure fiction and thus entertained the possibility of there being a phantasy within the phantasy world of his own world of chivalry. To be sure, Quixote resolved the conflicts between various orders of reality in various episodes, such as that of the wooden horse Clavileño, which should have been scorched when it passed the constellation of Capricorn. Still, the gnawing fact that Quixote's phantasied world of chivalry could contain an enclave of dreams subverted that world of chivalry from within, as it were, since Quixote had to ask whether that world itself could have been only a dream. Quixote's piecemeal withdrawal of the accent of reality from his private subuniverse highlighted for Schutz the paramount reality of everyday life, imposed upon all, and led him to praise Sancho, "who, in spite of all temptations of the transcendental, remains deeply rooted in the heritage of common sense."[24]

"Mozart and the Philosophers," read before the General Seminar in January 1956 and published in *Social Research* that summer of 1956, proposed to show that Mozart was more of a philosopher than his minimal acquaintance with philosophy might suggest. After considering the aesthetic theories of Mozart's time, which conceived art as imitating nature, and varied interpretations of his work by H. Cohen, Kiekegaard, and Dilthey, Schutz expanded Dilthey's view that for Mozart music served as "the natural expression of mental life." Mozart "built characters, actions, and situations on purely musical principles" and utilized the operatic orchestra to present moods, characters who could "speak in simultaneity," and typical attitudes, which varied according to diverse settings, much the way ideal types functioned in divergent economic settings. Schutz's descriptions of Mozart made him sound very much like Schutz, the value-free, tolerant social scientist:

> He was born not in order to set the world right but merely to express musically what exists in it. Nothing human was strange to his genius; he showed his full greatness precisely where the text revealed the diversity of life. He had to choose themes reaching from the transcendental world to the lowest region of sensual life, he had to create masters and servants, he had to show noble feelings and low motives, and he had to combine all of them. Only then was he himself.[25]

For Schutz, Mozart never intended to construct individual characters, but rather a succession of situations, which different characters interpreted differently, and thus his operas, rather than imitate nature, portrayed the basic structure of the social world. The central features of Mozart's art, then, consisted of translating outer time into inner time, amalgamating the listeners' *durée* with the performers', and, most basically, creating a community of intersubjectivity, which involved a simultaneity of the fluxes of inner time that a dramatist would only be able to present successively. Without explicitly philosophizing, Mozart captured perhaps better than anyone else how human beings met each other as a "We" and thereby philosophized better than the philosophers themselves.[26]

At the request of Maurice Merleau-Ponty, Schutz contracted to write a paper on Max Scheler for a volume entitled *Les philosophes célèbres*, but the complexity of the languages involved resulted in Mazenod press and Schutz exchanging over sixteen letters by the time the brief paper was published. This expository article on Scheler opened with Schutz characterizing Scheler as someone who lived in "continual mental haste" and who sought to show the place of humanity in the cosmos, as belonging to organic life, as emerging from evolution, and yet as transcending its environment as animals could not. Schutz explained Scheler's views on the levels of psychic existence, on the person and its acts in correlation with the apriori ranking of values, on the superiority of a coperformance approach to intersubjectivity over inference by analogy and empathy theories, and on the three types of knowledge (liberally educated, scientific, and religious) corresponding to their human types. After discussing the relative natural conception of the world and real and ideal factors, Schutz attributed the later Scheler's transformation to "the lifelong conflict between his sociological insight into the relativistic structure of the human condition and his faith in the existence of absolute values. . . ." Given Schutz's exchanges with Voegelin, one might speculate that if he had to choose between either side of this dilemma, he would have chosen the first over the second.[27]

In January 1954, Rabbi Louis Finkelstein invited Schutz to partake in the annual meeting of the Conference on Science, Philosophy, and Religion, to be held on August 31, 1954 at Harvard and to take this year for its theme symbols and values. Under pressure from his job, Schutz kept Finkelstein apprised of his progress and enlisted Natanson's editing skills before sending a draft to his intellectual comrades and to Finkelstein, who distributed all papers to all participants prior to the conference. Schutz introduced his essay by delineating the various questions eddying about the topic of signs and symbols and outlined his plan to approach symbolism through Husserl's concept of appresentation within the context of a philosophical anthropology, drawing on his work on multiple realities. Appresentation, namely the relationship by which one element of a pair referred to another not directly given in experience, could occur with reference to the following schemes: apperceptual (objects by themselves), appresentational (object referring), referential (object referred to), and interpretational (the order connecting the appresentational and referential schemes). After developing a set of principles to relate appresenters and what they appresented, Schutz elaborated on how one could pragmatically overcome transcendences through marks (a bookmark), indications (smoke indicating fire), signs (language), and symbols (Jacob's pillar). In the latter case, since the symbol was located in the world of everyday life (which here replaced the world of working) and referred to another province of meaning, e.g., the religious sphere, Schutz had to flesh out again his own theory of multiple realities. Drawing on Voegelin's work, he illustrated how societies, as social groups with their varied natural conceptions of the world, articulated a representative symbolic of themselves or even conceived themselves as representing a transcending reality (e.g., the order of Zeus).[28]

This entire discussion involved a progressive ascent from marks to symbols in which individuals attempting to overcome transcendences found it less and less within their power to do so. Thus one established a mark's meaning by oneself privately, overcoming the simple transcendence of what one left and would return to, and through indications one reached beyond oneself, grasping the unseen fire through the smoke; the connection, between appresenter and appresented, though, was less under private control. Similarly, on the intersubjective plane, signs and interpretational schemes bridging the gap between self and other might have worked effectively, but there remained a never-to-be-overcome transcendence insofar as the biographical situation and historical experiences constituting the other always differed from one's own. Finally, on the level of symbol, one encountered a transcendence beyond even the familiar realm of everyday life, and one's symbols gestured ever so inadequately toward what would never fall under one's control. To be sure, Schutz's remarks functioned more in epistemological and ontological terms, but there are salutary ethical implications at work insofar as Schutz recognizes once again the limits of intersubjective understanding and acknowledges trancendences beyond one's control—as Voegelin's gnostics never could have.[29]

Schutz wrote another major essay in this period: "Equality and the Meaning Structure of the Social World." That essay and what followed on it indicate an involvement by Schutz in the activities of a group of New York intellectuals after the Supreme Court's decision in *Brown v. Board of Education*. His participation in these activities will show us a new Schutz, a Schutz more willing to embrace normative claims than ever before and a Schutz who allowed societal injustice to evoke from him responses to which he was not accustomed.

Chapter 12

The Search for Equality

In 1954 the United States Supreme Court by its decision of *Brown v. Board of Education of Topeka* terminated the reign of the "separate but equal" doctrine that had been law since *Plessy v. Ferguson* approved of racial segregation in 1896. In reaction to this event, the organizers of the Conference on Science, Philosophy, and Religion, at which Schutz had presented his paper on symbolism in 1954, decided to focus on the general topic of equality for its 1955 annual meeting to be held at Columbia University. This chapter will discuss the paper Schutz presented at this meeting and his participation in this conference and in the follow-up Mohonk Ethics Institute of the summer of 1956. At that institute he clearly embraced a normative stance, reversing a disinclination engrained in him by his educational formation and criticized by Gurwitsch and, in particular, Voegelin. Yet this stance, which surpassed the positions of his earlier work, can also be shown to have emerged from them.[1]

"Equality and the Meaning Structure of the Social World"

In July 1955 Schutz mailed "Equality and the Meaning Structure of the Social World" to Finkelstein, reminding him that the paper, to be distributed with the other papers beforehand, did not address directly the topic he had suggested, namely, the "dynamics of social progress." Rather, as Schutz spelled out at the beginning, the paper investigated theoretically commonsense notions of equality and the various domains of relevances to which notions of equality were linked, and it contrasted in-group and out-group, and subjective and objective, understandings of equality. Since "equality" and "inequality" referred to degrees of excellence in performance, achievement, and status, they should be employed within the same domain of relevance. Hence, as Aristotle argued, flute players should be evaluated as equal (or unequal) on the basis of their ability to play, their wealth being irrelevant. Different social groups rank domains of relevances, valuing, for instance, art over wealth, and develop self-interpretations often at odds with out-group interpretations and capable of generating a "looking-glass effect" between groups.[2]

In the second half of the paper, Schutz presented how outsiders produce an alienating discrimination by exerting control over in-group members and forcing them to identify broad layers of their personality with a trait that they consider irrelevant. Outsiders discriminate by constituting falsely homogeneous domains of relevances, as when denying Marian Anderson an opportunity for singing because of her skin color, since singing and skin color pertain to different relevance-domains. However, typifications of another as belonging to a group are not by themselves discriminatory but rather require "an appropriate evaluation of this imposition from the subjective viewpoint of the afflicted individual." To exemplify the suppression of such a viewpoint, Schutz analyzed how Justice Brown in *Plessy v. Ferguson* exhibited the looking-glass effect when he anticipated the reactions of African Americans to the court's decision before it was issued or before they had the chance to give input. Brown claimed that if African Americans inferred from the decision that they were being assigned an inferior status, it would simply be an act of bad faith on their part; and he thereby immunized himself against any critique from their perspective. In addition, Schutz explained the pervasiveness of prejudices in the typifications that made the social world tick, prejudices that could not be eliminated by waving a "magic wand" and that required "a slow and patient modification of the system of relevances" through education. Basing himself on documents deriving from the United Nations Declaration of Human Rights and authored by Recasens Siches, Schutz discussed how discrimination imposes irrelevant natural or social categories upon individuals, and he distinguished minorities seeking *formal* equality (nondiscrimination) from those pursuing *real* equality (special rights or services). Majorities frequently misunderstand such minorities, much as Gunnar Myrdal had revealed that American blacks and whites misconstrue each other because of inverse relevance-rankings. Similarly, those taking "objective" equality of opportunity as the career open to all fail to understand the "subjective" obstacles that prevent individuals from taking advantage of such opportunities. Such obstacles might call for collective action if they are to be eliminated, as Crane Brinton thought, or a more modest pursuit of maximum self-realization permitted by one's situation, as Schutz proposed.[3]

This essay reflected Schutz's value-free perspective, since he simply described in-group and out-group perspectives in the experience of discrimination and in questions of group membership, equality, and equality of opportunity. However, Arthur Goddard, who translated and offered editorial assistance to Schutz and others, did not think that he had effectively abstained from value judgments, especially insofar as he cited U.N. documents as an authority. In so doing, he was seeking to capture *the* meaning of discrimination "beyond the bare observation of the disparity between in- and out-group and to arrive at some kind of prescriptive formula," beyond the limits of science. Goddard wondered how he would have been able to establish *any* thesis *at all* about the "wrongness" of discrimination, since, as a social scientist, he had renounced "any ultimate principle by which systems of relevances might be ordered." Goddard further objected that, when listing examples of typifying people according to features they considered irrelevant, he referred in the same breath to Hitler's Nuremberg laws *and* a [McCarthy] senatorial committee turning loyal civil servants into security risks. For Goddard, the legislation calling those to account who cooperated with "subversives" hardly deserved to be called discriminatory. Perhaps Schutz was so convinced that discrimination was morally wrong that he did not think it necessary to justify its wrongness, especially since his focus was on how it was constituted intersubjectively.[4]

Apart from slipping in the value judgments that Goddard detected, Schutz's social-scientific descriptions indirectly served ethical purposes. In a sense, one of the central purposes of his essay was to elucidate that in questions of discrimination and equality there were often at least *two* viewpoints involved, an in-group's and an out-group's. Furthermore, the entire equality essay is distinctive in that Schutz explicitly recognized that viewpoints pertain to groups as much as they do to individuals. In such an intergroup setting, what one may have taken to be obviously true may have in fact been only an out-group belief with which an in-group might have totally disagreed. For example, Justice Brown's looking-glass construction of how African Americans would react to *Plessy v. Ferguson* indicated how one could take one's group's beliefs for obviously true without recognizing one's position was only an out-group's and how one could further block even the possibility of such a recognition. One might argue, though, that Justice Brown covertly recognized the African American viewpoint insofar as he sought to suppress it via a looking-glass demonstration of its invalidity before the ink dried on his verdict and before African Americans had even entered the discussion. Because of this proneness to overlook outlooks at odds with one's own, Schutz insisted that the determination of the presence of discrimination required, beyond the evaluation of an imposed typification by the out-group, "an appropriate evaluation of this imposition from the subjective viewpoint of the afflicted individual." Schutz showed himself acutely attuned to this afflicted individual's viewpoint when he depicted how such individuals, identified with a trait they considered irrelevant, felt subjected to "degradation or oppression" and forced "to descend to the lowlands of the social stratum." Similarly, members of the out-group might be convinced that their offer of a formal equality of nondiscrimination was just, whereas the in-group, an excluded minority, might think that more positive measures had to be taken to ensure real equality.

Likewise, those providing for objective equality of opportunity might find themselves mystified as to why a minority person did not take advantage of the careers open to her talents, since they lacked any clue as to the subjective experience of the many obstacles hindering one from availing oneself of opportunities. Schutz *even considered the subjective viewpoint of Negrophobes*, whose prejudices, reinforced by their social world, would not disappear by waving a magic wand, and hence any effort by intellectuals to remove prejudices by informing them that biological science proved that there was no Negro race was doomed to failure. For Schutz, understanding the perspective of all involved was the condition of the possibility of resolving the problem of discrimination, just as nowadays it has become fashionable to take account of the viewpoints of all affected by any universal principle of ethics before seeking to implement it. But it is also possible that merely taking account of the subjective viewpoint of the other is not merely propaedeutic to ethics but actually fulfills an ethical mandate itself, perhaps even when it involves bracketing the ethical principles that so often block one's insight into another. Schutz eventually arrived at such a position, as will be seen by the end of this chapter.[5]

Aspects of Human Equality: The Fifteenth Symposium of the Conference on Science, Philosophy, and Religion

The Conference on Science, Philosophy, and Religion had sponsored intellectual discussions since 1940 for the purpose of promoting greater articulation about the democratic way of life, overcoming the "fragmentation of knowledge," and contributing to the common good. The participants in the 1955 meeting, the Fifteenth Symposium, held at Columbia, consisted of professors from the social sciences, biology, theology, law, and anthropology and included Jewish rabbis, Jesuit priests, Protestant ministers, an African American college president, and a woman professor, all of whose comments were recorded by unedited stenotype. All papers were published in a collection entitled *Aspects of Human Equality*, and at the conference's end Richard McKeon invited the participants after returning home to write down three or four pages about the direction of future discussions. For this purpose, Schutz contributed his brief paper "In Search of the Middle Ground," which will be considered here as a component of this symposium itself.[6]

After Richard McKeon initiated the discussion, Schutz commented on how abstract philosophical ideas filter down to commonsense persons who experience these ideas as "secularized," that is, as values detached from any philosophical or religious origin and transmitted from generation to generation as a part of a taken-for-granted tradition. The next day, Schutz envisioned the possibility that common sense, constituted by typifications and relevances shared by in-groups and out-groups, might serve as a possible locus in which the conference participants, with diverse theological or philosophical concepts of equality, might find a common ground. Later Schutz, following G. H. Mead, contended that the kindergarten playground was an ideal site to study how children in their games learned about equality and community formation by taking turns and observing the rules of the game. After Albert Hofstadter argued for careers open to one's personality and articulated five postulates on human dignity, brotherhood, equal opportunity, uniqueness, and community, Schutz agreed, except for two points. First, he opposed the idea that creativity was basic to the present time, the vast mechanization processes of which encouraged more and more conformism. Second, he objected to Hofstadter's fifth postulate calling for economic, educational, and social equality, since this postulate lacked the universality of the other four postulates and instead instanced the application of more abstract universal principles. When Professor John Plamenatz recommended that parents raise children to be responsible, considerate members of society, these considerations seemed to exceed the scope of philosophy, which ought to move on a universal plane, leaving decisions about child rearing and economic equality to concrete social groups, aided by the social sciences.[7]

On the third day, Professor Dorothy Lee argued that equality itself was derivative from respect for human dignity, which itself was revered in many societies with marked inequalities, and that insistence upon equality alone risked producing conformism on an international plane. Lee's comments sparked a reaction from Schutz, who agreed that Westerners, with their ideas of equality, and theoreticians, such as the participants in the conference, possessed an out-group perspective on "primitive [*sic*]" cultures whose in-group perspective Lee had attempted to capture. He pondered whether one would find equality as Westerners understood it in nontheoretical cultures' treatment of strangers and different age and sex groups.[8]

A few weeks later, he developed his small essay "In Search of the Middle Ground," a paper that Helmut Wagner found unique insofar as Schutz "abandoned his stance of aloofness from partisanship in practical social issues. . . . No longer the impartial, and, that is, uninvolved 'scientific observer,' he assumed the role of sympathetic observer lending advice to those for whom active involvement is a personal and moral obligation." Basically, he demarcated three possible types of "middle ground": a common language, a shared epistemology, and a unified pragmatic sense. For Schutz, it was important to develop in the future a common language by clarifying the topics to be studied, since in the equality conference the topics had ranged from fashioning universal ethical principles, to transforming the United States, to focusing on a common problem in cooperation with each other. In addition, participants had adopted a diversity of roles needing coordination: as responsible persons seeking an ethics; as "worried citizens of the United States of 1955, deeply troubled by the many manifestations of discrimination, prejudices, and other social evils"; and as scholars eager to investigate theoretically the problem of equality. As far as epistemology was concerned, Schutz was convinced that secularized common sense provided a middle ground on which philosophers, social scientists, and theologians might converge. But he hoped that the intellectual conference participants would focus on the commonsense actor's understanding of equality and discover their common ground in efforts to communicate with the "man in the street" about how to achieve the pragmatic goals of changing social attitudes and promoting racial equality and equality of opportunity.[9]

Those in attendance at the conference shared Schutz's sense of being troubled by discrimination, and hence Professor Perry Miller could jest that everyone thought that equality was a good thing except for Dr. Lee. Interestingly enough, much of the focus of their discussion had to do with a self-critical fear that the pursuit of equality itself might lead to a homogenizing disregard for the uniqueness of individuals. To fend off the possibility of such false equalization, they endeavored to ground equality in some underlying ethical concept such as the community of humanity, freedom, solidarity, human dignity, or natural law. Indeed, the metaphor of sportsmanship running throughout the conference reflected this concern, since sports implied recognizing natural inequalities and a willingness to acknowledge the other's excellence even if it were not one's own, thereby escaping the leveling *ressentiment* that frequently underpinned the pursuit of equality, as Nietzsche knew so well. Dorothy Lee, perhaps the most outspoken proponent of founding equality in an underlying ethical value—hence Miller's comment—repeatedly contended that equality existed to promote human dignity, to which it was subordinate. On this basis, she could also make the case that other cultures might have great respect for human dignity even without Western egalitarian practices and that equality (understood as interchangeability, equivalence, or conformity), could suppress uniqueness and result in totalitarianism—a point on which Hoftstadter concurred. In spite of these hesitancies, the conference at times succumbed to the very temptations it most feared when participants spoke of the United States "preparing the rest of the world to accept the concept of equality" or of its "Messianic role and function" on the world stage. Even Schutz's and Lee's reference to non-Western peoples as "primitive" revealed the implicit functioning of a standard to which others were expected to conform—though the resources for criticizing such a standard might not have been available in the mid-1950s.[10]

Dr. Lee's paper reminded Schutz that concepts of human dignity and equality were products of a highly theoretical attitude of which one needed to be self-critical, and hence he repeatedly stressed the limits of what philosophy by itself could do regarding concrete questions. In addition, he had continual recourse to common sense, and saw that even children's playground behavior could be educative for the theoretician. Although he did not emphasize the *ethical* grounding of the idea of equality as did other participants, he nevertheless delved beneath the abstract notion of equality by surfacing the *epistemological* insider/outsider divergences that enabled interlocutors to become self-aware of their own perspective and more attuned to others'. These tasks were every bit as important for approaching the question of equality as an attempt to provide an ethical foundation for equality that would avoid the totalization of others. His strategy in these conference discussions and his postconference essay resembled those deployed in his equality essay when it revealed how bigots (like Justice Brown) or intellectuals (in reference to Southern Negrophobes) had adopted an outsider's viewpoint, distant from the insider viewpoint of the other.[11]

The Institute of Ethics in 1956

When Rabbi Finkelstein invited Schutz to participate in a Lake Mohonk Institute on Ethics, a conference focused on equality of opportunity for education Schutz turned down a European trip and accepted because of the beautiful setting, the honorarium, and the promise of the institute to help resolve "problems of vital concern." Ever since 1950, the Conference on Science, Philosophy, and Religion had scheduled summer discussions at Lake Mohonk in preparation for its annual meeting in late August or September. The only records of Schutz's significant comments during the two weeks at Mohonk consisted of reports, memoranda, handwritten notes, and occasional interventions chronicled by A. Durwood Foster, of Duke University, the designated reporter. The institute produced no volume of essays, and Schutz's archival papers furnish no other evidence of his attendance at the August 27–30, 1956 meeting than a program, covered with his handwritten notes.[12]

In letters on March 16 and May 8, the Ford Foundation's Clarence Faust, director of the conference, broadened the topic from equal opportunity for education to "equality of opportunity and the various barriers to it." Finkelstein followed up with a letter assigning Schutz to group 2 (of six), which was to discuss the topic of barriers to equality of opportunity for the development of powers of social and civic judgment. All the groups were wary of pressing for equality of opportunity in a way that might deny factual inequalities of capacity. Schutz's group, though interested concretely in civic responsibility, shared with the others the commonly assigned tasks of determining the facts about barriers, their costs to the individual and the community, the philosophical framework in which the barriers were raised, and the philosophical ethic required to destroy them.[13]

In the general sessions, Schutz sounded a cautious note about how international institutions needed to display a context-sensitivity to different cultures, but his circumspection began even with Finkelstein's invitation to conference, on which he had underlined the words "raised" and "destroy" regarding barriers. He explained his reservations in a document he circulated at the institute entitled "Some Considerations concerning Thinking in Terms of Barriers." Schutz worried that the participants might think that equality of opportunity could be easily realized, were it not for artificially developed "barriers" that could be removed without any need for a creative determination of new directions. Further, he feared that sometimes barriers to equal opportunity might fill important functions in the social system, which would be damaged by their immediate removal, and his care about accurately understanding others prohibited him from attributing facilely to dominant groups the deliberate intention to deprive others of equality of opportunity. There was the additional danger of moving too quickly from the level of ethical principles to context, and hence Schutz inquired whether the folkways of a minority group resisting assimilation should be considered removable barriers to equal opportunity. Or should national sovereignty be considered a barrier to the U.N. or the U.N. a barrier to the self-realization of the United States, for instance? Schutz further pointed to obstacles to equality of opportunity that might not be easily removable insofar as they were constitutive features of the human condition. Such features would include the inevitable social distribution of knowledge, the impossibility of realizing all one's possibilities, historical and traditional functions essential for group maintenance, and factors maintaining the coexistence of groups or institutional orders. Just as Hayek argued that gradually and organically evolving social and economic systems resisted rationalistic "tinkering," so Schutz sounded a realist note, warning against any rush into ethical actions without considering their consequences and implications and thus recommending more a Weberian ethics of responsibility than one of conviction.[14]

Schutz also completed a memorandum to Harold Lasswell in preparation for the report their committee would produce one week later. In that memorandum, Schutz recommended discouraging uniformed judgment, and, to explain what a well-informed judgment was, he reiterated the three types of expert, man in the street, and well-informed citizen from his essay by that name ten years before. He then explained the social derivation of knowledge through interchanges with eyewitnesses, insiders, analysts, and commentators, and a new intermediary, the reporter. He then began to take some steps beyond "The Well-Informed Citizen" by inquiring into *how one develops well-formed judgments*. For instance, he elaborated on how the partiality of the perspectives on which knowledge depended posed questions about whom to trust, how to evaluate information, and how to make judgments in the face of social pressures, and required one to strive to see things in terms of others' relevance-systems. One could answer these questions and understand others by engaging in debate, adult education, nonpartisan roundtables, intergroup (including interracial) discussion groups, and educational television programs. However, Schutz ended the memorandum pessimistically, describing how little able well-informed citizens were to influence events, since, though they could educate their children, they were only mere atoms of public opinion capable of individually writing congresspeople or newspaper editors.[15]

By the end of the second week of the Institute, Schutz and Lasswell together had produced their report, each participating fully in its development. After Lasswell's oral presentation of the report to the other discussants, Schutz summarized the three basic areas in which citizens encountered obstacles (barriers to the equal opportunity to act as citizens ought to be able to act). These areas involved (1) acquiring information to make responsible civic judgments, (2) gaining insight into one's motivations, and (3) being given the chance to make decisions or influence others—the chance, as Schutz put it in a handwritten draft, of "being heard by those who have to make the decision."[16]

The written report on barriers to an equal opportunity to develop powers of social and civil judgment insisted that citizens recognize their responsibility for the common good by actively participating in processes of civic choice on the basis of adequate information. Citizens ought to exercise a critical attitude toward sources of information, and they ought to consider the normative grounds for their own goals as well as the relationship of alternative policies to probable results. They should be outspoken for opinions in the public interest, especially neglected opinions and those touching on their expertise, and should seek to remove violations of democratic practice, through persuasion first and severe sanctions if necessary, even while tolerating, as far as possible, the infirmities of others. Barriers in general limited citizens' ability to perform as required, and the report mentioned as an example of such a barrier a citizen's unwillingness "to seek relevant information about topics beyond the range of his immediate and narrowly personal interests."[17]

The bulk of this paper coauthored by Schutz and Lasswell consisted of a checklist of barriers in the United States. Government can promote a passive citizenry through such things as overcentralization, excessive stress on legality and constitutionality, censorship, overemphasis on security leading to an atmosphere of intimidation, undue trust in the invisible hand of the economy at the expense of goal-setting intelligence, and a dual-party system requiring unanimity and pursuing narrow immediate interests. Similarly, the mass media and educational and economic institutions can foster such passivity by ostracizing nonconformist positions, catering to frivolous interests, managing images, invading privacy, and ridiculing the person of conviction "as a crackpot or a pretentious intellectual or an uneducated haranguer." The report cited evidence that lower-class families "do not draw their children into an active posture toward public affairs," urged religious groups to take seriously "the social gospel," and invited professions to enhance possibilities for sound social and civic judgment. In the final section, on ethical problems, Schutz and Lasswell acknowledged that their report opened questions treatable by general ethical theory and urged that ordinary citizens clarify the normative grounds of their goals with others. They highlighted the anonymity introduced by television, the lack of "two-way" intercourse, and the inability of the isolated viewer to reach television presenters with replies or questions.[18]

This final segment on overcoming anonymity probably had its origins in a fragment in Schutz's handwriting among The Papers of Alfred Schutz entitled "Barriers of equality of opportunity of bringing about the alternative chosen by the individual or at least of being heard by those who make the decision." This fragment developed the third type of barrier that Schutz briefly mentioned after Lasswell's oral presentation, namely, the obstacles keeping the individual citizen from making decisions or influencing others to make them, and it included much more about anonymity than the brief mention of television in the report. The fragment began by discussing the dimensions of social distance and anonymity resulting from the structure of the social world, in which others are given as Consocii, more anonymous Contemporaries, and even more anonymous Predecessors and Successors. Schutz mentioned the immediacy and vividness possible among consocii, which allow one to answer questions and "be heard," but this intimacy contrasted with the anonymity experienced in dealing with the Contemporaries working for the government.

> An example of the extreme opposite case is the possibility for the individual voter to be heard by the once appointed government. They are [It is?] extremely limited: The individual citizen may write to his Congressman or the editor of his newspaper, he may form a protective committee, he may induce his local organization to action; all these steps have the functions of suggestion boxes in a large corporation. The suggestion is put in the box but nobody knows whether the box will be opened and if so whether the suggestion will be considered, still less whether it will be accepted.[19]

As a result of this account of political anonymity, developed within the context of the anonymity inherent in the structure of the social world, Schutz then proposed a solution reminiscent of Rousseau's cantons as the ideal locus for democratic practice:

> The only hope for a remedy consists in the assumption that by speaking out among the familiar group of consocii a kind of chain reaction can be created which might bring about the desired result. By the [this?] very reason of [?] the activity of the responsible citizen in the smallest circle accessible to him—the family, the classroom, the discussion group, the local political or professional organization—is of the highest importance and should be encouraged. By the same reason, all forms of expression in which the citizen speaks not as an individual but just as one of many (polls, etc.) should be discouraged.[20]

This model for democracy based on "small publics" placed in question for Schutz the present practice of democracy understood merely as majority rule: "It has, however, to be understood that at least the majority principle upon which the democratic way of life is founded is incompatible with the ideal of equality of opportunity to the single individual to make his personal opinion be heard and appreciated."[21]

Schutz, Ethics, and the Search for Equality

It is something of a new Schutz that one encounters in this chapter. One is hard-pressed to recall any other point when Schutz had associated himself so extensively with a group of people at once intellectually sophisticated *and explicitly morally committed*; never before had he spent such time in the company of religiously dedicated people of the Jewish, Catholic, and Protestant faiths. In spite of their diversity, several of the participants found the moral tenor of their own meetings—their own democratic, communal, and respectful interactions—worthy of remark. So explicitly morally committed were the participants that, taking the struggle for equality as presupposed among them, they worried about whether their own moral zeal might lead to immoral consequences, such as imposing uniformity upon unique individuals. Indeed, it was in response to the situation of a society beginning to desegregate and reverse centuries of injustice and in response to scholarly companions of high ethical character that Schutz publicly expressed moral commitments as he had rarely done before.[22]

In addition to expressing such commitments, he contributed to the moral search for equality by bringing his philosophical, especially epistemological, work to bear on the problem of discrimination. In his essay, he illuminated the viewpoint of "the afflicted individual," the African American victim of discrimination—a viewpoint often not consulted or even denied through a looking glass, and he also corrected misunderstandings to which intellectuals, like himself, were prone, such as thinking that the latest biological findings would convert Negrophobes. In the conference, stimulated by Dr. Lee's presentation, Schutz continued in this self-critical mode, stressing the potential for Western theoretical culture to misunderstand non-Western cultures, and he underlined the limits of philosophy in applying to concrete situations and stressed the educative role that common sense might play for theory. In sum, he opened theory and philosophy to their other just as the equality essay had attempted to open both the prejudiced individual and the intellectual to their others.

One can trace in the three documents from the 1956 Ethics Institute, Schutz's progress toward making his own ethical stance explicit. In the first document, "Some Considerations concerning Thinking in Terms of Barriers," Schutz appeared skeptical toward idealistic endeavors to remove barriers that might play important roles in social systems, that might maintain the identity of minority groups, or that might belong inescapably to the human condition. One can hear echoes here of Menger and Hayek on how rationalistic interventions into organically developed social systems can do more harm than good, or echoes of Weber on how ethicists must weigh the consequences of their forays into another sphere of activity, rather than push ahead with blind idealism. Though Schutz's education in Vienna might have disposed him to stress such realism, his second document, the memorandum to Lasswell, recovered a normative notion already expressed in "The Well-Informed Citizen" in 1946, namely, that well-informed judgment ought to prevail over uninformed judgment. But he went further, by indicating *how to acquire a well-informed judgment* through an intersubjective process of "knowledge formation" that required citizens to see things in terms not only of their own relevance-systems but also those of others and that would rely on debates, roundtables, and interracial discussion groups. The third document, the final report, not only detailed the barriers shutting out citizens from intersubjective processes of knowledge formation, but at the end probed the important possibility of affecting a decision's outcome, as the isolated television viewer cannot.[23]

In his fragment on being heard, he went even further by discerning within intersubjective knowledge formation an ethical value of ultimacy: *the single individual wishing to make his personal opinion heard and appreciated*. In order for this individual not to disappear into a bleak sea of anonymity, interchanges were required, particularly with small publics, families, discussion groups, and local organizations. Such discussions, while making eminently possible well-informed judgments, also served the purpose of bestowing on single individuals the recognition they deserved. Moreover, it would seem that Schutz was judging the success of democracy in terms of whether its individuals could be heard and appreciated. Hence, Schutz rejected as inadequate any reduction of democracy to mere majoritarianism by limiting it to casting a vote in large elections; this would render democracy comparable to dropping a note in a suggestion box, not knowing if the box will even be opened and leaving the active subjectivity unrecognized. On the contrary, it was the single individual wishing to be heard and appreciated who dictated the establishment of more interactive democratic practices.

To be sure, Schutz had not worked out a full ethical system here; as Thomas Luckmann once remarked pithily to this author, "He was not an ethicist." Thus, it is not clear whether his normative notion of democracy would be merely a political ideal that democracies should strive to realize or whether the idea of the individuals hoping to have their opinions heard and appreciated stands as an ethical ideal, more universal in scope, that any political system should strive to realize. Schutz was well aware that responsible participation in public affairs had to be rooted in the principle of practical reason (to use Kant's terminology), but Schutz never devoted a tract to defining practical reason or showed its relationship to logic or scientific rationality, as Kant and others did. Nevertheless, to define practical rationality would not have been a task beyond the ken of Schutz, who often wrote about the meaning of rationality, scientific and life-worldly, natural scientific and social scientific. Also there seem to be conflicting, but perhaps reconcilable, standards against which democracy was being assessed, since it is one thing for well-informed citizens to make their viewpoint prevail over that of the uninformed man in the street and another thing that individuals find their personal opinions heard and appreciated. In the first case, a democracy would be evaluated on the kind of knowledge (or lack of it) directing its activities and in the second on the quality of the relationships maintained between its citizens.[24]

But the ethical principles involved in ensuring that individuals be heard and that citizens be active in shaping their political destiny reflects the influence of the Austrian economic school upon him. Mises and Hayek did not share the premise of classical economics that iron laws of economics unfolded with necessity and governed economic actors mechanistically as if they were pawns. "There are no mysterious mechanical forces," Mises wrote; rather "there is I and you and Bill and Joe and all the rest. And each of us is both a producer and consumer." Mises and Hayek located the sources of the economy in the preferences, interchanges, and activities of individual consumers, in particular, and entrepreneurs. So Schutz did not locate the heart of political life in the large, anonymous vote of the majority, but rather in individual citizens joining with each other in small publics. Mises and Hayek emphasized the importance of the creative and active economic subject, not obeying economic laws working behind his or her back, but weighing preferences and taking creative entrepreneurial initiatives. So Schutz and Lasswell pressed for civic agency that would take active steps to be well-informed, critically examine sources of information, and resist governmental centralization and media pressures to uniformity. Even though some Austrian economists might have taken exception to the Schutz/Lasswell preference for active intelligent planning over submission to the invisible hand, Menger, at least, had thought that planning was needed, and Mises, while opposing planning, emphasized individual purposes over submission to market "mechanisms." Insofar as Mises conceived the entrepreneur as striving to satisfy consumer needs rather than to criticize them, Schutz and Lasswell might have argued that politics constituted a *different* domain requiring not only mutual interaction and reciprocal appreciation *but also* mutual critique in pursuit of the most inclusive common good.

Schutz, of course, throughout his career willingly endorsed both the Austrian turn to the subjective viewpoint of the economic actor and Weber's ideal-typic methodology, which best captured that viewpoint; and this methodological priority may explain his reluctance to commit himself to ultimate ethical values or principles. He was explicit with Voegelin that such principles ran the risk of imperiling one's tolerance for a pluralism of perspectives. However, in these political writings he saw his way through to a value of ethical ultimacy, capable of being articulated as a principle to govern democratic and political practices: namely, that individuals' opinions deserved to be heard and appreciated. Such an ethical principle is unique in that it does not suppress the other's subjective perspective but requires that it be taken seriously into account. Furthermore, this principle is entirely formal, mandating that one hear and appreciate the other's opinion, regardless of its material content, and the principle does not oblige one to agree in any way with the opinion that the other expresses, merely that such an opinion "be heard." As a result, the principle, by its imperative force and its formality, does not commit to any one viewpoint that might foster intolerance toward other viewpoints; it thus displays the value-freedom and openness to a diversity of motivation endemic to Austrian economics and Weberian sociology without succumbing to ethical relativism.

In a sense, the enunciation of this principle by Schutz near the end of a productive career casts an ethical light on all his works, which are almost entirely epistemological in nature. It is certainly easy to construe "Equality and the Meaning Structure of the Social World" as an epistemological work fulfilling the ethical purpose of letting the long-suppressed opinions and experience of "the afflicted individual" be heard and appreciated. But Schutz's lifetime project at its highest theoretical reaches was *also* about enabling the subjective viewpoint of the other person to be heard and appreciated. Schutz pursued this project by embracing Austrian economics and Weberian sociology, each of which gives pride of place to the subjective viewpoint of the actor. Because of this project, he could see the significance of Bergsonian temporality, marking the limits of understanding the other, or of the Husserlian effort to go behind a complete and constituted world to the subject's constituting activity—an effort that needed to be translated in terms of the social world. *Der sinnhafte Aufbau* is one immense effort to provide a philosophical vocabulary for the *verstehenden Soziologie*, that is, to make it possible to talk about understanding another person. Of course, in the more applied essays Schutz led the reader to see how the world looked to strangers, homecomers, Don Quixote, concert performers, or the black traveler denied access to a sleeping car. It comes as no surprise that Adolph Lowe, inviting Schutz to serve on a committee for a dissertation on emigrants, would appeal to his interest in "strangers" and "other queer human beings."[25]

Finally, one may speculate that in this normative principle, Schutz's own life story comes to expression, for he himself was often the stranger, the single individual needing to be recognized. One can think, for instance, of his experience of being asked never to return to the Austria for which he had risked his life in military service in World War I or of being a Jew in an anti-Semitic Germany or the United States. Perhaps his normative principle has its root in the feelings of being a businessperson in a philosopher's world or as a philosopher in a business world. He knew the need to be heard as a musician who thought that no journal would publish his maverick "Making Music Together," or an Austrian-trained philosopher/social scientist who later despaired of publishing in this country, as the next chapter will show. Perhaps what he went through sharpened his eye for strangers, for the viewpoint left out and needing recognition, for the victims of Nazi cruelty, the mail-order female workers "fined" in the name of "economic rationality," or the commonsense actor on the other side of science. Perhaps when he wrote of not being heeded by anonymous forces, he thought of a cousin committing suicide after being condemned by the rules of what he took to be a "Sunday school" morality or of African Americans who perhaps in 1954 finally glimpsed the possibility of being recognized. There is a pathos in Schutz's tone when he compares majoritarian democracy to dropping a suggestion in a box without knowing whether the box will ever be opened or the suggestion read or accepted. This pathos was born out of life itself.[26]

Chapter 13

Triumphs and Decline, 1957–58

The years 1957–58 were years of success for Schutz, perhaps the greatest being the presentation of his paper "The Problem of Transcendental Intersubjectivity in Husserl" at the Colloque philosophique de Royaumont—a presentation in which Schutz, the self-styled "heretic" and "maverick," won the acclaim of worldwide phenomenology. But these years were also times of decline, in which Schutz felt increasing alienation from the American academic and publishing establishment and in which he found his health gradually and seriously deteriorating.

Disputes and Success in the World of Phenomenology

The activities of the International Phenomenological Society focused on the major conferences to be held at Royaumont (April 23–29, 1957) and Venice (September 10–11, 1958). Perhaps taking the Royaumont gathering as an opportunity for establishing and interconnecting phenomenological organizations, Leo van Breda wrote Marvin Farber about the possibility of a European phenomenological society that would be affiliated with the International Phenomenological Society, which Farber and others had established in New York in 1939. While at Royaumont, Schutz, to whom Farber poured out his vitriol in private, negotiated an accord between Van Breda and Farber that protected the autonomy of each one's enterprises. Ever the peacemaker, Schutz reported to Farber the many kind comments Van Breda had made about him, including his nomination of Farber to be a board member of the European society, and Schutz recommended that *PPR* publish a paper of Van Breda's as a gesture of good will.[1]

Meanwhile, Schutz was also planning for *PPR* a manuscript on José Ortega y Gasset that might be lengthy, since Ortega y Gasset was unknown to the United States. After hearing about it from Schutz, Farber responded with his usual curt tone, limiting Schutz to 1,000–3,000 words and telling how he had returned manuscripts to younger scholars to be cut in half. Farber's letter evoked a bitter reaction from Schutz, who wrote a lengthy letter, which he reconsidered, condensed, and sent to Farber, who seemed to be telling him that the paper would be published, "if he behaved." He confessed that at his age it was good to abandon illusions, such as the illusion that one who had helped Farber since the beginning and had proved himself a loyal friend would not be placed on the same footing as younger scholars. Schutz ended his angry letter, "Young scholars from Cornell writing on Wittgenstein have to cut their paper in half for *PPR* publication. I cut my Ortega paper out." Receiving Schutz's softened version, Farber threw Schutz's anger back at him, "I can only express regret at your egregious misunderstanding of my letter, and at the unwarranted and unjustified inferences you express—which I simply reject." Though Farber anticipated receiving the Ortega y Gasset study for a Husserlian centennial edition planned for 1959, Schutz doubted that his paper would be suitable for that edition, inquired of Recasens Siches in Mexico about publishing it with *Dianoia*, and departed for the Venice conference in Europe, without informing Farber. This "unpleasant exchange of letters," as Schutz described it for Gurwitsch, demonstrated that Schutz experienced an increased sensitivity, which most people might feel if their achievements weren't respected or if they were treated as apprentices in a career in which they had distinguished themselves. Indeed, not being appreciated for who one is resembles not having one's opinion heard by unresponsive political structures.[2]

By the fall of 1958, the rift seemed to be healed, since Farber elicited Schutz's editorial advice and since Schutz requested two Husserl manuscripts on the life-world, on which he was preparing to write, and he kept Farber posted on the progess of his essay on type and *eidos*. Moreover, Schutz had agreed with Farber to look at a translation of Edith Stein's *Zum Problem der Einfühlung* by Stein's grandniece, Waltraut; though Schutz admired her great-aunt's character, he felt that the work was outdated and not relevant to English readers and that the entire translation needed revision. In spite of his own health problems and extensive commitments, he not only reviewed the manuscript, but continued his regular editorial duties, reading manuscripts and advising Farber on various proposals.[3]

Schutz's approached Van Breda about publishing Cairns's glossary of Husserlian terms, but Cairns refused to mail it, fearing the loss of twenty years of work and thereby prompting Schutz to joke that someone could greatly serve phenomenology by hiring a robber to steal the manuscript and mail it. Schutz had thanked Van Breda for organizing Royaumont and informed him of his plans to attend the Venice conference in 1958. A major crisis erupted, however, when Van Breda sent Schutz an article by Roman Ingarden that had appeared in the Italian journal *Archivio di Filosofia*. Ingarden had criticized the Husserl Archive for not sufficiently consulting those who had known Husserl personally regarding the publication of Husserl's work and for fostering concern for the development and continuity of Husserl's thought instead of thinking beyond Husserl by paying attention to his unresolved problems and contradictions.[4]

When Van Breda referred the matter to Schutz, he handled the entire situation masterfully, writing to Van Breda and objecting to Ingarden's use of the first-person plural to speak of Husserl's original followers (since Schutz did not agree); he also said he doubted that personal knowledge of Husserl necessarily produced magical editorial power. However, he did agree with Ingarden on the salutariness of trying to develop Husserl's thought, which did not stand or fall on getting the historical sequence of his works right or knowing what he had said at Göttingen or Freiburg. He perceptively observed that Ingarden's attacks were not personal, that they were published in an Italian journal that was not widely read, and that the root of Ingarden's problem might have had to do with how he had felt treated at Royaumont. He commended Van Breda for his work, including his welcome for "heretics" like himself, and later, in his usual style, informed Van Breda that Ingarden had said nice things about him at Venice in September 1958. At the very same time Schutz was in communication with Ingarden, praising his book on Bergson before mentioning quite frankly that Van Breda's work was invaluable and his staff too small. Schutz, though, strongly affirmed Ingarden's insight that one honored Husserl's thought in thinking beyond it. Although Ingarden continued differing with Schutz about the best order for publishing Husserl's works, he wrote Ilse after Alfred's death, lauding him as a rich human being and mature intellect. Once again Schutz managed to be forthright about his own position and still maintain cordial relationships with two parties at war with each other.[5]

Schutz offered advice to Van Breda about which manuscripts to publish first, helped track down unreturned manuscripts, and explored purchasing microfilm copies of the manuscript for the New School, a project that was only realized after Schutz's death when Marianne Lowe endowed it. Schutz's service of the worldwide phenomenological community also brought him into contact with Rudolf Böhm, who was in charge of collecting Husserl's manuscripts and correspondence at the Archives, to whom Schutz sent a copy to him of Husserl's Vienna Lecture, one of the three stenographed copies. He also mailed the correspondence in his possession: one letter to Husserl, nineteen letters and cards from Edmund and Malvine Husserl, twelve letters and cards from Fink, five letters from the Berlin Academy, and two copies of his reviews. Unsure whether his illness would permit him to travel to Europe, he inquired of Böhm early in 1959 about transcriptions of manuscripts, for which Böhm regretted having to charge him. Finally, on May 6, 1959, only days before his death, Schutz responded to a query from Böhm about the relationship between Husserl and Bergson. He said that because Husserl had ratified the protest proclamation against France at the opening of the First World War, there were tensions between the two thinkers, and Husserl had to deliver his Sorbonne lectures, later published as *Cartesian Meditations*, not in the department of philosophy but in the department for German philology. Schutz found it sad that the two great philosophers of this century, both Jews and both beset by similar problems, were separated from each other by national circumstances, although Hitler, paradoxically, brought them eventually into a closer relationship.[6]

Active Citizenship in the New School Community

Beginning in 1957, after Royaumont, Schutz made references throughout his correspondence to his deteriorating health. Nevertheless, he continued with his work at the New School, which included the usual teaching and service activities. He taught full-time in the spring of 1957, repeating his courses on methodology and social action in sociology and offering Contemporary Philosophy, which treated Bertrand Russell and neopositivism, Bergson, Husserl, Scheler, German and French existentialism, Hartmann, and Whitehead with a focus on ontology, philosophical anthropology, ethics, and epistemology. He took on a full teaching load in the academic year 1957–58, repeating courses on self and society, methodology, and applied theory, and giving a new course on causality that examined various interpretations of the concept, questions of teleology and motivation, and the different understandings of causality in the natural and social sciences. In the spring of 1958, he also offered a new course on familiar material, namely, a comparison between the thought of William James and Henri Bergson, for which he had read Ingarden's book on Bergson. When Hans Simons appointed Jonas to a committee on the bachelor of arts program at the New School, he asked Schutz to take the chair's position for the fall of 1958, even though he was concerned about Schutz's health and research commitments. Schutz, whose health at that moment seemed to be improving, generously accepted the responsibility, but was granted a sabbatical leave for the spring semester of 1959, for which, as was the New School custom, he was not to be paid. In the fall of 1958, in addition to the chair's duties, he taught seminars on sign and symbol, other minds, and language, with the latter course addressing topics such as the intersubjective context of language, the differences between human and animal "language," human development, language pathologies, and dialects.[7]

Alvin Johnson frequently consulted Schutz regarding editorial matters for *Social Research*, and their relationship remained convivial, with Schutz sharing with him, for example, the following joke, after Johnson had mentioned his own garden: "A minister admires the garden of one of his parishoners and remarks, 'With God as your partner you have succeeded in making a wonderful garden.' Answers the parishoner, 'You would be astonished to see what [would have] happened to my garden if I had left the whole job to my partner.'" Schutz also served on committees for master's theses and doctoral dissertations in philosophy and sociology. He showed his integrity and kindness in difficult cases, such as that of a student who had left the country without completing course work, returning manuscripts Schutz had lent her, or giving much hope that she would complete her master's thesis. Because of his work with her, Simons thanked him "as a fine educator" who had shown her "the patience and indulgence that gave her strength and poise." Another student, whom Schutz had assisted at the outset of his program and who had disappeared for two years, suddenly showed up in April 1959, complaining by phone about not receiving credit for two courses. Schutz had no record of grades for him, informed him of this, and entrusted the hostile letter he sent and the entire affair to Dean Staudinger. Schutz further displayed great kindness in his dealings with faculty members and administrators, praising a Neo-Kantian book written by Simons's father, recommending a colleague's manuscript for publication, rescuing Werner Marx again from a minor Jonas ploy, and sending the only sympathy note received by a faculty member whose father had died.[8]

The New School in these years was in financial straits, having no endowment, unable to provide financial aid for its students, paying very low salaries, and, on several occasions, making pitches to donors just to meet the payroll. Schutz put the philanthropist Lady Davis in touch with Alvin Johnson and informed Staudinger that Mrs. Marianne H. Lowe, a student and friend of the New School, was willing to contribute. She asked for her gift of $15,000 to be anonymous and for $2,000 of it to be earmarked for the library fund for the purchase of books in sociology and philosophy. Staudinger appointed Schutz to the library committee to recommend philosophy books. In addition, Schutz undertook a larger fund-raising project by inquiring about funding possibilities with Clarence Faust, who was in charge of the Ford Foundation Fund for the Advancement of Education and who had served as director of the 1956 Mohonk Ethics Institute. Since the Ford Fund supported not schools but programs, Schutz carefully studied the Woodring Report, which, prepared under the sponsorship of the Fund, discussed such a program. Besides, he consulted with the Columbia University sociologist R. M. MacIver, with whom Schutz had many contacts over the years. MacIver shared with him a sociological study he had done of a New York City junior high school entitled "Juvenile Delinquency Evaluation Project of the City of New York." After this research, Schutz prepared a proposal aimed at improving grammar and high school teaching of the social sciences, and Simons acclaimed the proposal for presenting the broader issues and explaining the unique contribution that the Graduate Faculty could make.[9]

Schutz's proposal argued that the young needed to understand more than the technological means for preserving their democratic heritage; they needed to understand the meaning of that heritage itself, that is, how its underlying ethical and religious values slowly evolved and what rationales underpinned economic and political practices. Schutz praised the American education his children had experienced, with the built-in discussion and debate that permitted full freedom of opinion, avoided authoritarian dogmas, and developed their faculties of judgment. He contrasted this education with the regulations at the Austrian *Gymnasium* in which he had studied and in which any student less than eighteen who engaged in any political discussion was threatened with immediate expulsion—hardly permitting the "being heard" that was pivotal in Schutz's contribution to the Ethics Institute. Schutz argued that Graduate Faculty courses could trace the connections between democracy and the free market, trade unions, equality of opportunity, desegregation, class structure, and the philosophical ideas of human dignity and freedom. Clearly drawing on views developed in years of cooperating with the Conference on Science, Philosophy, and Religion, as Embree noted, Schutz stated that the Graduate Faculty with its interdisciplinary, holistic, and philosophical outlook could locate the study of the social sciences within the more encompassing framework that was needed. In the end, Faust, who deeply admired Schutz, perceived too many practical difficulties in the program, but Schutz informed Simons that they had impressed Faust and that contact with him could be valuable for the future.[10]

Schutz participated in the many projects of the Graduate Faculty, inviting speakers, entertaining guests, requesting the University of Chicago Press to reissue Kallen's 1914 book on James and Bergson to honor the author's seventy-fifth birthday, and recommending essays for Hans Neisser's collection of essays from the Graduate Faculty. Further, when Humanities Press decided in 1958 to republish the final edition of Kaufmann's *Methodology of the Social Sciences* that appeared in 1946, Schutz went to great efforts to drum up publicity by soliciting book reviews, with mixed results, from Abel, Morganbesser, Nagel, Kallen, Brecht, Haberler, Johnson, Deyrup, Machlup, Natanson, Wolff, Froehlich, and Farber. It was a remarkable undertaking for a man whose own health was at low ebb, and a tribute to a friendship that had its rocky moments. For many of those from whom Schutz solicited reviews, the request itself was the last communication they would receive from him.[11]

President Simons undertook for Schutz the very service of helping him publish and win recognition that Schutz had rendered to others. In March of 1958, Simons urged Schutz to formulate a proposal for his projected book on the life-world with the plan of submitting it, along with one from Lowe, to the Rockefeller Foundation, and, if they were rejected, Simons promised to go to Bollingen Foundation and the Philosophical Library. Schutz was pessimistic from the start about the whole idea, writing Simons:

> I am rather pessimistic that your kind efforts, as far as *my* project is concerned, will lead to the desired result. I find myself, as far as Foundations are concerned, in a position similar to that of the New School: Our work does not fit in any of the pigeon holes prepared by them. My additional handicap is the fact that very few people share my conviction that the field of "basic research" in the social sciences is philosophy.[12]

The Rockefeller Foundation rejected both proposals, describing Schutz's endeavor as "really very far removed from those fields in which our Trustees have urged us to concentrate." Schutz drafted a response to thank Simons for showing him the rejection notification, and he agreed with melancholy and pride that his own work was far removed from the mainstream. He refused to apply for any more grants in this country and asked Simons not to approach other foundations. He reassured Simons that he had saved money to cover his leave of absence, and he jokingly commented that he deserved a sabbatical "every sixtieth year" and concluded, "It will be for the first time in my life that I can dedicate myself for a few months exclusively to writing."[13]

Schutz's sadness about being confined to the margins of the academic enterprise had been developing for a while, and it is tempting to speculate about its link with his earlier critique of majoritarian democracies that anonymize individuals deserving to be heard. In 1957 he considered publishing in Van Breda's Phenomenologica series, since the social sciences in the United States differed so much from the German *Geisteswissenschaften*, and, as he informed Farber, he planned his sabbatical in Europe "since it seems hopeless to me to find a publisher in this country." Finally, in his last letter to Luis Recasens Siches, in December 1958, he addressed the difficulties of publishing in the United States:

> I abandoned all hope to interest the North American philosophers in problems which are in the center of discussion in Europe, as I could discover when attending the Congress in Venice. In addition, all my friends have considerable difficulties with American publishers and it seems that the better the book, the greater those difficulties. There is, however, a good chance that I can have my book published in Europe without any trouble.[14]

The youthful embrace of American culture, after an initial resistance to it based on a reading of French authors, and willingness to make phenomenology speak American English through the works of James, Mead, and Dewey was long gone, perhaps ground down by what appeared to him like a lack of reciprocity.[15]

Schutz was tireless in assisting the New School in any way he could, reacting, for example, at Staudinger's request, to another university's report on graduate education and its doctoral program in the social sciences, and keeping administrators abreast of Aron Gurwitsch's interest in joining the faculty. Schutz had not only investigated the possibility of acquiring microfilmed copies of the Louvain Husserl manuscripts, but he had even secured funding for the project. However, when faced with resistance from the New School administration, he decided to wait for the new administration that would replace the retiring Simons and Staudinger over the next eighteen months.[16]

Encouraging and Advising Colleagues through Correspondence

As usual, Schutz corresponded most regularly with Aron Gurwitsch, but the two met more frequently than usual during the 1957–58 period. Gurwitsch taught summer school at the New School in 1957, and Schutz stopped en route home from a Maine vacation to visit Gurwitsch for a day in Cambridge in September and read to him the essay "Some Structures of the Life-World." In Europe, Schutz and Gurwitsch exchanged repeated letters during the summer of 1958 trying to arrange a meeting, but they were only able to meet in Venice during the philosophy meeting. Alice Gurwitsch discovered a photograph of Aron, Alfred, and Nathan Rotenstreich—the "Dioscuri," as Gurwitsch called it—and this photograph, besides being the only one taken of both friends together, captured the last face-to-face meeting they would ever have.[17]

They acquainted each other regularly with their triumphs at conferences or in print. Gurwitsch, for instance, kept Schutz informed about the publication of *Théorie du champ de la conscience* and implored him that the review for *Social Research* not end up in the wrong hands, and Schutz defended his friend's work against certain critics. Schutz, for his part, shared with Gurwitsch his paper on transcendental intersubjectivity and discussed the unsatisfactory, haggling-type conversation that followed on his presentation at Columbia of his paper, "Tiresias, or Our Knowledge of Future Events."[18]

Gurwitsch was continually seeking a more hospitable setting for his academic work, since he felt out of place at Brandeis and thought that the president of the university behaved vindictively toward him. In the spring of

1958, before Gurwitsch left for Europe, Schutz worked on the possibility that Gurwitsch might replace Jonas, who was taking a leave in 1959–60; but Gurwitsch, on leave from Brandeis in 1958–59, doubted that a second leave would be permitted. Nine months later, Schutz apprised Gurwitsch, now in Europe, of a new development. Schutz had procured a contribution to bring in his friend for the spring of 1960, and the current administration was considering replacing retiring Kurt Goldstein with him as professor in philosophy and psychology. However, Schutz was concerned about the precarious situation of the New School: it had financial problems and with the imminent retirement of Simons and Staudinger the university wanted to replace them with "Americans, and that says it all." Gurwitsch had considered a position at the University of Berlin, though Schutz finally dissuaded him by suggesting that that city at some point would be divided in two, leaving Gurwitsch in the East—an uncomfortable position for a independent Jew with little sympathy for dialectical materialism or existentialism. Gurwitsch's enthusiasm for the New School position seemed to increase with time, but it would finally be Schutz's death in the spring of 1959 that would open the door for Gurwitsch's full-time hiring as his replacement.[19]

They exchanged their philosophical papers and commented upon them. When Gurwitsch in "The Kantian and Husserlian Conceptions of Consciousness" argued that Husserlian intentionality surpassed Kant's and Leibniz's spontaneous consciousness by permitting the consciousness of identity to emerge, Schutz denied that intentionality could lead to the constitution of the objective world, since it presupposed the life-world as its basis. Schutz confessed to having become heretical in regard to the Husserlian project: "I have become so heretical that I no longer understand how the eidetic reduction can be performed, if only the identity of the noematic sense and not that of the objective object is presupposed." Schutz raised the further question of whether free variation in fantasy was really all that free, since it woud be constrained by ontological realms and the frameworks of open possibilities. Although Gurwitsch disagreed with Schutz's pessimism about Husserl—he thought that Husserl could solve problems that Kant could not handle, such as, presumably, the identity of objects—he agreed with Schutz that one had some knowledge of an object even before any search for its invariant features. Although most of their subsequent correspondence was taken up with questions about the New School, Schutz's work on type and *eidos* in Husserl's late philosophy led him to conclude that "every attempt at a clarification of the basic concepts of Husserlian philosophy demonstrates the indefensibility of the construction."[20]

Schutz continued to correspond with Eric Voegelin, who had taken a position at Munich and who concurred with Schutz's critique of Husserl on intersubjectivity, namely, that intersubjectivity was a matter of the ontology of the *Lebenswelt* rather than of phenomenology. Considering Husserl's work gnostic, Voegelin could not understand why Husserl continually sought to rectify his "denial of the world and its new creation out of the solitude of the meditating philosopher." Nevertheless, after Schutz's voyage to Europe in 1958, including a stopover in Louvain, Schutz remarked that Husserl still remained the old wizard (*Hexenmeister*) who always survived however many objections one might have against his philosophy—certainly a more positive assessment than Schutz was expressing around the same time to Gurwitsch. In addition, Voegelin also recommended to Schutz the recently published *Die dritte Walpurgnisnacht*, by Karl Kraus, which in Voegelin's opinion was the best thing written on National Socialism, especially due to its critical examination of Goebbels and totalitarian lies. While admiring Kraus, Schutz admitted to Voegelin that Kraus's technique was not equal to the massive evil that Hitler produced.[21]

One of his major correspondents in this period was Maurice Natanson, who had finally escaped Houston by landing a five-year contract at North Carolina. Schutz manifested a continual concern for Natanson's career, criticizing one of his presentations at a philosophy conference as a philosophical success but a "diplomatic failure," keeping on top of reviews of Natanson's book on Mead, reviewing his papers, and advising him where to submit them. Schutz also approached Lady Davis to aid him financially and helped him find summer school teaching, although once, when Natanson found out that Gurwitsch had a prior claim on summer teaching, Natanson threatened to picket the New School with a sign reading "I am just as smart as Aron Gurwitsch.'" Natanson worried that he might be asking too many things of Schutz: "I am really beginning to feel like a distant poor relation of yours and before much longer you will probably wince when you see a letter for me: 'What does he want now?' "[22]

When Natanson mentioned that his son Nicky's feet had regressed, that he had to be put in plaster casts for ten to twelve weeks, and that after that they would decide whether he would need an operation or casts for a longer period, Schutz's response was immediate. He told Natanson that he was sorry to learn that his poor boy had to undergo such an ordeal. He went on to refer to his own sad experiences: "Since we, too, had for many years the difficult task to keep a lively boy quiet and immovable, I know perfectly well what such a condition means to the whole family." In a touching conclusion to his letter in early January 1959, Natanson mentioned how he frequently returned to the things Schutz had written, reading them a sixth and seventh time and finding them fresh, expertly argued, and always profound. He ended his letter, "I must say here that the best thing I found in the Graduate Faculty, the thing without which there really would not have been any meaningful study there at all, was the presence of a magical person."[23]

Luis Recasens Siches wrote Schutz in September 1957 responding to a letter of more than one year before. Recasens Siches requested Schutz's paper on equality, encouraged his work on Ortega y Gasset, and criticized the relativism of Kelsen's newest book, *What Is Justice?* More than a year later, Recasens Siches notified Schutz that he had filed for divorce and had been given full parental rights over his children, one of whom his ex-wife had turned against him. In addition, he had twisted his back in an accident and produced an inflammation of the sciatic nerve that caused unbearable pain. These events had kept him from speaking to the editor of *Dianoia* about the possibility of Schutz publishing his Ortega y Gasset essay. Schutz, with delicate sympathy, responded, "In times of a crisis like this one, it is very hard, even for a friend, to say more than to express his sympathy," and he said he fully understood why the topic of his Ortega paper had not been broached.[24]

In the period 1957–58, Schutz continued his intellectual relationships with those associated with the Graduate Faculty. Adolph Lowe, for instance, sent Schutz a draft of a presentation for the General Seminar on functional analyses of economic growth and an outline for another paper. His interest in these papers, as usual, was not in predicting behaviors of forces but in showing how they should behave in order to be functional for the attainment of systemic goals, and he insisted that such functional analyses were prior to descriptive, prescriptive, or explanatory studies of empirical regularities. In this sense his functional approach was located at a pretheoretical level, much like that of Schutz's life-world, and Schutz could have argued that the life-world was even more fundamental than these functional analyses. Likewise, Thomas Luckmann, who had taken courses with Schutz while a graduate student at the New School, sought Schutz's reactions to papers on the sociology of speech and an essay on methodology that he had written for an introductory course he offered at Hobart and William Smith. In the letter explaining the latter paper, Luckmann observed at the end, "Of all my teachers in this field I owe the biggest and the most direct debt to you."[25]

Schutz advised the sociologist Kurt Wolff about publishing some of Scheler's work, and he informed him of the sad story of Ernst Grünwald, author of the 1934 *Das Problem der Soziologie des Wissens: Versuch einer kritischen Darstellung der wissenssoziologischen Theorien.* Apparently Grünwald had committed suicide after authoring a manuscript on language philosophy, and his parents sought to publish it with the help of Schutz. Schutz referred them to Voegelin, but then the *Anschluss* terminated all these plans. Schutz, returning after the war, was unable to find the parents, who, he assumed, had probably died in a gas chamber. In the rest of his answer to Wolff's query, he recommended that the following books be translated into English: Grünwald's book on the sociology of knowledge, Alexander Von

Schelting's *Max Webers Wissenschaftslehre*, Raymond Aron's *La soziologie allemande*, and his own "masterwork" *Der sinnhafte Aufbau der sozialen Welt*. Concerning the latter text, he commented to Wolff, "I have reread the book recently and according to my impartial judgment it has become better and more important (*noch aktueller*) over the last twenty-five years." In a final letter, Wolff sent Schutz a copy of Martin Luther King's *Strive toward Freedom*. He commented that it was "a great and elementary book, whose simplicity (a wrinkle) in its stand against all that assails and deforms, disconcerts, touches, stirs one up, and produces hope. Often tears will come to your eyes." Clearly, Wolff thought that the topic of racial relations, to which Schutz had devoted much energy at an earlier and healthier period of his life, would still be of significance for him.[26]

Schutz was involved in communication with various persons in the New York area, such as Louise Antz, a philosophy professor, who often invited Schutz to speak to the philosophy teachers she organized. Perhaps sensing the final outcome of his illness, she wrote, "Having lunch with you and our friends was one of the loveliest events of the year. I have cherished knowing you." Ernest T. Ferand, chair of the New York chapter of the American Musicological Society, invited Schutz to present "Mozart and the Philosophers" and provided George Schutz with music instruction. Schutz recommended him for a Fullbright Fellowship and praised his book on improvisation as so scholarly that he would have to spend a long time on it to be able to say something sensible. In addition, various international organizations elicited Schutz's participation, such as the Mount Pelerin Society, although he did not share the political views regularly associated with its members, such as their opposition to governmental intervention.[27]

In all these exchanges, in which one finds Schutz engaged in rich relationships with diverse persons, one can see him delighted with the intersubjective understanding to which he devoted so much of his philosophical work. In the file marked "Clippings" in Schutz's papers, there is a wonderful passage from John Cheever that Schutz preserved. It concretely describes what Schutz called "expressive movement" and captures the possibilities for understanding another person—the process that delighted and intrigued Schutz throughout his life:

> It is true of even the best of us that if an observer can catch us boarding a train at a way station; if he will mark our faces, stripped by anxiety of their self-possession; if he will appraise our luggage, our clothing, and look out of the window to see who has driven us to the station; if he will listen to the harsh or tender things we say if we are with our families, or notice the way we put our suitcase onto the rack, check the position of our wallet, our key ring, and

> wipe the sweat off the back of our necks; if he can judge sensibly the self-importance, diffidence, or sadness with which we settle ourselves, he will be given a broader view of our lives than most of us would intend.[28]

Success at Royaumont and in Publication

On January 3, 1957, the director of the Cultural Circle of Royamount invited Schutz to a conference on phenomenology to be held from April 23 to April 29, and on February 5, Schutz agreed to present on the problem of intersubjectivity in Husserl. At the conference, as was usual for Schutz, he renewed old friendships and made numerous new acquaintances, afterward sending offprints of his articles, reports on the meeting, and other communications related to the conference to such philosophers as Bachelard, Biemel, Cairns, Farber, Fink, Gurwitsch, Ingarden, Kuypers, Linshoten, Nédoncelle, Spiegelberg, Strasser, Van Breda, Voegelin, Von Peursen, and Wahl. He published the German text of his paper in *Philosophische Rundschau*, the only essay he published in German, as Richard Grathoff observed.[29]

The essay itself began by recounting Husserl's incomplete forays in *Ideas I* and the *Formal and Transcendental Logic* into the relationship between intersubjectivity and the constituting subjectivity that has no originary access to the other's subjective processes. To start the Fifth *Cartesian Meditation,* which sought to establish from within the ego the objectivity of the world as "for everyone," Husserl implemented a second *epoché*, screening off what was properly of the ego from what was not properly of it, from "everything that refers to other minds." This second *epoché* went beyond the phenomenological *epoché*, which, while bracketing belief in existence of the world, still left the world with the sense of being an intersubjective world whose objects were accessible to everyone. Schutz, however, objected that one would have to know what was not properly of the ego in order to abstract from it and that, therefore, one from the start must have already been in contact with an intersubjectively "preconstituted substratum," namely, the everyday social world. Furthermore, he asked whether the consciousness of the other person, supposedly belonging to what was properly of the ego, would not immediately institute a relationship with the other and hence create immediately an Us or a We. Moreover, the consciousness having as its intentional correlate what was not properly of the ego would nevertheless still refer to the intersubjective preconstituted substratum in which this consciousness was originally instituted, and hence it would seem to be impossible to refrain from *all* reference to other subjectivities. Finally, Husserl at times confused the ego executing the second *epoché*, the meditating observer, with the transcendental ego, to whom the world was pregiven in universal apperception and thus would already contain what was not properly of the ego within itself.[30]

In the second step, Husserl described how a body similar to one's living body appeared within one's primordial sphere and then, by a process of pairing, which did not involve logical derivation, one transferred the sense "another living body" to this other body. Schutz, though, argued that there was a basic dissimilarity in how one's own lived body was given to oneself (through inner, kinesthetic feelings) and how the other's body appeared (e.g., from without, visually). Further, Schutz contended that when one verified the presence of another's lived body on the basis that its behavior was "congruent" with what a living body should manifest, one would be drawing on, without admitting, the preconstituted substratum, especially the norms that every human being of one's cultural sphere observed. In the third phase of Husserl's account, the other body not only appresented another "I," but also everything belonging to its concretization, and a second appresented stratum overlay one's own experience of nature, namely nature as it could appear to the Other, that is, an objective world and common time-form. Schutz, who from his early Bergson period had insisted on the irrepeatability of one's temporality, questioned how the transfer of the sense "another's living body" could also constitute all the other's "stream of subjective processes" and the temporality of the Other essential to its constitution as a complete monad. Moreover, he denied that one could ensure a common, objective nature from the resources of one's own consciousness, without communication. In a brief interlude before his final discussion of *Cartesian Meditations*, Schutz opposed transfers of bodily localizations, contended that a social relationship preexisted communication, and rejected the idea of personal unities of a higher order.[31]

In the penultimate section of his essay, Schutz criticized the higher levels of community that Husserl built on the basis of the ego/alter ego relationship established earlier in the Fifth Meditation. The problem was that the *Cartesian Meditations* explicitly spoke of a transcendental We, a community; however, as Husserl himself acknowledged in his *Krisis*, the *epoché* created a solitude in which one dealt not with oneself or others as human beings but with mere phenomena, correlates of transcendental inquiry. As Schutz put it, "Each transcendental ego has now constituted for himself, as to its being and sense, his world, and in it all other subjects, including myself; *but* he has constituted them *just for himself and not for all other transcendental egos as well.*" Indeed, given this solitude of the transcendental meditator, it was doubtful whether there could even be a plurality of transcendental egos at all and whether one could even meditate with others. Schutz concluded that intersubjectivity was not a problem of constitution to be handled within the transcendental sphere, but rather a datum of the life-world that could be clarified through an ontology of the life-world, by uncovering the founding mundane intersubjectivity that Husserl's procedures in the Fifth Meditation occluded. Schutz contended that Husserl's moves within that meditation in effect transformed (and betrayed) the meaning of constitution itself, converting it from a clarification of sense-structure into a foundation of the structure of being, turning explication into creation. One sees here the disciplined Schutz, restricting himself to careful description and nothing beyond and stressing usual themes: the social life-world at the root of all reflective procedure and temporality, equally foundational, and distinguishing one individual from another so thoroughly as to destabilize any efforts to amalgamate them.[32]

In the comments after the presentation of the paper, Schutz highlighted the fact that he had presented before this "forum of highly competent phenomenologists" difficulties that he himself had been unable to overcome in twenty-five years of studying Husserl's theory. While his critique survived the ultimate test of this forum and while he might have been more pessimistic about phenomenology in private letters to Gurwitsch, in the discussion period after his paper he refused to jettison transcendental phenomenology or phenomenology in general. He even resisted the despair over transcendental phenomenology that his presentation seemed to have produced in M. Kelkel.[33]

After attending a New York University institute, Schutz, at the philosopher Sidney Hook's request, drew up "Some Equivocations in the Notion of Responsibility," which distinguished the first-person sense of responsibility from a third-person imputation of it and correlated this distinction with that between the subjective and objective meanings of actions. He also developed a dialectic between these two meanings, describing, for instance, what a true sense of guilt might be beyond (objective) external censure; for instance, he presented the paradox that designers of the atomic bomb suffered under a deep sense of (subjective) responsibility while their grateful government bestowed honors upon them. He recommended reformulating the problem of determinism in subjective and objective terms and extended first-person/third-person approaches to reponsibility to in-group/out-group relations. For instance, it was quite different if the Allied Powers, an out-group, were to hold Nazi leaders responsible than if the German people were to call to account their own in-group leaders. These contrasts between an anonymous third-person perspective and that of the first-person individual parallel Schutz's ethico-political antithesis between majoritarian democracy and the individual citizen, accountable and to be taken account of.[34]

Van Breda had scheduled Schutz to present "Some Structures of the Life-World" at the phenomenological colloqium at Venice and then rescheduled it for a Padua conference that he mysteriously canceled later. The paper, while prepared in 1957, was never read or published until Gurwitsch translated it for the third volume of the *Collected Papers* in 1966. The essay repeated Schutz's earlier accounts of key features of the life-world and incorporated a distinction between clear and distinct "knowledge about" from "knowledge of acquaintance," which grasped the superficial "what" of things without understanding "how" they worked. All knowledge differentiations depended upon the three types of relevances Schutz already developed, and, though Schutz may have felt that one of his relevances, the topical, accommodated Gurwitsch's thematic relevance, Gurwitsch could have defended the priority of thematic relevance, since everything Schutz said about relevances depended on making them thematic. Schutz analyzed in depth atypical experiences, documented the dialectic between what was thematic and the interpretational relevances brought to bear upon it, and emphasized the systematic interconnections between the types of relevances.[35]

In November 1958 Kurt Wolff invited Schutz to a symposium on the sociology of knowledge at the International Sociological Congress, but when Schutz found that the program failed even to mention the symposium, he withdrew, since he wished to spend his limited energies on projects that would make a difference. In December 1957 and March 1958, he published in the *Review of Metaphysics* two parts of an essay entitled "Max Scheler on Epistemology and Ethics," an essay for which Paul Weiss, who had requested it in February 1955, had granted Schutz all the time and space he needed. In an extraordinarily condensed and clear manner, Schutz exposited Max Scheler's epistemology and ethics in the space of thirty-four pages. He articulated Scheler's appropriation of Husserl's phenomenology; his epistemology, which grasped the (*intra* and *extra mentem*) thisness of a thing as opposed to its (*extra mentem*) thatness; his critique of Kant's philosophy as one of the "closed fist"; his ethics of the apriori value-ranking; and his philosophy of the Person.[36]

Via the ideal type of Tiresias, Schutz, in "Tiresias, or our Knowledge of Future Events," illuminated contingent commonsense knowledge of future events, which relied on a temporally developed and socially derived stock of knowledge, depended upon interests in the future, and intersected with knowledge of others. Knowledge of the future made use of generalized types as well as formalizations and idealizations that aimed at future occurrences not in their uniqueness but with an emptiness that the unique features of future events would fill in. Ironically, only in hindsight, after the event occurred, could one determine whether or how much the event was expected or unexpected. Having developed the knowledge/typification side of knowledge of the future, Schutz turned to relevances, especially since in the light of interests and a system of projects, one was able to come to terms with the imposed aspects of the ontological structure of the universe. Schutz, as in his writings on Goethe and rationality's limits, took full account of the future events that, lying beyond one's influence, one could anticipate as conforming with the past, even as he also allowed for indeterminate projects that could guide one's action to influence what was within one's power. Given the hopes and fears accompanying one's motivated action and the contingency of one's knowledge of the future—neither of which Tiresias experienced—Schutz cited the old Pythagorean poet's prayer that Socrates uttered in *Second Alcibiades*: "King Zeus, grant us good whether prayed for or unsought by us. But that which we ask amiss, do thou avert."[37]

This later Tiresias essay, unlike its earlier 1944 version, omits the undeveloped issue of "certainty" and concentrates on the reliability of typifications. At repeated junctures throughout, the later essay utilizes typifications to serve as the bridge between the past and future. The earlier version repeatedly situates projecting temporally, locating it with reference to the defining ends of a specious present—a concept mentioned only once in the later essay. Projecting in the later essay, however depends instead on typifications, though it is vague as to how they will be fully instantiated in the future and yet constitutive of the stock of knowledge. Whereas the earlier essay ends the third section by discussing future anticipations, the later essay deals with scientific prediction through types that remain valid "until future notice." This repeated emphasis on the validity of types until counterevidence appears suggests the influence of Schutz's essay on type and *eidos,* being written about the same time, and he corroborates this influence by specifically citing the view of Husserl's later work on how anticipations "explode." Finally, the earlier essay's view that one's past is active in one's projects in a trajectory whose full outcome and meaning only a prophet might have access to, suggests the oedipal overtones of that earlier essay.[38]

While preparing his essay on type and *eidos* in Husserl's later philosophy for the *PPR* issue in memory of Husserl, Schutz underwent double surgery and hospitalization, but he nevertheless managed to complete a 7,500–word manuscript on May 6, 1959. Hoping to illustrate Husserl's "operative" (vs. "thematic") conception of "typicality," Schutz explains how the presumptive idea of a universal originates on the prepredicative level when one expects on the basis of regular induction that other objects of a type will exhibit similar properties, "until future notice." Just as science systematically and methodically transforms nonessential types (e.g., that whales are fish) into essential ones, so everyday cognitive activity, taking off from the passive reception of the familiar type, fashions predicative judgments and constitutes universals. After summarizing Husserl's treatment of these themes in the *Krisis*, Schutz finds *Experience and Judgment* separating empirical from eidetic universals, with the latter book prescribing rules for experiencing all empirical particulars and transforming actualities into pure possibilities, such as the transcendental ego. In his concluding "Some Critical Remarks," Schutz contrasts how

Husserl developed the *eidos* out of the type in *Experience and Judgment* with his derivation of specific typicalities from essential ones in *Cartesian Meditations* and the *Krisis*. Schutz then criticizes Husserl for unthematized notions connected to typicality (e.g., similarity), an excessively visual orientation to similarity, confusion of essential and nonessential types, neglect of the social dimensions of transubjective typicality, and unclarity about the activity/passivity difference. In a final critique, Schutz wonders whether free variation aimed at *eidos* is not constrained from the start by the world's ontological structure and by natural attitude experience in terms of types, just as he had traced the transcendental constitution of intersubjectivity to origins in the preconstituted substratum of everyday life. Ilja Srubar pinpoints Schutz's difference with Husserl by observing that Schutz reversed the usual idea that the mundane had its limits in the eidetic when he asserted that the essence found its limits in the mundane.[39]

In a final paper, "Husserl's Importance for the Social Sciences," prepared for Herman Van Breda's memorial volume in honor of Edmund Husserl, Schutz prefixed remarks about his personal route into Husserl that were never published in *Collected Papers*. The body of the paper was divided into two parts. The first criticized several thinkers who believed that they were basing their approach to problems of the social world on Husserl's thought, and the second spoke positively of the aspects of Husserl's thought that were of continued relevance to these problems. Schutz, for instance, criticized Edith Stein, Gerda Walther, and Max Scheler for misuses of eidetic method in analyzing social reality (e.g., "collective persons"), though Scheler's later work on the "relative natural conception of the world" displayed improvement in recognizing the legitimate place of historical relativism, as did Merleau Ponty. Schutz analyzed Ortega y Gasset's differences with Husserl on empathy and the transcendental constitution of the alter ego, even though Ortega y Gasset neglected how the experience of the other's existence made possible a common environment. Positively, Schutz lauded Husserl's account of the natural attitude, which could provide a foundation for the social sciences, and his insights, which could clarify the foundational concepts of Max Weber's sociology. For example, Husserlian concepts could illuminate the meaning of projects that in turn gave meaning to human action; the idealizations, attentional modifications, and constitutional processes to be found in the stock of knowledge; and the open and problematic possibilities involved in choosing. Husserl's analysis of Here/There-based coordinate systems could clarify the reciprocity of perspectives; his account of temporality, intersubjectively shared time; his theory of appresentation, intersubjective interpretation and signs and symbols; and his notion of types, the structures of the social world.[40]

Little mention in the literature has been made of Schutz's relationship with his family, perhaps because during these two years he spent more time with his family than ever before. He took few, if any, business trips, which had always left their trace in the letters by providing details of family life. While in Royaumont, Alfred wrote Evelyn, telling her that he was "in his element" in Europe, since he was better known there than in the United States. Although he had feared to be seen as a "heretic" in the Royaumont meeting, he reported that he was pleased that most of those present concurred with him. Ilse accompanied Alfred on his trip to Venice from early June to mid-September in 1958, and it was she who informed the Gurwitsches, who were in Israel, that Alfred had to submit to double surgery in the spring of 1959. Among Schutz's personal papers, there was even a letter from George to his father in the hospital in February 1959, telling him to rest well. The next chapter will take up the final sickness and death of Alfred Schutz, an ordeal in which the love of his family for a father and husband will become all the more evident—and not only the love of his family, but also of his many friends.[41]

Chapter 14

Death and New Beginnings

Illness, Death, and Condolences

Schutz's illness compelled him to excuse himself from various New School events that even someone on sabbatical could not avoid, such as a luncheon with the new dean. He wrote Gurwitsch four days before his death that his heart problems had worsened and that since he was allergic to all available medicines, his only hope was to go to a sanatorium in Switzerland. The most thorough statement on his illness appeared in a letter to Eric Voegelin, in which Schutz mentioned that a chronic condition had developed in his heart due to an earlier infarct. In mid-February, an effort to reduce a build-up of inner fluids led to the need for an emergency operation, followed ten days later by another operation to remove the prostate. Five days after departing the hospital, he experienced heavy bleeding that made it necessary to return to the hospital and remain for six more weeks. After that stay, he found himself in the precarious situation of being allergic to most medicines, as he had mentioned to Gurwitsch, and of being thoroughly exhausted. As a result of these many health difficulties, he died on May 20, 1959.[1]

The condolences poured in. Marvin Farber, shocked to receive notice from Evelyn, considered him among the greatest of phenomenologists, "the finest exponent of the application of phenomenological analysis to social science." For Machlup, he was "the 'truest of the true,' he was the best, the most unsparing of friends, the wisest and most shrewd of my advisors, the greatest of those who stand near me." Gurwitsch, who wrote the memorial in *PPR*, praised his "perfect competence in highly diverse fields" and stated that for his friends "his friendship was one of the precious gifts of their lives." Gurwitsch summed up his character: "His mind was as penetrating, sharp, and keen as his heart was warm and generous. There was something radiant in him. He shouldered responsibilities that often seemed to surpass the capacities of a single man." Natanson acknowledged to Ilse what he had gained from Alfred "as a moral being" and commented on how he had combined a philosophical existence with his concrete humanity:

> I remember that after you and Alfred visited us in Forest Hills, he said of Charlie as we were walking out of the house, "This is the best thing you have shown me." He was interested in my technical productions, but also my concrete life. It was not just a matter of someone showing "interest" in my child; it was characteristic of his philosophical existence.[2]

Alvin Johnson, whose two letters of condolence Ilse considered her most proud, most cherished, "almost holy possessions," captured Schutz's own democratic, humanitarian leanings. He wrote,

> May I beg you to let me share your sorrow? For I too loved Alfred Schutz.
>
> I admired him as one of the greatest scholars I have known in my life. I loved him as a man who used his scholarship, not imperially, to subjugate inferior men, but humanly, to help them to a higher level of thought.[3]

In 1962, after Ilse had sent him a copy of the *Collected Papers, vol. 1: The Problem of Social Reality*, Johnson thanked her and described how in turning the pages, he was arrested by a paragraph or a sentence, and heard Schutz's own voice, serene and vibrant. He recalled Schutz's delight in seeing an idea penetrate a student's mind, and told Ilse that long after they were both gone, "there will be scholars who find in the work of Dr. Schutz an approach, a vital approach to the ultimate reality."[4]

Van Breda spoke eloquently of his character in his preface to volume 1 of *Collected Papers*:

> I would like to speak of the man, to evoke the acumen of his mind, his penetrating irony, his serenity and courage in exile, the wide range of his interests, the gift of youthfulness and sympathetic understanding which enabled him to assimilate successfully a new culture at the age of forty and to become accomplished in it.[5]

Richard Zaner in his introduction to *Reflections on the Problem of Relevance* presented a portrait from a graduate student's perspective:

> A man of great personal character, bearing, and engaging warmth, Schutz gave unstintingly of himself to his many students, despite the circumstance that in addition to teaching full-time with The Graduate Faculty, he had a more than full-time position as an executive in different corporations simultaneously. . . . In his teaching and in his

> writings, in courses and in counsel with students, he constantly insisted on the necessity of serious study of the works of thinkers of every persuasion and discipline. Tolerant and open in the finest philosophical tradition, he had little patience with narrow professionalism, whether educational or philosophical, but at no time did his impatience turn his wonderful sense of humor and irony into ill-tempered sarcasm. He constantly sought out what was common to the divergent currents of thought rather than what separated them.[6]

Posthumous Publications

In a letter of March 29, 1959, after leaving the hospital, Schutz bemoaned to Natanson this "sad way to spend my desired sabbatical," but then laid out three major projects: completion of what he had earlier called *Strukturen der Lebenswelt*, a new edition of *Der sinnhafte Aufbau* with an epilogue on Husserl's later works and American thinkers, and a collection of articles earlier designated as *The Problem of Social Reality*. He hoped to publish the latter with Bookmans, Inc., and outlined its three parts: on methodology (on common sense and social science), on phenomenology and the social sciences, and on symbolism, multiple realities, and language. Although Schutz's preferences were almost precisely followed in organizing that volume (a section on the structure of the social world in the first section was excluded), the general introductions he had desired for each of the three sections never materialized. He did, however, propose two additional volumes: *Studies in Applied Theory* and *Studies in Phenomenological Philosophy*, exactly the titles of volumes 2 and 3 of *Collected Papers*, respectively. He then asked Natanson whether the organization was appropriate and whether he would be able to edit *The Problem of Social Reality*, since Schutz wanted time to work on *Strukturen der Lebenswelt*. He mentioned that he trusted Natanson, who admired his work, and, besides, had received a grant to remunerate him. To conclude, with his usual respect for the full autonomy of those with whom he interacted, Schutz assured Natanson that if he were involved in his own work, he would understand, and the rejection of this proposition would change nothing in their friendship.[7]

Natanson responded immediately that he was as pleased to accept the proposal as he was disheartened by the circumstances making the offering of it possible and necessary. He then begged off of assuming responsibility for translating portions of *Der sinnhafte Aufbau*, having been scared "out of his wits" by Cairns's review of another author's faulty German translations, and he wondered to what degree Schutz might be willing to supervise his editing. At the end, he commented that his son Nick, Schutz's namesake, had announced with a three-year-old's assurance that the best composer ever was Rimsky Coffeecup.[8]

Schutz thanked him for accepting the editorship and for giving him peace of mind, since he knew Natanson would do an excellent job. He then outlined for him the contents he planned for volumes 2 and 3. The second volume finally contained all the articles Schutz had mentioned, with the exception of the T. S. Eliot article, which Ilse felt was in unfinished form, and an article on sociology of knowledge that he never wrote. It also came to include things he did not mention: "The Dimensions of the Social World," excerpts from *Der sinnhafte Aufbau*, translated by Professor Thomas Luckmann; "The Problem of Rationality in the Social World," his paper presented at Harvard in 1942; and the essay on Santayana. The third volume also eventually contained all that Schutz had requested and Gurwitsch's translation of "Some Structures of the Life-World," which he had not planned on including. Schutz was willing to collaborate with Natanson on the translations of *Der sinnhafte Aufbau* and assist with the editing, but he insisted that his book on the structures of the life-world would take priority. In all his haste to arrange his legacy, Schutz did not omit, though, to thank Natanson for the "sweet joke about Rimsky Coffeecup." On May 16, four days before his death, one of the many letters he wrote involved further editorial recommendations.[9]

The one posthumous work remaining to be discussed is *The Structures of the Life-World*, volumes 1 (1975) and 2 (1983). On the basis of Schutz's manuscripts (in the form of notebooks) Thomas Luckmann brought *The Structures of the Life-World* to its final form, acknowledging clearly his own role: "The book cannot be the book as Schutz would have written it. It is not even the book I think he would have written: a complete submersion of my own thought and work in his plan was neither possible nor, I am sure, was it something that Schutz would have wished under the circumstances." Schutz wrote the book, as Luckmann accurately recognized, "to bring together the results of his investigations into the structure of the world of everyday life and to present in one connected argument what was still scattered among various publications." Luckmann worked with Schutz's colored file cards indicating the divisions Schutz wished. Schutz's working papers and manuscripts were collected into six manuscripts, which Luckman, used along with the *Grosses Relevanzmanuskript*, which Zaner edited into *Reflections on the Problems of Relevances*. Luckmann also altered Schutz's plans, expanding a section on typifications in the third chapter on the subjective stock of knowledge; producing an entirely new chapter, the fourth, on knowledge and society; and abandoning a final chapter on the methodology of the social sciences that merely repeated earlier essays.[10]

In the first chapter, Schutz and Luckmann present the familiar features of the everyday life-world, whose objects are first given with sociocultural meaning; their taken-for-granted presuppositions can always become problematic, and, when conflicts arise regarding which typifying schemata are appropriate, theoretical tendencies are born. The second chapter explores the life-world's stratifications, including the provinces of meaning, the worlds spatially and temporally within reach, typified processes of biographical articulation, and the structure of the social world. A feature never presented before in Schutz's writing appears when elders or children are described as acting as bridges between present and past and future worlds.[11]

The third, the lengthiest chapter, relates the stock of knowledge to one's situation, including past and present situations, temporality, bodiliness, and the spatiotemporal and social structure of one's subjective experiences. This stock of knowledge includes ever-present, fundamental, nonlearned elements—for instance, knowledge about corporeality as such (e.g., breathing and swallowing); learned skills constitutive of the usual functioning of the body (e.g., walking); useful knowledge (e.g., playing the piano); and standardized recipes (e.g., a hunter reading tracks). While basic fundamental elements are invariant across societies, some habitual knowledge (skills, useful knowledge, and recipes) belongs to every stock of knowledge and some varies culturally (e.g., Romans did not walk like Huns did). The authors explain how the acquisition of knowledge is temporally articulated through polythetic steps during the course of a biography, including temporary interruptions. The stock of knowledge possesses its structure, with levels of familiarity, incompatibilities, degrees of credibility, negative knowledge, and systems of typifications and relevances, including the previously articulated three relevances in their interrelations and hypothetical relevances (e.g., a noise that sounds like a shot), which might turn out to be irrelevant. Attitudes, such as the fear of snakes, function as dispositions to act, in which are sedimented past lived experiences that can be retrospectively recovered as "because motives." Different "modes of consideration" are at play when one understands an action in terms of its in-order-to or because motives, and one ought not absolutize one mode over the other by favoring either the free project or the bound attitude.[12]

The fourth chapter of *The Structures of the Life-World*, developed by Luckmann alone, examines the social conditioning of the subjective stock of knowledge that presupposes presocial structural capacities that enable children to internalize the relative-natural worldview and to comprehend their "self" through intersubjective mirroring. Just as the *subjective* stock of knowledge is socially conditioned, so the *social* stock of knowledge has its origins, at least in part, when subjective knowledge is communicated to others. Socially transmitted signs permit one to detach knowledge from situation-bondedness by enabling one, for example, to speak of a river-crossing miles away instead having to lead another to it and single it out by wading through it. Anonymous signs, freed from concrete, subjective experiences, also make possible "falsification," since they leave out polythetic steps, subjective nuances, and historical contexts, even as they facilitate a social accumulation of knowledge and its higher forms (e.g., science). Further, the growing accumulation and development of the social stock of knowledge leads to increasing specialization and higher forms of knowledge, even opening possibilities for the self-reflective turn that results in analyses of logic and methodology and for theory, increasingly "de-pragmatized" and remote from everyday reality. Ideal-typical analyses permit construction of the formal types of simple and complex distributions of knowledge, depending on the degree to which a society's general knowledge is uniform and to which it has developed quasi-autonomous provinces of specialized knowledge. In a complex distribution, no individual can survey the specialized domains of knowledge, and, as a result, knowledge becomes an instrument of power, experts vie with other experts, the gap between laypersons and experts expands, and the well-informed citizen becomes all the more necessary.[13]

The fifth chapter, the first in the second volume of *The Structures of the Life-World*, opens by situating action and its understanding with reference to consciousness, as Schutz had done in his earliest works. One phantasies projects "within the framework of the practicable," but the voluntative fiat of a decision sets in motion a course of action that can undergo planned and unplanned interruptions, calling at times for the development of "decision trees." Though the idea of unrestricted rationality of action can illuminate the constitution of rational action in everyday reality, one ought to assess an act's rationality, not from the standpoint of omniscience, "but rather in regard to the knowledge that an actor *could* have had in a concrete, historical life-world." Schutz and Luckmann distinguish various forms of social action: between Consociates, immediate and either unilateral or reciprocal, and between Contemporaries, mediate and either reciprocal or unilateral. In unilateral mediate relationships, one hides one's action aimed at the other by packaging it among other acts, as do advertisers or propagandists, or one conceals one's authorship of an act or takes precautions against receiving an answer. In societies with a highly developed communication technology, unilateral mediate acts become preponderant and do not allow answers—precisely the problem that led to Schutz's critique of anonymous majoritarian democracy in his memorandum to Harold Laswell.[14]

The final chapter places Schutz's discussion of transcendencies in his essay on symbols within a new framework of little, medium, or great transcendencies, depending on whether these transcendencies have to do with something temporally or spatially "out of reach," other persons, or what lies beyond everyday life. Although "rationalist" worldviews absolutize the province of everyday life and deny the claims to reality of other provinces of meaning, it is possible to place in question the pragmatic motives of everyday life. One boundary of the life-world seems particularly uncrossable—namely, death—since one cannot even "experience" one's own death, even though one knows that one will die on the basis of others' deaths and one's own aging. While death places in question all one's life-world relevances, the meaning death assumes depends on the interpretations available in one's stock of knowledge and the degree of credibility one assigns them.[15]

At the end of this biography, it is tempting to speculate upon the major transitions in Schutz's own scholarly work, mindful, of course, that a complete account of these transitions would require a more careful textual analysis and could easily occupy a full chapter rather than a few paragraphs. It is clear that from the beginnings of his academic career in 1919 Schutz read Max Weber and that in the period 1924–28 he assimilated the work of Bergson before turning to Husserl around 1928 and producing *The Phenomenology of the Social World* in 1932. His *Phenomenology* gave him a basis with which to criticize through essays reductionistic tendencies in economics and the social sciences, particularly in the work of his mentor Mises, and to rehabilitate Weberian types, especially the *Homo oeconomicus*. Another key shift—perhaps more of a deepening of his phenomenology—took place in the manuscript "The Problem of Personality in the Social World," which developed notions of action and choice, integrated Leibnizian insights, and presented the *Wirkwelt* and its modifications, the various provinces of meaning, into which one "leapt." This manuscript, written in 1936–37, set the stage for "On Multiple Realities" (1945) and "Choosing among Projects of Action" (1951) and played a central role as late as 1954 in "Symbol, Reality, and Society" and posthumously in *Structures of the Life-World*. Just as the unpublished manuscript on personality bore fruit for more than twenty years, so Schutz's unpublished "Fragments toward a Phenomenology of Music" (1944) revealed the "tuning-in" relationship so basic to "Making Music Together" in 1951. In addition, a normative notion of democracy first appeared in the 1946 essay "The Well-Informed Citizen," and Schutz developed further normative dimensions of democracy in the 1956 Ethics Institute. Certainly Schutz must have been provoked to venture into the realm of normativity at least in part due to his exchange with Voegelin on Husserl's *Crisis* in 1943, in which the question of the validity of relevance schemes beyond their mere description was central. Schutz's understanding of relevance, the focus of a 1929 outline, continually developed throughout his career, particularly in the pragmatically oriented manuscripts of 1936–37, in the published works pursuant to those manuscripts, and in the relevance manuscripts authored from 1947 to 1951, which received fuller exposition in the posthumous *Structures of the Life-World*.

Early in the 1940s, Schutz's essays on applying scientific rationality to the less-rational social world found correlates in the Tiresias essay begun in 1942 and in the Goethe manuscripts (1948), with the final draft of Tiresias (1959) being also influenced by "Type and Eidos in Husserl's Late Philosophy" (1959). Although as early as 1940 Schutz showed himself critical of Husserl's approach to intersubjectivity in the Fifth Meditation, critical comments appear more regularly in the correspondence with Gurwitsch in the mid 1950s, particularly after translating (with Natanson) *Ideas 2* and *3* and writing on them. This critical strand, of course, climaxed in the 1957 Royaumont essay on transcendental phenomenology. To be sure, Schutz never abandoned phenomenology itself, and throughout his career one finds essays relying most heavily on Husserl and his own *Phenomenology*, even at the end of his life. The emerging picture is not one of major breaks in thought, but a development in which new themes burgeon, especially those of the personality essay (action, choice, *Wirkwelt*, finite provinces of meaning), rationality and the social world, and the critique of Husserl—all within a continually expanding vision. Indeed, *The Structures of the Life-World* was to be the work that brought these diverse strands into a single synthetic whole.[16]

According to Ilse Schutz, the influence of her husband's work spread after his death and the publication of posthumous works, due to efforts by Maurice Natanson, Fred Kersten, and Dorion Cairns. As a result of their efforts and others', the three volumes of *Collected Papers* have now appeared in Chinese, English, French, German, Italian, and Japanese, and other books have been translated into Danish, Hungarian, Polish, Portuguese, and Ukranian. A fourth volume of *Collected Papers,* under the editorship of Helmut Wagner and George Psathas in collaboration with Fred Kersten, appeared in 1996 and another volume is being planned. Lester Embree makes the following observation about the expansive presence and influence of Schutz's thought on the basis of the secondary literature:

> The secondary bibliography on Alfred Schutz developed by research assistants at Erlangen, Florida Atlantic, and Waseda Universities and published in 1999 on the website of the Center for Advanced Research in Phenomenology, Inc., contains over 1,400 items. These items are chiefly in English, French, German, Italian, Portuguese, Spanish, and Japanese and also chiefly in Communications, Economics, Education, Ethnology, Geography, History, Management Studies, Medicine, Nursing, Occupational Therapy, Philosophy, Political Sciences, Psychology, Psychotherapy, Psychiatry, Religious Studies, and Women's Studies. That is seventeen disciplines, sixteen outside of philosophy.[17]

Successors

Ilse Schutz learned to manage her husband's finances, arranged for a second edition of *Der sinnhafte Aufbau* in Vienna, and decided to publish *Collected Papers* with Martinus Nijhoff. All these endeavors reflected her decisiveness after seeking assistance from others: "But then I realized that everybody's life is so full of its own responsibilities and tasks, so they couldn't work full time on someone else's work. So I took it into my own hands and I devoted my entire time to it." Behind the scenes, until her death in 1990, she arranged and supervised projects, mediated disputes, and provided business expertise for the students and followers of Schutz in America and Germany who edited, translated, and won public acclaim for their own and Schutz's work. Evelyn Schutz Lang started as a successful systems analyst beginning in the 1950s, at a time when business was starting to make use of electronic data processing. She then founded a company in 1964 that managed the computer facilities of major corporations; she retired as the company president thirty-four years later. George was a protégé of Leonard Bernstein, and, as a composer and performer, he was involved in creating New York's *Mostly Mozart* programs. Following his father's example, he combined a life of business and music by inviting well-known European musicians to perform in New York.[18]

Gurwitsch finally came to the New School in 1959 as Schutz's successor. He played a key role in founding the Society for Phenomenology and Existential Philosophy in 1962 and in keeping "phenomenology" in its title. While at the New School he published *Studies in Phenomenology and Psychology*, and a collection of his essays on physics, logic, psychology, and the human sciences was posthumously published as *Phenomenology and the Theory of Science*. He died in 1973, having devoted much of his last decade to the production of *Leibniz: Philosophie des Panlogismus*, published in 1974. The earlier work he had done on a Leibnizian reading of Kant posthumously appeared as *Kants Theorie des Verstandes* in 1990.[19]

Eric Voegelin, successfully established the Institute of Political Science at Munich, where he experienced teaching success with graduate students in Munich and published *Anamnesis: Zur Theorie der Geschichte und Politik*. He then returned to the United States in 1969 as a distinguished scholar at Stanford, and in 1974 he published the fourth volume of his *Order and History*, *The Ecumenic Age*. Volume 5, *In Search of Order*, appeared in 1987, two years after his death.[20]

Marvin Farber continued serving as editor of *PPR* until his death in1974, and he held numerous administrative positions at other universities before completing his career as Distinguished Professor at the State University of New York at Buffalo. In 1966 he published *The Aims of Phenomenology*. This was largely a work of critical exposition of Husserl, but in his *Phenomenology and Existence*, published one year later, he stressed his own empiricist, realist, critical naturalist position.[21]

Fritz Machlup moved to Princeton in 1960 and then to New York University in 1971, and he continued publishing works that showed the influence of Schutz, such as his multivolume *The Production and Distribution of Knowledge in the United States* and *Methodology of Economics and Other Social Sciences*. When he died in 1983, he had published more than two dozen books and two hundred fifty articles.[22]

Maurice Natanson stayed at Chapel Hill, North Carolina, until changes in the early sixties led him to accept a visiting professorship at the University of California at Berkeley and a professorship at the University of California at Santa Cruz in 1965. He moved on to Yale University in 1976. He published extensively on philosophy and phenomenology, and philosophy/phenomenology and the social sciences, death, psychiatry, and literature. Among these publications were six books, including *Edmund Husserl: Philosopher of Infinite Tasks*, which won the National Book Award in 1974; *Anonymity: A Study in the Philosophy of Alfred Schutz*; and *The Erotic Bird: Phenomenology in Literature*, completed just before his death in 1996. Natanson's work extended Schutz's work into new areas, trying, for instance, to develop the *philosophy* that Schutz never wrote, so preoccupied was he with the *phenomenology* of the natural attitude. Hence Natanson took anonymity as a transcendental clue to such philosophy by focusing on what was constantly lost by anonymization and by utilizing it to locate what was individual, namely, the career of the individual I. He uncovered the presence of phenomenology in literature by illustrating how great literature depicted themes also addressed by phenomenological analysis, especially the taking for granted of human existence in the life-world. Natanson further illustrated how phenomenological practice could thematize the life-world and reconstruct it within transcendental subjectivity.[23]

Similarly, Thomas Luckmann and Peter Berger brought symbolic interactionism and Schutz's phenomenology into a sociological synthesis that explained how reality was socially constructed in its objective structures and the internalization of these structures in subjectivity. In addition, Luckmann published works on the sociology of language and sociology of religion.[24]

Schutz's thought had its influence upon various intellectual movements that succeeded him. For instance, his work served as a necessary but not sufficient condition for the emergence of ethnomethodology, which originated with Harold Garfinkel and drew upon the resources of symbolic interactionism and Talcott Parsons's sociology. Various commentators have debated the complex relationship between ethnomethodology and phenomenology, with Garfinkel repeatedly acknowledging phenomenology as a part of his own intellectual heritage, even though he himself had set out in distinctive directions.[25]

George Psathas has defined ethnomethodology as "a reflexive social practice, which seeks to explicate the methods of all social practices, including its own." Like Schutz's phenomenology, ethnomethodology seeks to criticize the suppositions of sociological theory, to return to common sense at the basis of such theory, to illuminate the features taken for granted in the natural attitude (through "breaching experiments"), and to take account of the subjective viewpoint of the actor. In accord with Schutz's understanding of social science, ethnomethodology has striven for value-free (nonjudgmental) descriptions of the practices of group members, utilizing concepts from Schutz's repertoire such as action in concert with others or the looking glass (e.g., Agnes, a transsexual, inteprets her family's interpretation of her interpretation of them). Like Schutz, ethnomethodology has depicted actors in a "humanistically significant" manner, refusing to portray them as rule-following judgmental "dopes" insofar as they adapt creatively to novel settings, live up to standards while learning what they are, and maneuver within novel situational possibilities that no rule system covers. Phenomenology may have most influenced ethnomethodology not to take social facts for brute givens, not even the practices of normal sexuality, which might be commonly taken to be "natural," but rather to disclose the accomplishments and achievements of group members that lie behind them and often remain anonymous. This ethnomethodological effort resembles Schutz's own struggle, from the moment he integrated Husserl's *Formal and Transcendental Logic* within his *Phenomenology*, to reveal the hidden performances of subjectivity behind any action given at face value.[26]

Of course, these similarities ought not obscure the differences between ethnomethodology and phenomenology. From the phenomenological side, critics have pointed out that ethnomethodology lacks sufficient appreciation for the objective quality of social fact, intentionality, the nature of the self, the transsituational character of meaning, the distinction between knowing and doing, and the difference between the planes of lay and sociotheoretical reflection. However, in the latter respect, defenders of ethnomethodology have contrasted the commonsense actor's interest in producing society with the sociologist's interest in knowing how that society is produced. Indeed, Psathas's view that the ethnomethodologist's own practice could itself be investigated ethnomethodologically breaks down the lay/theoretician distinction, but by employing the kind of self-reflexivity and self-referentiality that Husserl himself might find admirable. The real point of contention, however, might be located in the fact that Schutz describes the *structures* of the social world *eidetically*, whereas ethnomethodologists try to explain how concrete members, indexed to concrete social settings, accomplish activities. The structural-eidetic features of Schutz's analyses perhaps led Psathas to conclude that for him members of a social group would expect each new situation to be seen as typically the same, even though for Schutz, typifications are notoriously tentative and "explodable." Paradoxically, Schutz, who labored to uncover the anonymous subjective activity behind statically given products, ends up with a structural eidetic account of the social world that can appear as a static given when viewed from an ethnomethodological account of the ongoing processes by which members constitute a concrete social group. Of course, ethnomethodology's effort to recover this lost vitality, while criticizing Schutz, actually continues the trajectory that he himself commenced.[27]

Another movement affected by Schutz's work is the field of conversation analysis, which Garfinkel anticipated in discussions of "unpacking a conversation" and the importance of the serial ordering of expressions and which interactional studies by R. F. Bales and others preceded. In the late 1950s and early 1960s Harvey Sacks, in collaboration with Emanuel Schegloff and Gail Jefferson, played a principal role in founding this field. Sacks, in addition to studying with Garfinkel at the University of California in Berkeley, was also familiar with the work of Erving Goffman, also at Berkeley, and was influenced by Wittgenstein's ordinary language philosophy, Noam Chomsky's transformational grammar, anthropological studies, and Milman Parry's and Eric Havelock's studies of oral cultures. Sacks, Schegloff, and Jefferson have focused on such topics as the identification and recognition sequences in telephone conversations, summons-answer patterns, and turn-taking; and other studies have focused on the reception of compliments (Pomerantz), giving directions (Psathas), and emergency calls (Zimmerman). The method of conversation analysis, utilized in several hundred studies over three decades of research, has appeared in such diverse areas as anthropology, communication research, sociology, and sociological subbranches such as sociology of deviance and criminology, sociology of children, and various approaches to interaction.[28]

George Psathas has summarized the procedure of conversation analysis as follows:

> It takes up the problem of studying social life in situ, in the most ordinary of settings, examining the most routine, everyday, naturally occurring activities in their concrete details. Its basic position is that social actions are meaningful for those who produce them and that they have a natural organization that can be discovered and analyzed by close examination. Its interest is in finding the machinery, the rules, the structures that produce and constitute that orderliness. Such examination requires the avoidance of pre-formulated theoretical or

> conceptual categories and the adoption of an open-mindedness and willingness to be led by the phenomena of study.[29]

Although conversation analysis differs from ethnomethodology, since the latter has tended to use disruptive contrivances and to avoid systematic renditions of social life that can obscure its actuality, they also complement each other with conversation analysis affording a direct line of inquiry for the ethnomethodology that provides its roots. In Psathas's own summary and other descriptions of conversation analysis's focus on "the invisible practices of common sense"—which, as Garfinkel noted, require "discovery"—one hears echoes of Schutz's voice. In addition, when Psathas repeatedly emphasizes the importance of conversation analysis as an "explicatory" rather than "explanatory" method that rejects preformed, preformulated, and reductionistic category systems that impose themselves upon a phenomenon, obscuring or distorting it, one feels the impetus of Schutz. For Schutz continually strove to uncover the constitutive activities of a hidden subjectivity behind already formed products and to unearth the living stranger that anonymization processes may have buried.[30]

Appendix: The Courses Schutz Taught

Spring 1943 Introduction to Sociological Theory (Sociology)

Fall 1943 Theory of Social Action (Sociology)
Spring 1944 Mead (Philosophy and Sociology)

Fall 1944 Social Groups and Problems of Adjustment (Sociology)
Problems of a Sociology of Knowledge (Sociology)
Spring 1945 Theory of Social Action (Sociology)

Fall 1945 Social Groups and Problems of Adjustment (Sociology)
Spring 1946 Theory of Social Action (Sociology)

Fall 1946 Situations of Everyday Life and Current Events in the Light of Sociological Theory (Sociology)
Spring 1947 Problems of a Sociology of Knowledge (Sociology)

Fall 1947 Theory of Social Action (Sociology)
Spring 1948 Situations of Everyday Life (Sociology)

Fall 1948 Theory of Social Action (Sociology)

Fall 1949 Situations of Everyday Life (Sociology)
Self and Society (Sociology)
Spring 1950 Situations of Everyday Life (Sociology)
Problems of a Sociology of Language (Sociology)

Fall 1950 Theory of Social Action (Sociology)
The Concept of the "Social Role" (Sociology)
Theory of the Social Group (Sociology)
Spring 1951 Theory of the Social Group (Sociology)
Methodology of the Social Sciences (Philosophy)

Fall 1951 Self and Society (Sociology)
Problems of a Sociology of Knowledge (Sociology)
Spring 1952 Methodology of the Social Sciences (Philosophy)
Man and His Tools: Theory of Technical Progress

1952–53 Problems of a Sociology of Language (Sociology)
The Concept of the "Social Role" (Sociology)
Methodology of the Social Sciences (Philosophy)

1953–54 The Problem of Other Minds (Philosophy)
Theory of Social Action (Sociology)
Theory of the Social Group (Sociology)

1954–55 Problems of a Sociology of Knowledge (Sociology)
Self and Society (Sociology)
Methodology of the Social Sciences (Philosophy)

1955–56 Problems of a Sociology of Language (Sociology)
The Concept of the "Social Role" (Sociology)
Sign and Symbol (Philosophy)

Fall 1956 Theory of the Social Group (Sociology)
Equality, Prejudice, and Discrimination (Sociology)
Spring 1957 Methodology of the Social Sciences (Philosophy)
Theory of Social Action (Sociology)
Contemporary European Philosophy (Philosophy)

Fall 1957 Self and Society (Sociology)
Seminar in Applied Sociological Theory (Sociology)
Spring 1958 Methodology of the Social Sciences (Philosophy)
Causality (Philosophy)
William James and Henri Bergson (Philosophy)

(Courses announced but not given)
Fall 1958 Sign and Symbol (Philosophy)
Problems of a Sociology of Language (Sociology)
The Problem of Other Minds (Philosophy)

Notes

Chapter 1

1. "Alfred Schutz: Civil Service Application," folder 821, The Papers of Alfred Schutz, (henceforth PAS) Beinecke Rare Book and Manuscript Library, Yale University, General Manuscripts 129, Series III, Subject Files and Correspondence; "Personal and Financial Affidavits for Alfred Schutz," folder 823, PAS; Envelope labeled "Einwanderungsangelegenheit Eltern," from Otto ("Peter") Schutz, 13 May 1938, The Personal Papers of Alfred Schutz (henceforth PPAS) in possession of Evelyn S. Lang, New York; Family Documents, 1939, PPAS; Beller, *Vienna and the Jews*, 1–2, 49–50.

2. Ilse Schutz, interview by Anne Schwabacher at Fordham University, New York, 10 Nov. 1981, 16.

3. Affidavit sworn to in New York, 14 Dec. 1941, PAS.

4. Ibid.

5. To Peter and Hansi, 16 July and other undated letters, PPAS; Book Orders, folder 425, PAS; Clippings, Folder 485, PAS.

6. Poems dedicated to Parents, Christmas, 1914, PPAS. The German for the poem is the following: Betet mich an, ihr Schwachen, / Ihr, die ihr noch leugnet / Dass ihr Götter seid, / Sinkt in die Knie vor den Starken. / Ich habe mein Schicksal / In meiner Hand. / Ich schmiede selber / Mein eigenes Los. / Ich bin allem mir / Der einzige Gott. / Und ich bin stark.

7. "Vera's Tagebuch," PPAS. This translation is my own, and anywhere my translations appear, they will be acknowledged as my own.

8. Ilse Schutz, interview by Anne Schwabacher, 17; folders 821 and 825, PAS; "Civil Service Application," 7 Apr. 1943, PAS; Rozenblitt, *Jews of Vienna*, 72–73, 102–8. For Schutz's grade school education and love of Goethe at an early age, see Mori, "Alfred Schutz and the Imperial Capital Vienna," 6.

9. "Ford Foundation Applications Fund for the Advancement of Education," "Proposal to Clarence Faust given to President Hans Simons, Hans Staudinger, and Dean Arthur L, Swift," pp. 3–4, PAS. On the gymnasium system, see Beller, *Vienna and the Jews,* 1–2, 49–50.

10. Beller, *Vienna and the Jews,* 68.

11. Ilse Schutz, interview by Anne Schwabacher, 17–18; Biographical introduction to the Catalogue of The Papers of Alfred Schütz, The Beinecke Rare Book and Manuscript Library, Yale University, 4; Vita contained in file entitled "United States Office of Economic Warfare," folder 820, PAS. Ilja Srubar believed that he was an

educated person, joining the army as an *einfähriger Freiwilliger*, not an officer, but a soldier with special rights to visit courses needed to become an officer.

12. To Ilse Schutz, 8 May 1938, PPAS; to Ilse, and official document signed by Alfred Schutz with receipt of payment from the German Embassy in Paris, 18 May 1938, PPAS; note from the Bundesministerium für Heereswesen in Vienna, 30 May 1918, PPAS: honorable discharge from heavy artillery regiment, 3 Dec.1918, PPAS; picture of Alfred Schutz and military friends, 18 April (1918), PPAS.

13. Brook-Shepherd, *Austrians*, 4–6, 23–28, 38, 41–55, 65; Johnston, *Austrian Mind*, 15–18.

14. Brook-Shepherd, *Austrians*, 77–87, 88, 90–91.

15. Johnston, *Austrian Mind*, 47, 52, 266–70; Brook-Shepherd, *Austrians*, 116–18, 135, 137–50; Alfred Schutz, "Equality and the Meaning Structure of the Social World," 267–68; Ilse Schutz, interview by Anne Schwabacher, 7–8.

16. Brook-Shepherd, *Austrians*, 103–4.

17. Ibid., 115; Beller, *Vienna and the Jews*, 68; Johnston, *Austrian Mind*, 228, 240.

18. Brook-Shepherd, *Austrians*, 111–13, 134; Good, *Economic Rise* 165–66; Matis, "Austria, 234, 237; Preschlenova, "Austro-Hungarian Trade," 232–34; Hertz, *Economic Problem of the Danubian States*, 33, 40, 42, 218; Janik and Toulmin, *Wittgenstein's Vienna*, 50–54; Johnston, *Austrian Mind*, 22, 49–52.

19. McGrath, *Dionysian Art*, 10–11, 17, 40, 43, 45–46, 56–57, 60, 74, 87, 89, 100–104, 109, 112, 147, 172; Schorske, *Fin-de-Siècle Vienna*, 197, 199, 208, 236, 303.

20. McGrath, *Dionysian Art*, 27–28, 32, 196, 208–11, 215, 231, 237; Schorske, *Fin-de-Siècle Vienna*, 282.

21. Schorske, *Fin-de-Siècle Vienna*, 11, 13, 15, 20, 22, 36, 63–64, 69, 70, 72, 74–75, 87, 91, 212, 214, 217, 219, 221–23, 231, 247, 251, 281–309, 312, 323, 332, 343, 359, 363, 345, 346, 348, 358, 360–61; Janik and Toulmin, *Wittgenstein's Vienna*, 102–19. Johnston, *Austrian Mind*, 392. See Berger, "Das Problem der mannigfaltigen Wirklichkeiten," 229–51.

22. Janik and Toulmin, *Wittgenstein's Vienna*, 33–34, 46, 48, 64–66. See Schorske, *Fin-de-Siècle Vienna*, 9, 11, 18–19. To Marvin Farber, 26 Mar. 1951, 4 June 1951, PAS; Ilse Schutz, interview by Anne Schwabacher, 22; Johnston, *Austrian Mind*, 71, 99, 119–22, 174–80, 226, 335.

23. Brook-Shepherd, *Austrians*, 45, 95–103, 133; Beller, *Vienna and the Jews*, 20, 33–35, 70, 90–91, 106, 122–25, 132–35, 139, 142–43, 144–64, 167, 176, 188, 191, 193, 203, 215, 218, 230–36; Rozenblitt, *Jews of Vienna*, 1, 3, 6–7, 10–11, 17, 27, 29, 48–54, 71, 90–91, 104–5, 113, 123–24, 127, 128, 132, 142, 144, 148, 154–55, 157–58, 161–69, 170–71, 178–79, 185, 188–92, 193, 194, 195–96; Johnston, *Austrian Mind*, 3, 15, 27–28, 61, 71, 138, 344; Janik and Toulmin, *Wittgenstein's Vienna*, 54–56. Schorske, *Fin-de-Siècle Vienna*, 67; Ilse Schutz, interview by Anne Schwabacher, 3–4.

24. Schutz, "Equality and the Meaning Structure of the Social World," 257; Johnston, *Austrian Mind*, 3; Schutz, "On Multiple Realities," 231; and Alfred Schutz, "Symbol, Reality, and Society," 329–39; from Lois Natanson, 8 Jan. 1955, PAS; from

Maurice Natanson, 13 Nov. 1954, 26 Dec. 1955, PAS; to Aron Gurwitsch, 22 Feb. 1941 and 27 Mar. 1958, in *Philosophers in Exile,* 33–34, 286; to Fritz Machlup, 4 Jan. 1934, 13 Oct. 1938, PAS; to Eric Voegelin, 7 Dec.1942, 2 Nov. 1952, PAS; from Eric Voegelin, 6 Jan. 1949, 30 Apr. 1951, PAS; to Friedrich Hayek, Jan. 4, 1944, PAS; from Marvin Farber, 22 Aug. 1949, 15 Apr. 1957, PAS; to Rudolf Boehm, 6 May 1959, PAS; Clippings, PAS, Folder 485; from Hansi, 27 Mar.1939, PPAS; Ilse Schutz, interview by Anne Schwabacher, 24, 30, 50–51. On Christmas greetings and other matters, see: to Maurice Nédoncelle, 10 Mar. 1958, PAS; from Jacques Maritain, no date, PAS; Christmas card from Philip Merlan, PAS; from Susan Aron, 2 Sept. 1940, PAS; from Luis Recasens Siches, Christmas, 1955, PAS; from the Spiegelbergs, Christmas, 1947; Christmas, 1948, PAS; to Richard Hays Williams, 22 Dec. 1941, PAS; from Franciska Glas to Ilse Schutz, 30 July 1938, PPAS; from Hansi, 20 Dec. 1938, PPAS. Evelyn Schutz attended Fielston High School, run by the Ethical Cultural Society, according to George Schutz, interview by Michael Barber, Woodstock, New York, 11 Mar. 2002.

25. Brook-Shepherd, *Austrians*, 151, 182, 216–17, 222–33; Janik and Toulmin, *Wittgenstein's Vienna* 247; Johnston, *Austrian Mind,* 73.

26. Brook-Shepherd, *Austrians*, 234–35; Charles A. Gulick, *Labor's Workshop of Democracy*, 59, 64–65, 70, 89–99, 164–65, 144, 176, 354; Ilse Schutz, interview by Anne Schwabacher, 18; Johnston, *Austrian Mind,* 73; Mototaka Mori situates Schutz within the Liberal group at the University of Vienna in opposition to Socialists (under Max Adler) and Christian Socialists (under the leadership of Othmar Spann); see Mori, "Alfred Schutz and the Imperial Capital Vienna," 10, 12.

27. Brook-Shepherd, *The Austrians*, 239, 252–54; Gulick, Labor's Workshop of Democracy, 99, 110–13, 192, 194; see Janik and Toulmin, *Wittgenstein's Vienna,* 237, 241 on the efforts of intellectuals like Kelsen and others to effect political and social reform after the monarchy.

28. Brook-Shepherd, *Austrians*, 256–75, 286–94, 296, 300–2, 307–33, 342–45; Gulick, *Leber's Workshop of Democracy* 129–32, 171, 178, 247–55, 342.

29. Curriculum vitae prepared for the Office of Economic Warfare in 1943, PAS. For a list of the courses Schutz took after he registered in the fall of 1918 at the university, see Mori, "Alfred Shutz and the Imperial Capital Vienna," table 1.

30. Alfred Schutz, interview by Bettina Greaves, The Schutz Archives at Waseda University, Tokyo, under the direction of Professor Hisashi Nasu, 20 Nov. 1958, 3–5; Fritz Machlup, interview by George Schutz, 1976.

31. Wagner, *Alfred Schutz*, 12; Engel-Janosi, . . . *Aber ein stolzer Bettler*, 59, 61–64, 69–10, 110–19, in particular deals with the Mises circle; see Fritz Machlup, interview by George Schutz, 1976. Prendergast, "Alfred Schutz and the Austrian School of Economics," 1976: 6.

32. Alfred Schutz, interview by Bettina Greaves, p. 3; Schutz, "Toward a Viable Sociology", 75–83; Alfred Schutz, "Understanding and Acting," 84–87; Wagner, *Alfred Schutz*, 12; Haberler, "Mises' Private Seminar," 190–92; Fritz Machlup, interview by George Schutz.

33. Folder 632, PAS (This translation is mine.); Haberler, "Mises' Private Seminar," 192.

34. For examples of such letters see the following: to Felix Kaufmann, 19 Apr. 1932, 24 Sept. 1932, 24 June 1935, 26 Sept. 1935, 29 May 1938, 31 July 1938, 26

Dec. 1938, Correspondence between Felix Kaufmann and Alfred Schutz (henceforth CFK/AS), from Felix Kaufmann, 28 Oct. 1935, Correspondence between Felix Kaufmann and Alfred Schutz; from Fritz Machlup, 10 Jan. 1936, 22 Mar. 1938, 12 Apr. 1938, 12 May 1938, 20 June 1938, 4 May 1940, PAS; to Fritz Machlup, 26 Jan. 1936, 23 May 1936, 29 Mar. 1938, 26 Apr. 1938, 12 Oct. 1938, PAS; to Eric Voegelin, 2 Sept. 1940, 12 Jan. 1943, PAS; from Eric Voegelin, 26 July 1946, PAS. See Felix Kaufmann, review of *Der sinnhafte Aufbau der sozialen Welt*, by Alfred Schutz: 1712–16; from Friedrich Hayek, 13 Oct. 1938, 3 Nov. 1938, 26 Nov. 1938, PAS; to Gottfried Haberler, 4 Sept. 1941, 15 Sept. 1941, PAS. On stocks and other concrete matters see: to Fritz Machlup, 31 Mar. 1937, 8 Dec. 1942, 15 Jan. 1943, 11 Mar. 1943, 14 Apr. 1946, 16 Apr. 1946, 27 Apr. 1946, 9 Nov. 1954, 14 Nov. 1954, 9 Dec. 1954, PAS; from Fritz Machlup, 4 Jan. 1939, PPAS; Fritz Machlup to Mr. L.A. Chamberlain, 15 Mar. 1954, PAS; from Walter Froehlich, 27 Mar. 1946, 6 Apr. 1946, 26 Apr. 1946, 6 Oct.1951, PAS.

35. Schutz, interview by Bettina Greaves, 3, 5, 6–7, 8; to Ludwig von Mises, 25 July 1940, PAS; cable to Fritz Machlup, 29 July 1940, PAS; to Walter Froehlich, no date, PAS; from Ludwig von Mises, 16 Sept.1938, PPAS; Ilse Schutz to Mises, no date (within the June 1938 folder), PPAS. In the interview with Greaves, Schutz criticizes Mises on two counts: his obsession with a pure liberalism with no welfare or socialist provisions of any kind, a stance Schutz thought was not politically possible; and his refusal to make use of mathematics in economics, a refusal Schutz traced to his poor relationship with his mathematician-brother, Richard Mises. Only after their mother's death were they again on speaking terms. See Schutz, interview by Greaves, 9; see also to Fritz Machlup, 14 Mar.1948, PAS; from Fritz Machlup, 28 Mar. 1948, PAS; from Viktor Stadler, 28 Jan. 1939, PPAS.

36. To Marvin Farber, 28 Sept. 1955, 2 Sept. 1942, PAS; from Hans Kelsen, 27 Sept. 1942, 27 June 1945, 3 Aug. 1945, PAS; to Hans Kelsen, 17 Sept. 1942, 7 Oct.1942, PAS.

37. See Sato, "Tomoo Otaka and Alfred Schutz in the 1930s," 1–16. This article contains a letter from Ilse Schutz that described Schutz's relationship with Otaka and was included in the preface of the Japanese translation of *Der sinnhafte Aufbau der sozialen Welt*, which appeared in Tokyo in 1982.

38. Ilse Schutz, interview by Anne Schwabacher, 21–22.

39. Ilse Schutz, interview by Rudi Hartmann in New York, 14 May 1981, 2; George Schutz, interview by Lester Embree, 8 Oct. 1990.

40. "Venedig," 28 Nov. 1922, in *Poems,* Plays by Alfred Schutz, 10 Feb.10, 1925, PPAS (my translation). "Und so es immer mit all'olen Dingen / Die uns begegnen auf unserer Bahn: / Wir glauben zu greifen, sie zu erringen / Und sie sind doch fern . . . und alles ist Wahn. / Und wir, wir gleiten vorbei. / Und so ist immer: Auf unseren Weg / Kommt einmal ein Mensch, ein Mensch uns entgegen. / Er wäre vielleicht . . . Doch wir sind traurig / Und bleiben einsam auf unserem Wegen. / Und gleiten und gleiten vorbei."

41. Embree, "Editor's Introduction," 9–14.

42. Winternitz, "The Role of Music in Leonardo's Paragone," 270.

43. Ilse Schutz, interview by Anne Schwabacher, 19, 28; Vita for United States Office of Economic Warfare, folder 822, PAS; Vita for Civil Service Application, folder 822, PAS; Resumé Fragments, folder 933, PAS.

44. Vita for United States Office of Economic Warfare; Vita for Civil Service Application; Resumé Fragments; from Emil Reitler, 24 Sept. 1943, in Personal and Financial Affidavits for Alfred Schutz, PAS;

45. To Ilse Schutz, 28 Aug. 1936, 31 Aug. 1936, 5 Sept. 1936, 15 Dec. 1936, 28 July 1938, 2 Aug. 1938, 5 May 1939, 9 May 1939, PPAS; from Ilse Schutz, 27 Mar. 1937, 10 June 1937, 20 June 1937, 22 June 1937, 6 Oct. 1937, 9 May, 1939, 10 May 1939, 13 May 1939, PPAS; Ilse Schutz, interview by Rudi Hartmann, 4.

46. Ilse Schutz, interview by Anne Schwabacher, 10 Nov. 1981, 1–14.

47. Ibid.,14–15, 19–20; from Ilse Heim, 19 July 1923, 18 July 1924, PPAS; to Ilse Heim, 25 July 1924 (my translation), 17 Sept. 1924, PPAS; to Liesl Gerstel, 8 Sept. 1925, PPAS; Editorial from Hans Reinhold Steinbach, PPAS.

48. Emmanuel Winternitz, "A Poem with a Hyancinth Dedicated to the Schutz Married Couple," 1927, PAS; to Ilse Schutz, 10 Aug. 1926, PPAS (my translation).

49. Ilse Schutz, interview by Anne Schwabacher, 23.

50. Ibid.; to Ilse Schutz, 5 Oct. 1935, PPAS (my translation).

51. To Ilse Schutz, 10 Sept.1933, PPAS (my translation); see also from Ilse Schutz, 7 Sept. 1933, PPAS.

52. Ilse Schutz, interview by Anne Schwabacher, 23a–24, 48; Ilse Schutz, interview by Rudi Hartmann, 4.

53. Ilse Schutz, interview by Rudi Hartmann, 11, 13; Ilse Schutz, interview by Anne Schwabacher, 20, 42. Richard Zaner cites Ilse's own descriptions of the process of writing in a letter to him: "His book, *Der sinnhafte Aufbau der sozialen Welt*, he dictated to me during many nights and weekends. I took it down in shorthand, typed it and he worked it over again and again, either again dictating, or writing the next version in longhand, which I transcribed then again into typewritten manuscripts. In later years and especially when he wrote in English [whose common vernacular and technical vocabulary Schutz mastered in remarkably short time, Zaner adds] he preferred to write every first draft in longhand. I typed it then and he corrected and changed it again, so there were often three or four or even more versions till he finally was satisified." See Zaner, introduction to *Reflections on the Problem of Relevance*, xxiii n. 53. George Schutz recollected that Ilse typed in seven carbons everything that Alfred gave her George Schutz, interview by Michael Barber. See from Ilse Schutz, 23 July 1929, 25 July 1929, 26 July 1929, 30 July 1929, 31 July 1929, 5 Aug 1929, 6 Oct. 1931, 10 Nov. 1931, 2 Feb. 1935, 23 May 1935, 22 June 1935, 30 June 1935, 5 July 1935, 6 July 1935, 11 July 1935, 16 July 1935, 25 July 1935, 20 Apr. 1936, 28 Apr. 1936, 7 July 1936, 9 July 1936, 27 Mar 1937, 11 Apr. 1937, 26 Oct. 1937, 22 Aug. 1938, PPAS; to Ilse Schutz, 21 July 1935, PPAS.

Chapter 2

1. Schutz, "Husserl and His Influence on Me,": 41; Schutz, "Life Forms and Meaning Structure," 42–43; Schutz, *Collected Papers*, 4: 79, 84–86, 89, 90, 92, 206–7; Fritz Machlup, interview by George Schutz; Eberle, "Die deskriptive Analyse der Oekonomie durch Alfred Schütz," 75; Prendergast, "Alfred Schutz and the Austrian School of Economics," 14–15; Schutz, *Phenomenology of the Social World*, xxxi, 43, 226; to Marianne Weber, 27 Apr. 1932, PAS; from Marianne Weber, 10 May 1932, PAS.

2. Schutz, *Phenomenology of the Social World,* 5; Weber, "Der Sinn der 'Wertfreiheit' " 493–94, 497, 510; Weber, "Meaning of Ethical Neutrality in Sociology and Economics," 18–19, 21–22, 33. See Weber,"'Die 'Objektivität' sozialwissenschaftlicher und sozialpolitischer Erkenntnis," 150–51, 175–76; " 'Objectivity' in Social Science and Social Policy," 54, 76–77; see Srubar, "Wertbeziehung und Relevanz zu Schütz' Weber-Rezeption," 44, 47.

3. Weber, *Wirtschaft und Gesellschaft*, 2–3, 10, 13; Weber, *Economy and Society:* 6–7, 21, 26. See Weber, "Politik als Beruf," 537–42, 547; "Politics as Vocation," 216–19, 224. See Weber, "'Die 'Objektivität' sozialwissenschaftlicher und sozialpolitischer Erkenntnis," 169–70, 171–72, 192–93, 197–98, 203–4; Weber, " 'Objectivity' in Social Science and Social Policy," 71, 73, 92, 96–97, 102–3; Weber, *Max Weber:* 74; Weber, *Protestant Ethic and the Spirit of Capitalism*, 181–83; see Weber, "Der Sinn der 'Wertfreiheit' der soziologischen und ökonomischen Wissenschaften," 515; Weber, "Meaning of 'Ethical Neutrality' in Sociology and Economics," 37. See Weber, "Zur Lage der bürgerlichen Demokratie in Russland," 46–47, 49–51; Weber, "Prospects for Democracy in Tsarist Russia," 270, 273. See Weber, "Der Sozialismus," 509–11; Weber "Socialism," 261–62; Schutz, *Phenomenology*, 5–7; Weber, *Wirtschaft und Gesellschaft*, 10; Weber, *Economy and Society*, 1:21.

4. Schutz, *Phenomenology of the Social World,* 5–7; Weber, " 'Die 'Objektivität' sozialwissenschaftlicher und sozialpolitischer Erkenntnis," 171–72, 192–93, 197–98, 203–4; Weber, "'Objectivity' in Social Science and Social Policy," 73, 92, 96–97, 102–3; Weber, *Wirtschaft und Gesellschaft*, 10; Weber, *Economy and Society*, 21.

5. Max Weber, "R. Stammlers 'Überwindung' der materialistischen Geschichtsauffassung," 331–36; Weber, "Concept of 'Following a Rule,' " 106–10. See Weber, *Wirtschaft und Gesellschaft*, 4–5; Weber *Economy and Society*, 10–11. See Weber, "Kritischen Studien auf dem Gebiet der kulturwissenschaftlichen Logik," 275–81, 286–87; Weber, "Critical Studies in the Logic of the Cultural Sciences," 173–78, 184–85. See Weber, *Hinduismus und Buddhismus*, 366–67, 370–72; Weber, "Religions of Asia," 193–94, 197–99.

6. Weber, *Wirtschaft und Gesellschaft*, 7; Weber, *Economy and Society*, 14–15; Runciman, "Introduction to 'The Methodology of the Social Sciences,' " 65; Schutz, "Concept and Theory Formation in the Social Sciences," 48–66.

7. Schutz, *Phenomenology of the Social World,* xxxi, 7–12; Alfred Schutz, "Positivistic Philosophy" 123–49, es. 126.

8. Schutz, *Phenomenology of the Social World,* 17–19, 54–63.

9. Ibid., 23–31.

10. Ibid., 31–38.

11. Ibid., 144–50, 151–59, 208.

12. Ibid., 220–41; Weber, *Wirtschaft und Gesellschaft*, 5–6, Weber, *Economy and Society*, 11–12.

13. Schutz, *Phenomenology of the Social World,* 241–49; Weber, *Wirtschaft und Gesellschaft*, 60; Weber, *Economy and Society*, 110; Prendergast, " Alfred Schutz and the Austrian School of Economics," 18.

14. Schutz, "Husserl and his Influence on Me," 41; see also Srubar, "Einleitung: Schutz' Bergson-Rezeption," 8.

15. Schutz, *Life Forms and Meaning Structure*, 4; to see what Wagner leaves out (the second number is Srubar's pagination in Schutz *Theorie der Lebensformen*): 47/

102–3; 50–51/107–8; 55/115–16; 57/119; 58/121; 63–64/127–29; 64–65/130–31; 66/132–33; 89–90/166–69; 92–93/172–74; 106–7/192–93.

16. Schutz, "Life Forms and Meaning Structure," a translation of "Lebensformen and Sinnstruktur," 83; 53–54/112; 70/138; 77–78/113 n. 40/148–50/199 n. 21; Srubar, "Einleitung: Schutz' Bergson-Rezeption," 19–22.

17. Ibid., 34/83, 46/100–1; 49–52/106–10, 67/134, 71/140, 73–76/143–47, 98–99/180–82; Schutz, "Meaning Structures of Language," a translation of "Erleben, Sprache und Begriff," 135/221.

18. Schutz, "Life Forms and Meaning Structure," 23 (no correlative in Srubar's edition).

19. Ibid., 71/140, 98–99/180–82.

20. Ibid.,19/332, 21/334, 41/92, 43/95, 53/111, 59/123, 77/147–48, 79/151, 99–109/182–97; Schutz, "Meaning Structures of Language,"127–28/210–12, 128–34/210–19, 135–51/220–44; Schutz, "Meaning Structure of Literary Art Forms," a translation of "Sinnstruktur der Novelle: Goethe," 160–62/254–56; on the unity of the I, see Schutz, "Meaning Structures of Language," 136/222; see Wagner's comments on 4, 125 in Schutz, *Life Forms and Meaning Structure*. Srubar, *Kosmion*, 60–63; Srubar, "Einleitung: Schutz' Bergson-Rezeption," 35.

21. Schutz, "Life Forms and Meaning Structure," 23/no correlate in German, 34/83, 70/138–39, 98–99/181–82, 115 n. 56/no correlate in German; Schutz, "Meaning Structures of Language," 140–41/229–30. See Max Scheler, *Formalism in Ethics*, 72–99; Scheler, *Nature of Sympathy*, 234–37. See also Heidegger, *Being and Time*, 122–48; Srubar, "Einleitung: Schutz' Bergson-Rezeption," 24, 69; Wagner, *Bergsonian Bridge*, 59–64; see Schutz, "On Multiple Realities," 255–56.

22. Schutz, "Life Forms and Meaning Structure," 32/80, 53/110–11, 59/123, 70/139, 78–79/149–51, 99/182; Schutz, "Meaning Structures of Language," 136/222; Wagner, "Bergsonian Period of Alfred Schutz," 198; Wagner, *Bergsonian Bridge*, 44, 59, 64, 105, 125, 131; Srubar, "Einleitung: Schutz' Bergson-Rezeption," 67; Schutz, "Husserl and His Influence on Me," 42; Schutz, *Phenomenology of the Social World*, 46–53; Husserl, *Zur Phänomenologie des inneren Zeitbewusstseins (1893–1917)*, 81–82, 116–20, translated under the title *On the Phenomenology of the Consciousness of Internal Time (1893–1917)*, 85–86, 120–24; Srubar, *Kosmion*, 93–95, 104, 105. John Brough, translater of Husserl's work on consciousness of internal time, has also written in the areas of aesthetics and temporality.

23. Schutz, "Life Forms and Meaning Structure," 34/82, 43/95–96; Schutz, "Meaning Structures of Language," 127–28/211–12; Wagner, "Bergsonian Period of Alfred Schutz," 190; Wagner, *Bergsonian Bridge*, 34–35; Wagner, "Editor's Note," 122; Srubar, *Kosmion*, 126–28; Srubar, "Einleitung: Schutz' Bergson-Rezeption," 57–58, 64.

24. Schutz, *Phenomenology of the Social World*, 99.

25. Schutz, "Life Forms and Meaning Structure," 49/105, 66/133–34, 68–69/136–37, 71–72/140–42; Schutz, "Meaning Structures of Language," 142/230–31; Schutz, "Meaning Structures of Literary Art Forms," 160–62/252–55; Schutz, "Understanding and Acting," 86.

26. Schutz, "Life Forms and Meaning Structure," 44–48/96–104, 62–66/126–34, 74/143–45; Wagner, "Bergsonian Period of Alfred Schutz," 191.

27. Schutz, *Phenomenology of the Social World*, 66–69; Schutz, "Choosing among Projects of Action," 72, 86, 91–92; Schutz, "Political Economy," 4, 98–99; Schutz,

"Basic Concepts and Methods of the Social Sciences," 127; Bergson, *Time and Free Will*, 140–221.

28. Schutz, *Phenomenology of the Social World,* 12–13, 102–7.

29. Schutz, "Husserl's Importance for the Social Sciences," 141; Schutz, "On Multiple Realities," 212, 215, 240; Schutz, "Language, Language Disturbances, and the Texture of Consciousness," 275, 284; Schutz, "Symbol, Reality, and Society," 293, 300, 338, 344; Schutz, "Don Quixote and the Problem of Reality," 139; Schutz, "Making Music Together," 170; Schutz, "Mozart and the Philosophers," 196; Schutz, "Problem of Transcendental Intersubjectivity in Husserl," 72–73; Schutz, "Realities from Daily Life to Theoretical Contemplation," 29; Schutz, "Toward a Viable Sociology," 80–81; Schutz, "Fragments toward a Phenomenology of Music," 249, 255, 257. See Kallen, *William James and Henri Bergson*, 104–5, 197; George Santayana, *Winds of Doctrine and Platonism and the Spiritual Life,* 67–68, 74, 77, 86–87; Srubar comments on Schutz's awareness of the *Lebensphilosophie* tradition of Dilthey and Nietzsche, which he never endorsed, in "Einleitung: Schutz' Bergson-Rezeption," 23; see Wagner, "Bergsonian Period of Alfred Schutz," 195, on Schutz's rejection of Bergson's biological interpretation of psychological processes.

30. Schutz, "Life Forms and Meaning Structure," 72–73/141–42; Schutz, "Meaning Structure of Language," 128–29/212–14; Schutz, "Meaning Structures of Literary Art Forms," 161/253–54.

31. Schutz "Life Forms and Meaning Structure," 33/82, 99/181–82; Wagner, *Bergsonian Bridge*, 10–11; Schutz, *Phenomenology of the Social World,* 36, 103 (two references); Bergson, *Duration and Simultaneity,* 32, 111.

Chapter 3

1. Schutz, "Husserl and His Influence on Me," 41–43; Prendergast, "Alfred Schutz and the Austrian School of Economics," 4–5.

2. From Edmund Husserl, 3 May 1932, PAS. The translation is mine.

3. Schutz, "Husserl and His Influence on Me," 43–44; Schutz, review of *Méditations cartésiennes*, 2404–16; Schutz, review of *Formale und transzendentale Logik:* 773–84; from Eugen Fink, 25 Oct. 1932, 22 Dec. 1932, 14 Feb. 1933, PAS; Vita sent by Alfred Schutz to Richard Tirana, Reoccupation Division, Board of Economic Warfare, 18 Mar. 1943, PAS; from Gerhard Husserl, 1 Oct. 1940, PAS; to Gerhard Husserl, 5 Oct. 1940, PAS; to Felix Kaufmann, 16 Sept. 1940, PAS; from Felix Kaufmann, 18 Sept. 1940, PAS; from Marvin Farber, 26 Dec. 1945.

4. Schutz, "Husserl and His Influence on Me," 41–42; Schutz, *Phenomenology of the Social World,* 33, 43–44, 65, 97; Alfred Schutz, "Phenomenology and the Social Sciences," 132.

5. Schutz, "Husserl and His Influence on Me," 42; Schutz, *Phenomenology of the Social World,* 12, 46–53; Husserl, *On the Phenomenology of the Consciousness of Internal Time (1893–1917),* 4–6, 24–25, 31–32, 36–55, 79–80, 122–23, 130–33, 162, 290, 350–54. See also Brough, "Translator's Introduction," xxiii, xxviii, xxxv, xxxviii–xxxix; Schutz, *Phenomenology of the Social World,* 46–53. On the "monothetic"/ "polythetic" distinction, see Edmund Husserl, *Ideas Pertaining to a Pure Phenom-*

enology and to a Phenomenological Philosophy, 1:283–84; Schutz, *Phenomenology of the Social World,* 68.

6. Husserl, *On the Phenomenology of the Consciousness of Internal Time (1893–1917),* 34, 41–43, 77–89, 84–89, 122–23, 237–40, 331, 382, 391–93; Brough, "Translator's Introduction," xix, xxiii, xxxv, xxxvi, xxxviii–xxxix, xliii–xlv, xlvi–xlviii, xlviii–li, liii, lv; Schutz, *Phenomenology of the Social,* 46–53.

7. Schutz, *Phenomenology of the Social World,* 53–66, 86–96; Edmund Husserl, *On the Phenomenology of the Consciousness of Internal Time (1893–1917),* 54–55; see Cox, *Schutz's Theory of Relevance*, 158, and Schutz, "Type and Eidos in Husserl's Late Philosophy," 113–14.

8. Schutz, *Phenomenology of the Social World,* 65, 229–39.

9. Ibid., 36. See also Husserl, *Formal and Transcendental Logic*, 263; see also Alfred Schutz, review of *Formal and Transendental Logic,* 166–73. See also Schutz, *Phenomenology of the Social World,* 31–37, and Schutz, "Husserl and His Influence on Me," 42.

10. Schutz, *Phenomenology of the Social World,* 37, see also 31–37; "indications" (*Anzeichen*) refers to the technical terminology of Edmund Husserl in *Logical Investigations*, 1:184.

11. Schutz, *Phenomenology of the Social World,* 66–69, 74–86.

12. Ibid., 98–99, 102–7, 109, 120–21, 123, 176–214. See Schutz, "Husserl's Importance for the Social Sciences," 141.

13. Schutz, *Phenomenology of the Social World,* 136–38.

14. Ibid., 97, see also 33; from Eugen Fink, 22 Dec. 1932, PAS; to Marvin Farber, 12 June 1940, PAS; to Aron Gurwitsch, 20 Apr. 1952, *PE*, 178; 23 Aug. 1954, *PE*, 230–31; 1 Jan. 1956, *PE*, 246–47.

15. Schutz, "Husserl and His Influence on Me," 42; Schutz, "Phenomenology and the Social Sciences," 120, 122, 126–27, 132; Husserl, *Cartesian Meditations*, 132–36; Husserl, "Author's Preface to the English Edition," 7–8; Schutz, *Phenomenology of the Social World,* 43–44, 220–21, 241; Kockelmans, "Deskriptive oder interpretieriende Phänomenologie" 37–38.

16. Schutz, "Concept and Theory Formation in the Social Sciences," 63; Weber, "Der Sinn der 'Wertfreiheit' der soziologischen und ökonomischen Wissenschaften," 493–94, 497, 510; Weber, "Meaning of Ethical Neutrality in Sociology and Economics," 18–19, 21–22, 33.

17. Menger, *Principles of Economics*, 58, 115; Kirzner, *Founding Era,* xv–xvi, xxiv; Blaug, "Was There a Marginal Revolution?" 8, 11; Littlechild, *Fallacy of the Mixed Economy*, 14–15; Mises, *Human Action*, 121; Mises, *Epistemological Problems of Economics*, 153; Knight, introduction to *Principles of Economics*, 13–15. Joseph Schumpeter, after leaving Austria, was professor of economics at Harvard, and, along with Parsons, invited Schutz to speak there in 1940.

18. Mises, *Human Action*, 315; Mises, *Epistemological Problems of Economics*, 93.

19. Menger, *Investigations,* 64, 84; Menger, *Principles of Economics*, 115, 146; Mises, *Human Action*, 121–25, 204–5; Stephen Kresge, introduction to *Hayek on Hayek,* 7–8; Hayek, "Place of Menger's *Grundsätze*," 200–1.

20. Menger, *Investigations*, 58–61, 63, 68, 72, 84; Schutz, "Concept and Theory Formation in the Social Sciences," 53, 58; Schutz, "Social World and the Theory of

Social Action," 6–7; Alfred Schutz, "Problem of Rationality in the Social World," 79–80, 84–85; Smith, *Austrian Philosophy,* 337; Fabian and Simons, "Second Austrian School of Value Theory," 84; Grassl, "Markets and Morality," 147–49, 156, 160; Hayek, "Place of Menger's *Grundsätze*," 200–1; Hayek, "Economics and Knowledge," 37, 43–45; Kirzner, *Age of Mises and Hayek* ix; Kresge, introduction to *Hayek on Hayek,* 7–8. On marginal utility see: Mises, *Human Action*, 31, 56, 121–25, 204–5; Eberle, "Die deskriptive Analyse der Oekonomie durch Alfred Schütz," 73–75.

21. Menger, *Investigations*, 8–9, 10, 16, 54, 63–64, 71, 79, 84, 87, 88, 91, 117, 133, 135, 147, 172–77; Menger, *Principles of Economics*, 58, 116, 121, 123, 146; Kirzner, *Founding Era*, x, xv; see Prendergast, "Alfred Schutz and the Austrian School of Economics," 10, 22.

22. Mises, *Epistemological Problems of Economics*, 34–35, 148, 208; Mises, *Human Action*, 10, 19, 63–64, 95–96, 101, 121, 208, 232–34, 239–44, 377, 287; Mises, *Epistemological Problems of Economics*, 181; Eberle, "Die deskriptive Analyse der Oekonomie durch Alfred Schütz," 87.

23. Mises, *Epistemological Problems of Economics*, 95–96, see also 19, 34, 85, 94, 109; Mises, *Human Action*, 69, 85–86.

24. Mises, *Human Action*, 3, 232–34.

25. Ibid., 3, 63–64, 232–33, 240; Mises, *Epistemological Problems of Economics*, 34–35.

26. Mises, *Human Action*, 113, 153, 377, 387; Kirzner, *Founding Era*, xxv.

27. Hayek, "Economics and Knowledge," 45–46; Hayek, "Kinds of Rationalism," 84–95; Hayek, *Hayek on Hayek*, 50–51, 72–73; Kresge, introduction to *Hayek on Hayek,* 18, 32; Littlechild, *Fallacy of the Mixed Economy,* 10, 21. For more on the differences between Hayek and Mises, see Kirzner, *Age of Mises and Hayek*, xii.

28. Wagner, *Alfred Schutz*, 164; Hayek, *Road to Serfdom*, 54, 59, 71, 121, 148, 154, 166, 199, 205, 211, 228, 230; Hayek, "Moral Element in Free Enterprise," 230; Hayek, *Hayek on Hayek*, 58;

29. Schutz, "Basic Problems of Political Economy," 88–92; Schutz, "Political Economy," 98–100, 104; Alfred Schutz, "Choice and the Social Sciences," 574, 585; Schutz, "Concept and Theory Formation in the Social Sciences," 59; Helling, "Alfred Schütz, Felix Kaufmann, and the Economists of the Mises Circle," 43–68; Prendergast, "Alfred Schutz and the Austrian School of Economics," 11–14, 16–22.

30. Sombart, *Die drei Nationalökonomien* 74–83, 289–91, 302–4, 305; Mises, *Epistemological Problems of Economics*, 137–42; Schutz, *Phenomenology of the Social World,* 24–31, 241–49; Schutz, "Concept and Theory Formation in the Social Sciences," 63; Rasmussen, "Explorations of the Lebenswelt," 22–23, and Wolff, "Discussion of Wagner, Imber, and Rasmussen,"31 (reprint from *Human Studies,* 137).

31. Schutz, "Political Economy," 99; Mises, *Human Action*, 62–63, 232–34, 239–43; Mises, *Epistemological Problems of Economics*, 108–9; Schutz, "Meaning Structures of Language," 156 n. 28.

32. Schutz, "Political Economy," 103; Schutz, "Problem of Rationality in the Social World," 87.

33. Schutz, "Political Economy," 102–4; Schutz, *Phenomenology of the Social World,* 243–44.

34. Mises, *Epistemological Problems of Economics*, 84; Schutz, "Choice and the Social Sciences," 568–69, 574–75, 584; Schutz, "Political Economy," 104; Schutz,

"Problem of Rationality in the Social World," 78, 86; Schutz, "On Multiple Realities"; Prendergast, "Alfred Schutz and the Austrian School of Economics," 23.

35. Eberle, "Die deskriptive Analyse der Oekonomie durch Alfred Schütz," 103–14; Schutz, "Political Economy,"103–4.

36. Schutz, "Choice and the Social Sciences," 578.

37. Schutz, "The Well-Informed Citizen," 125.

38. To Marvin Farber, 28 Sept. 1955, PAS; Johnston, *Austrian Mind,* 95–96; to Fritz Machlup, 10 Sept. 1934, PAS; to Hans Kelsen, 17 Sept. 1942, 7 Oct. 1942, PAS; from Hans Kelsen, 27 June 1945, PAS; Paulson, introduction to *Normativity and Norms*, xxiii–xxx; Paulson, "Hans Kelsen's Earliest Legal Theory," 36–37; Kelsen, *Pure Theory of Law*, 19, 64, 67, 75, 77, 79, 81, 87, 90, 98–113, 135, 172–73, 178, 190–91, 195–98, 210, 218–20, 285–87; Hans Kelsen, "'Foreword' to the Second Printing," 13–14, 17–19; Kelsen, *Introduction to the Problems of Legal Theory*, 14, 15–16, 17, 33–34, 44, 46, 56, 58, 63–65, 97, 101; Kelsen, *What Is Justice?* 4, 5, 6, 11, 10–13, 17–18, 20–22, 350; Kaufmann, *Logik und Rechtswissenschaft*, 50, 51, 54, 59, 84, 114, 128; Kaufmann, *Die Kriterien des Rechts*, 5–48, 63–64, 100, 113, 123, 124, 147, 164; Kelsen, " 'Foreword' to the Second Printing," 8; Kaufmann, "Juristischer und soziologicher Rechtsbegriff," 15, 31, 39.

39. Wagner, *Alfred Schutz*, 11; Schutz, "Scholar of Multiple Involvements," 138; Kaufmann, *Logik und Rechtswissenschaft*, 63–82; 83–91; Kaufmann, *Die Kriterien des Rechts*, 78, 95, 102, 104, 109, 111–12, 113, 123, 131–33, 138–39, 142–43, 148, 155–56; Felix Kaufmann, *Methodology of the Social Sciences*, 210; Kaufmann, "Juristischer und sociologischer Rechtsbegriff," 30, 31; Schutz, "Foundations of the Theory of Social Organization," 208, n. 5; Kersten, "Editor's Preface," 203; to Marvin Farber, 2 Sept. 1942, PAS; Pound, *Social Control through Law*, 67, 107, 109; Treviño, introduction to *Social Control through Law*, xlvii; to Marvin Farber, 12 June 1940, PAS.

40. Eric Voegelin, in his notes for a 1957 course entitled "The Nature of Law," felt that Kelsen cut short his own regressive procedure by not grounding law itself in morality (see Eric Voegelin, "The Nature of Law, Mimeograph for Law Course," PAS, Folder 861, 39–78); Pound, *Social Control through Law*, 29, 96–97, 108–9; from Luis Recasens Siches, 9 Sept., 1957, PAS.

Chapter 4

1. Alfred Schutz, folder 673, PAS; to Fritz Machlup, 12 October 1938, PAS; Schutz, "Das Problem der Personalität in der Sozialwelt," folders 222–26, PAS; Ilse Schutz, interview by Anne Schwabacher, 24.

2. Schutz, "Das Problem der Personalität in der Sozialwelt," folder 222, 7066–67, 7072–73, 7077–78, 7080–95. See James, *Principles of Psychology*, 2:501, 519, 521, 528; Scheler, *Problems of a Sociology of Knowledge*, 35, 53–54, 61–62; Scheler, "Zu Lehre von Grund aller Dinge," 192. See Srubar, *Kosmion*, 159 and Schutz, "Political Economy,"103–4; Schutz, "Choice and the Social Sciences," 578.

3. Schutz, "Die Einheit des Leibes," folder 223, 7102–33, PAS (my translation); Ilja Srubar, "Alfred Schütz's Konzeption der Sozialität des Handelns," 145–56.

4. Schutz, "Die Tempora des Ich and ihre perspektivische Aufgliederung," folder 224, 7149–51, PAS (my translation), see also 7134–48, PAS; see Schutz, "Some Leading Concepts of Phenomenology," 115–16; Natanson, *Anonymity,* 120ff.

5. Schutz, "Die Tempora des Ich and ihre perspecktivische Aufgliederung," 7157–58.

6. Ibid., 7152–58.

7. Ilja Srubar notes (*Kosmion,* 133) correctly that Schutz's pragmatic turn took place in this 1936–37 manuscript, before he ever set foot on American soil; Alfred Schutz, "Die Konstitution der Wirkwelt und ihrer Modifikationen," folder 225, 7159–78, PAS, see 7184 on the orientation to theory; see also 7179–88; see also "Die Welt des Traumes," folder 226, 7191, 7193, 7201–2, 7207–11, PAS; see also Schutz, "On Multiple Realities," 230, 234, 255–59.

8. To Raoul Rabinerson, 15 Dec. 1939, PAS; Ilse Schutz, interview by Anne Schwabacher, 30–31.

9. Schutz, "Diary of a Visit to the United States," 23 Mar., 1 Apr., 3 Apr., and 5 Apr., 1937. PPAS.

10. Ibid., 19 Mar., 21 Mar., 27 Mar., 15 Apr., 16 Apr. 1937.

11. Ibid., 21 Mar., 26 Mar., 31 Mar. 1937; Fritz Machlup, interview by George Schutz; Alfred Schutz to Gerhard Husserl, 28 Feb. 1937, The Papers of Dorion Cairns, courtesy of Lester Embree.

12. Schutz "Diary of a Visit to the United States," 18 Mar., 20 Mar., 22 Mar., 25 Mar., 30 Mar., 3 Apr., 14 Apr. 1937.

13. Ibid., entries for 21 Mar., 2 Apr., 4 Apr., 10–11 Apr., 15 Apr. 1937; see Shaw, *Candida,* 111–92. Schutz, Personal and Financial Affidavits for Alfred Schutz, 3 July 1941, PAS. See Winternitz, "Role of Music in Leonardo's Paragone," 270.

14. Schutz, "Diary of a Visit to the United States," 19 Mar., 22 Mar., 23 Mar., 31 Mar., 14 Apr. 1937.

15. Ibid., 22 Mar., 23 Mar., 28 Mar., 1 Apr., 6 Apr. 1937.

16. Ibid., 15 Apr. 1937.

17. Ibid.

18. Ibid., 16 Apr. 1937.

Chapter 5

1. Brook-Shepherd, *Anschluss,* 29, 52, 58, 62, 127, 131, 139–42, 149–58, 164, 172–78, 188–99, 201–3, 209–10; Brook-Shepherd, *Austrians*, 326–33, 342–45; Ilse Schutz, interview by Anne Schwabacher, 28; Schuschnigg, *Austrian Requiem*, 197, 199, 277.

2. From Max Mintz, 22 Mar., 23 Mar. 1938, PPAS; From Ilse Schutz, undated (in "1938 and 1939 Undated File"), PPAS.

3. To Fritz Machlup, 26 Apr. 1938, PAS. My translation.

4. From Ilse Schutz, 29 Mar. 1938, PPAS; from Hansi and Peter, 21 Mar. 1938, 28 Mar. 1938; 10 Apr. 1938, PPAS; from Vilma Thierry, 6 April 1938, 15 Apr. 1938, PPAS; from Eric Heim 11 Apr. 1938, PPAS; from Friedrich Hayek, 17 Apr. 1938, PPAS.

5. From Hansi and Peter, 21 Mar. 1938, 8 Apr. 1938, 10 Apr. 1938, 13 Apr. 1938, 4 May 1938, 6 May 1938, 16 May 1938, 23 May 1938, 30 May 1938, 1 June 1938, 2 June 1938, 3 June 1938, 7 June 1938, 9 June 1938, 11 June 1938, PPAS; to Fritz Machlup, 25 May 1935, 22 Mar. 1938, 29 Mar. 1938, 25 May 1938, 3 Mar. 1939, PAS; from Fritz Machlup, 5 Apr. 1938; 12 May 1938, PAS; from Hella Hayek, 2 Apr. 1938, PPAS; from Friedrich Hayek, 23 Apr. 1938, PPAS; from Vilma Thierry, 10 May 1938, 20 May 1938; 27 May 1938, PPAS; from Felix Kaufmann, 22 May 1938, 27 May 1938, 2 June 1938, PPAS; Schutz, "Scholar of Multiple Involvements," 139; Fritz Machlup, interview by George Schutz.

6. From Max Mintz, 11 Apr. 1938, 16 Apr. 1938, 29 Apr. 1938, 22 May 1938, 29 May 1938, PPAS; From Paul Emödi, 12 April 1938, PPAS; from Renée Hiemasch, 17 May 1938, 25 May 1938, 7 June 1938, PPAS; from Liesl Gerstl, 29 May 1938, 8 June 1938, PPAS; from Liesl Gerstl and Dr. Duschak, 8 Apr. 1938, 5 May, 1938, PPAS; from Vilma Thierry, 5 May 1938, 27 May 1938, PPAS; from Karl Menger, 7 May 1938, PPAS; from Fritz Machlup, 12 May 1938, PPAS; from Fritz Ehrmann, 17 May 1938, 29 May 1938, PPAS; from P. Laforgue, 10 June 1938, PPAS.

7. From M. Kathrein Reitler and Company, 19 Apr. 1938, PPAS; to Emil Reitler, 2 May 1938, PPAS; to Peter and Hansi, 26 Jan. 1939 in an envelope labeled "Letters Concerning Immigration of Parents: Letters to Alfred's Mother," PPAS; from Ilse Schutz to Hansi and Peter, 15 Dec. 1939, in an envelope labeled "Letters Concerning Immigration of Parents: Letter to Alfred's Mother," PPAS.

8. From M. I. Goldschmidt to Ilse Schutz (copy to Alfred Schutz), 12 May 1938, PPAS; to Ilse Schutz, 8 May 1938, PPAS (my translation); from Ilse Schutz, 3 Apr. 1938, 11 Apr. 1938, 13 Apr. 1938, 19 April 1938, 29 April 1939, 2 May 1938, 5 May 1938, 21 May 1938, 23 May 1938, 25 May 1938, 29 May 1938, 30 May 1938, 31 May 1938, 4 June 1938, 8 June 1938, PPAS; to Ilse Schutz, 9 Apr. 1938; 12 May 1938, 15 May 1938, 18 May 1938, PPAS; "Receipt of Payment from German Embassy," 18 May 1938, PPAS. Marcel Beaufils was a musician and novelist; Pierre Monteux, a violinist; Lionel Robbins, professor of economics at the London School of Economics.

9. Ilse Schutz, interview by Anne Schwabacher, 26–27.

10. From Hansi, 13 June 1938, 25 June 1938, 30 Aug. 1938, PPAS; from Hansi and Peter, 15 June 1938, 27 June 1938, 29 June 1938, 4 July 4 1938, 5 July 1938, 9 July 1938, 28 July 28 1938; 4 August 1938, 8 August 1938, 9 August 1938, 11 August 1938, PPAS; from Peter to Ilse Schutz, 5 July 1938, PPAS; from Ilse Schutz to Fanny, 15 June 1938, PPAS; from Franziska Glas to Ilse Schutz, 30 July 1938, PPAS; from Olly Werner, 8 July 1938, PPAS; from Kathrein & Co. Vienna, 27 July 1938, PPAS; to Firma Kathrein & Co., 18 July 1938, PPAS; from Landlord, 17 June 1938, PPAS; Ilse Schutz, interview by Anne Schwabacher, 28; to Monsieur le Directeur de le Tennis Pension de Famille, 24 June 1938, PPAS; from Ilse Schutz (at Hotel Bellevue), 29 June 1938; from Ilse, no date, 4 Oct. 1938, PPAS; to Ilse Schutz, 1 Aug. 1938, 3 Oct. 1938, PPAS; to "Dear Friend," 18 June 1938, PPAS; itemized lists and costs by Georges Mènard with cover letter of 10 Dec. 1938 from O. Bauer, Paris architect, in envelope labeled, "Documents and Letters Concerning Leaving Vienna under Hitler 1938 and Applications for Residence Permit in Paris," PPAS; from O. Bauer to Ilse Schutz, 24 Aug. 1938 with "Living and Furniture Contents, Paris, 1938, for

Immigration from Vienna to Paris" 26 Apr. 1939, PPAS; from Ludwig Andertum, 15 June 1938, PPAS; from Emanuel Winternitz, 15 June 1938, 23 June 1938, 24 June 1938, telegram of 29 June 1938, 1 July 1938; telegram of 6 July 1938, 12 July 1938, 18 July 1938, 1 Aug. 1938, 8 Aug. 1938, 30 Aug. 1938, 31 Aug. 1938, 25 May 25 1939, PPAS; Letter of Gerhard to Walter Fröhlich, 24 June 1938, PPAS; from Gerhard, 28 June 1938, PPAS; from Felix Kaufmann, 20 June 1938, PPAS; from Fritz Machlup, 30 June 1938, 7 Aug. 1938, PPAS; from Lissy Vögelin to Ilse Schutz, 18 May 1939, PPAS; from Eric Voegelin, 25 Sept. 1938, PPAS; from Ludwig von Mises, 16 Sept. 1938, PPAS.

11. From Edward Rebhan, 22 June 1938, 13 July 1938, 27 Aug. 1938, 6 Sept. 1938, 14 Oct. 1938, 5 Jan. 1939, 28 Jan. 1939, 4 Apr. 1939, PPAS; to Edward Rebhan, 18 Oct. 1943, 20 Oct. 1938, PPAS; from Dr. Münz, 20 Oct. 1938, PPAS; from Gretl Rebhan to Ilse Schutz, 24 Sept. 1938, PPAS; from Gretl and Eddie Rebhan, 21 Dec. 1938, PPAS; from a medical doctor in Italy, 22 June 1938, PPAS; from Carl Nathan, 18 June 1938, PPAS; to Carl Nathan, 2 Nov. 1938, PPAS; to Dr. Walter Block, 2 Nov. 1938, PPAS; from William Klein, 25 June 1938, PPAS; to Fritz Machlup, 25 May 1938, PAS; from Fritz Machlup, 24 Dec. 1938, 4 Jan. 1939, PPAS; from Georg Steinbach, 23 July 1938, 21 Sept. 1938, PPAS; to Georg Steinbach, 29 Sept. 1938, PPAS; from Lois (Schutz's mother's doctor), 15 Aug. 1938, 26 Aug. 1938, 5 Sept. 1938, 25 Nov. 1938, PPAS; from Kurt Arway, 15 Aug. 1938, 20 Aug. 1938, PPAS; from Erich Heim, 16 Aug. 1938, 23 Aug. 1938, 1 Sept. 1938, 14 Sept. 1938, 15 Oct. 1938, 4 Nov. 1938, PPAS; from Ilse Schutz, 31 July 1938, PPAS; from First British American Corporation of London, 24 Aug. 1938, PPAS; to Mr. Epstein, 31 Aug. 1938, PPAS; from Stephan von Kuffner, 7 Sept. 1938, PPAS; from Arnold Rosenthal, 13 Sept. 1938, PPAS; to Oswald Glasberg (Waldja), 18 Oct. 1938, PPAS; from Oswald Glasberg to Erich Stadler (copy for Schutz), 5 Feb. 1939, PPAS; from Fritzi to Alfred Schutz, 23 Oct. 1938, 16 Dec. 1938, PPAS; from Fritz Nathanson, 28 Oct. 1938, PPAS; from E, 9 Nov. 1938, PPAS; from Ella Breuer to Ilse Schutz, 13 Nov. 1938, PPAS; from Rudolf Zeiszig, 22 Dec. 1938, PPAS; from M. I. Goldschmidt, 24 Dec. 1938, PPAS; from Marianne and Edith Glaser to Ilse Schutz, 24 Dec. 1938, PPAS; from C. Brunschweig, 21 Jan. 1939, PPAS; from *Revue Thomiste*, 23 Mar. 1939, PPAS; from Renèe Hiemasch, 5 July 1938, 23 July 1938, 7 Aug. 1938, 27 Aug. 1938, 7 Sept. 1938, 8 Oct. 1938, 31 Oct. 1938, PPAS; from Anna Kaff, 12 July 1938, 8 Aug. 1938, PPAS; from Erich Stadler, 31 July 1938, 11 Sept. 1938, 15 Oct. 1938, 21 Oct. 1938, 6 Mar. 1939, PPAS; from Marcel Friedmann, 5 Aug. 1938, PPAS; from Alice (Liesl) Gerstl, 30 Aug. 1938; 15 Oct. 1938; 29 Jan. 1939, PPAS; from Walter Froehlich, 15 July 1938, 17 Mar. 1939, PPAS; from Viktor Stadler, 15 Oct. 1938, 24 Oct. 1938, 26 Oct. 1938, 5 Nov. 1938, 10 Dec. 1938, 2 Jan. 1939, 13 Jan. 1939, 28 Jan. 1939; 29 Jan. 1939, PPAS; from Max Mintz, 16 Oct. 1938, PPAS; from Eric Voegelin, 25 Oct. 1938, 2 Apr. 1939, PPAS; from Oskar Schutz, 27 Nov. 1938, 7 Jan. 1939, PPAS; from Amy Emödl to Ilse, 12 Jan. 1939; PPAS; from Paul Landsberg, 3 July 1938, 18 Aug. 1938, PPAS; from Felix Kaufmann, 9 July 1938, 15 Nov. 1938, PPAS; from Stefan Possony, 17 Sept. 1938, PPAS; from Friedrich Hayek, 26 Dec. 1938, PPAS; from Academia Verlagsbuchhandlung, 25 Feb. 1939, PPAS; from V. Carthica 25 March 1939, PPAS; from Société de Études Philosophiques, 2 Apr. 1939, PPAS; from D. K. Kapmahls, 3 Apr. 1939, PPAS; List of members of Colloque Walter Lippmann, 29

Aug. 1938, PPAS. Eugen Fink, Husserl's assistant from 1930 onward, produced important essays in phenomenology. Jean Héring was a French phenomenologist who wrote on eidetic, constitutive phenomenology and phenomenology of religion. Ludwig Landgrebe, Husserl's assistant until 1930, worked on phenomenology and history. Paul Landsberg was a student of Max Scheler. John Wild was an American phenomenologist and existentialist who taught at Harvard.

12. To Alfred Levy, 24 Jan. 1939, PPAS; from Hansi and Peter, 20 June 1938, 26 June 1938, 9 July 1938, 24 July 1938, 12 Aug. 1938, 20 Aug. 1938, 26 Aug. 1938, 3 Sept. 1938, 14 Sept. 1938, 28 Oct. 1938, 8 Nov. 1938, 9 Nov. 1938, 11 Nov. 1938, 12 Nov. 1938 (in a envelope labeled: "Letters Concerning Immigration of Parents: Letter to Alfred's Mother"), 13 Nov. 1938, 14 Nov. 1938, 16 Nov. 1938, 18 Nov. 1938, 9 Dec. 1938, 29 Dec. 1938, 25 Jan. 1939, 2 Feb. 1939, 17 Feb. 1939, 18 Feb. 1939, PPAS; from Gisa Heim to Ilse Schutz, 14 July 1938; 21 July 1938, 13 Aug. 1938, 27 Aug. 1938, 1 Sept. 1938, PPAS; from Peter to Alfred and Ilse Schutz, 3 Sept. 1938, 16 Sept. 1938, 19 Nov. 1938, 24 Nov. 1938, PPAS; from Erich Heim to Ilse Schutz, 4 Aug. 1938, 23 Aug. 1938, PPAS; from Ilse Schutz, 7 Sept. 1938, PPAS; from Otto Weissberger, 6 Sept. 1938, 18 Nov. 1938, PPAS; from Erich Heim, 14 Sept. 1938, 4 Oct. 1938, PPAS; to Hanus Weisl, 20 Sept. 1938, PPAS; from Hanus Weisl, 25 Sept. 1938, 21 Oct. 1938, PPAS.

13. From Hansi and Peter, 19 Nov. 1938, 23 Nov. 1938, 24 Nov. 1938, 25 Nov. 1938, 27 Nov. 1938, 2 Dec. 1938, 4 Dec. 1938, 6 Dec. 1938, 10 Dec. 1938, 12 Dec. 1938, 14 Dec. 1938, 17 Dec. 1938, 22 Dec. 1938, 29 Dec. 1938, 31 Dec. 1938, 4 Jan. 1939, 6 Jan. 1939, 14 Jan. 1939, 19 Jan. 1939, 20 Jan. 1939, 30 Jan. 1939, 16 Feb. 1939, 24 Feb. 1939, 25 Feb. 1939, 14 Mar. 1939, 29 Mar. 1939, PPAS; from Ilse Schutz to her cousin Ernest in Zagreb, 25 Nov. 1938, PPAS; to Alfred Levy, 6 Dec. 1938, PPAS; Notes, immediately following letters of 23 Nov. 1938, PPAS. Schutz's parents on 19 Nov. 1938 anticipated leaving on 19 Dec. 1938; on 4 Dec. 1938, they expected to go on 3 Jan. 1939; on 22 Dec., 24 Jan. 1939; on 29 Dec., 12 Jan. 1939; on 31 Dec., 15–20 Jan.; on 30 Jan, 14 Feb.; on 16 Feb., 20 Feb.; on 14 Mar., 21 Mar.; on 29 Mar., 5–6 Apr., the actual dates on which they left. Health certificate from the Leopoldstatt Police Depatment, PPAS, in an envelope labeled "Letters Concerning Immigration of Parents, Letter to Alfred's Mother," 16 Dec. 1938, PPAS. On health problems see from Hansi and Peter, 26 June 1938, 30 June 1938, 25 Aug. 1938, 26 Aug. 1938, PPAS.

14. From Ernest, Ilse's cousin, to Ilse, 16 Nov. 1938, PPAS; from Hansi and Peter, 11 July 1938, 18 July 1938, 24 July 1938, 25 July 1938, 20 Aug. 1938, 21 Sept. 1928, 14 Sept. 1938, 26 Sept. 1938, 1 Oct. 1938, 5 Oct. 1938, 13 Oct. 1938, 14 Oct. 1938, 16 Oct. 1938, 18 Oct. 1938, 27 Oct. 1938, 28 Oct. 1938, 5 Nov. 1938, 6 Nov. 1938, 8 Nov. 1938, 13 Nov. 1938, 18 Nov. 1938 (my translation), 19 Nov. 1938 (my translation), 12 Dec. 1938, 6 Jan. 1939, 7 Jan. 1939, 19 Jan. 1939, 22 Jan. 1939, 4 Feb. 1939, 14 Feb. 1939, 26 Feb. 1939, PPAS; from Peter to Ilse, 3 Sept. 1938, PPAS; Letter of Hansi to Alfred Schutz (in Amsterdam), 3 Oct. 1938, PPAS; to Ilse Schutz, 28 July 1938, 1 Aug. 1938, 2 Aug. 1938, 3 Oct. 1938, PPAS; to Hansi and Peter, 26 Jan. 1939, in an envelope labeled "Letters Concerning Immigration of Parents, Letter to Alfred's Mother,"PPAS.

15. From Eddie Rebhan, 4 Apr. 1939, PPAS. My translation.

16. Clipping entitled "Ausländer, die in Frankreich Militardienst leisten" in PPAS, after 17 July 1939; to Robert Lambert, 18 Apr. 1939, PPAS. Ilse Schutz, interview by Anne Schwabacher, 31–33.

17. From Paul Weinberg (Amsterdam), 20 Apr. 1939, PPAS; from Ludwig von Mises, 31 May 1939, PPAS; from Ernie (Ilse's cousin), 1 June 1939, PPAS; to Ilse Schutz, 2 June 1939, 7 June 1939, PPAS; from Marcel Friedmann, 6 Apr. 1939, PPAS; from Emanuel Winternitz (in Cambridge, Massachusetts) to Ilse Schutz (in New York), 25 May 1939, PPAS; from Viktor Stadler, 10 Apr. 1939, 29 May 1939, PPAS; from Liesl Gerstl, 11 Apr. 1939, PPAS; from Siegfried Kracauer to Ilse Schutz, 30 Apr. 1939, PPAS; from Eddie Rebhan, 4 May 1939, 25 May 1939, PPAS; to Edward Rebhan, 17 June 1939, PPAS; from Georg Steinbach to Ilse Schutz, 9 May 1939, PPAS; from Georg Steinbach, 18 May 1939, 21 June 1939, PPAS; from Liesl Gerstl to Ilse Schutz, 19 May 1939, PPAS; from Lucy Friedmann to Ilse Schutz, 20 June, 1939. See Grathoff, Introduction to *Philosophers in Exile*, xv, xx, xxii, and Grathoff, Introduction 'Riders of the Apocalypse,' 2; On being a banker by day and a phenomenologist by night see letter of Schutz to Gurwitsch, November 9, 1940, in *PE*, 26; Embree, "Biographical Sketch of Aron Gurwitsch," xxiii. Hannah Arendt was a political philosopher who later ended up at the New School; Raymond Aron, a French political theorist; Gaston Berger, a student of Husserl and phenomenologist working in the area of epistemology; Lucien Goldman, a sociologist; Eric Itor Kahn, a musician and member of the Albineri Trio; Alexandre Koyré, a student of Husserl who wrote on logical paradoxes, philosophy of religion, and Hegel; Siegfried Kracauer, an art historian; Gabriel Marcel, a French existentialist philosopher; Jacques Maritain, a French Thomist philosopher; Maurice Merleau-Ponty, a French phenomenologist; Hélène Metzger, a historian of science; Louis Rougier, a political theorist; Gunther Stern, a philosopher and the husband of Hannah Arendt; and Jean Wahl, a phenomenologist.

18. From Rudolph Zieszig, 7 Apr. 1939, PPAS; from Ernest to Ilse Schutz, 19 Apr. 1939, 2 May 1939, PPAS; to Ilse Schutz, 5 May 1939, 19 May 1939, 22 May 1939, 26 May 1939, PPAS; to Herr Schiff, 20 May 1939, PPAS; from Hansi and Peter to Ilse Schutz via Lucy Friedmann, 8 May 1939, PPAS; from Gisa, 11 May 1939, PPAS; from Erich Heim to Mr. Sieff, 1 May 1939, PPAS; from Erich Heim, 27 May 1939, PPAS.

19. From Ilse Schutz, 3 May 1939 (my translation) (see also from Ilse, 7 May 1939), PPAS; from Gabbitas, Thring, and Company to Ilse Schutz, 2 May 1939, 26 May 1939, PPAS; to Ilse Schutz, telegram of 3 May 1939, 5 May 1939, 6 June 1939, 7 June 1939; from Continental-Bankiers in Trustkantoor, Amsterdam, 20 Apr. 1939, PPAS; from Marcel Friedmann, 2 May 1939, PPAS; to Mr. Lacy Kuz (New York), 2 May 1939, PPAS; from Ilse Mintz to Ilse Schutz, 4 July 1939, PPAS; Ilse Schutz, interview by Anne Schwabacher, 23a.

20. From Ilse Schutz, 13 May 1939 PPAS (my translation); see also from Ilse, 9 May 1939, 10 May 1939, 14 May 1939, 15 May 1939, 21 May 1939, 23 May 1939, 5 June 1939, PPAS; to Ilse Schutz, 9 May 1939, 22 May 1939, 2 June 1939, PPAS; Ilse Schutz, interview by Anne Schwabacher, 34–36; from Marcel Friedmann 9 May 1939, PPAS.

21. From Felix Kaufmann and Max Mintz, 11 May 1939, PPAS; from Felix Kaufmann, 12 May 1939, PPAS; from Felix Kaufmann, 17 Mar. 1940, 29 Oct. 1944,

15 Sept. 1945, 21 Sept. 1945, PAS; to Felix Kaufmann, 16 Sept. 1940, 17 Sept. 1945, PAS; Alfred Schutz to Felix Kaufmann, 25 May 1939; 1 June, 1941, 21 Oct. 1944, from Ilse Schutz, 13 May 1939, PPAS; to Marvin Farber, 27 Nov. 1958, PAS.

22. Ilse Schutz, interview by Anne Schwabacher, 36–37; the menu for dinner, 14 July 1939, The New Amsterdam, PPAS.

23. Levinas, *Totality and Infinity,* 245.

Chapter 6

1. Ilse Schutz, interview by Anne Schwabacher, 37–38; to Fritz Machlup, 19 Sept. 1939, PAS; George Schutz, interview by Michael Barber.

2. To Raoul Rabinerson, 15 Dec. 1939, PAS.

3. Duhamel, *La possession du monde*, 39, 46, 50, 53, 80, 85–87, 93, 107, 111, 124, 132, 140, 177, 192–93, 221, 241–43, 244–45, 253–54, 257–58, 260–68; Maurois, *En América*, 11, 23, 42, 47, 49–50, 52, 56–59, 67, 77, 90, 104, 108, 111. See Ilse Schutz, interview by Anne Schwabacher, 30, 35.

4. To Raoul Rabinerson, 15 Dec. 1939, PAS.

5. To Fritz Machlup, 11 Apr. 1939, 30 June 1939, 26 July 1939, 30 July 1939, 14 Aug. 1939, PAS; to Ilse Schutz, 1 Feb. 1940, PPAS; Ilse Schutz, interview by Anne Schwabacher, 38–39, Fritz Machlup, interview by George Schutz.

6. To Aron Gurwitsch, 10 Apr. 1940, PAS; to Aron Gurwitsch, 10 Nov. 1939, *PE*, 13; from Aron Gurwitsch, 29 Apr. 1940, *PE*, 14; from Marcel Friedmann, 8 Mar. 1940, 20 Mar. 1940, 5 Apr. 1940, PPAS; from Walter Froehlich, 6 June 1940, PPAS; from Hansi, 12 Mar. 1940, PPAS; from Hansi and Peter, 14 Jan. 1941, PPAS; to Fritz Machlup, 23 Nov. 1939; 16 Apr. 1940, PAS; from Dr. Martin Buchband, 31 Mar. 1940, PPAS; see grades for courses, 1940 file, PPAS; from Mr. Ernest Hamburger, 5 March 1942, PAS.

7. From Hansi and Peter, 24 July 1939, 25 July 1939, 29 July 1939, 1 Aug. 1939, 2 Aug. 1939, 7 Aug. 1939, 8 Aug. 1939, 10 Aug. 1939, 14 Aug. 1939, 16 Aug. 1939, 21 Aug. 1939, 23 Aug. 1939, 4 Sept. 1939, 8 Sept. 1939, 11 Sept. 1939, 21 Sept. 1939, 23 Sept. 1939, 25 Sept. 1939, 28 Sept. 1939, 29 Sept. 1939, 14 Oct. 1939, 15 Oct. 1939, 16 Oct. 1939, 17 Oct. 1939, 18 Oct. 1939, 21 Oct. 1939, 13 Dec. 1939, 14 Dec. 1939, 8 Jan. 1940, 11 Jan. 1940, 14 Jan. 1940, 24 Jan. 1940, 12 June 1940, 6 July 1940, 4 Sept. 1940, 27 Sept. 1940, 7 Nov. 1940, PPAS; from Hansi and Peter to Ilse Schutz, 8 May 1939, PPAS; to Peter and Hansi, 29 Mar. 1941, 2 May 1941, PPAS. From September 4, 1939, until December 26 of that year, Schutz's parents sent thirty-eight letters. See: to Ilse Schutz, 5 May 1939, 9 May 1939, 19 May 1939, 31 Jan. 1940, PPAS; from Ilse Schutz, 31 Jan. 1940, PPAS; to Otto Schutz, 26 Apr. 1941, PPAS; to Asto Rougier, 18 May 1941, PPAS; from Paul Blühdorn, 21 July 1940, 7 Aug. 1940, 16 Dec. 1940, PPAS; to Paul Blühdorn, 1 Aug. 1940, PPAS; from Oswald Glasberg, 31 Oct. 1940, PPAS; Sworn document by Alfred Schutz regarding a $700 loan to Oswald Glasberg, 16 Dec. 1940, PPAS; telegrams regarding affidavit preparations for the parents of Alfred Schutz, 1941 file, PPAS; to Aron Gurwitsch, 26 Apr. 1941, *PE*, 38; to Alexander Weiner, 2 July 1941, 14 July 1941, 6 Aug. 1941, PPAS; telegram to Otto Schutz, 5 Sept. 1941, PPAS; documents, PPAS.

8. From Oswald Glasberg, 20 July 1940, Aug. 13, 1940, 12 Sept. 1940, 30 Sept. 1940, 27 Dec. 1940; from file entitled Letters to Oswald Glasberg, PPAS: to Oswald

Glasberg, 5 Aug. 1940, 6 Aug. 1940, 8 Aug. 1940, 14 Aug. 1940, 23 Aug. 1940, 27 Aug. 1940, 3 Sept. 1940, 26 Sept. 1940, 15 Oct. 1940, 16 Oct. 1940, 25 Oct. 1940; to Dr. Fleishacker, 6 Aug. 1940, PPAS; from file entitled Letters to Oswald Glasberg, PPAS: to Col. Chesley W. Jurney, 23 Sept. 1940; from Randy Griz of Sopic Corporation to Alfred Schutz, 4 Mar. 1941, PPAS; Cablegram to Della and Berthold, 7 Mar. 1941, PPAS; from Della, 17 Mar. 1941, PPAS. For correspondence on other relatives, see from Hansi and Peter, 24 Oct. 1939, 1 Dec. 1939, 8 Dec. 1939, 11 Jan. 1940, 18 Jan. 1940, 4 Sept. 1940, 24 Dec. 1940, PPAS; from Berthold and Della, 19 Aug. 1940, 23 Oct. 1940, PPAS; from Richard and Malva Schutz to Alfred Schutz, no date, but after 23 Sept. 1940, PPAS; from Oskar Schutz, 27 Dec. 1940, 31 Dec. 1940, 17 Mar. 1941, 5 May 1941, 1 June 1941, 13 June 1941, 24 July 1941, PPAS; to Oskar Schutz, 12 Apr. 1941, cable of 29 May 1941, 11 Aug. 1941, PPAS; to Mr. Dietsch, Committee for Catholic Refugees from Germany, 3 Apr. 1941, 24 May 1941, PPAS; to Fr. Mark Seybold, 3 Apr. 1941, PPAS; to Suzanne R. Aron, 20 Sept. 1940, PAS; to Frau Malvine Husserl, no date, PAS; from Klara Lustiger, 22 Aug. 1939, PPAS; from Ilse Schutz, 24 Jan. 1940; to Max Mintz, 11 Sept. 1940, PPAS; from Fritz Machlup, 4 May 1940, PAS; to Dear Professor, 16 Sept. 1940, PPAS; from Suzanne Aron, 2 Sept. 1940, PAS; to Suzanne Aron, 20 Sept. 1940, PAS; from Raymond Aron, 7 May 1941, PAS; to Raymond Aron, 12 June 1941, PAS; from Marcel Friedmann, 8 Mar. 1940, 12 Dec. 1940, 20 Dec. 1940, 6 Jan. 1941, 9 Jan. 1941, 14 Jan. 1941, 29 Jan. 1941, 11 June 1941, 22 Oct. 1941, 5 May 1942, PPAS; to Dr. Herbert Furth, 14 Oct. 1940, 19 Dec. 1940, PAS; from Eddie Rebhan, 20 Apr. 1941, PPAS; from Samuel Ellsworth to Edward Rebhan, 19 May 1941, PPAS; to International Students' Service, 11 June 1941, PPAS; to Mrs. Sol Rothschild, 11 Oct. 1939, 19 Oct. 1939, 1 Nov. 1939, 18 Jan. 1940, 18 Mar. 1940, PPAS; from Aron Gurwitsch, 29 Apr. 1940, *PE*, 13–14; 5 Aug. 1940, *PE*, 14–15; 17 Aug. 1940, *PE*, 16; 23 Aug. 1940, *PE*, 17–18; 7 Nov. 1940, *PE*, 25; 10 June 1941, *PE*, 38–40, 18 Mar. 1942, *PE*, 53–54; 30 May 1942, *PE*, 56–57; 11 July 1942, *PE*, 57–58; 19 July, 1942, *PE*, 59–60; to Aron Gurwitsch, 20 Aug. 1940, *PE*, 16–17; 2 Nov. 1940, *PE*, 19; 26 Jan. 1941, *PE*, 32–33; 28 Mar. 1942, PE, 54.

9. To Ilse Schutz, 24 Jan. 1940, 27 Jan. 1940, 1 Feb. 1940, PPAS.

10. To Marvin Farber, 12 June 1940, PAS (my translation); from Marvin Farber, postcard of 19 Dec. 1938, 2 May 1939, 24 May 1940, PAS; Grathoff, introduction to *Philosophers in Exile*, xxvi; Schutz, vita for United States Office of Economic Warfare, folder 820, PAS; Schutz's notes on the constitution of the International Phenomenological Society, no date, Folder 620, PAS; to Aron Gurwitsch, 10 Nov. 1939, *PE*, 12–13.

11. Husserl, "Notizen zur Raumkonstitution" 23–37; Schutz, "Editor's Preface to Edmund Husserl's 'Notizen zur Raumkonstitution'," 21–23 (also published in vol. 4 of *Collected Papers*, 174–76); from Marvin Farber, 1 July 1940, 13 July 1940, 17 July 1940, 22 July 1940, 8 Aug. 1940, postcard of 30 Sept. 1940, postcard of 21 Oct. 1940, 9 Dec. 1940, 4 Jan. 1941, 7 Feb. 1941, 29 Apr. 1941, 1 May 1941, 25 June 1941, 14 Mar. 1942, PAS; to Marvin Farber, 19 July 1940, 5 Aug. 1940, 26 Sept. 1940, 2 Oct. 1940, 6 Nov. 1940, 12 May 1941, 6 Aug. 1941, 10 Sept. 1941, 28 Mar. 1942, PAS; see Farber, *Foundation of Phenomenology*; Marvin Farber to Felix Kaufmann (copy to Schutz), 1 Nov. 1941, PAS; to Jean Hèring, 20 Sept. 1940, PAS; to Frau Staudinger,

3 Dec. 1940, PAS; to Theodor Adorno, 3 Sept. 1940, PAS; to Goetz Briefs, 11 Sept. 1940, PAS. See also Wagner, "Marvin Farber's Contribution," 226–29.

12. To Jacques Maritain, 3 June 1940, 24 July 1940, 30 Sept., 1940, 10 Oct. 1940, 20 Nov. 1940, 29 Apr. 1941, 13 May 1941, 31 May 1941, 3 June 1941, PAS; from Jacques Maritain, 27 Oct. 1940, PAS; from Marvin Farber, 27 Aug. 1940, 6 Sept. 1940, 5 May 1941, 24 May 1941, PAS; to Marvin Farber, 3 Sept. 1940, 10 Sept. 1941, PAS; Marvin Farber to Jacques Maritain, 17 May 1941, PAS.

13. To Felix Kaufmann, 19 Apr. 1932, 31 July 1938, 16 Sept. 1940, *CFK/AS*; from Felix Kaufmann, 26 Dec. 1938, 29 Mar. 1940, 18 Sept. 1940, 2 June 1941, 24 May 1942, 27 July 1944, 29 Oct. 1944, 15 Sept. 1945, 17 Sept. 1945, 21 Sept. 1945, *CFK/AS*; Wagner, *Alfred Schutz*, 66.

14. From Ethelind Austin, secretary of the Department of Philosophy, Harvard University, 25 Aug. 1939, PAS; Conference on Method in Philosophy and the Sciences, folder 456, PAS; from Marvin Farber, 18 Dec. 1938, PAS; see chapter 3, 61–70; Schutz, "Phenomenology and the Social Sciences," 118–39.

15. Schutz, "Problem of Rationality in the Social World," 6–24; to Talcott Parsons, Sept. 1939, PAS; to Aron Gurwitsch, 8 Nov. 1941, *PE*, 43; to Friedrich Hayek, 4 Nov. 1942; to Fritz Machlup, 23 June 1940, PAS; Grathoff, introduction to *The Theory of Social Action,* xxiii–xxiv.

16. From Maurice Mandelbaum, 29 Apr. 1940, PAS; to Maurice Mandelbaum, 31 Oct. 1940, PAS; to Horace Kallen, 6 Nov. 1940, PAS; from Horace Kallen, 9 Dec. 1940, PAS; to Aron Gurwitsch, 2 Nov. 1940, *PE*, 19. Mandelbaum was professor of philosophy at Dartmouth and later Johns Hopkins, and he was active in the American Philosophical Association.

17. Schutz, "William James's Concept of the Stream of Thought," 1–14; from Aron Gurwitsch, 5 Aug. 1939, *PE*, 3; 7 Nov. 1940, *PE*, 21–25; to Aron Gurwitsch, 19 Aug. 1939, *PE*, 6–11; 16 Nov. 1940, *PE*, 27–29; see Gurwitsch, "On the Object of Thought," 142–43; Letter of Fred Kersten to Michael Barber, September 10, 2001.

18. To Richard Hays Williams, 17 Nov. 1940, PAS; from Marvin Farber, 1 May 1941, PAS; to Marvin Farber, 6 Aug. 1941, PAS; to Aron Gurwitsch, 8 Nov. 1941, *PE*, 43; to Fritz Machlup, 17 Apr. 1942, PAS; Schutz, "Scheler's Theory of Intersubjectivity," 150–64.

19. Schutz, "Scheler's Theory of Intersubjectivity," 164–79, see 169 n. 43–179; to Aron Gurwitsch, 21 Nov. 1941, *PE*, 45–46; 1 Mar. 1942, *PE*, 51–52; 11 Dec. 1941, *PE,* 52–53; from Aron Gurwitsch, 30 Nov. 1940, *PE*, 46–49; 11 July 1942, *PE*, 58; 19 Dec. 1940, *PE*, 31; Series I, Writings, Box 3, Folders 1 and 2, 1455–74, 1461–65, PAS.

20. Grathoff, introduction to *The Theory of Social Action*, xxiii–xxiv, xxv; to Talcott Parsons, 17 Mar. 1941, *TSA*, 97–98; 15 Nov. 1940, *TSA*, 4–5; from Talcott Parsons, 30 Oct. 1940, *TSA*, 3; to Fritz Machlup, 16 Apr. 1940, 7 Dec. 1940, PAS; from Fritz Machlup, 23 June 1940, PAS; from Richard Hays Williams, 25 June 1940, PAS; to Richard Hays Williams, 6 Nov. 1940, 17 Nov. 1940, PAS; see Schutz "Phenomenology and the Social Sciences," 118, Author's Note.

21. Schutz, "Parsons' Theory of Social Action: *A Critical Review by Alfred Schutz*," in *TSA*, 8–21.

22. Ibid., 21–60.

23. Ibid., 36–37.

24. Ibid., 14, 25, 36, 37, 41, 43, 50; from Talcott Parsons, 16 Jan. 1941, 63, 64, 66–67, *TSA*; 23 January 1941, 73, 74, 75–77, *TSA*; 2 Feb. 1941, 82, 83, 88, 92, *TSA*; to Talcott Parsons, 17 Mar. 1941, 97, 100, 101, *TSA*; Maurice Natanson, foreword to *The Theory of Social Action*, x–xi; see Embree, "Methodology Is Where Human Scientists and Philosophers Can Meet," 369, 371.

25. From Talcott Parsons, 2 Feb. 1941, 84–85, 87–90, *TSA*; 29 Mar. 1941, 108, *TSA*; to Talcott Parsons, 17 Mar. 1941, 96, *TSA*.

26. For the tensions, see for instance, from Talcott Parsons, 16 Jan. 1941, 63, 66, *TSA*; 23 Jan. 1941, 76, 92, *TSA*; 29 Mar. 1941, 107–9, *TSA*; to Talcott Parsons 17 Mar. 1941, 95–99, 105–6, *TSA*; April 21, 1941, 110–11, *TSA*; from Gottfried Haberler, 20 May 1941, PAS; from Eric Voegelin, 28 May 1941, PAS; see Rehorick and Buxton, "Recasting the Parsons-Schutz Dialogue," 151–69.

27. To Talcott Parsons, 17 Mar. 1941, 96, *TSA*; see Grathoff, introduction to *Philosophers in Exile*, xxiv.

Chapter 7

1. To Marvin Farber, 9 Feb. 1942, 13 Mar. 1942, 20 July 1942, 27 July 1942, 4 Aug. 1942, 2 Sept. 1942, 16 Dec. 1942, 20 Jan. 1943, 17 Feb. 1943, 27 Feb. 1943, 4 May 1945, PAS; from Marvin Farber, 17 July 1942, 19 Oct. 1942, 14 July 1944, 9 Sept. 1944, 4 Nov. 1944, 25 Nov. 1944, PAS; from Kurt Wolff, 15 Feb. 1943, PAS; to Kurt Wolff, 17 Feb. 1943, PAS; from Luis Recasens Siches, 24 Aug. 1942, PAS; to Luis Recasens Siches, 16 Oct. 1942, PAS.

2. To Marvin Farber, 20 July 1942, 2 Sept. 1942, 6 Sept. 1943, 3 Jan. 1944, 2 Jan. 1945, PAS; from Marvin Farber, 17 July 1942, 31 July 1943, 12 Oct. 1943, 8 Jan. 1944, 28 Mar. 1944, postcard of 29 Apr. 1944, 19 Aug. 1944, postcard of 15 Apr. 1945, PAS; from Herbert Spiegelberg, 24 June 1943, 6 Sept. 1943, 20 Sept. 1944, 10 Nov. 1943, PAS; from Herbert Spiegelberg to Marvin Farber, 23 June 1943, 6 July 1943, PAS; tentative plan for a sourcebook, PAS, folder 796.

3. From Marvin Farber, 27 Feb. 1943, 1 June 1945, 8 June 1945, PAS; to Marvin Farber, 5 June 1945, 12 June 1945, PAS.

4. From Marvin Farber, 4 Apr. 1942, 6 July 1943, 25 Oct. 1943, 16 Dec. 1943, 19 June 1944, 19 Aug. 1944, 29 Nov. 1944, 6 Jan. 1945, 11 Jan. 1945, PAS; to Marvin Farber, 20 Dec. 1943, PAS.

5. From Alvin Johnson, 22 Dec. 1942, PAS; from Hans Staudinger, 25 Sept. 1943, PAS; course listings for the New School for Social Research, collected by Helmut Wagner; Ilse Schutz, interview by Anne Schwabacher, 41–42; to Helmut Kuhn, 6 Mar. 1943, PAS.

6. Course listings, 18 Aug. 1943, PAS.

7. To Professor Eduard Heimann, 18 Feb. 1943, PAS; Heimann, "Just War of Unjust Nations," 2–6.

8. From Irene B. Opton, 15 Jan. 1943, 8 Sept. 1943, 9 Oct. 1943, 11 Feb. 1944, 18 Feb. 1944, 2 Mar. 1944, 14 Apr. 1944, 25 May 1944, 3 July 1944, PAS; to Irene Opton, 4 Mar. 1944, 5 May, 1944, PAS; from Richard Tirana, 18 Mar. 1943, 12 May

1943, 20 May 1943, PAS; to Richard Tirana, 31 Mar. 1943, May 20, 1943, PAS; from Board of Economic Warfare, 25 May 1943, PAS; "Agricultural Credit in Germany," by Alfred Schutz, Sept. 1943, folder 820, PAS; to Gottfried Haberler, 27 Mar. 1943, 14 Feb. 1944, PAS; from Gottfried Haberler, 30 Mar. 1943, PAS; to Fritz Machlup, 24 Nov. 1943, PAS; from Fritz Machlup, 2 Sept. 1943, PAS; from Herbert Furth, 12 Apr. 1943, 20 Apr. 1943, PAS; to Aron Gurwitsch, 1 Oct. 1943, *PE*, 68.

9. To Ilse Schutz, 11 Feb.1942, PPAS; from Ilse Schutz, 2 Aug. 1945, PPAS; to Fritz Machlup, 17 Sept. 1945, PAS.

10. Ilse Schutz, interview by Anne Schwabacher, 39–40; from A. K. Renne, 20 May 1942, PPAS; from Evvy Jeral, 20 May, 1942, PPAS; from Riedl, 21 May 1942, PPAS; from F. Z. Reitler, 21 May 1942, PPAS; from A. G. Redley, 21 May 1942, PPAS; from Marcel Friedmann, 25 May 1942, PPAS; from Max Mintz, 19 May 1942, PAS; from Felix Kaufmann, 24 May 1942, PAS; from Aron Gurwitsch, 20 May 1942, *PE*, 55; to Aron Gurwitsch, 22 May 1942, *PE*, 55; to Marvin Farber, 27 May 1942, PAS; from Erich Heim, 3 July 1942, PPAS; to Fritz Machlup, 28 Aug. 1943, PAS; Family Documents, PPAS; from Evelyn Schutz from Camp Sheldrake, undated 1942, PPAS; to Liesl, 30 Dec. 1942, PPAS; to Hansi, 2 Aug. 1945, PPAS.

11. From Marcel Friedmann, 22 Oct. 1941, 5 May 1942, PPAS; to Marcel Friedmann, 30 Dec. 1942, PPAS; from Marcel Friedmann to Annie Unger, 3 Oct. 1942, PPAS; to Ludwig von Mises, 25 July 1940, PAS; to Robert Horecki, 21 Jan. 1942, PAS; to Walter Froehlich, 24 Jan. 1942, 12 Mar. 1942, PAS; to Fritz Machlup, 8 Nov. 1943, PAS; to Gottfried Haberler, 4 Sept. 1941, 15 Sept. 1941, PAS; from Hans Kelsen, 27 June 1945, 3 Aug. 1945, PAS.

12. From Fritz Machlup, 10 Jan. 1936, 28 Apr. 1940, 19 Sept. 1940, 10 Dec. 1940, 24 Sept. 1941, PAS; to Fritz Machlup, 5 Oct. 1940, 7 Dec.1940, PAS; see Pinney, "Institutional Man," 543–62; Frank H. Knight, "'What Is Truth' in Economics?" 1–8, 11–31.

13. From Fritz Machlup, 9 May 1940, 21 Feb. 1941, 24 Sept. 1941, 24 Aug. 1944, 25 Sept. 1945, PAS; to Fritz Machlup, 25 Oct. 1940, 7 Dec. 1940, 8 Dec. 1942, 15 Jan. 1943, 11 Mar. 1943, 2 Sept. 1943, 18 Oct. 1943, 22 Oct. 1943, 24 Nov. 1943, 17 Aug. 1944, 17 Sept. 1945, PAS; to Gustav Machlup (Fritz's brother), 13 Mar. 1943, PAS.

14. From Eric Voegelin, 23 Nov. 1942, 27 Jan. 1943, 23 Apr. 1943, 12 Jan. 1945, 29 Mar. 1945, PAS; to Eric Voegelin, 7 Dec. 1942, PAS.

15. To Eric Voegelin, 12 Jan. 1943, 7 Apr. 1943, PAS; from Eric Voegelin, 3 Apr. 1943, PAS; see Voegelin, "Siger de Brabant," *PPR* 4 (1944): 512, see also 507–10; Dempf, *Kritik der historischen Vernunft*, 179–80; Dempf, *Sacrum Imperium,* 335, 341–42, 344–47, 348–49, 354; Voegelin, *New Science of Politics,* 110–19, 127, 132, 143, 172–77, 186–87; see Dempf, *Theoretische Anthropologie*, 78, 101, 188, 191–98, 236; from John Courtney Murray, 25 June 1956, PAS.

16. From Eric Voegelin, 16 Jan. 1943, 28 Sept. 1943, PAS; from Felix Kaufmann, 27 July 1944, PAS.

17. Voegelin, *Anamnesis,* 4, 80, 92, 112–13, 126, 145, 176–77; Voegelin and Strauss, *Faith and Political Philosophy,* 18–19, 58, 64, 142–43, 153–54, 159, 172, 177–80, 197–98, 202, 214–15, 284, 306, 357; Voegelin, *Ecumenic* Age,71–72, 177, 185, 197–98, 202, 215, 224, 236–37, 241, 252, 315; Voegelin, *In Search of Order*,

36–37, 58–59, 103; Pangle, "Platonic Political Science in Strauss and Voegelin," 332–33; Voegelin, *New Science of Politics*, 122, 129, cf. 107–32; from Aron Gurwitsch, 2 Nov. 1952, *PE*, 183; 24 Jan. 1953, *PE*, 195; Voegelin, *Israel and Revelation,* 142; Voegelin, "German University and the Order of German Society," 25; Voegelin, *World of the Polis*, 12–13. See also Barber, "Values as Critique and the Critique of Values," 213–18; from Eric Voegelin, 16 Jan. 1943, PAS.

18. From Eric Voegelin, 23 Nov. 1940, PAS; from Eric Voegelin to Alfred Schutz on Edmund Husserl, 17 Sept. 1943, in Voegelin and Strauss, *Faith and Political Philosophy*, 19–34.

19. Schutz, "Husserl's *Crisis of Western Sciences*," 177–86; from Leo Strauss, 3 Jan. 1944, PAS.

20. From Eric Voegelin, 28 Dec. 1943, PAS; Schutz, "Husserl's *Crisis of Western Sciences*,"178.

21. From Eric Voegelin, 21 Apr. 1945, 6 Oct. 1945, PAS; Voegelin, "Theory of Legal Science," 570, folder 875, PAS.

22. From Aron Gurwitsch, 19 July 1942, *PE*, 59–60, 18 Aug. 1942, *PE*, 61–62; 21 Dec. 1942, *PE*, 65–66; to Aron Gurwitsch, 25 Aug. 1942, *PE*, 62; 24 Dec. 1942, *PE*, 66–67; 1 Oct. 1943, *PE*, 68.

23. From Felix Kaufmann, 29 Oct. 1944, 15 Sept. 1945, 21 Sept. 1945, PAS; to Felix Kaufmann, 17 Sept. 1945, PAS; Schutz "Life-World and Scientific Experience," 110–11.

24. Fritz Machlup, interview by George Schutz; Kaufmann, *Metodología de las ciencias sociales*, 205, 269, 299–300, 265, 328, 336–37; from Felix Kaufmann, 5 July 1934, 24 July 1934, 26 July 1934, 5 Mar. 1935, 24 June 1935, 25 July 1934, 28 Oct. 1935, *CFK/AS*; Prendergast, "Alfred Schutz and the Austrian School of Economics," 7; and Schutz, *Phenomenology of the Social World,* xxxii.

25. On the empirical controllability of social scientific claims, see Kaufmann, *Metodología de las ciencias sociales*, 83; Schutz, "Concept and Theory Formation in the Social Sciences," 51–52. On methodological individualism, see Schutz, "Problem of Rationality in the Social World," 84–85; Kaufmann, *Metodología de las ciencias sociales*, 320. On the marginal utility principle, see Kaufmann, *Metodología de las ciencias sociales*, 340–41, 344, 350, 352, and 365; Schutz, "Political Economy," 94–95, 96–100, 102–4. On data and deductive methods, see Kaufmann, *Metodología de las ciencias sociales*, 52, 188, 290, 301–6, 366–68; Kaufmann, "On the Subject-Matter and Method of Economic Science," 381–401; Schutz, "Political Economy," 95–100, 104. On the preference for diversity of methods as opposed to purity, see Schutz, "Political Economy," 95; Kaufmann, *Metodología de las ciencias sociales*, 309–25. On how methodology needs tutoring from social scientists, Schutz, "Problem of Rationality in the Social World," 88, and Embree, "Schutz on Science," 265–70; see also Kaufmann, "Remarks on the Methodology of the Social Sciences," 75–78. See Korsgaard, *Creating the Kingdom of Ends* 276–91.

26. Schutz, "On Multiple Realities," 250; from Felix Kaufmann, 29 Oct. 1944, 15 Sept. 1945, PAS; to Felix Kaufmann, Sept. 17, 1945, PAS; Kaufmann, *Methodology of the Social Sciences*, 18, 31, 47, 53, 65, 69, 91, 93, 222; see Kaufmann, "Logical Rules of Scientific Procedures," 457–71, esp. 465, 467; Schutz, "Die Konstitution der Wirkwelt and ihrer Modifikationen," part C: "Die theoretische Welt der kontemplativen

Betrachtung," folder 225, 135–49, PAS; Schutz, "On Multiple Realities," 245–59; Embree, "Schutz's Phenomenology of the Practical World," 126–27; Schutz, "Political Economy," 103; Schutz, *Phenomenology* of the Social World, 43–44; Husserl, "Vienna Lecture," 277–78, 280, 282–87, 291, 298.

27. Emanuel Winternitz, "Role of Music in Leonardo's Paragone," 270–71; George Schutz, inteview by Lester Embree; Fritz Machlup, interview by George Schutz; Winternitz, *Musical Instruments*.

28. To Friedrich Hayek, 4 Nov. 1942, PAS; from Friedrich Hayek, 25 Dec. 1942, PAS; Schutz, "Problem of Rationality in the Social World," (lecture), 7, 19; Schutz, "Problem of Rationality in the Social World" (ed. Brodersen), 65–66, see also pp. 65, 69, 71, 73, 74–77, 79, 81–82.

29. Schutz, "Homecomer," 114–15.

30. Ibid.,106–19; to the *American Journal of Sociology*, 28 Nov. 1944, PAS; from Reuben Hill, 22 May 1945, PAS; to Reuben Hill, 5 June 1945, PAS; from Herbert Spiegelberg, 27 July 1945, PAS.

31. To Aron Gurwitsch, 1 Oct. 1943, *PE*, 68; Schutz, "Some Leading Concepts of Phenomenology," 99–117; from Leo Strauss, 9 Nov. 1943, PAS.

32. To Aron Gurwitsch, 19 Sept. 1945, *PE*, 76–77.

33. Schutz, *Phenomenology of the Social World,* 52–63, and see Chapter 4, 99, 103; Schutz, "On Multiple Realities," 207–29. I am indebted here to Lester Embree, "Schutz's Phenomenology of the Practical World," 124–28; see also to Aron Gurwitsch, 21 June 1954, *PE*, 226.

34. Schutz, "On Multiple Realities," 229–59; to Eugen Fink, 23 May 1957, PAS; from Maurice Natanson, 21 July 1954, PAS; from Herbert Spiegelberg, 15 Jan. 1946, PAS; from Aron Gurwitsch, 3 Sept. 1945, *PE*, 75; see Gurwitsch, *Field of Consciousness*, 382–413; from Eric Voegelin, 6 Oct. 1945, PAS; see Grathoff, "Zum Begriff des 'Finiten'," 25–37; Webb, *Presence of the Past,* 50.

35. Schutz, "Fragments toward a Phenomenology of Music," 243–75.

36. Kersten, "Preface to 'Fragments on the Phenomenology of Music'," 6–22; see Schutz, "Fragments toward a Phenomenology of Music," 244, 246–50, 254, 263–68; see Smith, introduction to *In Search of Musical Method*, 2.

37. From Hans Staudinger to Alfred Schutz, 28 June 1944, PAS; from Marvin Farber, 14 July 1944, 19 Aug. 1944, 9 Sept. 1944, PAS; Ilse Schutz, interview by Anne Schwabacher, pp. 52–53.

38. To Aron Gurwitsch, 11 May 1946, *PE*, 80–81; from Aron Gurwitsch, 9 June 1946, 20 June 1946, *PE*, 81; from Fritz Machlup, 23 Apr. 1946, PAS; to Marvin Farber, 11 May 1946, PAS; from Eric Voegelin, 18 Apr. 1946, 1 May 1946, PAS; from Walter Froehlich, 9 June 1946, PAS; to Ilse Schutz, 14 July 1946, 18 July 1946, 17 Aug. 1946, 9 Sept. 1946, 12 Sept. 1946, 16 Sept. 1946, 19 Sept. 1946, 22 Sept. 1946, PPAS; from Ilse Schutz, 16 July 1946, 11 Sept. 1946, 20 Sept. 1946, PPAS; from Dr. Knapp to Mrs. A. Schutz, 24 Sept. 1946, PPAS.

39. To Ilse Schutz, 24 Sept. 1946, 25 Sept. 1946, 27 Sept. 1946, 28 Sept. 1946, 30 Sept. 1946, PPAS.

40. To Aron Gurwitsch, 17 Nov. 1946, *PE*, 87; 20 Apr. 1947, *PE*, 90; 3 Sept. 1947, *PE*, 94–95; 4 Feb. 1948, *PE*, 97; to Fritz Machlup, 1 Jan. 1946, 25 May 1947, PAS; from Marvin Farber 1 May 1947, PAS; from Eric Voegelin 1 Aug. 1947, 31 Dec.

1947, PAS; to Stephan Kuffner, 19 Aug. 1947, PAS; to Ilse Schutz, 20 Mar. 1947, 30 Mar. 1947, 4 June 1947, 16 June 1947, 22 June 1947, 25 June 1947, 3 July 1947, PPAS; from Ilse Schutz, 26 Mar. 1947, 30 May 1947, 4 June 1947, 20 June 1947, 29 June 1947, 1 July 1947, 13 July 1947, PPAS; from Walter Froehlich, 6 Jan. 1948, PAS; Ilse Schutz, interview by Anne Schwabacher, 54; "Clippings," folder 449, PAS; to George Schutz, 9 June 1947, 16 June 1947, 1 July 1947, PPAS; from George Schutz, 7 June 1948, PPAS; to Hansi, 9 Aug. 1947, PPAS.

41. Ilse Schutz, interview by Anne Schwabacher, 54–55.

Chapter 8

1. To Marvin Farber, 16 Dec. 1942, PAS; to Aron Gurwitsch, 9 Nov. 1942, *PE*, 64–65; 11 June 1945, *PE*, 74; from Aron Gurwitsch, 16 July 1944, *PE*, 69–72; Gurwitsch, "On Contemporary Nihilism," 170–98.

2. Schutz, "Stranger," 91–105.

3. From Aron Gurwitsch, 16 July 1944, *PE*, 69–72.

4. Gurwitsch, "On Contemporary Nihilism," 170–98.

5. Aron Gurwitsch, "Some Philosophical Roots of Nazism," cited in Embree, "Two Husserlians Discuss Nazism," 79–80; from Aron Gurwitsch to Eric Voegelin, 3 April 1949, courtesy of Lester Embree.

6. To Aron Gurwitsch, 11 June 1945, *PE*, 74; Schutz, "Stranger," 99, 104–5; Schutz, "On Multiple Realities," 213 n. 7.

7. Schutz, *Phenomenology of the Social World,* 44, 97; from Eric Voegelin, 21 Apr. 1945, PAS.

8. Schutz, "Gnosticism and Orthodoxy," 4:227.

9. From Eric Voegelin, 2 Nov. 1952, PAS; Schutz, "Gnosticism and Orthodoxy," 227; George Schutz, interview by Michael Barber.

10. From Eric Voegelin, 21 Apr. 1945, PAS (my translation).

11. Schutz,"The Homecomer," 116–19.

12. From Eric Voegelin, 28 Dec. 1943, PAS (my translation).

13. Ibid., see chapter 7, 10–11; this chapter, 2–3; Schutz, "Husserl's *Crisis of Western Sciences*," 178. For a full discussion of the gradual publication of various parts of Husserl's *Crisis*, see Carr "Translator's Introduction," xvi–xxi.

14. From Eric Voegelin, 15 Sept. 1952, PAS (my translation).

15. To Eric Voegelin, 10 Oct. 1952, PAS; see Zaner, "introduction," viii.

16. From Eric Voegelin, 10 Jan. 1953, PAS (my translation); see Maurice Natanson, "Disenchantment and Transcendence" in *Phenomenology, Role, and Reason,* 317.

17. To Eric Voegelin, 10 Oct. 1952, PAS.

18. Ibid., 6–7 (my translation); Schutz, "Gnosticism and Orthodoxy," 229, 230, 232, 233.

19. From Eric Voegelin, 1 Jan. 1953, PAS.

20. From Eric Voegelin, 19 Oct. 1952, PAS.

21. See above chapters 2–3; Weber, "Science as a Vocation," 147–48.

22. Habermas, "Discourse Ethics," 45–50; from Eric Voegelin, 15 Sept. 1952, PAS.

23. From Aron Gurwitsch, 19 Dec. 1940, *PE*, 31; 16 July 1944, *PE*, 69–72; Husserl, "Vienna Lecture," 298–99; Gurwitsch, "On Contemporary Nihilism," 170–98; Embree, "Everyday Social Relevancy in Gurwitsch and Schutz," 47.

24. Schutz, "Gnosticism and Orthodoxy," 223.

25. From Eric Voegelin, 28 Sept. 1943, 28 Dec. 1943, 21 Apr. 1945, 6 Oct. 1945, 7 Nov. 1949, 30 Apr. 1951, 15 Sept. 1952, 1 Jan. 1953, 10 Jan. 1953, 31 May 1957, PAS; to Eric Voegelin, 10 Oct. 1952, PAS; see Voegelin, *Autobiographical Reflections*, 73; Voegelin, *New Science of Politics*, 13–22; from Eric Voegelin to Alfred Schutz on Edmund Husserl, 17 Sept. 1943; Voegelin and Strauss, *Faith and Political Philosophy*, 20, 24–34; Husserl, "Vienna Lecture," 286.

26. Two other correspondents highlight this lack of an ethical viewpoint in Schutz's thought, noticed by Gurwitsch and Voegelin: Herbert Spiegelberg and Kurt Wolff. See Spiegelberg, "Defense of Human Equality," 144–46; from Herbert Spiegelberg, 21 Dec. 1940, 6 Sept. 1943, 20 Oct. 1944, PAS; from Kurt Wolff, 5 June 1945; 11 Oct. 1955, 2 Nov. 1955, PAS; to Kurt Wolff 21 Apr. 1952, PAS; Wolff, "Before and after Sociology," 155–57, 266–69; Wolff, *Survival and Sociology*, 46–47, 51–52, 55 n. 23; H. Wolff, *Transformation in the Writing*, 126; Schutz, *Phenomenology of the Social World*, 241; Powell, "What and Why of Experience," 115; Parsons, "Constitutive Phenomenology," 341; Schutz, "Symbol, Reality, and Society," 318.

Chapter 9

1. To Marvin Farber, 19 Oct. 1951, PAS; see also to Marvin Farber 23 May 1948, no date (folder 523), PAS; Alfred Schutz, Curriculum Vitae for United States Office of Economic Warfare, folder 820, PAS; to Fritz Machlup, 17 Sept. 1945, 25 Sept. 1945, 1 Jan. 1947, 14 Mar. 1948, 28 Mar. 1948, 26 May 1949, 20 Nov. 1949, PAS; from Fritz Machlup, 18 Sept. 1945, PAS; Letter of Recommendation for Alfred Schutz to Señor Luis Montes de Oca, Presidente Ejecutivo, Banco Internacional, S.A., 10 Mar. 1947, PAS; to Ilse Schutz, 7 June 1949, PAS; to Ilse Schutz, 3 Sept. 1946, 12 Oct. 1946, 18 Mar. 1947, 30 Mar. 1947, 15 June 1947, 8 July 1947, 3 July 1948, 22 July 1948, 7 Aug. 1948, 7 June 1949, 26 June 1949, 28 June 1949, 4 July 1949, 16 July 1949, 19 Oct. 1950, 22 Oct. 1950, 27 Oct. 1950, 30 Oct. 1950, PPAS; from Ilse Schutz, 6 July 1949, PPAS; from Gottfried Haberler, 7 Jan. 1948, PAS; to Aron Gurwitsch, 10 July, 1946, *PE*, 82–83; 20 Apr. 1947, *PE*, 90–91; 4 Oct. 1950, *PE*, 118–19; 2 Dec. 1950, *PE*, 122–23; 16 July 1951, *PE*, 137; to Eric Voegelin, 9 Feb. 1949, PAS.

2. From Alvin Johnson, 22 Dec. 1942, 28 Feb. 1944, 21 Feb. 1945, 2 Mar. 1945, PAS; from Bryn Hovde, 29 May 1947, 2 June 1948, 25 Feb. 1949, PAS; from Hans Simons, 24 Apr. 1950; Brodersen, "Editor's Note," xiii; from Albert Salomon, no date (folder 777), PAS; from Howard White, 22 Nov. 1949, PAS; from Horace Kallen, 11 Jan. 1950, PAS; Schutz, "Scholar of Multiple Involvements," 134–39; from *12th Street, A Quarterly*, 14 Apr. 1950, PAS; to Marvin Farber, 19 Oct. 1951, PAS; from Hans Staudinger, 9 Mar. 1950, PAS; from Carl Mayer, 11 Oct. 1945, 29 Oct. 1951, PAS; to Aron Gurwitsch, 30 Oct. 1951, *PE*, 146–47; to Herbert Spiegelberg, 30 Oct. 1951, PAS; from Erich Hula, dean of the New School, 22 Jan. 1946, PAS.

3. To Kurt Riezler, 12 Nov. 1948, PAS; from Aron Gurwitsch, 9 Nov. 1948, *PE*, 102–5; 27 Nov. 1948, *PE*, 107–8; from Eric Voegelin, 6 Jan. 1949, PAS; to Eric Voegelin, 4 Feb. 1949, PAS.

4. Course listings; to Aron Gurwitsch, 4 Feb. 1949, *PE*, 110–11; 26 Jan. 1950, *PE*, 114; 16 Mar. 1951, *PE*, 132–33. Fred Kersten and Evelyn S. Lang have provided information about how Schutz taught and revised courses; see Alfred Schutz, "Notes for a Course on the Problems of a Sociology of Language, Fall Semester, 1958," reconstructed by Fred Kersten, in *Collected Papers*, vol. 5, ed. Lester Embree (forthcoming).

5. To Marvin Farber, 2 Jan. 1945, 4 May 1945, 11 May 1946, PAS; from Marvin Farber, 4 July 1945, 1 Oct. 1945, 28 Oct. 1945, postcard of 2 Dec. 1945, postcard of 8 Dec. 1945, 16 Jan. 1946, postcard of 5 July 1946, 11 Oct. 1946, 11 Nov. 1946, 19 Nov. 1946, 23 May 1948, 9 June 1948, 28 Aug. 1948, 3 Sept. 1948, 8 Sept. 1948, 22 Aug. 1949, 20 July 1950, PAS; from Herbert Spiegelberg, 15 Jan. 1946, PAS; Copy of the purchase of a bow for 5,000 francs at E. Maucotel and P. Deschamp, 13 July 1948, PAS; Schutz, "Editor's Preface to Edmund Husserl, 'Die Welt der lebendigen Gegenwart,' " 323; Stern, "Toward a Solution of the Problem of Solipsism," 679–87; Kuhn, "Exhortatio ad Philosophiam," 83–98. Wagner, "Marvin Farber's Contribution to the Phenomenological Movement," 231.

6. From Marvin Farber, 9 Feb. 1947, 22 Aug. 1949, 10 Dec. 1950, 30 Dec. 1950, 17 May 1951, PAS.

7. To Helmut Kuhn, 25 Jan. 1948, PAS; Halberstam, *Fifties* 9, 11, 12, 15, 16, 25, 27, 49; Goldman, *Crucial Decade—and After,* 7, 8, 9–10, 21–22, 34–35, 37–38, 57–60, 72, 76–77.

8. From Helmut Kuhn to Marvin Farber, 25 Dec. 1947, PAS; from Marvin Farber, 25 Dec. 1947, 3 Jan. 1948, PAS; see Carnap,"Two Concepts of Probability," 513–32; Carnap, "Remarks on Induction and Truth," 590–602; Carnap, "Rejoinder to Felix Kaufmann," 609–11; Riepe, "Conclusion," 381; Mathur, "Marvin Farber, 26; Roderick M. Chisholm, foreword to *The Search for an Alternative,* vii, x; for Farber's own praise of Lenin and a criticism of Husserl's political neutrality, see Farber, *Search for an Alternative*, 216–38, esp. p. 227 on Husserl; Wagner, "Marvin Farber's Contribution to the Phenomenological Movement," 223; from Cornelius Krusé to Helmut Kuhn, 8 Jan. 1948, PAS; from Helmut Kuhn, 16 Jan. 1948, PAS; from Aron Gurwitsch, 3 Sept. 1945, *PE*, 76.

9. From Marvin Farber to Helmut Kuhn, 20 Jan. 1948, PAS; to Helmut Kuhn, 25 Jan. 1948, 16 Oct. 1958, PAS; to Helmut Kuhn, 25 Jan. 1948, in *PE*, 97–98; from Aron Gurwitsch, 2 Feb. 1948, *PE*, 96; to Aron Gurwitsch, 4 Feb. 1948, *PE*, 96–97.

10. Farber, "Experience and Transcendence" 1–23; from Herbert Spiegelberg, 7 Oct. 1951, 16 Dec. 1951, PAS; to Herbert Spiegelberg, 30 Oct. 1951, PAS; Schutz, "Choosing among Projects of Action," 67–96 and Schutz, *Problem of Social Reality*, 66–96; from Aron Gurwitsch, 16 Oct. 1951, *PE*, 144–45; 6 Nov. 1951, *PE*, 147; to Aron Gurwitsch, 30 Oct. 1951, *PE*, 146–47; from Aron Gurwitsch to Marvin Farber, appended to letter of 16 Oct. 1951, *PE*, 145–46; from Marvin Farber to Aron Gurwitsch, 22 Oct. 1951, in *PE*, 147–48; from Marvin Farber, 9 Nov. 1949, 26 Mar. 1951, PAS; to Marvin Farber, 4 June 1951, PAS.

11. From Walter Froehlich, 18 June 1940, 1 Nov. 1940, 20 June 1942, 17 July 1943, 6 Sept. 1945, 27 Mar. 1946, 6 Apr. 1946, 26 Apr. 1946, 13 May 1946, 20 Oct.

1948, 25 Feb. 1949, 6 Oct. 1951, 29 Feb.1952, 22 Feb. 1953, 5 May 1955, 17 June 1955, 20 Jan. 1957, 5 Jan. 1959, PAS; to Walter Froehlich, undated, before 16 Sept. 1940, 16 Sept. 1940, 24 Jan. 1942, 12 Mar. 1942, 14 Apr. 1946, 27 May 1948, PAS; Obituary for Viktor Stadler (with Ilse's handwriting stating that he, next to Winternitz, was Schutz's closest friend in Vienna), 13 June 1946, folder 799, PAS; from Viktor Stadler, 1 Jan. 1940, PAS; from Steffi Froehlich to Ilse Schutz, 6 Jan. 1941, PAS; from Fritz Machlup, 15 Apr. 1946, 23 Apr. 1946, PAS; to Fritz Machlup, 27 Apr. 1946, 27 June 1947, 9 Oct. 1947, PAS; from Eric Voegelin, 18 Apr. 1946, 1 May 1946, PAS; from Eric Schiff, 22 June 1947, PAS; from Friedrich Hayek, 11 Apr. 1950, PAS; from Else Staudinger, 3 Jan. 1947; from Walter Biemel, 18 Sept. 1947, 2 Oct. 1947, 5 Nov. 1949, 5 Dec. 1949, PAS; to Hannah Machlup, 6 Sept. 1951, PAS; from Hannah Machlup, 22 Sept. 1951.

12. To Mavin Farber, 4 June 1951, PAS; from Marvin Farber, 30 Dec. 1950, PAS; from Ilse Schutz, 4 June 1947, 29 June 1947, 1 July 1948, 22 June 1949, 20 July 1949, 2 Nov. 1950, PPAS; to Ilse Schutz, 5 Sept. 1946, 17 Oct. 1946, 22 June 1947, 14 June 1949, 16 June 1949, 18 June 1949, 19 June 1949, 23 June 1949, 26 June 1949, 29 June 1949, 4 July 1949, 17 July 1949, 23 July 1949, PPAS; to Hansi, 9 Sept. 1945, 9 Aug. 1947, PPAS; from George Schutz, 7 June 1948, 29 June 1949, PPAS.

13. To Ilse Schutz, 21 Aug. 1948, PPAS.

14. From Ilse Schutz, 13 June 1948, 13 July 1948, 18 July 1948, 25 July 1948, 31 July 1948, 14 June, 1949, cable of Aug. 1948, PPAS; to Ilse Schutz, 29 June 1948, 3 Aug. 1948, 19 Aug. 1948, PPAS; to Hansi, 2 Aug. 1945, 20 June 1948, 27 July 1948, 31 July 1948, 19 Aug. 1948, PPAS; from Ilse Schutz to Hansi, 9 Aug. 1948, PPAS.

15. To Raymond Aron, 26 Aug. 1949, PAS; from Marcel Beaufils, 7 Aug. 1946, PAS; to Marcel Beaufils, 28 Dec. 1952, PAS; from W. Eucken, 10 May 1949, PAS; to Eric Voegelin, 1 Nov. 1949, PAS; from Karl Popper, 20 Mar. 1950, PAS; from Hans Vanden Waal, 28 Oct. 1948, PAS; from Fritz Machlup, 14 Nov. 1946, 8 Nov. 1949, 29 Oct. 1951, 12 Dec. 1951, PAS; to Fritz Machlup, 9 Dec. 1947, 26 May 1949, 20 Nov. 1949, PAS; Machlup, *Basing-Point System;* Machlup, *Economics of Sellers' Competition,* see 494 n. 13; from Eric Voegelin, 26 July 1946, 2 May 1948, 18 May 1948, 30 Aug. 1948, 22 Mar. 1949, 29 Mar. 1949, 6 June 1949, 5 Nov. 1949, 20 May 1950, 27 July 1950, 26 Dec. 1951, 12 Sept. 1953, PAS; to Eric Voegelin, 26 Aug. 1949, 1 Nov. 1949, 17 May 1950, 30 Oct. 1951, 28 Dec. 1951, 9 Sept. 1953, PAS; see Riezler, *Man,* 21; "Draft of a Letter of Recommendation for a Guggenheim Fellowship," undated, folder 838, PAS.

16. To Aron Gurwitsch, 21 Dec. 1945, *PE*, 79–80; 11 May 1946, *PE*, 80–81; 18 Oct. 1946, *PE*, 84–85; 20 Apr. 1947, *PE*, 90–91; 22 June 1947, *PE*, 91–92; 3 Sept. 1947, *PE*, 94–95; 12 Nov. 1948, *PE*, 105–6; 25 Nov. 1948, *PE*, 106–7; 12 Dec. 1948, *PE*, 108–9; 24 Dec. 1950, *PE*, 127–28; 16 Mar. 1951, *PE*, 132; from Aron Gurwitsch, 9 Dec. 1945, *PE*, 77–79; 20 June, 1946, *PE*, 81–82; 19 Aug. 1946, *PE*, 83–84; 17 Nov. 1946, *PE*, 87–88; 23 Mar. 1947, *PE*, 89–90; 11 Aug. 1947, *PE*, 92–93; 3 Oct. 1947, *PE*, 95–96; 22 May 1948, *PE*, 101–2; 9 Nov. 1948, *PE*, 102–5; 27 Nov. 1948, *PE*, 107–8; 17 Dec. 1948, *PE*, 108–9; 4 Oct. 1950, *PE*, 118–19; "*Curriculum Vitae* of Aron Gurwitsch," in *PE*, 104–5.

17. Schutz, "Sartre's Theory of the Alter Ego," 180–203; to Aron Gurwitsch, 18 Oct. 1946, *PE*, 84–86; 3 Sept. 1947, *PE*, 94–95; September 3, 1947, 94–95; from Aron Gurwitsch, 15 Dec. 1946, *PE*, 88–89; 11 Aug. 1947, *PE*, 92–94; 22 May 1948,

PE, 101–2; see Schutz, *Reflections on the Problem of Relevance*, 171–74; Schutz, "Edmund Husserl's *Ideas*, Volume II," 21.

18. Gurwitsch, "Présuppositions philosophiques de la logique," 395–405, from Aron Gurwitsch, 17 Dec. 1950, *PE*, 123–24; to Aron Gurwitsch, 24 Dec. 1950, *PE*, 125–28; 8 Jan. 1951, *PE*, 128–29; 13 Jan. 1951, *PE*, 129–30; Schutz, *"Zu Wilhelm Meisters Wanderjahre,"* Series I, Writings, Folders 28–30, 885–1039, PAS, see in particular pp. 934–36.

19. From Aron Gurwitsch, 4 Feb. 1950, *PE*, 115–16; 24 June 1951, *PE* 135–36; 1 Aug. 1951, *PE*, 138–39; to Aron Gurwitsch, 24 Dec. 1950, *PE*, 124–28; 16 July 1951, *PE*, 137; 29 Aug. 1951, *PE*, 139–42; see Schutz, "Type and Eidos," 115; see Gurwitsch, "Gelb-Goldstein's Concept," 359–84; see "Clippings," folder 494, PAS; Endress, "Alfred Schutz and Karl Mannheim," 1–17; see Grathoff, "Introduction to 'The Field of Consciousness,' " 134.

20. Schutz, "Well-Informed Citizen," 120–34; Srubar, "Where Does the Political Emerge From?" 1–22; Kim, "Schutz's Account of the Life-World," 1–24; Husserl, *Ideas* vol. 1, #100, p. 246.

21. From Aron Gurwitsch, 2 Dec. 1950, *PE*, 122–23; 8 Jan. 1951, *PE*, 128–29; Atomic Bomb Clippings, Folder 406, PAS; "Clippings," folder 449, PAS; to Hansi, 9 Aug. 1945, PPAS.

22. Schutz, "Sartre's Theory of the Alter Ego," 180–203.

23. Schutz, "Language, Language Disturbances, and the Texture of Consciousness," 260–86; to Aron Gurwitsch, 4 Feb. 1949, *PE*, 110–11; 26 Jan. 1950, *PE*, 114; 4 Oct. 1950, *PE,* 119; from Aron Gurwitsch, 4 Feb. 1950, *PE*, 115–17; Course listings.

24. Schutz, "Scholar of Multiple Involvements," 134; to Eric Voegelin, 10 Oct. 1952, PAS; from Herbert Furth, 11 Apr. 1950, PAS; Helling, "A. Schutz and F. Kaufmann," 35–55 (*Human Studies* reprint, 141–61).

25. Schutz, "Choosing among Projects of Action,"67–96; Schutz, "Das Problem der Personalität in der Sozialwelt," 7066–90; Schutz, "Die Konstitution der Wirkwelt und ihrer Modifikationen," 7159–78; Schutz, "On Multiple Realities," 235.

26. Schutz, "Choice and the Social Sciences," 573–90.

27. Schutz, "Making Music Together," 159–78; Schutz, "Husserl *Parisian Lectures* of 1929," 193–95; George Schutz, interview by Lester Embree; see Vaitkus, *How Is Society Possible?* 148, 163–89.

28. Schutz, *"Zu Wilhelm Meisters Wanderjahre,"* 885–1039, see esp. pp. 934–36, as well as pp. 887, 899–900, 906, 922–23, 937, 957–63, (see esp. 934 for a list of unexplained events); to Aron Gurwitsch, 24 Dec. 1950, *PE*, 124–28.

29. Ibid., 898, 899–916, 916, 937, 972, 975–76, 981, 982, 983, 986, 987, 989, 991, 993, 995–96, 999, 1004; on fate see 955, 990, 1015, 1029; from Eric Voegelin, 30 Aug. 1948, PAS; from Albert Salomon, 3 July 1948, PAS.

30. Schutz, *"Wilhelm Meisters Lehrjahre,"* Series I, Box 12, Folder 230, 17, PAS.

31. Ibid., 1, 3–4, 5, 9, 10–11, 13, 16–27.

32. To Ilse Schutz, 22 June 1947, PPAS; Schutz, *"Wilhelm Meisters Lehrjahre,"* 17.

33. To Aron Gurwitsch, 3 Sept. 1947, *PE*, 94; 4 Oct. 1950, *PE*, 118–20.

34. Schutz and Luckmann, *Structures of the Life-World*, 1:3–18; 36–58.

35. From Ilse Schutz to Richard M. Zaner, cited by Zaner, introduction, xxii–xxiii.

36. Luckmann, preface to vol. 1 of *The Structures of the Life-World*, xxiii–xxiv; Zaner, introduction, viii.

37. Schutz, *Reflections on the Problem of Relevances*, 2, 4–5, 8, 10–15, 16–74; on the interaction between motivational and interpretative relevances, see also 69–70.

38. Ibid., 75–32.

39. Ibid., 133–82; from Aron Gurwitsch, 22 May 1948, *PE*, 101.

40. To Alvin Johnson, 10 Apr. 1950, 24 Apr. 1950, PAS; see Schutz, "T.S. Eliot's Concept of Culture," 4, 25, 44; from Fritz Machlup, 24 Sept. 1941, PAS; see column by Paul Henry Lang on democratic nature of choral music, folder 936, PAS.

Chapter 10

1. To Marvin Farber, 19 Oct. 1951, 14 Oct. 1954, PAS; from Marvin Farber, 4 Jan. 1953, PAS; to I. Hosiosky, 29 Apr. 1954, PAS; from Hans Simons, 30 July 1954, 1 July 1955, PAS; from Fritz Machlup, 28 Nov. 1955, PAS; Wagner, *Alfred Schutz*, 70; to Aron Gurwitsch, 4 Feb. 1949, *PE*, 110; 4 Dec. 1952, *PE*, 193; 11 May 1953, *PE*, 205–6; 2 Oct. 1953, *PE*, 216; 13 Oct. 1954, *PE*, 234; 1 May 1956, *PE*, 254–55; 18 Nov. 1956, *PE*, 259; from Walter Froehlich, 17 June 1955, PAS; to Ilse Schutz, 1 Jan. 1953, 4 Jan. 1953, 25 Sept. 1953, 4 Nov. 1953, 11 Nov. 1953, 27 Dec. 1953, 31 Dec. 1953, 13 Sept. 1954, 18 Sept. 1954, 21 Sept. 1954, 30 Sept. 1954, PPAS; from Ilse Schutz, 15 Sept. 1954, 28 Sept. 1954, PPAS; to Albert Salomon, 3 Sept. 1954, PAS; to Alvin Johnson, 13 Oct. 1954, PAS; from Eduardo Nicol, 28 Feb. 1955, PAS; from Maurice Natanson, 2 Oct. 1955, PAS.

2. To Ilse Schutz, 1 Jan. 1953, 30 Sept. 1954, PPAS; from Ilse Schutz, 31 Dec. 1953, 15 Sept. 1954, 25 Sept. 1954, PPAS.

3. To Hansi, 19 Nov. 1952, 17 July 1954, 21 July 1954, 26 July 1954, 1 Aug. 1954, 4 Aug. 1954, 8 Aug. 1954, 12 Aug. 1954, 21 Sept. 1954, from Evelyn Schutz, 6 Aug. 1956, PPAS; from Ilse Schutz, 24 Oct. 1953, PPAS; George Schutz, interview by Michael Barber.

4. To Ilse Schutz, 24 Sept. 1952, 4 Nov. 1953, 27 Dec. 1953, 21 July 1954, 6 Feb. 1955, PPAS; from Ilse Schutz, 26 July 1953, 17 Aug. 1953, 24 Oct. 1953, 27 Oct. 1953, 31 Oct. 1953, 4 Nov. 1953, 6 Nov. 1953, 31 Dec. 1953, 15 Sept. 1954, 28 Sept. 1954, 1 Oct. 1954, PPAS; from Evelyn Schutz, 6 Aug. 1956, PPAS; to Maurice Natanson, 17 Oct. 1955, 25 Sept. 1956, PAS; to Dr. Eugene S. Wilson, 23 Apr. 1955, PAS; George Schutz, interview by Michael Barber.

5. George Schutz, interview by Lester Embree; George Schutz, interview by Michael Barber.

6. George Schutz, interview by Lester Embree; Fritz Machlup, interview by George Schutz.

7. Fritze Machlup, interview by George Schutz; George Schutz, interview by Lester Embree.

8. From Emodi Handorff to Ilse Schutz, Easter 1953, PPAS; to Ilse Schutz, 4 Nov. 1953, PPAS; to Hansi, 26 July 1954, 1 Aug. 1954, PPAS; George Schutz, interview by Michael Barber.

9. From Marvin Farber, 7 July 1953, 3 Aug. 1953, 15 Aug. 1953, 13 Dec. 1953, PAS; to Marvin Farber, 19 Jan. 1954, PAS.

10. From Marvin Farber, 23 Jan. 1954, 7 Feb. 1954, 20 Feb. 1954, 6 Mar. 1954, 11 Apr. 1954, 27 Apr. 1954, 21 Aug. 1954, 28 Aug. 1954, 10 Sept. 1954, PAS; to Marvin Farber, 19 Jan. 1954, 25 Feb. 1954, 21 Jan. 1954, 10 Mar. 1954, 14 Oct. 1954, PAS; from Herbert Spiegelberg, 2 Apr. 1953, PAS; Carr, "Translator's Introduction," xvi–xxi.

11. To H.L. van Breda, 21 Sept. 1949, PAS.

12. From H. L. van Breda, 7 Dec. 1946, 12 Nov. 1947, 26 July 1949, 9 Nov. 1949, 25 Jan. 1950, PAS; to H. L. van Breda, 21 Sept. 1949, 5 Jan. 1950, 9 Aug. 1954, PAS; From H. L. van Breda to Y. H. Krikorian, 2 July 1956, PAS; from Marvin Farber, 15 July 1943, 23 Oct. 1944, 15 Aug. 1953, 29 Sept. 1953, 19 Sept. 1955, 30 Sept. 1955, 31 Oct. 1955, 19 Nov. 1955, 22 Dec. 1955, 2 June 1956, postcard of 21 June 1956, 1 Oct. 1956, 22 Oct. 1956, 27 Oct. 1956, PAS; to Marvin Farber, 28 Sept. 1955, 11 Oct. 1955, 25 Oct. 1955, (no day) Oct. 1956, PAS.

13. To Aron Gurwitsch, 19 Jan. 1952, *PE*, 149; 23 Feb. 1952, *PE*, 161–62; from Hans Simons, 24 Apr. 1950, 18 July 1952, 1 June 1953, 25 July 1953, 30 July 1954, 25 Oct. 1954, 1 July 1955, 12 July 1956, PAS; to Hans Simons, 25 July 1952, PAS; to Hans Staudinger, 22 May 1953, PAS.

14. Course listings; Catalogue, the Graduate Faculty of the New School for Social Research; to Alvin Dobsevage of the New York Philosophical Society, 3 Feb. 1954, PAS; from Esther Dworetsky, 29 Mar. 1955, PAS.

15. To Leila Freedberger, secretary of the Alumni Association, 28 Jan. 1955, PAS; Embree, "Editor's Introduction," 4–5; see "Clippings," folder 494, PAS.

16. Memorandum to Dr. Saul Padover, 28 Nov. 1952, PAS; memorandum from Hans Neisser, 8 Jan. 1953, PAS; from Hans Neisser, 1 June 1953, PAS; memorandum to the Department of Philosophy, 15 Jan. 1953, PAS; to Dr. Deyrup, 26 Jan. 1953, 1 May 1956, PAS; to Hans Simons, 4 Jan. 1952, 29 Feb. 1952, PAS; from Hans Simons, 1 June 1953, 31 Jan. 1954, 26 Oct. 1954, PAS; to Hans Staudinger, 22 May 1953, PAS; from Hans Staudinger, 2 May 1955, PAS; from Alvin Johnson, 10 Apr. 1950, 25 Apr. 1950, 6 Dec. 1950, 7 Jan. 1952, 4 Mar. 1952, 6 Oct. 1954, 19 Apr. 1955, 22 Nov. 1955, 23 Nov. 1955, 17 Jan. 1956, PAS; to Alvin Johnson, 24 Apr. 1950, 4 Jan. 1952, 29 Feb. 1952, 13 Oct. 1954, 4 Dec. 1954, 9 Dec. 1954, 7 Jan. 1955, 17 Jan. 1956, PAS; see Jaspers, *Origin and Goal of History;* from Alvin Johnson to Lady Davis, 27 Apr. 1955, PAS. Johnson cites Maurice Wertheim's comment that he "ought to be in Wall Street or the penitentiary" in letter from Alvin Johnson to Lady Davis, 27, April 1955, PAS; see to *Social Research*, 11 Oct. 1955, 6 Dec. 1955, 22 May 1956, 28 May 1956, PAS; from *Social Research*, 1 Dec. 1955, 23 Oct. 1956, PAS; to Aron Gurwitsch, 27 Sept. 1955, *PE*, 243.

17. Schutz "Scope and Function of the Department of Philosophy," 112–17; memorandum of the dean of the Graduate Faculty to the chairman of the Board, 13 Jan. 1954, PAS; from Willma Carlson, 6 Jan. 1954, PAS; from Hans Staudinger, 23 Nov. 1953, 13 Apr. 1954, PAS; to Hans Staudinger, 22 Feb. 1954, PAS; announcement of Alfred Schutz to the Department of Philosophy, 28 Jan. 1954, PAS; from Dr. Deyrup, 4 Dec. 1953, PAS.

18. From Werner Marx, 7 Mar. 1954, PAS; to Werner Marx, 10 Nov. 1954, PAS; to Hans Jonas, 29 Feb. 1956, PAS.

19. To Hans Jonas, 27 Jan. 1954, 17 Mar. 1954, 24 Mar. 1954, 21 Oct. 1954, PAS; from Hans Jonas, 18 Mar. 1954, 21 Mar. 1954, PAS; from Hans Jonas to Alvin

Johnson, 4 July 1954, PAS; see Kersten, "Image-Making and the Nature of the Imagination," 47–89; from Hans Staudinger to Hans Jonas, 3 Mar. 1954, 8 Mar. 1954, 18 Mar. 1954, 23 Mar. 1954, PAS; from Hans Jonas to Hans Staudinger, 3 Mar. 1954, 30 Dec. 1954 (copy to Alfred Schutz), PAS.

20. From Hans Simons, 26 Oct. 1954, PAS; to Hans Simons, 4 May 1956, PAS; from Hans Jonas, 17 Jan. 1956, PAS; from Reuben Abel to Alfred Schutz and Hans Jonas, 5 Apr. 1956, PAS; memorandum to Hans Staudinger, 23 Feb. 1956, PAS; to Hans Staudinger, 20 Dec. 1955, 10 Jan. 1956, PAS; from Hans Staudinger, 6 Jan.1956, PAS.

21. From Hans Jonas, 10 Jan. 1956, PAS.

22. To Hans Jonas, 29 Feb. 1956, PAS.

23. Cairns, "My Own Life," 1–13; see Schutz, "Some Structures of the Life-World," 122–23, 130, 132 for the possible influence of Cairns.

24. Ilse Schutz, interview by Anne Schwabacher, 41; from Albert Salomon, no date, folder 777, 18 June 1948, 3 July 1948, 29 June 1954, 19 Apr. 1955, 8 July 1957, PAS; to Albert Salomon, 3 Sept. 1954, 5 Nov. 1955, PAS; from Bryn J. Hovde, 26 May 1954, PAS; see Salomon, *Tyranny of Progress*.

25. From Adolph Lowe, 2 Dec. 1944, 11 Feb. 1944, 2 Mar. 1948, 14 Sept. 1955, PAS.

26. From Adolph Lowe, 10 Oct. 1955, 19 Oct. 1955, 23 Nov. 1955, 1 Dec. 1955, PAS; see Schutz, "Social Science and the Social World," 140–46.

27. To Mary Henle, 27 Jan. 1953, PAS; from Horace Kallen, 11 Jan. 1950, undated (folder 628), PAS; to Horace Kallen, 26 Feb. 1952, 12 May 1952, 21 Dec. 1956, PAS; from Karl Löwith, 4 Feb. 1954, PAS; receipt for purchase of *Gesammelte Werke* of Wilhelm von Humboldt for DM 113, 11 Feb. 1953, folder 667, PAS; to Swiss Bank Corporation (money to Löwith's account), 3 Mar. 1953, PAS; from Leo Strauss, 24 Oct. 1953, 11 Oct. 1955, PAS; to Leo Strauss, 20 Oct. 1955, PAS; from Anna Huth, 5 Nov. 1956, PAS.

28. To Arvid Brodersen, 29 Oct. 1951, 12 May 1952, 22 Apr. 1954, 23 Nov. 1955, 27 Mar. 1958, PAS; from Arvid Brodersen, 26 Mar. 1958, PAS; to Aron Gurwitsch, 19 Jan. 1952, *PE*, 149; from Helmut Wagner, 16 Nov. 1952, 17 May 1953, 14 Dec. 1953, 8 May 1955, 16 June 1955, 28 Oct. 1955, 17 Jan. 1956, 14 Oct. 1956, 28 Oct. 1957, 16 May 1958, PAS; to Helmut Wagner, 9 July 1954, 11 May 1955, 21 Oct. 1958, PAS; from Eduard Heimann to Helmut Wagner, 3 May 1955, PAS; vita of Helmut Wagner, folder 892, PAS; to Aron Gurwitsch, 27 Sept. 1955, *PE*, 243–44.

29. To Maurice Natanson, 29 Jan. 1951, PAS.

30. To Horace Kallen, 26 Feb. 1952, PAS; from Maurice Natanson, 20 Nov. 1951, 11 Dec. 1951, 8 Jan. 1952, 31 Mar. 1952, undated postcard from Houston, 13 Nov. 1954, 18 Jan. 1955, 26 Jan. 1955, 25 May 1955, 6 July 1955, 2 Oct. 1955, 16 Nov. 1955, 12 Dec. 1955, 8 Apr. 1956, 7 Sept. 1956, 17 Sept. 1956, PAS; to Maurice Mandelbaum, 7 Jan. 1955, PAS.

31. From Maurice Natanson, 1 Oct. 1953, PAS.

32. To Marvin Farber, 19 Jan. 1954, PAS; from Maurice Natanson, 1 Oct. 1953, 14 Nov. 1953, 20 Jan. 1954, 3 Apr. 1954, PAS; to Maurice Natanson, 13 Oct. 1954, PAS; clipping on a student who shot his teacher in Sicily, folder 716, PAS;

33. From Maurice Natanson, 1 Nov. 1956, PAS; see also from Natanson, 6 July 1955, 20 Oct. 1955, 16 Nov. 1955, 26 Dec. 1955, 20 Feb. 1956, 20 June 1956, PAS.

34. From Maurice Natanson, 7 Jan. 1954, 15 Feb. 1955, 12 Oct. 1955, PAS; to Maurice Natanson, 10 Mar. 1954, PAS.

35. To Maurice Natanson, 7 Nov. 1952, 14 Nov. 1953, 18 Dec. 1953, 13 Oct. 1954, 18 Mar. 1955, 1 July 1955, 17 Oct. 1955, 20 Oct. 1955, 25 Sept. 1956, PAS; from Maurice Natanson, 23 June 1954, 24 Sept. 1954, 13 Nov. 1954, 10 May 1955, 22 June 1955, 6 July 1955, 11 Dec. 1955, 25 Dec. 1955, PAS; gift certificate receipt, 20 Oct. 1955, PAS; from Lois Natanson, no date in folder 713, 8 Jan. 1955, 31 Oct. 1955, PAS; to Aron Gurwitsch, 23 Feb. 1952, *PE*, 162; from Aron Gurwitsch to Alfred Schutz, 9 Mar. 1952, *PE*, 162–64.

36. From Maurice Natanson, 23 June 1953, 20 Jan. 1954, 3 Apr. 1954, 30 June 1954, 24 Sept. 1954, 18 Oct. 1954, 13 Nov. 1954, 2 Oct. 1955, 26 Dec. 1955, 5 Jan. 1956, 7 Sept. 1956, PAS; to Maurice Natanson, 21 June 1954, 2 July 1954, 13 Oct. 1954, 18 Mar. 1955, 3 Nov. 1955, 25 Sept. 1956, PAS; see Natanson, *Social Dynamics of George H. Mead;* see also Natanson, "Concept of the Given in Peirce and Mead," 143–57. Other articles of Natanson that Schutz read include: "La historia como ámbito finito de sentido," later published as "History as a Finite Province of Meaning," 175–76; review of *Phénoménologie de Husserl*, 563–67; "Phenomenology from the Natural Standpoint," 241–45; review of *Martin Buber,* 113–17.

37. From Maurice Natanson, 16 Oct. 1952, 21 July 1954, 1 Nov. 1956, PAS; Natanson, *Social Dynamics of George H. Mead*, 59, 81–82; Natanson, review of *Martin Buber*, 115–17.

38. From Maurice Natanson, 14 Nov. 1951, 31 Mar. 1955, 2 Oct. 1955, PAS; to Maurice Natanson, 18 Mar. 1955, 17 Oct. 1955, 3 Nov. 1955, PAS; Natanson, "Sartre's Fetishism," 95–99; the passage to which Natanson referred can be found in Schutz, "Phenomenology and the Social Sciences" the first paragraph on p. 182, corresponding to the first full paragraph on p. 135 in *The Problem of Social Reality*; Natanson, "History as a Finite Province of Meaning," 175–76; Ames, "Mead and Husserl on the Self," 320–31; Natanson, "Phenomenology from the Natural Standpoint," 241–45.

Chapter 11

1. From Fritz Machlup, 11 Mar. 1952, 2 July 1952, 14 Nov. 1953, 17 Apr. 1954, 22 Apr. 1954, 10 Nov. 1954, 14 Nov. 1954, (no day) Jan. 1955, 17 Apr. 1955, 7 Aug. 1955, 28 Nov. 1955, 1 May 1956, 4 Mar. 1957, PAS; to Fritz Machlup, 25 June 1952, 20 Aug. 1952, 17 Apr. 1953, 22 Sept. 1953, 4 Dec. 1953, 17 Feb. 1954, 5 Nov. 1954, 9 Nov. 1954, 9 Dec. 1954, 26 Sept. 1955, 8 May 1956, 19 Mar. 1957, PAS; Machlup, *Methodology of Economics;* to Aron Gurwitsch, 11 May 1953, *PE*, 205–7; Nagel, review of *The Counter-Revolution of Science,* 560–65; see Machlup, *Economics of Sellers' Competition;* Friedman, *Essays in Positive Economics*, 41; Machlup, "Do Economists Know Anything?" 168–77, 182; from Fritz Machlup to Gustav Machlup, 16 Nov. 1953, PAS; see also Machlup, "Problem of Verification in Economics" 1–21; from Fritz Machlup to E. S. Wilson, director of admissions at Amherst, 10 Feb. 1955, PAS;

2. To Eric Voegelin, 10 Jan. 1952, 10 Jan. 1953, 12 Mar. 1953, 9 Sept. 1953, PAS; from Eric Voegelin, 12 Jan. 1952, 1 Jan. 1953, 14 Jan. 1953, 20 May, 1953, 3 Sept. 1953, 28 Sept. 1953, 23 Dec. 1953, 31 Oct. 1954, 31 May 1955, 17 Oct. 1956,

31 Dec. 1956, PAS; Schutz, "Gnosticism and Orthodoxy," 221–22, 224–33; Voegelin, *New Science of Politics*, 37; see Voegelin, *Israel and Revelation*, 25–53, 73–112; Voegelin, "The Origins of Totalitarianism," 21; from Guggenheim Foundation to Alfred Schutz, 31 Dec. 1954, PAS; from Louisiana University Press to Alfred Schutz, 12 Apr. 1955, PAS; to Donald Ellegood, 22 Apr. 1955, PAS.

3. Program of "Organizational Behavior Project Conference on 'Problems of Model Construction in the Social Sciences,'" 15–16 Mar. 1952, folder 544, PAS; to Harold Garfinkel, 21 Mar. 1952, PAS; to Kenneth Burke, 16 Sept. 1952, 16 Dec. 1952, 11 June 1953, PAS; from Kenneth Burke, 10 Nov. 1952, PAS; Schutz, "Making Music Together," 174; Burke, "On Human Behavior Considered 'Dramatistically,' " 274–76, 279, 283–85, 286, 289, 292; see Schutz, *Reflections on the Problem of Relevance*, 155–56; Burke, *A Grammar of Motives* 294–97.

4. Compare: to Aron Gurwitsch, 19 Jan. 1952, *PE*, 149–53 and Gurwitsch, *Field of Consciousness*, 318, 334, 341, 346, 351, 356–58, 368–70; see Lester Embree, "Everyday Social Relevancy," 45–61; compare to Aron Gurwitsch, 25 Jan. 1952, *PE*, 153–60, and *Field of Consciousness*, 392, 394, 399, 414–20; Gurwitsch, *Marginal Consciousness*, 69–70, 78; from Aron Gurwitsch, 17 Feb. 1952, *PE*, 160–61; compare to Aron Gurwitsch, 17 Mar. 1952, *PE*, 164–70, and *Field of Consciousness*, 212, 221, 233–34, 236, 240, 243, 258–61, 265, 270, 289; see Langsdorf, "Der Rand des Bewusstseins, 31–50.

5. From Aron Gurwitsch, 4 Apr. 1952, *PE*, 172–75; 3 Oct. 1952, *PE*, 179–80; to Aron Gurwitsch, 20 Apr. 1952, *PE*, 175–79; 12 Oct. 1952, *PE*, 181–83.

6. From Aron Gurwitsch, 2 Nov. 1952, *PE*, 183–84; 24 Jan. 1953, *PE*, 194–95; 5 Apr. 1953, *PE*, 202–3; 11 June 1953, *PE*, 209–10; 24 June, 1953, *PE*, 212–13; to Aron Gurwitsch, 10 Nov. 1952, *PE*, 186–87; 4 Dec. 1952, *PE*, 191–93; 9 Apr. 1953, *PE*, 203–4; 15 June 1953, *PE*, 210–12; excerpts from Aron Gurwitsch to Eric Voegelin, 2 Nov. 1952, in *PE*, 184–85.

7. Nagel, review of *The Counter-Revolution of Science*, 560–565; from Aron Gurwitsch, 15 May 1953, *PE*, 207–9; 11 June 1953, *PE*, 210; to Aron Gurwitsch, 4 Dec. 1952, *PE*, 191; 9 April 1953, *PE*, 203–4; 11 May 1953, *PE*, 205–6.

8. From Aron Gurwitsch, 2 Nov. 1952, *PE* 183–84; 16 Nov. 1952, *PE*, 190–91; 6 Feb. 1953, *PE*, 196–97; 5 Apr. 1953, *PE*, 202–3; 24 June, 1953, *PE*, 212–13; 5 Sept. 1953, *PE*, 213–14; 7 Nov. 1955, *PE*, 244–46; 22 Feb. 1956, *PE*, 249–50; 8 Apr. 1956, *PE*, 251–52; 29 Apr. 1956, *PE*, 252–54; to Aron Gurwitsch, 10 Nov. 1952, *PE*, 186–87; 4 Dec. 1952, *PE*, 193; 9 Feb. 1953, *PE*, 197–99; 27 Feb. 1956, *PE*, 250–52; 1 May 1956, *PE*, 254–56; 18 Nov. 1956, *PE*, 259.

9. To Aron Gurwitsch, 2 Oct. 1953, *PE*, 216; 3 Dec. 1953, *PE*, 217–19; 20 Dec. 1953, *PE*, 220; 17 Jan. 1954, *PE*, 222–23; 21 Jan. 1954, *PE*, 223–24; 21 June 1954, *PE*, 226–27; from Aron Gurwitsch, 22 Nov. 1953, *PE*, 216–17; 5 Dec. 1953, *PE*, 219–20; 6 June 1954, *PE*, 224–25; 27 June 1954, *PE*, 227–28; Gurwitsch, "Kantian and Husserlian Conceptions of Consciousness," 148–60.

10. To Aron Gurwitsch, 21 June 1954, *PE*, 226–27; 13 Oct. 1954, *PE*, 234–38; from Aron Gurwitsch, 27 June 1954, *PE*, 227–28; 10 Sept. 1954, *PE* 231–34; see Grathoff, "Das Problem der Intersubjektivität," 87–20.

11. From Aron Gurwitsch, 7 Aug. 1954, *PE*, 229; 30 Nov. 1954, *PE*, 238–39; 7 Apr. 1955, *PE*, 241–42; 24 May, 1955, *PE*, 241–42; 21 Sept. 1955, *PE*, 242–43;

7 Nov. 1955, *PE*, 244–46; 29 Apr. 1956, *PE*, 252–54; to Aron Gurwitsch, 23 Aug. 1954, *PE*, 230–31; 27 Sept. 1955, *PE*, 243–44; 1 Jan. 1956, *PE*, 246–47; 1 May 1956, *PE*, 254–56; Gurwitsch, "Last Work of Edmund Husserl," 397–447.

12. From Aron Gurwitsch, 3 May 1953, *PE*, 204; 11 June 1953, *PE*, 209–10 n. 1; 3 Jan. 1954, *PE*, 221; 3 Jan. 1954, *PE*, 221; 27 June 1954, *PE*, 228; 10 Sept. 1954, *PE*, 233; 7 Apr. 1955, *PE*, 240; 7 Nov. 1955, *PE*, 244–45; 22 Feb., 1956, *PE*, 249–50; 8 Apr. 1956, *PE*, 251–52; 4 Aug. 1956, *PE*, 256–57; to Aron Gurwitsch, 9 Apr. 1953, *PE*, 203–4; 11 May, 1953, *PE*, 206; 3 Oct. 1954, *PE*, 237; Jan. 1955, *PE*, 239; 7 Apr. 1955, *PE*, 240; 14 Apr. 1955, *PE*, 240–41; 21 Sept. 1955, *PE*, 242; 27 Sept. 1955, *PE*, 243–44; 27 Feb. 1956, *PE*, 250–51; 1 May 1956, *PE*, 255; 1 Oct. 1956, *PE*, 257–58; see Spiegelberg, *Phenomenological Movement;* announcement of concert by Eric Itor Kahn, 29 Apr. 1958, PAS; from Eric Itor Kahn, 26 Nov. 1941, 20 May 1942, 13 Sept. 1945, PAS.

13. From L. M. Lachmann, 2 May 1956, 17 June 1956, 2 July 1956, 19 Sept. 1956, PAS; to L. M. Lachmann, 10 May 1956, PAS; see review of *On Freedom and Free Enterprise,* 954–55, folder 890, PAS; to Lewis Beck, 12 Sept. 1955, PAS; from Lewis Beck, 28 Sept. 1955, PAS; to Howard Becker, 7 Dec. 1951, 23 Jan. 1952, 17 Oct. 1955, PAS; from Howard Becker, 12 Dec. 1951, PAS; from Lewis Coser, 21 Nov. 1953, 16 May 1956, 6 June 1956, PAS; to Lewis Coser, 28 May, 1956, PAS; from Fritz Machlup, 17 Apr. 1955, PAS; from Tomoo Otaka, 25 July 1953, PAS.

14. From Richard Snyder, 30 June 1954, 16 Sept. 1954, 23 Nov. 1954, PAS; to Richard Snyder, 6 Sept. 1954, PAS.

15. To Jeremiah Kaplan, telegram of 19 Nov. 1958, PAS.

16. From Jeremiah Kaplan, 24 June 1954, 28 Aug. 1954, 13 Sept. 1954, 3 Feb. 1955, 15 Sept. 1955, 4 Dec. 1956, PAS; to Jeremiah Kaplan, 3 Sept. 1954, 6 Sept. 1954, 31 Jan. 1955, 16 Feb. 1955, 12 Sept. 1955, 30 Nov. 1956, 17 May 1957, 21 Oct. 1958, telegram of 19 Nov. 1958, PAS; from John C. McKinney, 16 Aug. 1955, PAS; to John McKinney, 12 Sept. 1955, PAS; to Hans Staudinger, 26 Mar. 1957, PAS.

17. To Marvin Farber, 19 Oct. 1951, PAS; from Eric Voegelin, 28 Dec. 1951, 15 Sept. 1952, PAS; Schutz, "Scope and Function of the Department of Philosophy," 115–17; Schutz, "Santayana on Society and Government," 201–25; see Santayana, *Scepticism and Animal Faith,* 20–21, 68–69, 75, 99, 103–6; Santayana, *Dominations and Powers,* 69, 117, 119, 194, 242, 269, 274, 295, 298, 316, 350–52, 399, 410, 447, 461–62; Srubar, *Kosmion*, 189.

18. Santayana, *Character and Opinion in the United States*, 77.

19. *Ibid*., 70, 72, 74, 75, 77, 79, 82–84, 87, 88, 94, 114, 121, 134; Santayana *Winds of Doctrine*, 209, 213; from Fred Kersten to Michael Barber, 10 Sept. 2001.

20. From Aron Gurwitsch, 3 Oct. 1952, *PE,* 179, 3 Jan. 1954, *PE,* 221; to Aron Gurwitsch, 4 Dec. 1952, *PE,* 191; Husserl, *Ideen,* vol. 2 trans. by Richard Rojcewicz and André Schuwer, under the title *Ideas Pertaining to a Pure Phenomenology and to a Phenomenological Philosophy*, vol. 2 Schutz, "Edmund Husserl's *Ideas,* Volume II," 15–39; from Marvin Farber, 8 Mar. 1952, 17 Apr. 1952, 12 July 1952, 5 Aug. 1952, 26 Oct. 1952, 4 Jan. 1953, 3 May 1953, 14 June 1953, 15 July 1953, 3 Aug. 1953, 29 Sept. 1953, 12 Dec. 1953, PAS; to Marvin Farber, 25 July 1952, April 17, 1952, 30 Nov. 1953, PAS; from Marvin Farber to Arthur Goddard, 18 Nov. 1953, PAS; Schutz "Making Music Together," 161–62; Schutz, "Phenomenology and The Foundations of the Social Sciences," 40–49; Husserl, *Ideen,* vol. 3, trans. Ted. E. Klein and

William E. Pohl, under the title *Ideas Pertaining to a Pure Phenomenology and to a Phenomenological Philosophy*, vol. 3.

21. From Aron Gurwitsch, 15 May 1953, *PE*, 207; to Aron Gurwitsch, 23 Feb. 1951, *PE*, 161; from Harold Garfinkel, 5 Dec. 1949, 13 Aug. 1951, 7 Sept. 1951, 24 Mar. 1952, PAS; to Harold Garfinkel, 4 Sept. 1951, 21 Mar. 1952, PAS; to Fritz Machlup, 25 June 1952, PAS; to G. S. Brunner, 21 Mar. 1952, PAS; to Oskar Morgenstern, 21 Mar. 1952, PAS; to Kenneth Burke, 16 Sept. 1952, PAS.

22. Cf. Alfred Schutz, "Common-Sense," 74–80 with Schutz, "Problem of Rationality in the Social World," 27–34; from Garfinkel, 8 Oct. 1953, PAS; to Harold Garfinkel, 19 Jan. 1954, PAS; Garfinkel, "Notes on 'The Sociological Attitude,'" PAS.

23. Schutz, "Positivistic Philosophy,"125–28, 128–39, 140, 142, 143–49; to Aron Gurwitsch, 9 Apr. 1953, *PE*, 203; 11 May 1953, *PE*, 205–6; from Aron Gurwitsch, 13 May 1953, *PE*, 207; Nagel and Hempel, "Symposium," 44–45, 48–49, 50–55, 58–60, 79–84; Schutz, "Concept and Theory Formation in the Social Sciences," 48–64; Williame, *Les fondements phénoménologiques,* 188.

24. To Luis Recasens Siches, 7 Sept. 1954, PAS; from Luis Recasens Siches, Christmas 1955, PAS; Schutz, "Don Quixote and the Problem of Reality," 135–58.

25. Schutz, "Mozart and the Philosophers," 192. Hermann Cohen was a neo-Kantian philosopher at Marburg at the end of the nineteenth century and early twentieth century. Søren Kierkegaard was a Danish philosopher of religion. Wilhelm Dilthey, a German philosopher, stressed a human science approach to consciousness and psychology.

26. Ibid., 179–200.

27. From Maurice Merleau-Ponty, 19 Dec. 1955, PAS; to Maurice Merleau-Ponty, 20 Feb. 1956, PAS; from Editions d'art Lucien Mazenod, 21 Dec. 1955, 21 Jan. 1956, 13 Apr. 1956, 16 July 1956, 1 Feb. 1957, PAS; to Editions d'art Lucien Mazenod, 21 Jan. 1956, 13 Apr. 1956, 8 May 1956, 17 May 1956, 18 Mar. 1957; Schutz, "Max Scheler's Philosophy," 133–44.

28. From Louis Finkelstein, 7 Jan. 1954, PAS; to Louis Finkelstein, 4 Feb. 1954, 5 Apr. 1954, 24 May 1954, 22 June 1954, 30 June 1954, 1 July 1954, PAS; to Maurice Natanson, 13 July 1954, PAS; from Maurice Natanson, 21 July 1954, PAS; to Jessica Feingold, 19 July 1954, PAS; from Jessica Feingold, 21 July 1954, PAS; see Program of a Conference on Symbols and Society, Aug. 30–Sept. 2, 1954, PAS; Schutz, "Symbol, Reality, and Society," 287–356; to Aron Gurwitsch, 21 June 1954, *PE*, 226–27; 13 Oct. 1954, *PE*, 234–38; from Aron Gurwitsch, 10 Sept. 1954, *PE*, 231–34.

29. Barber, "Finitude Rediscovered," 73–80; from Kurt Wolff, 11 Oct. 1955, PAS; Morris, "Comment on Schutz's Paper on Symbolism" folder 462, PAS; Schutz, "Experience and Transcendence," 234–41; for notebook materials of Schutz on this topic, see Schutz and Luckmann, *Structures of the Life World*, vol. 2, 266–77.

Chapter 12

1. From Louis Finkelstein to Alfred Schutz, 6 Jan. 1955, 21 June 1956, 21 Apr. 1958, PAS. In a newspaper interview, Clarence Faust specifically connects the conference on equality with the Supreme Court decision; see "Clippings," folder 485, PAS. George Schutz recollects how his father was quite aware that African Americans had

a different perspective on many issues from whites and that whites were often unable to understand them (George Schutz, interview by Michael Barber).

2. To Louis Finkelstein, 10 Jan. 1955, 11 May 1955, PAS; from Louis Finkelstein, 9 May 1955, PAS; from Jessica Feingold, 14 June 1955, PAS; to Jessica Feingold, 21 July 1955, 28 July 1955, PAS; Schutz, "Equality and the Meaning Structure of the Social World," 226–49.

3. Ibid., 250–73; see Embree, "Alfred Schutz on Reducing Social Tensions," 81–102; to Luis Recasens Siches, 20 Oct. 1955, PAS; from Luis Recasens Siches, 8 June 1956, PAS; from Adolph Lowe, 14 Sept. 1955, PAS. Crane Brinton was a historian. Gunnar Myrdal, a sociologist, wrote on race matters in his famous *An American Dilemma.*

4. From Arthur Goddard, 18 Sept. 1955, PAS; Schutz, "Equality and the Meaning Structure of the Social World," 257, 262; from Shirley and Arthur Goddard, 8 Aug. 1940, PPAS.

5. Schutz, "Equality and the Meaning Structure of the Social World," 256, 260–62, 266, 267–68.

6. Bryson et al., *Aspects of Human Equality,* 407–8; Schutz, "In Search of the Middle Ground," 147–51; Clarence Faust, ed., "Unedited Stenotype Report, 'Aspects of Human Equality,' Meeting of Fellows, Conference on Science, Philosophy, and Religion," folder 465, PAS: Tues. afternoon, 29 Aug. 1955, 7, 10, 18, 20; Tues. morning, 30 Aug. 1955, 87; Thurs. morning, 1 Sept. 1955, 32; Thursday luncheon, 1 Sept. 1955, 53, 55, 58; Embree, "Ethical–Political Side of Schutz," 238–39. The group included such renowned persons as Thomas Adam (professor of political science, New York University), Lyman Bryson (professor of education, Columbia University), Thurston Davis, S.J. (editor, *America*), Clarence H. Faust (Ford Foundation, Fund for the Advancement of Education), Louis Finkelstein (chancellor, professor of theology, the Jewish Theological Seminary of America), Eli Ginzberg (professor of economics, Columbia University), Simon Greenberg (professor, vice-chancellor, Jewish Theological Seminary of America), William Haller (Fellow, Folger Shakespeare Library), Hudson Hoagland (Worcester Foundation for Experimental Biology, professor of physiology, Boston University), Albert Hofstadter (professor of philosophy, Columbia University), Charles S. Johnson (president, Fisk University), F. Ernest Johnson (professor of education, Columbia University), John LaFarge, S.J. (Catholic Interracial Council), Dorothy Lee (professor of anthropology, Merrill-Palmer School); R. M. MacIver, (professor of political philosophy and sociology, Columbia University), Richard McKeon (professor of philosophy and Greek, University of Chicago), Perry Miller (professor of American literature, Harvard), John P. Plamenatz (professor, Nuffield College, Oxford University), Ordway Tead (board of higher education, City of New York), and Quincy Wright (professor of international law, University of Chicago).

7. "Unedited Stenotype Report, 'Aspects of Human Equality,'" Tuesday morning session, 30 Aug. 1955, 40–53, 60–62 (Schutz's comments), 87–109, 109–17 (Schutz's comments), 126–39; see Scheler on "functionalization of essences" in *Problems of a Sociology of Knowledge*, 41; Scheler, *On The Eternal in Man*, 209–13; "Unedited Stenotype Report, 'Aspects of Human Equality,' " Tues. afternoon, 30 Aug. 1955, 126–39, 140–44, 154 (Schutz's comments), 158–65, 165–66 (Schutz's comments); Thurs. morning, 1 Sept. 1955, 1–13; 13–15 (Schutz's comments); see Mead, "Genesis of the Self and Social Control," 284–85.

8. "Unedited Stenotype Report, 'Aspects of Human Equality,'" Wed. morning, 31 Aug. 1955, 167–91; 191–92 (Schutz's comments).

9. Schutz, "In Search of the Middle Ground," 147–51.

10. "Unedited Stenotype Report, 'Aspects of Human Equality,'" Monday afternoon, 29 August 1955, 13; on the need to root the idea of inequality in an underlying ethics see Johnson, "Concept of Human Equality," 30; Plamenatz, "Equality of Opportunity," 94; Greenberg "Comments by Simon Greenberg,' " 109–10; Hofstadter, "Career Open to Personality," 113, 132; Lee, "Equality of Opportunity as a Cultural Value," 255, 256–58, 262, 265, 269–70; Faust, "Equality in American Education," 318–19; Hofstadter comments, "Unedited Stenotype Report, 'Aspects of Human Equality,' " Tues.afternoon, 30 Aug. 1955, 142–52, and Thursday morning, 1 Sept. 1955, 23–24; McKeon comments, Mon. evening, August 19, 1955, 50; Lee comments, Wed. morning, 31 Aug. 1955, 185–87; Hofstadter comments, Tues. morning, 30 Aug. 1955, 89; Tues. afternoon, 30 Aug. 1955, 132, 169; on messianic pretensions, see "Unedited Stenotype Report, 'Aspects of Human Equality,' " Tues. morning, 30 Aug. 1955, 101–4.

11. Schutz comments, "Unedited Stenotype Report, 'Aspects of Human Equality,'" Wed. morning, 31 Aug. 1955, 191–92.

12. To Aron Gurwitsch, 1 May 1956, *PE*, 255; from John Courtney Murray, 25 June 1956, PAS; to Louis Finkelstein, 22 Mar. 1956, PAS; Embree, "Ethical-Political Side of Schutz," 238–39.

13. Embree, "Ethical-Political Side of Schutz," 239–43; from Clarence Faust, 8 May 1956, PAS; from Louis Finkelstein, 10 May 1956, PAS.

14. Embree, "Ethical-Political Side of Schutz," 243–45; to Clarence Faust, 12 May 1956, PAS; from Louis Finkelstein, 10 May 1956, PAS; Schutz, "Some Considerations concerning Thinking in Terms of Barriers," 287–89.

15. Embree, "Ethical-Political Side of Schutz," 250–69; Schutz, "Memorandum [to Dr. Doctor Harold Laswell]," 291–95. Harold Lasswell was a sociologist whose principal work discussed the effects of bureaucracy on democracy

16. Embree, "Ethical-Political Side of Schutz," 271–77.

17. Embree, "Ethical-Political Side of Schutz," 297–98.

18. Ibid., 300–11.

19. Schutz, "Barriers of Equality of Opportunity."

20. Ibid.

21. Ibid. See also Schutz, "Ethical Issue Involved" Embree, "Ethical-Political Side of Schutz," 269–71, 276–77.

22. "Unedited Stenotype Report, 'Aspects of Human Equality,'" Mon. afternoon, 29 Aug. 1955, 7, 10, 18, 20; Thurs. luncheon, 1 Sept. 1955, 53, 55, 58; Schutz, "In Search of the Middle Ground," 148; to Louis Finkelstein, 22 Mar. 1956, PAS.

23. Schutz, "The Ethical Issue Involved," 276–77, see Schutz's summary of the report in Embree, "Ethical-Political Side of Schutz," 273.

24. Embree, "Ethical-Political Side of Schutz," 276

25. From Aldoph Lowe, 11 Feb. 1948, PAS.

26. To Marvin Farber, 21 Oct. 1958, PAS; draft of a letter to Hans Staudinger, 25 Apr. 1958, PAS; to Aron Gurwitsch, 20 Dec. 1958, *PE*, 304; Koev, "Alfred Schutz," 60–61.

Chapter 13

1. From Marvin Farber, 19 Mar. 1957, 7 Apr. 1957, 13 Apr. 1957, 15 Apr. 1957, 12 May 1957, PAS; from Marvin Farber to Fr. Leo van Breda, (no day) April 1957, PAS; to Marvin Farber, 9 May 1957, 13 June 1957, PAS.

2. To Marvin Farber, no date (draft reacting to letter of Farber, 16 April, 1958), 18 Apr. 1958, 1 May 1958, PAS; from Marvin Farber, 23 Apr. 1958, 25 Apr. 1958, 2 May 1958, 18 June 1958, 27 June 1958, PAS; to Aron Gurwitsch, 16 Mar. 1958, *PE*, 282; 1 May 1958, *PE*, 289; to Luis Recasens Siches, 14 Apr. 1958, PAS; Hermida-Lazcano, "The Taken-for-Granted World," 43–69.

3. From Marvin Farber, 21 Jan. 1957, 13 Feb. 1957, 22 July 1957, 3 Sept. 1957, 12 Oct. 1957, 8 Feb. 1958, 10 Apr. 1958, 18 June 1958, 28 June 1958, 16 July 1958, 26 July 1958, 5 Oct. 1958, 23 Nov. 1958, PAS; to Marvin Farber, 21 Oct. 1958, 20 Nov. 1958, 27 Nov. 1958, PAS; from Waltraut Stein, 12 Nov. 1958, 27 Jan. 1959, PAS; to Waltraut Stein, 15 Jan. 1959, PAS. Edith Stein was a phenomenologist who worked with Max Scheler and Edmund Husserl.

4. To H. L. van Breda, 1 July 1957, 6 July 1957, 17 Sept. 1957, 10 Oct. 1957, 8 Nov. 1957, 29 Nov. 1957, PAS; to H. L. van Breda, 16 July 1957, 21 Aug. 1957, 23 Sept. 1957, 31 Oct. 1957, PAS; Cairns, *Guide for Translating Husserl;* from Marvin Farber, 5 Oct. 1958, PAS; from Roman Ingarden to H. L. van Breda, 18 Nov. 1957, PAS.

5. To H. L. van Breda, 8 Nov. 1957, 13 Dec. 1957, 3 Jan. 1958, 21 Oct. 1958, PAS; from H. L. van Breda, 11 Jan. 1958; from Roman Ingarden, 17 Jan. 1958, 22 Feb. 1958, PAS; to Roman Ingarden, 25 Jan. 1958, PAS; from Roman Ingarden to Ilse Schutz, 12 Nov. 1959, PAS. Roman Ingarden, the Polish professor of philosophy, had studied under Husserl at Göttingen and Freiburg and worked on phenomenology and aesthetics.

6. To H. L. van Breda, 3 Jan. 1958, 20 Nov. 1958, PAS; from H.L.Van Breda, 23 Apr. 1958, 2 Oct. 1958, 24 Nov. 1958, PAS; to Andrew Osborn, 16 Oct. 1958, PAS; from Susan M. Haskins to Alfred Schutz, 20 Oct. 1958, PAS; from Hans Staudinger to Marianne Lowe, 30 May 1957, folder 802, PAS; from Hans Staudinger, 9 Apr. 1958, PAS; from Alvin Johnson to Lady Davis, 27 Apr. 1955, PAS; from Louis Bloomfield, 19 July 1957; to Louis Bloomfield, 7 Feb. 1957, PAS; to Aron Gurwitsch, 3 Feb. 1959, *PE*, 310; to Rudolf Böhm, 1 July 1957, 16 Sept. 1957, 24 Apr. 1958, 4 Dec. 1958, 14 Feb. 1959, 16 Apr. 1959, 6 May 1959, 16 May 1959; PAS; from Rudolf Böhm, 2 May 1958, 23 Jan. 1959, 9 Apr. 1959, PAS; see "Clippings," folder 449, PAS.

7. To Aron Gurwitsch, 20 Dec. 1958, *PE*, 302; 6 June 1957, *PE*, 267; to Werner Marx, 17 Sept. 1957, PAS; to Hans Simons, 13 Feb. 1958, PAS; from Hans Simons, 12 July 1956, 12 July 1957, 23 June 1958, 24 June 1958, 10 July 1958, PAS; from Eric Voegelin, 9 May 1958, PAS; to Eric Voegelin, 3 Feb. 1959, PAS; to Marvin Farber, 27 Nov. 1958, PAS; to Rudolf Böhm, 14 Feb. 1959, PAS; to Kurt Wolff, 14 Feb. 1959, 16 Apr. 1959, PAS; to Walter Froehlich, 25 Aug. 1958, PAS; from Maurice Natanson, 6 Feb. 1958, 12 Jan. 1959, 29 Mar. 1959, PAS; to Luis Recasens Siches, 17 Sept. 1957, PAS; to Helmut Wagner, 21 Oct. 1958, PAS; to Arvid Brodersen, 23 Nov. 1955, PAS; course listings; to Hans Staudinger, 27 Sept. 1957, PAS; to I. Hososky, 2 Dec. 1958, PAS; see T. Luckmann, *Life-World and Social Realities* 85–86.

8. From Alvin Johnson, 12 Sept. 1957, 31 Oct. 1957, 25 Feb. 1958, 21 Oct. 1958, 1 Dec. 1958, PAS; to Alvin Johnson, 16 Sept. 1957, 10 Oct. 1957, 25 Oct. 1957, 4 Mar. 1958, 27 Mar. 1958, 21 Oct. 1958, PAS; from Arvid Brodersen, 26 Mar. 1958, PAS; from Miguel Chareco to Hans Staudinger, 27 July 1957, PAS; from Hans Simons, 21 Aug. 1957, 19 Sept. 1957, 24 June 1958, PAS; to Hans Simons, 1 Oct. 1957, (in Staudinger file) PAS; to Hans Staudinger, 16 Apr. 1959, PAS; from Miriam Borkaw, 31 Dec. 1957, PAS; to Princeton University Press, 9 Jan. 1958, PAS; to Werner Marx, 14 Feb. 1959, PAS; from Werner Marx, 18 Feb. 1959, PAS; from Bernard Rosenberg, 11 Nov. 1958, PAS.

9. To Hans Staudinger, 17 May 1957, PAS; from Hans Staudinger to Marianne Low, 30 May 1957, PAS; to Aron Gurwitsch, 19 Jan. 1952, *PE*, 149; 16 Mar. 1958, *PE*, 282; memorandum from Hans Staudinger, 15 Nov. 1957, Apr. 1958, PAS; clipping from *The New York Times*, 12 Feb. 1956, on Senator Javits asking for student aid, folder 734, PAS; clipping on Hans Simons, *New York Post*, 15 May 1955, folder 791, PAS; draft entitled "The New School College," 5 Aug. 1957, folder 533, PAS; clipping from the *New York Herald*, folder 533, PAS; B. Luckmann, "Alfred Schütz und Aron Gurwitsch an der New School," 315–37; B. Luckmann, "Small Life Worlds of Modern Man," 580–96; from Louis M. Bloomfield, 9 July 1957, PAS; from Hans Simons, 21 Aug. 1957, PAS; from Hans Simons to friend, 7 June 1957, PAS; from Robert MacIver, 21 Jan. 1943, 27 Jan. 1943, 26 Sept. 1945, 19 Jan. 1955, 7 Nov. 1957, PAS; to Robert MacIver, 10 Jan. 1955, PAS; from Otto Kirchheimer to Alfred Schutz, 22 May 1957, PAS; from Otto Kirchheimer to Robert MacIver, 16 May 1957, PAS; to Clarence Faust, 10 Dec. 1957, Text IV, in Embree, "Ethical-Political Side of Schutz," 313–18.

10. To Clarence H. Faust, 10 Dec. 1957, in Embree, "Ethical-Political Side of Schutz," 313–18; Embree, "Ethical-Political Side of Schutz," 280; from Clarence Faust, 10 Feb. 1958, PAS; Memorandum from Hans Simons, no date, folder 533; 29 Oct. 1957, PAS; from Hans Simons, 5 Feb. 1958, 19 Feb. 1958, PAS; to Hans Simons, 14 Nov. 1957, 30 Nov. 1957, 13 Feb. 1958, PAS; from Hans Staudinger to Hans Neisser, Alfred Schutz, and Hans Simons, 9 Jan. 1958, PAS; Memorandum from Hans Staudinger to Hans Simons, 15 Jan. 1958, PAS.

11. To Eduard Heiman, 19 Nov. 1956, PAS; from Hans Aufricht, 10 May 1957, PAS; to Hans Aufricht, 23 May 1957, PAS; from Hans Simons, 26 Nov. 1956, 25 Mar. 1957, PAS; from Hans Neisser, 18 Oct. 1957, PAS; to Hans Neisser, 18 Dec. 1956, PAS; to Werner Stark, 24 Apr. 1958, PAS; Committee on Philosophy in Education (APA) Report, 19 Oct. 1957, PAS; to editor of the University of Chicago Press, 17 Jan. 1958, PAS; to Roger W. Shugg, 20 Mar. 1958, PAS; from Roger W. Shugg, 26 Mar. 1958, PAS; from Alexander J. Morin, 6 June 1958, PAS; to Else Kaufmann, 6 Nov. 1958, 28 Nov. 1958, PAS; to Marvin Farber, 27 Nov. 1958, 4 Dec. 1958, PAS; to Arnold Brecht, 28 Nov. 1958, PAS; to Gottfried Haberler, 28 Nov. 1958, PAS; from Gottfried Haberler, 2 Dec. 1958, PAS; to Alvin Johnson, 28 Nov. 1958, PAS; from Alvin Johnson, 1 Dec. 1958, PAS; to Fritz Machlup, 28 Nov. 1958, PAS; from Fritz Machlup, 2 Dec. 1958, PAS; to Maurice Natanson, 1 Nov. 1958, PAS; to Kurt Wolff, 28 Nov. 1958, PAS; from Kurt Wolff, 4 Dec. 1958, PAS.

12. To Hans Simons, 23 Mar. 1958, PAS.

13. From Hans Simons, 26 Mar. 1958, PAS; from Norman S. Buchanan to Hans Simons, 1 Apr. 1958, PAS; draft of a letter to Hans Simons, 25 Apr. 1958 (in Staudinger file, folder 802), PAS.

14. To Luis Recasens Siches, 4 Dec. 1958, PAS.

15. To H. L. van Breda, 10 Oct. 1957, PAS; to Marvin Farber, 21 Oct. 1958, PAS.

16. From Dean Hans Staudinger to Mr. Ralph Walker, chair of the board of trustees, 17 Sept. 1958, PAS; to Hans Staudinger, 23 Oct. 1958, 2 Dec. 1958, 3 Feb. 1959, PAS; from dean of Maxwell Graduate School of Citizenship and Public Affairs to Hans Staudinger, 17 Nov. 1958, PAS; announcement of Harlan Cleveland to Select Graduate Faculty, 12 Feb. 1959, PAS; to Hans Simons, 2 Dec. 1958, PAS; to Aron Gurwitsch, 20 Dec. 1958, *PE*, 304; 3 Feb. 1959, *PE*, 310; from H. L. van Breda, 21 Oct. 1958, PAS; to H. L. van Breda, 20 Nov. 1958, 24 Nov. 1958, PAS; on the reign of the two "Hanses," see B. Luckmann, "Alfred Schütz und Aron Gurwitsch an der New School," 323.

17. To Aron Gurwitsch, 25 Apr. 1957, *PE*, 266; 6 June 1957, *PE*, 267; 16 Sept. 1957, *PE*, 271; 3 Oct. 1957, *PE*, 273; 7 Dec. 1957, *PE*, 279; 1 May 1958, *PE*, 289; 21 July 1958, *PE*, 292; from Aron Guwitsch, 30 Sept. 1957, *PE*, 272; 16 July 1958, *PE*, 291; 24 Sept. 1958, *PE*, 295–97; Schutz, "Some Structures of the Life-World," 116–32.

18. From Aron Gurwitsch, 27 Jan. 1957, *PE*, 260; 10 Mar. 1957, *PE*, 261; 30 Sept. 1957, *PE*, 272; 31 Oct. 1957, *PE*, 275; 15 Jan. 1958, *PE*, 280–81; 22 Mar. 1958, *PE*, 283–84; 25 Nov. 1958, *PE*, 298–99; 9 May 1959, *PE*, 314; to Aron Gurwitsch, 15 Mar. 1957, *PE*, 262; 24 Apr. 1957, *PE*, 265–66; 6 June 1957, *PE*, 267–71; 16 Sept. 1957, *PE*, 271; 16 Mar. 1958, *PE*, 282–83; 27 Mar. 1958, *PE*, 286–87; 1 Nov. 1958, *PE*, 297–98; to Marvin Farber, 9 May 1957, 4 Apr. 1959, 16 Apr. 1959, PAS; Gurwitsch, "Problem of Existence in Constitutive Phenomenology," 118, 122–23; Alfred Schutz, "Husserl's Importance for the Social Sciences," 86–98, and in *Problem of Social Reality*, 140–49; Schutz and Luckmann, *Structures of the Life-World;* Gurwitsch, "Beitrag zur phänomenologischen Theorie der Wahrnehmung," 419–37 and as "Contribution to the Phenomenology of Perception," 332–49; see also book orders, folder 435, PAS; Gurwitsch, *Leibniz;* Evans, "Afterword," 322–23; see Gurwitsch, *Kants Theorie des Verstandes*.

19. From Aron Gurwitsch, 22 Mar. 1958, *PE*, 284; 19 Apr. 1958, *PE*, 287; 1 July 1958, *PE*, 289–90; 16 July 1958, *PE*, 291; 10 Aug. 1958, *PE*, 295; 25 Nov. 1958, *PE*, 298–300; 19 Dec. 1958, *PE*, 301; 9 Jan. 1959, *PE*, 306; 20 Jan. 1959, *PE*, 308; 9 May 1959, *PE*, 312–14; to Aron Gurwitsch, 25 Apr. 1957, *PE*, 266; 16 Mar. 1958, *PE*, 282–83; 27 Mar. 1958, *PE*, 285–87; 19 Apr. 1958, *PE*, 287; 1 May 1958, *PE*, 289; 21 July 1958, *PE*, 292–93; 20 Dec. 1958, *PE*, 302–5; 3 Feb. 1959, *PE*, 309–10; from Hans Staudinger to Henry David, 22 May 1959, PAS; see Guggenheim Fellowship application, 1957, folder 569, PAS; McGlynn, "Note on Philosophy in German Universities Today," 248–52.

20. From Aron Gurwitsch, 31 Oct. 1957, *PE*, 274; 12 Dec. 1957, *PE*, 279–80; 10 Aug. 1958, *PE*, 295; 25 Nov. 1958, *PE*, 300; to Aron Gurwitsch, 7 Dec. 1957, *PE*, 275–79; 21 July 1958, *PE*, 292–94; 1 Nov. 1958, *PE*, 298; 3 Feb. 1959, *PE*, 310; Gurwitsch, "On the Conceptual Consciousness," 391–95; Gurwitsch, "Kantian and Husserlian Conceptions of Consciousness," 150–59.

21. From Eric Voegelin, 12 Feb. 1957, 31 May 1957, 18 June 1957, 28 Feb. 1958, 9 May 1958, 3 Aug. 1958, 12 Aug. 1958, 20 Oct. 1958, 26 Dec. 1958, 23 Mar.

1959, 30 Apr. 1959, PAS; to Eric Voegelin, 2 Jan. 1958, 16 Oct. 1958, 3 Feb. 1959, PAS; clipping from *Süddeutsche Zeitung*, 29–30 Nov. 1958, 15, on Voegelin's Antritt lecture; Kraus, *Die dritte Walpurgisnacht* 38, 46, 51–58, 60–63, 66, 70–71, 79, 81, 84, 97–99, 111, 120, 123, 126, 134, 143–44, 145–46, 150, 154–55, 159, 160, 164–66, 173, 175, 179; Ilse Schutz, interview by Anne Schwabacher, 22; to Fritz Machlup, 4 Jan. 1934, PAS; see obituary for Victor Stadler, folder 799, PAS, in which Ilse Schutz remarks that Stadler belonged to Kraus's inner circle and had introduced Schutz to him.

22. From Maurice Natanson, 11 Jan. 1957, 11 Feb. 1957, 5 Apr. 1957, 25 Sept. 1957, Saturday 1957 (folder 719), 5 Dec. 1957, 24 Jan. 1958, 6 Feb. 1958, 8 Mar. 1958, 25 Oct. 1958, PAS; to Maurice Natanson, 17 May 1957, May 1957, 26 May 1957, 27 Nov. 1957, 1 Nov. 1958, PAS; from Harold Laswell to Maurice Natanson, 30 Jan. 1957, PAS; from Hans Jonas to Maurice Natanson, 20 Dec. 1957, PAS; to Martin Lean, 24 Apr. 1958, PAS; Natanson, "Death and Situation," 218; Natanson, "Study in Philosophy and the Social Sciences," 276, 283, 284; Kaminsky, review of *The Social Dynamics of George Herbert Mead,* 417; to Louis Bloomfield, 7 Feb. 1957, PAS.

23. From Maurice Natanson, 28 Aug. 1957, 6 Feb. 1958, 25 Oct. 1958, 12 Jan. 1959, PAS; to Maurice Natanson, 27 Nov. 1957, 1 Nov. 1958, PAS; from Quentin Lauer, 19 Jan. 1957, PAS.

24. From Luis Recasens Siches, 9 Sept. 1957, 24 Apr. 1958, 11 Nov. 1958, PAS; to Luis Recasens Siches, 17 Sept. 1957, 4 Dec. 1958, PAS. After an extensive search, Lester Embree reported no direct correspondence between Schutz and Ortega.

25. From Adolph Lowe, 23 Mar. 1957, August 1957 (folder 666), 23 Apr. 1958, PAS; from Thomas Luckmann, 28 Sept. 1958, PAS; to Thomas Luckmann, 21 Oct. 1958, letter with no date (folder 668), PAS; see T. Luckmann, preface to *The Structures of the Life-World*, vol. 1, xxv.

26. To Kurt Wolff, 29 May 1958, 12 May 1959, PAS; Grünwald, *Das Problem der Soziologie des Wissens,* Schelting, *Max Webers Wissenschaftslehre,* Aron, *La soziologie allemande contemporaine*.

27. To Marvin Farber, 10 Oct. 1940, PAS; untitled comments by Louis Antz *Philosophic Mind*, 8 Dec. 1939 and 22 Nov. 1940, folder 756, PAS; to Louise Antz, no date (folder 402), 4 Dec. 1940, 26 Apr. 1954, 27 Jan. 1959, PAS; from Bettina Bien, 29 July 1958, 21 Nov. 1958, PAS; see Bien, *Works of Ludwig von Mises;* from Ernest T. Ferand, 26 Sept. 1957, PAS; to Ernest T. Ferand, 2 Oct. 1957, PAS; from K. F. Koehler, Verlag Stuttgart, 16 Jan. 1958, PAS; from Irving Louis Horowitz, University of Buenos Aires, 8 Dec. 1958, PAS; to Irving Louis Horowitz, 15 Jan. 1959, PAS; from Hans Moeller, 18 Dec. 1956, PAS; to Hans Moeller, 15 Jan. 1957, PAS; from Gerhard Hirschfield, 28 Mar. 1958, 21 July 1958, PAS; from Jacques Rueff, 26 Mar. 1957, PAS; from Dr. A. Hunold, 28 Dec. 1953, PAS; report of the Venice meeting of the Mount Pelerin Society, 6–10 Sept. 1954, PAS; statement of aims of the Mount Pelerin Society, 8 Apr. 1947, PAS; program for the seventh meeting of the Mount Pelerin Society in Berlin, 29 Aug.–3 Sept. 1956, PAS; resolution of A. Hunold, 5 Dec. 1956, PAS; tenth anniversary meeting of the Mount Pelerin Society in St. Moritz, Switzerland, 2–8 Sept. 1957, PAS; eleventh anniversary meeting of the Mount Pelerin Society at Princeton, 8–13 Sept. 1958, PAS; see letter of Evelyn Schutz to Michael Barber, February 20, 2003.

28. Clipping, folder 449, PAS.

29. From director of the Cultural Circle of Royaumont to Alfred Schutz, 3 Jan. 1957, PAS; to director of the Cultural Circle of Royaumont, 5 Feb. 1957; to Madame Nadia Tegrine Bora, 9 May 1957, PAS; from H. L. van Breda to participants in the Colloque Philosophique de Royaumont, 20 May 1957, PAS; to Professor J. Linshoten, 23 May 1957, PAS; to D. K. Kuypers, 23 May 1957, PAS; to Maurice Nédoncelle, 10 Oct. 1957, 29 May 1958, PAS; from Maurice Nédoncelle, 4 Dec. 1957, PAS; Nédoncelle, *Vers und philosophie de l'amour;* review of Gaston Bachelard's *La poétique de l'espace*, folder 454, PAS; Bachelard, *La poètique de l'espace*; to Herbert Spiegelberg, 23 May 1957, PAS; to Stefan Strasser, 7 Feb. 1957, PAS; from Stefan Strasser, 25 Sept. 1957, PAS; to C. A. von Peursen, 23 May 1957, PAS; to Jean Wahl, 23 May 1957, 25 Sept. 1957, PAS; to Walter Biemel, 23 May 1957, 21 Oct. 1958, PAS; from Walter Biemel, 10 Nov. 1958, PAS; to Eugen Fink, 23 May 1957, PAS; from M. A. Bera, 22 June 1958, 16 July 1958, 30 July 1958, PAS; to M. Gandillac, 16 Oct. 1958, PAS; Richard Grathoff, *PE*, 283n; Schutz, "Das Problem der transzendentalen Intersubjektivität bei Husserl," 81–107 (later published as Schutz, "Problem of Transcendental Intersubjectivity," 51–91); from Mrs. H. G. Gadamer, 17 Sept. 1957, PAS; to Frau H. G. Gadamer, 24 Sept. 1957, PAS.

30. Schutz, "Problem of Transcendental Intersubjectivity," 51–61.

31. Ibid., 61–73.

32. Ibid., 73–84; see Fink, "L'analyse intentionnelle," 53–87.

33. Schutz, "Problem of Transcendental Intersubjectivity," 65–66, 84–91; from Dorion Cairns, 4 Apr. 1957 (courtesy of Lester Embree) 1, 3, 5, 7, 9–11, 16, 18–20 (handwritten numbers 13, 23); from Stefan Strasser, 25 Sept. 1957, PAS; from Leo Strauss, 18 July 1958, PAS; Husserl, *Cartesian Meditations*, 10–16; from Herbert Spiegelberg, 21 May 1957, PAS; to Herbert Spiegelberg, 17 Sept. 1957, PAS; to Roman Ingarden, 25 Jan. 1958, PAS; Richard Zaner, "Making Music Together While Growing Older," 1–18; to Aron Gurwitsch, 13 Oct. 1954, *PE*, 236–37; Schutz, "Scheler's Theory of Intersubjectivity," 174; Schutz, "Concept and Theory Formation in the Social Sciences," 55–56.

34. From Sidney Hook, 26 Nov. 1956, 15 Feb. 1957, PAS; to Sidney Hook, 12 Feb. 1957, PAS; Schutz, "Some Equivocations in the Notion of Responsibility," 274–76; see "Clippings," folder 449, PAS.

35. From Aron Gurwitsch, 16 Sept. 1957, 30 Sept. 1957, *PE*, 272; *PE*, 271; 20 Sept. 1957, *PE*, 272 n.1; 12 Dec. 1957, *PE*, 279–80; to Aron Gurwitsch, 3 Oct. 1957, *PE*, 273; 7 Dec. 1957, *PE*, 279; 12 July 1958, *PE*, 290–91; 1 May 1958, *PE*, 289; Embree, "Everyday Social Relevancy in Gurwitsch and Schutz," 45–61; Schutz, "Some Structures of the Life-World," 116–32, (on Gurwitsch, see 126).

36. To Kurt Wolff, 28 Nov. 1958, 14 Feb. 1959, PAS; from Kurt Wolff, 23 Dec. 1958, PAS; from Kurt Wolff to participants in the Sociology of Knowledge Symposium, 25 Jan. 1959, 6 Feb. 1959, 1 Mar. 1959, PAS; from Kurt Wolff to T. B. Bottomore, executive secretary, International Sociological Association, 25 Jan. 1959, PAS; to Maurice Natanson, 3 Feb. 1959, PAS; from Paul Weiss, 4 Feb. 1955, PAS; to Paul Weiss, 16 Feb. 1955, 12 May 1957, PAS;, from V. C. Chappell

(Weiss's secretary), 23 Feb. 1955, 27 May 1955, 10 Feb. 1956, PAS; to V. C. Chappell, 26 May 1955, 21 Feb. 1956, PAS; Schutz, "Max Scheler's Epistemology and Ethics," 145–78; see Jasper, *Die grossen Philosophen;* Scheler, *Formalism in Ethics and Non-Formal Ethics of Values* and *On the Eternal in Man.* In his investigations, Schutz produced notes on Kant far exceeding what made its way into section D, "Scheler's Criticism of Kant's Philosophy" in the essay "Max Scheler's Epistemology and Ethics" (see Series I, Writings, box 3, folders 37–38, 1285–1381, PAS. Schutz repeatedly noticed Scheler's resistance to the constructive role that according to Kant the mind plays with reference to suprasense aspects of the world. Scheler attributed it to his fear of "transcendental contingency," and to his neglect of such things as the richness of emotional life, the effect of history and ethnicity upon rationality, and the distinction between authonomy of insight and of volition; see Schutz, Series I, Writings, box 3, folders 37–38, 1293–94, 1305, 1344, 1355, 1359, 1363, 1366, 1371, 1379, and folder 41, 1433, PAS. Paul Weiss, professor of philosophy at Yale University, served as editor of the *Review of Metaphysics.*

37. To Aron Gurwitsch, 16 Mar. 1958, *PE*, 282–83; 27 Mar. 1958, *PE*, 286; to Alvin Johnson, 21 Oct. 1958, PAS; from Alvin Johnson, 21 Oct. 1958, PAS; Schutz, "Tiresias," 277–93.

38. Schutz, "Tiresias," 281–83 versus "Teiresias," 51–52; on the focus on typifications, see "Tiresias," 282, 284, 286, 289–90, versus the specious present in "Teiresias," 52–53, 54, 56–57, 59. On "exploding: anticipations," contrast "Tiresias," 286 with "Teiresias," 56. Fred Kersten in an insightful article entitled "Phenomenology, History, and Myth" links Schutz's essay on type and eidos with the Tiresias essay. Tiresias exemplifies a mythic attempt to break free of the contingencies of the present, whose life-world richness Schutz's essay on type and eidos attempts to reinstate and clarify, as a counterpart to the more refined interpretations of modern scientific reflection. See Fred Kersten, "Phenomenology, History, and Myth" 241, 245, 248–49, 262, 263 n. 87, 264–265–269.

39. To Marvin Farber, 21 Oct. 1958, 27 Nov. 1958, 4 Apr. 1959, 6 May 1959, PAS; from Marvin Farber, 6 Apr. 1959, PAS; to Aron Gurwitsch, 20 Dec. 1958, *PE*, 302–5; 3 Feb. 1959, *PE*, 310; Schutz, "Type and Eidos," 92–115; Srubar, *Kosmion*, 265. Cf. Gorman, *Dual Vision*, 72–73; see Wiggins and Schwartz, "Psychiatric Diagnosis," 204.

40. To H. L. van Breda, 29 May 1958, PAS; Schutz, "Husserl's Importance for the Social Sciences,"140–49; to Ferrater Mora, Department of Philosophy, Bryn Mawr, 15 May 1958, PAS; Schutz, "Husserl and His Influence on Me," 44.

41. To Aron Gurwitsch, 6 June 1957, *PE*, 268; 7 Dec. 1957, *PE*, 275; from Ilse Schutz, 23 Apr. 1957, 26 Apr. 1957, PPAS; from Hans Staudinger to Marianne Lowe, no date (1957?), PAS; to Evelyn Schutz, 24 Apr. 1957, PPAS; from Ilse Schutz to Alice and Aron Gurwitsch, 2 Mar. 1959, *PE*, 312; letter of Georgie to Dad, 18 Feb. 1959, PPAS; George Schutz had offered to stop college to spend more time together, but instead his father promised to be more available during his sabbatical year. Unfortunately, he died just before his son's graduation from the University of Rochester in 1959 (George Schutz, interview by Michael Barber).

Chapter 14

1. From Hans Simons, 4 Mar. 1959, PAS; to Hans Simons, 13 Mar. 1959, PAS; from Hans Staudinger to Ilse Schutz, 5 Mar. 1959, PAS; from Richard H. Kennington, 24 Mar. 1959, PAS; to Gaston Berger, 16 Apr. 1959, PAS; to Martin Landau, 14 Feb. 1959, 6 May 1959, PAS; from Martin Landau, 20 Jan. 1959, PAS; to Bernard Liebowitz, 6 May 1959, PAS; to Saul K. Padover, 6 May 1959, PAS; from Alice and Aron Gurwitsch to Ilse Schutz, 2 Mar. 1959, *PE*, 312; to Aron Gurwitsch, 16 May 1959, *PE*, 315; to Marvin Farber, 4 Apr. 1959, PAS; to Eric Voegelin, 4 Apr. 1959 (misplaced in Farber file), PAS.

2. From Maurice Natanson to Ilse Schutz, 27 May 1959, PAS; from Marvin Farber to Dear Friends, 26 May 1959, PAS; to Marvin Farber, 16 Apr. 1959, PAS; from Fritz Machlup to Ilse Schutz, 1 June 1959, PAS; Gurwitsch, "Alfred Schuetz (1899–1959)" *PPR* 20 (1959): 141–43, also cited in *PE*, 319–20.

3. From Alvin Johnson to Ilse Schutz, 21 May 1959, PAS; from Ilse Schutz to Mrs. De Lima, 30 June 1967, PAS.

4. From Alvin Johnson to Ilse Schutz, 7 Nov. 1962, PAS.

5. Van Breda, preface to *The Problem of Social Reality*, vii.

6. Zaner, "Introduction," xxii.

7. To Maurice Natanson, 3 Feb. 1959, 29 Mar. 1959, PAS.

8. From Maurice Natanson, 1 Apr. 1959, PAS.

9. To Maurice Natanson, 17 Apr. 1959, 16 May 1959, PAS; from Maurice Natanson, 6 May 1959, PAS.

10. T. Luckmann, preface to vol. 1 of *The Structures of the Life-World*, xvii, xxi–xxiv; Zaner, introduction, viii.

11. Schutz and Luckmann, *Structures of the Life-World,* 1: 3–20, 21–98.

12. Ibid., 1: 99–241; vol. 2: 20.

13. Ibid., 1: 243–331.

14. Ibid., 2: 1–97.

15. Ibid., 2: 99–157.

16. See Schutz, "Outline of a Theory of Relevance" 3–5.

17. Embree, "Appeal of Alfred Schutz beyond Philosophy," forthcoming; Ilse Schutz, interview by Rudi Hartmann, 14.

18. Ilse Schutz, interview by Anne Schwabacher, 55; Ilse Schutz, interview by Rudi Hartmann, 14; Embree, "In Memoriam, Ilse Schutz (1902–1990)," 223–24.

19. Gurwitsch, *Studies in Phenomenology and Psychology;* Gurwitsch, *Phenomenology and the Theory of Science*, Gurwitsch, *Leibniz;* Gurwitsch, *Kants Theorie des Verstandes.*

20. Voegelin, *Anamnesis.* Voegelin, *Ecumenic Age;* Voegelin, *In Search of Order;* Heilke, *Eric Voegelin,* 3–8.

21. Farber, *Aims of Phenomenology*, Farber, *Phenomenology and Existence;* Riepe, *Phenomenology and Natural Existence*, 1–13.

22. Machlup, *Production and Distribution of Knowledge;* Machlup, *Methodology of Economics;* Dreyer, preface vii–xiii; Eisner, "Machlup on Academic Freedom," 3–20.

23. Crowell, "Conversation with Maurice Natanson," 289–334; Natanson, *Edmund Husserl;* Natanson, *Anonymity;* Natanson, *Erotic Bird.* On the philosophy of Schutz and phenomenology and literature see: Natanson, *Anonymity*, 124–25, 127, 139, 143; Natanson, *Erotic Bird*, 8, 64, 82, 116, 121, 142–45; see Natanson, "Philosophy and Psychiatry," 261.

24. Berger and Luckmann, *Social Construction of Reality;* Luckmann, *Die unsichtbare Religion;* Luckmann, *Sociology of Language*.

25. Mary F. Rogers, *Sociology, Ethnomethodology, and Experience,* 82, 115, 117, 135, 187; Garfinkel, *Studies in Ethnomethodology,* 36, 37, 76, 272; Garfinkel, "Studies of the Routine Grounds of Everyday Activities," 3; Garfinkel, "A Conception of, and Experiments with, 'Trust,' " 187; Psathas, "Approaches to the Study of the World of Everyday Life," 5 n. 3; Clayman and Maynard, "Ethnomethodology and Conversation Analysis," 3–4, 29 n. 3; Garfinkel, "Perception of the Other," 26, 30, 59, 151; Hama, "Alfred Schutz's Theory of Science and Ethnomethodology," 4.

26. Psathas, "Approaches to the Study of the World of Everyday Life," 16, see also 3, 6, 15; Rogers, *Sociology, Ethnomethodology, and Experience,* 85–86, 88–89, 91, 103–5, 113, 117, 127, 132; Garfinkel, *Studies in Ethnomethodology*, 37, 104, 111, 128, 147, 152–57, 180–82; Garfinkel, "Studies of the Routine Grounds of Everyday Activities," 12; Garfinkel "Conception of, and Experiments with, 'Trust,' " 195–97.

27. Rogers, *Sociology, Ethnomethodology, and Experience,* 91–92, 113, 119, 121, 125, 126, 129; Psathas, "Approaches to the Study of the World of Everyday Life," 7–15.

28. Rogers, *Sociology, Ethnomethodology, and Experience,* 106; Garfinkel, *Studies in Ethnomethodology*, 41; Garfinkel, "Studies of the Routine Grounds of Everyday Activities," 4; Psathas, *Conversation Analysis,* 3–8, 15, 23, 27, 39, 58, 67–68; Clayman and Maynard, "Ethnomethodology and Conversation Analysis," 1–9; see Grathoff, "Über Typik und Normalität im alltäglichen Milieu," 103.

29. Psathas, *Conversation Analysis,* 1–2.

30. Clayman and Maynard, "Ethnomethodology and Conversation Analysis," 5, 17, 20, 25–28; Have, *Doing Conversation Analysis,* 15; Psathas, *Conversation Analysis,* 2, 8, 10, 11, 43–44, 51, 53, 65, 66.

Bibliography

Ames, Van Meter. "Mead and Husserl on the Self." *Philosophy and Phenomenological Research* 15 (1955): 320–31.

Aron, Raymond. *La soziologie allemande contemporaine*. Paris: Presses Universitaires de France, 1981. Translated by Mary Bottomore and Thomas Bottomore under the title *German Sociology* (Glencoe, Ill.: Free Press, 1957).

Bachelard, Gaston. *La poétique de l'espace*. Paris: Presses Universitaires de France, 1957.

Barber, Michael D. "The Ethics behind the Absence of Ethics in Alfred Schutz's Thought." *Human Studies* 14 (1991): 129–40.

———. "Finitude Rediscovered." *Philosophy and Theology* 1 (1990): 73–80.

———. *Social Typifications and the Elusive Other: The Place of Sociology of Knowledge in Alfred Schutz's Phenomenology*. London: Associated University Presses, 1988.

———. "Values as Critique and the Critique of Values: Voegelin and Schutz on Theory in the Social Sciences." In *Schutzian Social Science*, edited by Lester Embree, 213–33. Dordrecht: Kluwer Academic Publishers, 1999.

Beller, Steven. *Vienna and the Jews, 1867–1938: A Cultural History*. Cambridge: Cambridge University Press, 1990.

Berger, Peter L. "Das Problem der mannigfaltigen Wirklichkeiten: Alfred Schütz und Robert Musil." In *Sozialität und Intersubjektivität: Phänomenologische Perspektivender Sozialwissenschaften im Umkreis von Aron Gurwitsch und Alfred Schütz*, edited by Richard Grathoff and Bernhard Waldenfels, 229–51. Munich: Wilhelm Fink, 1983.

Berger, Peter L., and Thomas Luckmann. *The Social Construction of Reality: A Treatise in the Sociology of Knowledge*. New York: Doubleday, 1966.

Bergson, Henri. *Duration and Simultaneity, with Reference to Einstein's Theory*. Translated by Leon Jacobson. Indianapolis: Bobbs-Merrill, 1965

———. *Time and Free Will: An Essay on the Immediate Data of Consciousness*. Translated by F. L. Pogson. New York: Harper and Brothers, 1960.

Bien, Bettina. *The Works of Ludwig von Mises*. Irvington-on-Hudson, N.Y.: Foundation for Economic Education, 1970.

Blaug, Mark. "Was There a Marginal Revolution?" In *The Marginal Revolution in Economics: Interpretation and Evaluation*, edited by R. D. Collison Black, A. W. Coats, Caufurd D. W. Goodwin, 3–14. Durham, N.C.: Duke University Press, 1973.

Brodersen, Arvid. "Editor's Note." In *Studies in Social Theory*, edited by Arvid Brodersen. Vol. 2 of *Collected Papers*. The Hague: Martinus Nijhoff, 1964.

Brook–Shepherd, Gordon. *The Anschluss*. Philadelphia: J. B. Lippincott, 1963).

———. *The Austrians: A Thousand-Year Odyssey*. New York: Carroll & Graf, 1997.

Brough, John Barnett. "Translator's Introduction." In *On the Phenomenology of the Consciousness of Internal Time (1893–1917)*. Dordrecht: Kluwer Academic Publishers, 1991.

Bryson, Lyman, Clarence H. Faust, Louis Finkelstein, and R. M. MacIver, eds. *Aspects of Human Equality: Fifteenth Symposium of the Conference on Science, Philosophy, and Religion*. New York: Conference on Science, Philosophy, and Religion in Their Relation to the Democratic Way of Life and Harper and Brothers, 1956.

Bryon, Lyman, Louis Finkelstein, Hudson Houghland, and R. M. MacIver, *Symbols and Society: Fourteenth Symposium of the Conference on Science, Philosophy, and Religion*. New York: Conference on Science, Philosophy, and Religion in Their Relation to the Democratic Way of Life and Haper & Bros., 1955.

Burke, Kenneth. *A Grammar of Motives*. Berkeley and Los Angeles: University of California Press, 1969.

———. "On Human Behavior Considered 'Dramatistically.'" Appendix to *Permanence and Change: An Anatomy of Purpose*, 274–94. Indianapolis: Bobbs-Merrill, 1965.

Cairns, Dorion. *Guide for Translating Husserl*. The Hague: Martinus Nijhoff, 1973.

———. "My Own Life." Edited by Lester Embree. In *Phenomenology, Continuation, and Criticism: Essays in Memory of Dorion Cairns*, edited by F. Kersten and R. Zaner, 1–13. The Hague: Martinus Nijhoff, 1973.

———. The Papers of Dorion Cairns. Courtesy of Lester Embree.

Carnap, Rudolf. "Rejoinder to Felix Kaufmann." *Philosophy and Phenomenological Research* 6 (1946): 609–11.

———. "Remarks on Induction and Truth." *Philosophy and Phenomenological Research* 6 (1946): 590–602.

———. "Two Concepts of Probability." *Philosophy and Phenomenological Research* 5 (1945): 513–532.

Carr, David. "Translator's Introduction." In *The Crisis of European Sciences and Transcendental Phenomenology: An Introduction to Phenomenological Philosophy*, translated by David Carr. Evanston, Ill.: Northwestern University Press, 1970.

Chisholm, Roderick M. Foreword to *The Search for an Alternative: Philosophical Perspectives of Subjectivism and Marxism*, by Marvin Farber. Philadelphia: University of Pennsylvania Press, 1984.

Clayman, Stephen E., and Douglas W. Maynard. "Ethnomethodology and Conversation Analysis." In *Situated Order: Studies in the Social Organization of Talk and Embodied Activities*, edited by Paul ten Have and George Psathas, 1–30. Studies in Ethnomethodology and Conversational Analysis, no. 3. Washington, D.C.: International Institute for Ethnomethodology and Conversation Analysis and University Press of America, 1995.

Cox, Ronald R. *Schutz's Theory of Relevance: A Phenomenological Critique*. The Hague: Martinus Nijhoff, 1978.

Crowell, Steven. "A Conversation with Maurice Natanson." In *The Prism of the Self: Philosophical Essays in Honor of Maurice Natanson*, edited by Steven Galt Crowell, 289–34. Dordrecht: Kluwer Academic Publishers, 1995.

———, ed. *The Prism of the Self: Philosophical Essays in Honor of Maurice Natanson*. Dordrecht: Kluwer Academic Publishers, 1995.

Dempf, Alois. *Kritik der historischen Vernunft*. Munich: R. Oldenbourg, 1957.

———. *Sacrum Imperium: Geschichts- und Staatsphilosophie des Mittelalters und der politischen Renaissance*. Munich: R. Oldenbourg, 1929.

———. *Theoretische Anthropologie*. Munich: Leo Lehnen Verlag, 1950.

Dreyer, Jacob S., ed. *Breadth and Depth in Economics: Fritz Machlup—The Man and His Ideas*. Lexington, Mass.: Lexington Books, 1978.

———. Preface to *Breadth and Depth in Economics: Fritz Machlup—The Man and His Ideas*. Edited by Jacob S. Dreyer. Lexington, Mass.: Lexington Books, 1978.

Duhamel, Georges. *La possession du monde*. 30th ed. Paris: Mercure de France, 1916.

Eberle, Thomas S. "Die deskriptive Analyse der Ökonomie durch Alfred Schütz." In *Alfred Schütz: Neue Beiträge zur Rezeption seines Werkes*, edited by Elisabeth List and Ilja Srubar, 69–119. Amsterdam: Rodopi, 1988.

Review of *On Freedom and Free Enterprise: Essays in Honour of Ludwig von Mises*. *Economist* 180, no. 5900 (22 Sept. 1956): 954–55.

Eisner, Robert. "Machlup on Academic Freedom." In *Breadth and Depth in Economics: Fritz Machlup—The Man and His Ideas*, edited by Jacob S. Dreyer, 3–20. Lexington, Mass.: Lexington Books, 1978.

Embree, Lester. "Alfred Schutz on Reducing Social Tensions." In *Phenomenology of the Political*, edited by Kevin Thompson and Lester Embree, 81–102. Dordrecht: Kluwer Academic Press, 1999.

———, ed. *Alfred Schutz's "Sociological Aspect of Literature": Construction and Complementary Essays*. Dordrecht: Kluwer Academic Publishers, 1998.

———. "The Appeal of Alfred Schutz beyond Philosophy, e.g. Jurisprudence." In *The Legacy of Alfred Schutz*, edited by Martin Endress, Hisashi Nasu, and George Psathas. Dordrecht: Kluwer Academic Publishers, forthcoming. Already published as "O atractivo de Alfred Schutz en disciplinas for a da filosofia, como a xurisprudencia," translated into Italian by Maria Luz Pintos, *Agora, Papeles de Filosofia* 19 (2000): 15–30.

———. "Biographical Sketch of Aron Gurwitsch." In *Life-World and Consciousness: Essays for Aron Gurwitsch*, edited by Lester Embree, xvii–xxx. Evanston, Ill.: Northwestern University Press, 1972.

———. "Editor's Introduction." In *Alfred Schutz's "Sociological Aspect of Literature": Construction and Complementary Essays*, edited by Lester Embree, 3–14. Dordrecht,: Kluwer Academic Publishers, 1998.

———. "The Ethical-Political Side of Schutz: His Contributions at the 1956 Institute on Ethics concerned with Barriers to Equality of Opportunity." In *Schutzian Social Science*, edited by Lester Embree, 235–318. Dordrecht: Kluwer Academic Publishers, 1999.

———. "Everyday Social Relevancy in Gurwitsch and Schutz." *Annals of Phenomenological Sociology* 2 (1977): 45–61.

———. "In Memoriam, Ilse Schutz (1902–1990)." *Human Studies* 14 (1991): 219–24.

———. "Methodology Is Where Human Scientists and Philosophers Can Meet: Reflections on the Schutz-Parsons Exchange." *Human Studies* 3 (1980): 367–73.

———, ed. *Schutzian Social Science*. Dordrecht: Kluwer Academic Publishers, 1999.

———. "Schutz on Science." In *Worldly Phenomenology: The Continuing Influence of Alfred Schutz on North American Human Science*, edited by Lester Embree, 251–71. Washington, D.C.: Center for Advanced Research in Phenomenology and University Press of America, 1988.

———. "Schutz's Phenomenology of the Practical World." In *Alfred Schütz: Neue Beiträge zur Rezeption seines Werkes*, edited by Elisabeth List and Ilja Srubar, 121–44. Amsterdam: Rodopi, 1988.

———. "Two Husserlians Discuss Nazism: Letters between Dorion Cairns and Aron Gurwitsch in 1941." *Husserl Studies* 8 (1991): 77–105.

———, ed. *Worldly Phenomenology: The Continuing Influence of Alfred Schutz on North American Human Science*. Washington, D.C.: Center for Advanced Research in Phenomenology and University Press of America, 1988.

Endress, Martin. "Alfred Schutz and Karl Mannheim: Antipodes in the Sociology of Knowledge?" In *The Legacy of Alfred Schutz: International Conference on His Centennial*, edited by Hisashi Nasu, eleventh paper, 1–17. Tokyo: Waseda University, 1999.

Engel-Janosi, Friedrich. *Aber ein stolzer Bettler: Erinnerungen aus einer verlorenen Generation*. Graz: Verlag Styria, 1974.

Evans, J. Claude. "Afterword." In *Philosophers in Exile: The Correspondence of Alfred Schutz and Aron Gurwitsch, 1939–1959*, edited by Richard Grathoff, 321–26. Bloomington: Indiana University Press, 1989.

Fabian, Reinhard, and Peter M. Simons. "The Second Austrian School of Value Theory." In *Austrian Economics: Historical and Philosophical Background*, edited by Wolfgang Grassl and Barry Smith, 37–101. New York: New York University Press, 1986.

Farber, Marvin. *The Aims of Phenomenology: The Motives, Methods, and Impact of Husserl's Thought*. New York: Harper and Row, 1967.

———. "Experience and Transcendence: A Chapter in Recent Phenomenology and Existentialism." *Philosophy and Phenomenological Research* 12 (1951): 1–23.

———. *The Foundation of Phenomenology*. Cambridge: Cambridge University Press, 1943.

———. *Phenomenology and Existence: Toward a Philosophy within Nature*. New York: Harper and Row, 1967.

———. *The Search for an Alternative: Philosophical Perspectives of Subjectivism and Marxism*. Philadelphia: University of Pennsylvania Press, 1984.

Faust, Clarence. "Equality in American Education: Notes on Development with Respect to Racial Equality in Education." In *Aspects of Human Equality: Fifteenth Symposium of the Conference on Science, Philosophy, and Religion*, edited by Lyman Bryson, Clarence H. Faust, Louis Finkelstein, and R. M. MacIver, 299–312. New York: Conference on Science, Philosophy, and Religion in Their Relation to the Democratic Way of Life, and Harper and Brothers, 1956.

Fink, Eugen. "L'analyse intentionnelle et le problème de la pensée spéculative." In *Problèmes actuels de la phénoménologie*, edited by H. L. van Breda, 53–87. Bruges: Desclée de Brouwer, 1951.

Friedman, Milton. *Essays in Positive Economics*. Chicago: University of Chicago Press, 1953.

Garfinkel, Harold. "A Conception of, and Experiments with, 'Trust' as a Condition of Stable Concerted Action." In *Motivation and Social Interaction: Cognitive Determinants*, edited by O. J. Harvey, 187–238. New York: Ronald Press, 1963.

———. "The Perception of the Other: A Study in Social Order." Ph.D. diss., Harvard University, 1952.

———. *Studies in Ethnomethodology*. Englewood Cliffs, N.J.: Prentice-Hall, 1967.

———. "Studies of the Routine Grounds of Everyday Activities." In *Studies in Social Interaction*, edited by David Sudnow, 1–30. New York: Free Press; London: Collier Macmillan, 1972.

Goldman, Eric. *The Crucial Decade—and After: America, 1945–1960*. New York: Vintage Books, 1961.

Good, David. *The Economic Rise of the Habsburg Empire, 1750–1914*. Berkeley and Los Angeles: University of California Press, 1984.

Gorman, Robert. *The Dual Vision: Alfred Schutz and the Myth of Phenomenological Science*. Boston: Routledge and Kegan Paul, 1977.

Grassl, Wolfgang. "Markets and Morality: Austrian Perspectives on the Economic Approach to Human Behavior." In *Austrian Economics: Historical and Philosophical Background*, edited by Wolfgang Grassl and Barry Smith, 139–81. New York: New York University Press, 1986.

Grathoff, Richard. Introduction to *Philosophers in Exile: The Correspondence of Alfred Schutz and Aron Gurwitsch, 1939–1959*. Edited by Richard Grathoff. Bloomington: Indiana University Press, 1989.

———. "Introduction to 'Riders of the Apocalypse.' " In *Philosophers in Exile: The Correspondence of Alfred Schutz and Aron Gurwitsch, 1939–1959*, edited by Richard Grathoff, 2. Bloomington: Indiana University Press, 1989.

———. "Introduction to 'The Field of Consciousness.' " In *Philosophers in Exile: The Correspondence of Alfred Schutz and Aron Gurwitsch, 1939–1959*, edited by Richard Grathoff, 134. Bloomington: Indiana University Press, 1989.

———. Introduction to *The Theory of Social Action: The Correspondence of Alfred Schutz and Talcott Parsons*. Edited by Richard Grathoff. Bloomington: Indiana University Press, 1978.

———, ed. *Philosophers in Exile: The Correspondence of Alfred Schutz and Aron Gurwitsch*. Trans. Claude Evans. Bloomington: Indiana University Press, 1989.

———. "Das Problem der Intersubjektivität bei Aron Gurwitsch und Alfred Schütz." In *Sozialität und Intersubjektivität: Phänomenologische Perspektiven der Sozialwissenschaften im Umkreis von Aron Gurwitsch und Alfred Schütz*, edited by Richard Grathoff and Bernhard Waldenfels, 87–120. Munich: Wilhelm Fink, 1983.

———. "Über Typik und Normalität im alltäglichen Milieu." In *Alfred Schütz und die Idee des Alltags in den Sozialwissenschaften*, edited by Walter M. Sprondel and Richard Grathoff, 89–110. Stuttgart: Ferdinand Enke, 1979.

———. "Zum Begriff des 'Finiten' in der 'Finite Provinces of Meaning' von Alfred Schütz." In *Phenomenology as a Dialogue*, a special issue of *Critique and Humanism*, edited by Kolyo Koev, 25–37. Sofia, Bulgaria: National Public Opinion Center, 1990.

Grathoff, Richard, and Bernhard Waldenfels, eds. *Sozialität und Intersubjektivität: Phänomenologische Perspektiven der Sozialwissenschaften im Umkreis von Aron Gurwitsch und Alfred Schütz*. Munich: Wilhelm Fink, 1983.

Greenberg, Simon. "Comments by Simon Greenberg on Plamenatz's 'Equality of Opportunity.'" In *Aspects of Human Equality: Fifteenth Symposium of the Conference on Science, Philosophy, and Religion*, edited by Lyman Bryson, Clarence H. Faust, Louis Finkelstein, and R. M. MacIver, 107–10. New York: Conference on Science, Philosophy, and Religion in Their Relation to the Democratic Way of Life and Harper and Brothers, 1956.

Grünwald, Ernst. *Das Problem der Soziologie des Wissens: Versuch einer kritischen Darstellung der wissenssoziologischen Theorien*. Vienna: Wilhelm Braumüller, 1934.

Gulick, Charles A. *Labor's Workshop of Democracy*. Vol. 1 of *Austria: From Hapsburg to Hitler*. Berkeley and Los Angeles: University of California Press, 1948.

Gurwitsch, Aron. "Alfred Schuetz (1899–1959)" *Philosophy and Phenomenological Research* 20 (1959): 141–143. Also published in *Philosophers in Exile: The Correspondence of Alfred Schutz and Aron Gurwitsch,* 1939–1959, edited by Richard Grathoff, 319–20. Bloomington: Indiana University Press, 1989.

———. "Beitrag zur phänomenologischen Theorie der Wahrnehmung." *Zeitschrift für philosophische Forschung* 13 (1959): 419–37. Translated by Frederick Kersten under the title of "Contribution to the Phenomenology of Perception." In *Studies in Phenomenology and Psychology*, 332–49. Evanston, Ill.: Northwestern University Press, 1966.

———. *The Field of Consciousness*. Pittsburgh: Duquesne University, 1964.

———. "Gelb-Goldstein's Concept of 'Concrete' and 'Categorial' Attitude and the Phenomenology of Ideation." In *Studies in Phenomenology and Psychology*, 359–84. Evanston, Ill.: Northwestern University Press, 1966.

———. "The Kantian and Husserlian Conceptions of Consciousness." In *Studies in Phenomenology and Psychology*, 148–60. Evanston, Ill.: Northwestern University Press, 1966.

———. *Kants Theorie des Verstandes*. Edited by Thomas M. Seebohm. Dordrecht: Kluwer Academic Publishers,1990.

———. "The Last Work of Edmund Husserl." In *Studies in Phenomenology and Psychology*, 397–447. Evanston, Ill.: Northwestern University Press, 1966.

———. *Leibniz: Philosophie des Panlogismus*. Berlin: Walter de Gruyter, 1974.

———. *Marginal Consciousness*. Edited by Lester Embree. Athens: Ohio University Press, 1985.

———. "On Contemporary Nihilism." *Review of Politics* 7 (1945): 170–98.

———. "On the Conceptual Consciousness." In *Studies in Phenomenology and Psychology*, 390–96. Evanston, Ill.: Northwestern University Press, 1966.

———, "On the Object of Thought." In *Studies in Phenomenology and Psychology*, 141–47. Evanston, Ill.: Northwestern University Press, 1966.

———. *Phenomenology and the Theory of Science*. Edited by Lester Embree. Evanston, Ill.: Northwestern University Press, 1974.

———. "Présuppositions philosophiques de la logique." *Revue de Métaphysique et le Morale* 56 (1951): 395–405. Translated by A. Rosenthal under the title "Philosophical Presuppositions of Logic," in *Studies in Phenomenology and Psychology*. (Evanston, Ill.: Northwestern University Press, 1966) 350–58.

———. "The Problem of Existence in Constitutive Phenomenology." In *Studies in Phenomenology and Psychology*, 116–23. Evanston, Ill.: Northwestern University Press, 1966.

———. "Some Philosophical Roots of Nazism." Cited in "Two Husserlians Discuss Nazism: Letters between Dorion Cairns and Aron Gurwitsch in 1941," by Lester Embree. *Husserl Studies* 8 (1991): 79–80.

———. *Studies in Phenomenology and Psychology*. Evanston, Ill.: Northwestern University Press, 1966.

Haberler, Gottfried. "Mises' Private Seminar." Appendix in *"Planning for Freedom" and Twelve Other Essays and Addresses*, by Ludwig von Mises, 190–92. Memorial third edition South Holland, Ill.: Libertarian Press, 1974.

Habermas, Jürgen. "Discourse Ethics: Notes on a Program of Philosophical Justification." In *Moral Consciousness and Communicative Action*, translated by Christian Lenhardt and Shierry Weber Nicholsen, 43–115. Cambridge, Mass.: MIT Press, 1990.

Halberstam, David. *The Fifties*. New York: Villard Books, 1993.

Hama, Hideo. "Alfred Schutz's Theory of Science and Ethnomethodology." In *The Legacy of Alfred Schutz: International Conference on His Centennial*, edited by Hisashi Nasu, fourteenth paper, 1–7. Tokyo: Waseda University, 1999.

Have, Paul ten. *Doing Conversation Analysis: A Practical Guide*. London: Sage Publications, 1999.

Have, Paul ten, and George Psathas, eds. *Situated Order: Studies in the Social Organization of Talk and Embodied Activities*. Studies in Ethnomethodology and Conversational Analysis, no. 3. Washington, D.C.: International Institute for Ethnomethodology and Conversation Analysis and University Press of America, 1995.

Hayek, Friedrich "Economics and Knowledge." In *Individualism and the Economic Order*, 33–56. Chicago: University of Chicago Press, 1948.

———. *Hayek on Hayek: An Autobiographical Dialogue*. Edited by Stephen Kresge and Leif Wenar. Chicago: University of Chicago Press, 1989.

———. "Kinds of Rationalism." In *Studies in Philosophy, Politics, and Economics*, 82–95. Chicago: University of Chicago Press, 1967.

———. "The Moral Element in Free Enterprise." In *Studies in Philosophy, Politics, and Economics*, 229–36. Chicago: University of Chicago Press, 1967.

———. "The Place of Menger's *Grundsätze* in the History of Economic Thought." In *The Essence of Hayek*, edited by Chiaki Nishiyama and Kurl R. Leube, 195–207. Stanford, Calif.: Hoover Institution Press, 1984.

———. *The Road to Serfdom*. Chicago: University of Chicago Press, 1944.

Heidegger, Martin. *Being and Time*. Translated by John Macquarrie and Edward Robinson. San Francisco: Harper San Francisco, 1962.

Heilke, Thomas W. *Eric Voegelin: In Quest of Reality*. Lanham, Md.: Rowman and Littlefield, 1999.

Heimann, Eduard. "The Just War of Unjust Nations." *Christianity and Crisis* 3 (1943): 2–6.

Helling, Ingeborg K. "Alfred Schütz, Felix Kaufmann, and the Economists of the Mises Circle: Personal and Methodological Continuities." In *Alfred Schütz: Neue Beiträge zur Rezeption seines Werkes*, edited by Elisabeth List and Ilja Srubar, 43–68. Amsterdam: Rodopi, 1988.

———. "A. Schutz and F. Kaufmann: Sociology between Science and Interpretation." In *Alfred Schutz: Appraisals and Developments*, edited by Kurt Wolff. Dordrecht: Mortinus Nijhoff, 1984. Reprint from *Human Studies* 7, no. 2 (1984): 141–61.

Hermida-Lazcano, Pablo. "The Taken-for-Granted World: A Study of the Relationship between A. Schutz and J. Ortega y Gasset." *Human Studies* 19 (1996): 43–69.

Hertz, Frederick. *The Economic Problem of the Danubian States: A Study in Economic Nationalism*. London: Victor Gollancz, 1947.

Hofstadter, Albert. "The Career Open to Personality: The Meaning of Equality of Opportunity for an Ethics of Our Time." In *Aspects of Human Equality: Fifteenth Symposium of the Conference on Science, Philosophy, and Religion*, edited by Lyman Bryson, Clarence H. Faust, Louis Finkelstein, and R. M. MacIver, 111–42. New York: Conference on Science, Philosophy, and Religion in Their Relation to the Democratic Way of Life, and Harper and Brothers, 1956.

Husserl, Edmund. "Author's Preface to the English Edition." In *Ideas: General Introduction to Pure Phenomenology*, translated by W. R. Boyce Gibson, 5–22. New York: Collier Books; London: Collier Macmillan, 1931.

———. *Cartesian Meditations: An Introduction to Phenomenology*. Translated by Dorion Cairns. The Hague: Martinus Nijhoff, 1960.

———. *The Crisis of European Sciences and Transcendental Phenomenology: An Introduction to Phenomenological Philosophy*. Translated by David Carr. Evanston, Ill.: Northwestern University Press, 1970.

———. *Formal and Transcendental Logic*. Translated by Dorion Cairns. The Hague: Martinus Nijhoff, 1969.

———. *Ideas Pertaining to a Pure Phenomenology and to a Phenomenological Philosophy*. Vol. 1: *General Introduction to a Pure Phenomenology*. Translated by F.Kersten. The Hague: Martinus Nijhoff, 1982.

———. *Ideas Pertaining to a Pure Phenomenology and to a Phenomenological Philosophy*. Vol. 2: *Studies in the Phenomenology of Constitution*. Translated by Richard Rojcewicz and André Schuwer. Dordrecht: Kluwer Academic Publishers, 1989.

———. *Ideas Pertaining to a Pure Phenomenology and to a Phenomenological Philosophy*. Vol. 3: *Phenomenology and the Foundations of the Sciences*. Translated by Ted E. Klein and William E. Pohl. The Hague: Martinus Nijhoff, 1980.

———. *Ideen zu einer reinen Phänomenologie and phänomenologischen Philosophie*. Vol. 2; *Phänomenologische Untersuchungenzur Konstitution*. Edited by Marly Beimel. The Hague: Martinus Nijhoff, 1952.

———. *Ideen zu einer Phänomenologie un phänomenologische Philosophie*. Vol. 3, *Die Phänomenologie und die Fundamente der Wissenschaften*. Edited by Marly Biemel. The Hague: Martinus Nijhoff, 1952.

———. *Logical Investigations*. Translated by J. N. Findlay. Edited by Dermot Moran. 2 vols. London: Routledge, 2001.

———. "Notizen zur Raumkonstitution: Fortsetzung der Untersuchungen zur phänomenologischen Interpretation der kopernikanischen Lehre." *Philosophy and Phenomenological Research* 1 (1940): 23–37.

———. *On the Phenomenology of the Consciousness of Internal Time (1893–1917)*. Translated by John Barnett Brough. Dordrecht: Kluwer Academic Publishers, 1991. Originally published as *Zur Phänomenologie des inneren Zeitbewusstseins (1893–1917)*, (see below).

———. "The Vienna Lecture." Appendix A in *The Crisis of European Sciences and Transcendental Phenomenology: An Introduction to Phenomenological Philosophy*, translated, by David Carr, 269–99. Evanston, Ill.: Northwestern University Press, 1970.

———. *Zur Phänomenologie des inneren Zeitbewusstseins* (1893–1917). Edited by Rudolph Boehm. The Hague: Martinus Nijhoff, 1966.

James, William. *The Principles of Psychology*. 2 vols. 1918. Reprint, New York: Dover, 1950.

Janik, Alan, and Stephen Toulmin. *Wittgenstein's Vienna*. New York: Simon and Schuster, 1973.

Jaspers, Karl. *Die grossen Philosophen*. Munich: R. Piper, 1957.

———. *The Origin and Goal of History*. Translated by Michael Bullock. New Haven, Conn.: Yale University Press, 1953.

Johnson, F. Ernest. "The Concept of Human Equality." In *Aspects of Human Equality: Fifteenth Symposium of the Conference on Science, Philosophy, and Religion*, edited by Lyman Bryson, Clarence H. Faust, Louis Finkelstein, and R. M. MacIver, 25–31. New York: Conference on Science, Philosophy, and Religion in Their Relation to the Democratic Way of Life and Harper and Brothers, 1956.

Johnston, William. *The Austrian Mind: An Intellectual and Social History, 1848–1938*. Berkeley and Los Angeles: University of California Press, 1972.

Kallen, Horace. *William James and Henri Bergson: A Study in Contrasting Theories of Life*. Chicago: University of Chicago Press, 1914.

Kaminsky, Jack. Review of *The Social Dynamics of George Herbert Mead*, by Maurice Natanson. *Philosophy and Phenomenological Research* 18 (1958): 417.

Kaufmann, Felix. The Correspondence between Felix Kaufmann and Alfred Schutz. Courtesy of Dirk Tänzler. Sozialwissenschaftliches Archive, Geisteswissenschaftliche Sektion, Fachbereich Geschichte und Soziologie, Universität Konstanz.

———. "Juristischer und soziologicher Rechtsbegriff." In *Gesellschaft, Staat, und Recht: Untersuchungen zur reinen Rechtslehre*, edited by Alfred Verdross, 14–41. Frankfurt am Main: Sauer & Auvermann, 1967.

———. *Die Kriterien des Rechts*. Tübingen, 1924. Reprint, Aalen: Scientia Verlag, 1966.

———. "The Logical Rules of Scientific Procedures." *Philosophy and Phenomenological Research* 2 (1941): 457–71.

———. *Logik und Rechtswissenschaft: Grundriss eines Systems der reinen Rechtslehre*. Tübingen: J. C. B. Mohr (Paul Siebeck), 1922.

———. *Metodología de las ciencias sociales*. Translated by Eugenio Imaz. Mexico City: Fondo de Cultura Economica, 1946.

———. *Methodology of the Social Sciences*. London: Oxford University Press, 1944.

———. "On the Subject-Matter and Method of Economic Science." *Economica* 42 (1933): 381–401.

———. "Remarks on the Methodology of the Social Sciences." *Sociological Review* 28 (1936): 64–84.

———. Review of *Der sinnhafte Aufbau der sozialen Welt*, by Alfred Schutz. *Deutsche Literaturzeitung für Kritik der internatanalen Wissenschaften* 36 (1932): 1712–16.

Kelsen, Hans. "'Foreword' to the Second Printing of *Main Problems in the Theory of Public Law* (1923)." In *Normativity and Norms: Critical Perspectives on Kelsenian Themes*, edited by Stanley L. Paulson, and Bonnie Litschewski Paulson, 1–22. Oxford: Clarendon Press, 1998.

———. *Introduction to the Problems of Legal Theory*. Translated by Bonnie Litschewski Paulson and Stanley L. Paulson. Oxford: Clarendon Press, 1992. A translation of the 1st ed. of *Reine Rechtslehre* (1934).

———. *Pure Theory of Law*. Translated by Max Knight from the second revised and enlarged German edition. Berkeley and Los Angeles: University of California Press, 1967.

———. *What Is Justice? Justice, Law, and Politics in the Mirror of Science*. Berkeley and Los Angeles: University of California Press, 1957.

Kersten, Fred. "Editor's Preface to 'The Foundations of the Theory of Social Organization.'" In vol. 4 of *Collected Papers*, by Alfred Schutz, edited by Helmut Wagner and George Psathas in collaboration with Fred Kersten, 203. Dordrecht: Kluwer Academic Publishers, 1996.

———. "Image-Making and the Nature of the Imagination." *Études Phénoménologiques* 17 (2002): 47–89.

———. "Phenomenology, History, and Myth." In *Phenomenology and Social Reality: Essays in Memory of Alfred Schutz*, edited by Maurice Natanson, 234–69. The Hague: Martinus Nijhoff, 1970.

———. “Preface to ‘Fragments on the Phenomenology of Music.’” In *In Search of Musical Method*, edited by F.J. Smith, 6–22. London: Gordon and Breach Science Publishers, 1976.

Kim, Hongwoo. “Schutz’s Account of the Life-World: In Search for a Political Sphere.” In *The Legacy of Alfred Schutz: International Conference on His Centennial*, edited by Hisashi Nasu, fourth paper, 1–24. Tokyo: Waseda University, 1999.

Kirzner, Israel M., ed. *The Age of Mises and Hayek*. Vol. 3 of *Classics in Austrian Economics: A Sampling in the History of a Tradition*. London: William Pickering, 1995.

———. *The Founding Era*. Vol. 1 of *Classics in Austrian Economics: A Sampling in the History of a Tradition*. London: William Pickering, 1995.

Knight, Frank. Introduction to *Principles of Economics*, edited and translated by James Dingwall and Bert F. Hoselitz, 9–35. Glencoe, Ill.: Free Press, 1950.

———. “‘What Is Truth’ in Economics?” *Journal of Political Economy* 48 (1940): 1–33.

Kockelmans, Joseph. “Deskriptive oder interpretierende Phänomenologie in Schütz’s Konzeption der Sozialwissenschaft.” In *Alfred Schütz und die Idee des Alltags in der Sozialwissenschaften*, edited by Walter M. Sprondel and Richard Grathoff, 27–43. Stuttgart: Ferdinand Enke, 1979.

Koev, Kolyo. “Alfred Schutz and the Problem of Everyday Life Average Structures.” In *Phenomenology as a Dialogue*, a special issue of *Critique and Humanism*, edited by Kolyo Koev, 54–73. Sofia, Bulgaria: National Public Opinion Center, 1990.

———, ed. *Phenomenology as a Dialogue*, a special issue of *Critique and Humanism*. Sofia, Bulgaria: National Public Opinion Center, 1990.

Korsgaard, Christine. *Creating the Kingdom of Ends*. Cambridge: Cambridge University Press, 1996.

Kraus, Karl. *Die dritte Walpurgisnacht*. Munich: Kösel-Verlag, 1955.

Kresge, Stephen. Introduction to *Hayek on Hayek: An Autobiographical Dialogue*, by Friedrich Hayek, edited by Stephen Kresge and Leif Wenar, 1–35. Chicago: University of Chicago Press, 1989.

Kuhn, Helmut. “Exhortatio ad Philosophiam.” *Philosophy and Phenomenological Research* 8 (1947): 83–98.

Langsdorf, Lenore. “Der Rand des Bewusstseins: Eine Kritik an Gurwitsch’s Konzeption der sozialen Welt.” In *Sozialität und Intersubjektivität: Phänomenologische* Perspektiven der Sozialwissenschaften im Umkreis von Aron Gurwitsch und Alfred *Schütz*, edited by Richard Grathoff and Bernhard Waldenfels, 31–50. Munich: Wilhelm Fink, 1983.

Lee, Dorothy. “Equality of Opportunity as a Cultural Value.” In *Aspects of Human* Equality: *Fifteenth Symposium of the Conference on Science, Philosophy, and Religion*, edited by Lyman Bryson, Clarence H. Faust, Louis Finkelstein, and R. M. MacIver,

255–71. New York: Conference on Science, Philosophy, and Religion in Their Relation to the Democratic Way of Life and Harper and Brothers, 1956.

Levinas, Emmanuel. *Totality and Infinity: An Essay on Exteriority*. Translated by Alphonso Lingis. The Hague: Martinus Nijhoff, 1979.

List, Elisabeth, and Ilja Srubar, eds. *Alfred Schütz: Neue Beiträge zur Rezeption seines Werkes*. Amsterdam: Rodopi, 1988.

Littlechild, S. C. *The Fallacy of the Mixed Economy: An "Austrian" Critique of Economic Thinking and Policy*. London, U.K.: Institute of Economic Affairs, 1978.

Luckmann, Benita. "Alfred Schütz und Aron Gurwitsch an der New School." In *Sozialität und Intersubjektivität: Phänomenologische Perspektiven der Sozialwissenschaften im Umkreis von Aron Gurwitsch und Alfred Schütz*, edited by Richard Grathoff and Bernhard Waldenfels, 315–37. Munich: Wilhelm Fink, 1983.

———. "The Small Life Worlds of Modern Man." *Social Research* 37 (1970): 580–96.

Luckmann, Thomas. *Life-World and Social Realities*. London: Heinemann Educational Books, 1983.

———. Preface to vol. 1 of *The Structures of the Life-World*, by Alfred Schutz and Thomas Luckmann, translated by Richard M. Zaner and H. Tristram Engelhardt. Evanston, Ill.: Northwestern University Press, 1973.

———. *The Sociology of Language*. Indianapolis: Bobbs-Merrill, 1975.

———. *Die unsichtbare Religion*. Frankfurt am Main: Suhrkamp, 1991.

Machlup, Fritz. *The Basing-Point System*. Philadelphia: Bakiston, 1949.

———. "Do Economists Know Anything?" *American Scholar* 22 (1953): 167–82.

———. *The Economics of Sellers' Competition: Model Analysis of Sellers' Conduct*. Baltimore: Johns Hopkins University Press, 1952.

———. *Methodology of Economics and Other Social Sciences*. New York: Academic Press, 1978.

———. "The Problem of Verification in Economics." *Southern Economic Journal* 22 (1955): 1–21.

———. *The Production and Distribution of Knowledge*. Princeton, N.J.: Princeton University Press, 1962.

Mathur, D. C. "Marvin Farber and the Program of Naturalistic Phenomenology." In *Phenomenology and Natural Existence: Essays in Honor of Marvin Farber*, edited by Dale Riepe, 26–40. Albany: State University of New York Press, 1973.

Matis, Herbert. "Austria: Industrialization in a Multinational Setting." In *The Industrial Revolution in National Context: Europe and the USA*, edited by Mikuláš Teich and Roy Porter, 226–46. Cambridge: Cambridge University Press, 1996.

Maurois, André. *En América*. Edited by Robert M. Waugh. New York: American Book Company, 1936.

McGlynn, James V. "A Note on Philosophy in German Universities Today." *Philosophy and Phenomenological Research* 19 (1958): 248–252.

McGrath, William. *Dionysian Art and Populist Politics in Austria*. New Haven, Conn.: Yale University Press, 1974.

Mead, George Herbert. "The Genesis of the Self and Social Control." In *Selected Writings*, edited by Andrew J. Reck, 267–93. Indianapolis: Bobbs-Merrill, 1964.

Menger, Carl. *Investigations into the Method of the Social Sciences with Special Reference to Economics*. Edited by Louis Schneider. Translated by Francis J. Nock. New York: New York University Press, 1985.

———. *Principles of Economics*. Edited and translated by James Dingwall and Bert F. Hoselitz. Glencoe, Ill.: Free Press, 1950.

Mises, Ludwig von. *Epistemological Problems of Economics*. Translated by George Reisman. Princeton, N.J.: D. Van Nostrand, 1960.

———. *Human Action: A Treatise on Economics*. 3rd rev. ed. Chicago: Contemporary Books, 1963.

Myrdal, Gunnar. *An American Dilemma: The Negro Problem and Modern Democracy.* New York: Harper & Bros., 1964

Mori, Mototaka. "Alfred Schutz and the Imperial Capital Vienna." In *The Legacy of Alfred Schutz: International Conference on His Centennial*, edited by Hisashi Nasu, second paper, 1–19. Tokyo: Waseda University, 1999.

Morris, Charles. "Comment [on Alfred Schutz's "Symbol, Reality and Society."] In *Symbol and Society: Fourteenth Symposium of the Conference on Science, Philosophy, and Religion,* edited by Lyman Bryon, Louis Finkelstein, Hudson Hoagland, and R. M. MacIver, 202–3. New York Conference on Science, Philosophy, and Religion in the Relation to the Democratic Way of Life and Harper & Bros., 1955.

Nagel, Ernest. Review of *The Counter-Revolution of Science: Studies in the Use of Reason*, by F. A. Hayek. *Journal of Philosophy* 49 (1952): 560–65.

Nagel, Ernest, and Carl Hempel. "Symposium: Problems of Concept and Theory Formation in the Social Sciences." In *Science, Language, and Human Rights*, 43–86. Proceedings of the American Philosophical Association, vol. 1. Philadelphia: University of Pennsylvania Press, 1952.

Nasu, Hisashi, ed. *The Legacy of Alfred Schutz: International Conference on His Centennial*. Tokyo: Waseda University, 1999.

Natanson, Maurice. *Anonymity: A Study in the Philosophy of Alfred Schutz*. Bloomington: Indiana University Press, 1986.

———. "The Concept of the Given in Peirce and Mead." *Modern Schoolman* 32 (1955): 143–57.

———. "Death and Situation." In *Literature, Philosophy, and the Social Sciences: Essays in Existentialism and Phenomenology*, 212–20. The Hague: Martinus Nijhoff, 1962.

———. "Disenchantment and Transcendence." In *Phenomenology, Role, and Reason: Essays on the Coherence and Deformation of Social Reality*, 307–24. Springfield, Ill.: Charles C. Thomas, 1974.

———. *Edmund Husserl: Philosopher of Infinite Tasks*. Evanston, Ill.: Northwestern University Press, 1973.

———. *The Erotic Bird: Phenomenology in Literature*. With a foreword by Judith Butler. Princeton, N.J.: Princeton University Press, 1998.

———. Foreword to *The Theory of Social Action: The Correspondence of Alfred Schutz and Talcott Parsons*. Edited by Richard Grathoff. Bloomington: Indiana University Press, 1978.

———. "La historia como ámbito finito de sentido." *Convivium* 2 (1957): 143–50.

———. "History as a Finite Province of Meaning." In *Literature, Philosophy, and the Social Sciences: Essays in Existentialism and Phenomenology*, 172–77. The Hague: Martinus Nijhoff, 1968. First published as "La historia como ámbito finito de sentido" (see above).

———. *Literature, Philosophy, and the Social Sciences: Essays in Existentialism and Phenomenology*. The Hague: Martinus Nijhoff, 1962.

———. *Phenomenology, Role, and Reason: Essays on the Coherence and Deformation of Social Reality*. Springfield, Ill.: Charles C. Thomas, 1974.

———, ed. *Phenomenology and Social Reality: Essays in Memory of Alfred Schutz*. The Hague: Martinus Nijhoff, 1970.

———. "Phenomenology from the Natural Standpoint: A Reply to Van Meter Ames." *Philosophy and Phenomenological Research* 17 (1956): 241–45.

———. "Philosophy and Psychiatry." In *Phenomenology, Role, and Reason: Essays on the Coherence and Deformation of Social Reality*, 232–64. Springfield, Ill.: Charles C. Thomas, 1974.

———, ed. *Philosophy of the Social Sciences: A Reader*. New York: Random House, 1963.

———. Review of *Martin Buber: The Life of Dialogue*, by Maurice S. Friedman. *Social Research* 24 (1957): 113–17.

———. Review of *Phénoménologie de Husserl*, by Quentin Lauer. *Philosophical Review* 65 (1955): 563–67.

———. "Sartre's Fetishism: A Reply to Van Meter Ames." *Journal of Philosophy* 48 (1951): 95–99.

———. *The Social Dynamics of George H. Mead*. The Hague: Martinus Nijhoff, 1973.

———. "A Study in Philosophy and the Social Sciences." In *Philosophy of the Social Sciences: A Reader*, edited by Maurice Natanson 271–85. New York: Random House, 1963.

Nédoncelle, Maurice. *Vers und philosophie de l'amour*. Paris: Aubier, 1946.

Pangle, Thomas L. "Platonic Political Science in Strauss and Voegelin." In *Faith and* Political Philosophy: *The Correspondence between Leo Strauss and Eric Voegelin, 1934–1964*, edited by Peter Emberley and Barry Cooper, 321–47. University Park: Pennsylvania State University Press, 1993.

Parsons, Arthur. "Constitutive Phenomenology: Schutz's Theory of the We-relation." *Journal of Phenomenological Psychology: Studies in the Science of Human Experience and Behavior* 4 (1973): 331–61.

Paulson, Stanley. Introduction to *Normativity and Norms: Critical Perspectives on Kelsenian Themes*. Edited by Stanley L. Paulson and Bonnie Litschewski Paulson. Oxford: Clarendon Press, 1998.

———. "Hans Kelsen's Earliest Legal Theory: Critical Constructivism." In *Normativity and Norms: Critical Perspectives on Kelsenian Themes*, edited by Stanley L. Paulson, and Bonnie Litschewski Paulson; 23–43. Oxford: Clarendon Press, 1998.

Pinney, Harvey. "The Institutional Man." *Journal of Political Economy* 48 (1940): 543–62.

Plamenatz, John. "Equality of Opportunity." In *Aspects of Human Equality: Fifteenth Symposium of the Conference on Science, Philosophy, and Religion*, edited by Lyman Bryson, Clarence H. Faust, Louis Finkelstein, and R. M. MacIver, 79–107. New York: Conference on Science, Philosophy, and Religion in Their Relation to the Democratic Way of Life and Harper and Brothers, 1956.

Pound, Roscoe. *Social Control through Law*. New Haven, Conn.: Yale University Press, 1942. Reprint, with a new Introduction by A. Javier Treviño, New Brunswick, N.J.: Transaction, 1997.

Powell, Brenda. "The What and Why of Experience: The Contrapuntal Relationship between Cognitive Style and Systems of Relevance." *Annals of Phenomenological Sociology* 2 (1977): 107–33.

Prendergast, Christopher. "Alfred Schutz and the Austrian School of Economics." *American Journal of Sociology* 92 (1986):1–26.

Preschlenova, Roumyana. "Austro-Hungarian Trade and the Economic Development of Southeastern Europe before World War 1." In *Economic Transformations in East and Central Europe: Legacies from the Past and Policies for the Future*, edited by David F. Good, 231–60. London: Routledge, 1994.

Psathas, George. "Approaches to the Study of the World of Everyday Life." *Human Studies* 3 (1980): 3–17.

———. *Conversation Analysis: The Study of Talk-in-Interaction*. Vol. 35 of *Qualitative Research Methods*. Thousand Oaks, Calif.: Sage Publications, 1995.

Rasmussen, David M. "Explorations of the Lebenswelt: Reflections on Schutz and Habermas," 21–26. In *Alfred Schutz: Appraisals and Developments*, edited by Kurt Wolff, Dordrecht: Martinus Nijhoff, 1984. Reprint from *Human Studies* 7, no. 2 (1984): 127–32.

Rehorick, David, and William Buxton. "Recasting the Parsons-Schutz Dialogue: The Hidden Participation of Eric Voegelin." In *Worldly Phenomenology: The Continuing Influence of Alfred Schutz on North American Human Science*, edited by Lester Embree, 151–69. Washington, D.C.: Center for Advanced Research in Phenomenology and University Press of America, 1988.

Riepe, Dale. "Conclusion." In *Phenomenology and Natural Existence: Essays in Honor of Marvin Farber*, edited by Dale Riepe, 390–91. Albany: State University of New York Press, 1973.

———, ed. *Phenomenology and Natural Existence: Essays in Honor of Marvin Farber*. Albany: State University of New York Press, 1973.

Riezler, Kurt. *Man: Mutable and Immutable*. Chicago: Regnery, 1950.

Rogers, Mary F. *Sociology, Ethnomethodology, and Experience: A Phenomenological Critique*. Cambridge: Cambridge University Press, 1983.

Rozenblitt, Martha L. *The Jews of Vienna, 1867–1914: Assimilation and Identity*. Albany: State University of New York Press, 1983.

Runciman, W. G. "Introduction to 'The Methodology of the Social Sciences.'" In *Max Weber: Selections in Translation*, edited by W. G. Runciman, 65–68. Cambridge: Cambridge University Press, 1978.

Salomon, Albert. *The Tyranny of Progress: Reflections on the Origins of Sociology*. New York: Noonday Press, 1955.

Santayana, George. *Character and Opinion in the United States*. New York: W. W. Norton, 1934.

———. *Dominations and Powers: Reflections on Liberty, Society, and Government*. New York: Charles Scribner's Sons, 1954.

———. *Scepticism and Animal Faith: Introduction to a System of Philosophy* 1923. Reprint, New York: Dover, 1955.

———. *Winds of Doctrine, and Platonism and the Spiritual Life*. New York: Harper and Brothers, 1957.

Sato, Yoshikazu. "Tomoo Otaka and Alfred Schutz in the 1930s—Their Social Theory and Its Socio-Cultural Background." In *The Legacy of Alfred Schutz: International Conference on His Centennial*, edited by Hisashi Nasu, first paper, 1–16. Tokyo: Waseda University, 1999.

Scheler, Max. *Formalism in Ethics and Non-Formal Ethics of Values*. Translated by Manfred S. Frings and Roger L. Funk. Evanston, Ill.: Northwestern University Press, 1973.

———. *The Nature of Sympathy*. Translated by Peter Heath. New Haven, Conn.: Yale University Press, 1954.

———. *On the Eternal in Man*. Translated by Bernard Noble. New York: Harper and Brothers, 1960.

———. *Problems of a Sociology of Knowledge*. Translated by Manfred S. Frings. Edited by Kenneth W. Stikkers. London: Routledge and Kegan Paul, 1980.

———. "Zu Lehre von Grund aller Dinge." In *Erkenntnislehre und Metaphysik*, edited by Manfred S. Frings, 185–222. Vol. 2 of *Schriften aus dem Nachlass*, Bern: Francke Verlag, 1979.

Schelting, Alexander von. *Max Webers Wissenschaftslehre: Das logische Problem der historischen Kulturerkenntnis: Die Grenzen der Soziologie des Wissens*. Tübingen: J. C. B. Mohr (Paul Siebeck), 1934.

Schorske, Charles E. *Fin-de-Siècle Vienna: Politics and Culture*. New York: Vintage Books, 1981.

Schuschnigg, Kurt von. *Austrian Requiem*. Translated by Franz von Hildebrand. New York: G. P. Putnam's Sons, 1946.

Schutz, Alfred. "Barriers of Equality of Opportunity of Bringing about the Alternative chosen by the Individual or at Least of Being Heard by Those Who Make the Decision." In "The Ethical-Political Side of Schutz: His Contributions at the 1956 Institute on Ethics concerned with Barriers to Equality of Opportunity," by Lester Embree. In *Schutzian Social Science*, edited by Lester Embree, 269–71. Dordrecht: Kluwer Academic Publishers, 1999.

———, "Basic Concepts and Methods of the Social Sciences." In vol. 4 of *Collected Papers*, edited by Helmut Wagner and George Psathas in collaboration with Fred Kersten, 121–30. Dordrecht: Kluwer Academic Publishers, 1996.

———. "Basic Problems of Political Economy." In vol. 4 of *Collected Papers*, edited, by Helmut Wagner and George Psathas in collaboration with Fred Kersten, 88–92. Dordrecht: Kluwer Academic Publishers, 1996.

———. "Choice and the Social Sciences." In *Life-World and Consciousness: Essays for Aron Gurwitsch*, edited by Lester Embree, 565–96. Evanston, Ill.: Northwestern University Press, 1972.

———. "Choosing among Projects of Action." In *The Problem of Social Reality*, edited by Maurice Natanson, 67–96. Vol. 1 of *Collected Papers*. The Hague: Martinus Nijhoff, 1962.

———. *Collected Papers*. Vol. 4. Edited by Helmut Wagner and George Psathas in collaboration with Fred Kersten. Dordrecht: Kluwer Academic Publishers, 1996.

———. "Common-Sense and Scientific Interpretation of Human Action." In *The Problem of Social Reality*, edited by Maurice Natanson, 3–47. Vol. 1 of *Collected Papers*. The Hague: Martinus Nijhoff, 1962.

———. "Concept and Theory Formation in the Social Sciences." In *The Problem of Social Reality*, edited by Maurice Natanson, 48–66. Vol. 1 of *Collected Papers*. The Hague: Martinus Nijhoff, 1962.

———. "Don Quixote and the Problem of Reality." In *Studies in Social Theory*, edited by Arvid Brodersen, 135–58. Vol. 2 of *Collected Papers*. The Hague: Martinus Nijhoff, 1964.

———. "Editor's Preface to Edmund Husserl, 'Die Welt der lebendigen Gegenwart und die Konstitution der äusserleiblichen Umwelt.'" *Philosophy and Phenomenological Research* 6 (1946): 323.

———. "Editor's Preface to Edmund Husserl's 'Notizen zur Raumkonstitution.'" *Philosophy and Phenomenological Research* 1 (1940): 21–23. Also published in vol. 4 of *Collected Papers*, edited by Helmut Wagner and George Psathas in collaboration with Fred Kersten (Dordrecht: Kluwer Academic Publishers, 1966), 174–76.

———. "Edmund Husserl's *Ideas*, Volume II." In *Studies in Phenomenological Philosophy*, edited by Ilse Schutz, 15–39. Vol. 3 of *Collected Papers*. The Hague: Martinus Nijhoff, 1966.

———. "Equality and the Meaning Structure of the Social World." In *Studies in Social Theory*, edited by Arvid Brodersen, 226–73. Vol. 2 of *Collected Papers*. The Hague: Martinus Nijhoff, 1964.

———. "Erleben, Sprache, und Begriff." In *Theorie der Lebensformen: Frühe Manuskripte aus der Bergson-Periode*, edited by Ilja Srubar, 209–50. Frankfurt am Main: Suhrkamp, 1981. Translated by Helmut Wagner under the title "Meaning Structures of Language," in *Life Forms and Meaning Structure*, by Alfred Schutz. (London: Routledge and Kegan Paul, 1982), 125–57.

———. "The Ethical Issue Involved." In "The Ethical-Political Side of Schutz: His Contributions at the 1956 Institute on Ethics concerned with Barriers to Equality of Opportunity," by Lester Embree. In *Schutzian Social Science*, edited by Lester Embree, 276–77. Dordrecht: Kluwer Academic Publishers, 1999.

———. "Experience and Transcendence." In vol. 4 of *Collected Papers*, edited by Helmut Wagner and George Psathas in collaboration with Fred Kersten, 234–41. Dordrecht: Kluwer Academic Publishers, 1996.

———. "The Foundations of the Theory of Social Organization." In vol. 4 of *Collected Papers*, vol. 4, edited by Helmut Wagner and George Psathas in collaboration with Fred Kersten, 203–20. Dordrecht: Kluwer Academic Publishers, 1996.

———. "Fragments toward a Phenomenology of Music." In vol. 4 of *Collected Papers*, edited by Helmut Wagner and George Psathas in collaboration with Fred Kersten, 243–75. Dordrecht: Kluwer Academic Publishers, 1996.

———. "Gnosticism and Orthodoxy: Contrast in Fundamental Metaphysical and Theological Positions." In vol. 4 of *Collected Papers*, edited by Helmut Wagner and George Psathas in collaboration with Fred Kersten, 221–33. Dordrecht: Kluwer Academic Publishers, 1996.

———. "The Homecomer." In *Studies in Social Theory*, edited by Arvid Brodersen, 106–19. Vol. 2 of *Collected Papers*.The Hague: Martinus Nijhoff, 1964.

———. "Husserl and His Influence on Me." Edited by Lester Embree. *Annals of Phenomenological Sociology* 2 (1977): 41–44.

———. "Husserl's *Crisis of Western Sciences*." In vol. 4 of *Collected Papers*, edited, by Helmut Wagner and George Psathas in collaboration with Fred Kersten, 177–86. Dordrecht: Kluwer Academic Publishers, 1996.

———. "Husserl's Importance for the Social Sciences." In *The Problem of Social Reality*, edited by Maurice Natanson, 140–49. Vol. 1 of *Collected Papers*. The Hague: Martinus Nijhoff, 1962. First published as "Husserl's Importance for the Social Sciences," in *Edmund Husserl: 1859–1959*, edited by H. L. van Breda and J. Taminaux (The Hague: Martinus Nijhoff, 1959), 86–98

———. "Husserl's *Parisian Lectures* of 1929." In vol. 4 of *Collected Papers*, edited by Helmut Wagner and George Psathas in collaboration with Fred Kersten, 193–95. Dordrecht: Kluwer Academic Publishers, 1996.

———. "In Search of the Middle Ground." In vol. 4 of *Collected Papers*, edited by Helmut Wagner and George Psathas in collaboration with Fred Kersten, 147–51. Dordrecht: Kluwer Academic Publishers, 1996.

———. "Language, Language Disturbances, and the Texture of Consciousness." In *The Problem of Social Reality*, edited by Maurice Natanson, 260–86. Vol. 1 of *Collected Papers*. The Hague: Martinus Nijhoff, 1962.

———. "Lebensformen und Sinnstruktur." In *Theorie der Lebensformen: Frühe Manuskripte aus der Bergson-Periode*, edited by Ilja Srubar, 79–207. Frankfurt-am-Main: Suhrkamp, 1981. Translated by Helmut Wagner under the title of "Life Forms and Meaning Structure," in *Life Forms and Meaning Structure*, by Alfred Schutz (see below).

———. "Letter of Alfred Schutz to Clarence H. Faust, The Fund for the Advancement of Education." In "The Ethical-Political Side of Schutz: His Contributions at the 1956 Institute on Ethics concerned with Barriers to Equality of Opportunity," by Lester Embree. In *Schutzian Social Science*, edited by Lester Embree, 313–18. Dordrecht: Kluwer Academic Publishers, 1999.

———. "Life Forms and Meaning Structure." In *Life Forms and Meaning Structure*, 31–117. London: Routledge and Kegan Paul, 1982.

———. "The Life-World and Scientific Experience." In vol. 4 of *Collected Papers*, edited by Helmut Wagner and George Psathas in collaboration with Fred Kersten, 110–11. Dordrecht: Kluwer Academic Publishers, 1996.

———. "Making Music Together: A Study in Social Relationship." In *Studies in Social Theory*, edited by Arvid Brodersen, 159–78. Vol. 2 of *Collected Papers*. The Hague: Martinus Nijhoff, 1964.

———. "Max Scheler's Epistemology and Ethics." In *Studies in Phenomenological Philosophy*, edited by Ilse Schutz, 145–78. Vol. 3 of *Collected Papers*. The Hague: Martinus Nijhoff, 1966.

———. *Life Forms and Meaning Structure.* Translated by Helmut Wagner. London: Routledge and Kegan Paul, 1982.

———. "Max Scheler's Philosophy." In *Studies in Phenomenological Philosophy,* edited by Ilse Schutz, 133–44. Vol. 3 of *Collected Papers.* The Hague: Martinus Nijhoff, 1966.

———. "Meaning Structure of Literary Art Forms." In *Life Forms and Meaning Structure,* 158–79. London: Routledge, 1982.

———. "Meaning Structures of Language." In *Life Forms and Meaning Structure,* 125–57. London: Routledge, 1982.

———. "Memorandum [to Dr. Harold Lasswell]." In "The Ethical-Political Side of Schutz: His Contributions at the 1956 Institute on Ethics concerned with Barriers to Equality of Opportunity," by Lester Embree. In *Schutzian Social Science,* edited by Lester Embree, 291–95. Dordrecht: Kluwer Academic Publishers, 1999.

———. "Mozart and the Philosophers." In *Studies in Social Theory,* edited by Arvid Brodersen, 179–200. Vol. 2 of *Collected Papers.* The Hague: Martinus Nijhoff, 1964.

———. "Notes for a Course on the Problems of a Sociology of Language, Fall Semester, 1958." Reconstructed by Fred Kersten and edited by Lester Embree for *Collected Papers,* vol. 5, in preparation.

———. "On Multiple Realities." In *The Problem of Social Reality,* edited by Maurice Natanson, 207–59. Vol. 1 of *Collected Papers.* The Hague: Martinus Nijhoff, 1962.

———. "Outline of a Theory of Relevance." In vol. 4 of *Collected Papers,* edited by Helmut Wagner and George Psathas in collaboration with Fred Kersten, 3–5. Dordrecht: Kluwer Academic Publishers, 1996.

———. The Papers of Alfred Schutz. Beinecke Rare Book and Manuscript Library, Yale University. New Haven, Conn. Abbreviated in the notes as PAS.

———. "Parson's Theory of Social Action: *A Critical Review by Alfred Schutz.*" In *Theory of Social Action,* edited by Richard H. Grathoff, 8–60. Bloomington: Indiana University Press, 1978.

———. The Personal Papers of Alfred Schutz. Ms. Evelyn S. Lang, New York, N.Y. Abbreviated in the notes as PPAS.

———. "Phenomenology and the Foundations of the Social Sciences (*Ideas,* Volume III by Edmund Husserl)." In *Studies in Phenomenological Philosophy,* edited by Ilse Schutz, 40–50. Vol. 3 of *Collected Papers.* The Hague: Martinus Nijhoff, 1966.

———. "Phenomenology and the Social Sciences." In *The Problem of Social Reality,* edited by Maurice Natanson, 118–39. Vol. 1 of *Collected Papers.* The Hague: Martinus Nijhoff, 1962. First published in *Philosophical Essays in Memory of Edmund Husserl,* edited by Marvin Farber. (Cambridge, Mass.: Harvard University Press, 1940), 164–86.

———. *The Phenomenology of the Social World.* Translated by George Walsh and Frederick Lehnert. Evanston, Ill.: Northwestern University Press, 1967. Originally published as *Der sinnhafte Aufbau der sozialen Welt: Eine Einleitung in die verstehende Soziologie* (Vienna: Springer, 1932).

———. "Political Economy: Human Conduct in Social Life." In vol. 4 of *Collected Papers*, edited by Helmut Wagner and George Psathas in collaboration with Fred Kersten, 93–105. Dordrecht: Kluwer Academic Publishers, 1996.

———. "Positivistic Philosophy and the Actual Approach of Interpretative Social Science: An Ineditum of Alfred Schutz from Spring 1953." Edited by Lester Embree. *Husserl Studies* 14 (1997): 123–49.

———. "Das Problem der transzendentalen Intersubjektivität bei Husserl." *Philosophische Rundschau: Eine Vierteljahrschrift für philosophische Kritik* 5 (1957): 81–107.

———. "The Problem of Rationality in the Social World." In *Studies in Social Theory*, edited by Arvid Brodersen, 64–88. Vol. 2 of *Collected Papers*. The Hague: Martinus Nijhoff, 1964.

———. "The Problem of Rationality in the Social World: A Lecture Delivered at the Faculty Club of Harvard University on April 13th, 1940." In vol. 4 of *Collected Papers*, edited by Helmut Wagner and George Psathas in collaboration with Fred Kersten, 6–24. Dordrecht: Kluwer Academic Publishers, 1996.

———. *The Problem of Social Reality*. Edited by Maurice Natanson. Vol. 1 of *Collected Papers*. The Hague: Martinus Nijhoff, 1962.

———. "The Problem of Transcendental Intersubjectivity in Husserl." In *Studies in Phenomenological Philosophy*, edited by Ilse Schutz, 51–91. Vol. 3 of *Collected Papers*. The Hague: Martinus Nijhoff, 1966.

———. "Realities from Daily Life to Theoretical Contemplation." In vol. 4 of *Collected Papers*, edited by Helmut Wagner and George Psathas in collaboration with Fred Kersten, 25–50. Dordrecht: Kluwer Academic Publishers, 1996.

———. *Reflections on the Problem of Relevance*. Edited by Richard M. Zaner. New Haven, Conn.: Yale University Press, 1970.

———. Review of *Formal and Transcendental Logic,* by Edmund Husserl. In vol. 4 of *Collected Papers,* edited by Helmut Wagner and George Psathas in collaboration with Fred Kersten, 166–73. Dordrecht: Kluwer Academic Publishers, 1996.

———. Review of *Formale und transzendentale Logik*, by Edmund Husserl. *Deutsche Literaturzeitung für Kritik der internationalen Wissenschaften* 54 (1933): 773–84. Translated under the title "Review of *Formal and Transcendental Logic* (see above).

———. Review of *Méditations cartésiennes*, by Edmund Husserl. *Deutsche Literaturzeitung für Kritik der internationalen Wissenschaften* 51 (1932): 2404–16.

———. "Santayana on Society and Government." In *Studies in Social Theory*, edited by Arvid Brodersen, 201–25. Vol. 2 of *Collected Papers*. The Hague: Martinus Nijhoff, 1964.

———. "Sartre's Theory of the Alter Ego." In *The Problem of Social Reality*, edited by Maurice Natanson, 180–203. Vol. 1 of *Collected Papers*. The Hague: Martinus Nijhoff, 1962.

———. "Scheler's Theory of Intersubjectivity and the General Thesis of the Alter Ego." In *The Problem of Social Reality*, edited by Maurice Natanson, 150–79. Vol. 1 of *Collected Papers*. The Hague: Martinus Nijhoff, 1962.

———. "A Scholar of Multiple Involvements: Felix Kaufmann." In vol. 4 of *Collected Papers*, edited by Helmut Wagner and George Psathas in collaboration with Fred Kersten, 134–39. Dordrecht: Kluwer Academic Publishers, 1996.

———. "The Scope and Function of the Department of Philosophy within the Graduate Faculty." In vol. 4 of *Collected Papers*, edited by Helmut Wagner and George Psathas in collaboration with Fred Kersten, 112–17. Dordrecht: Kluwer Academic Publishers, 1996.

———. "Sinnstruktur der Novelle: Goethe." In *Theorie der Lebensformen: Frühe Manuskripte aus der Bergson-Periode*, edited by Ilja Srubar, 251–78. Frankfurt am Main: Suhrkamp, 1981. Translated by Helmut Wagner under the title "Meaning Structure of Literary Art Forms" (see above).

———. "Social Science and the Social World." In vol. 4 of *Collected Papers*, edited by Helmut Wagner and George Psathas in collaboration with Fred Kersten, 140–46. Dordrecht: Kluwer Academic Publishers, 1996.

———. "The Social World and the Theory of Social Action." In *Studies in Social Theory*, edited by Arvid Brodersen, 3–19. Vol. 2 of *Collected Papers*. The Hague: Martinus Nijhoff, 1964.

———. "Some Considerations concerning Thinking in Terms of Barriers." In "The Ethical-Political Side of Schutz: His Contributions at the 1956 Institute on Ethics concerned with Barriers to Equality of Opportunity," by Lester Embree. In *Schutzian Social Science*, edited by Lester Embree, 287–89. Dordrecht: Kluwer Academic Publishers, 1999.

———. "Some Equivocations in the Notion of Responsibility." In *Studies in Social Theory*, edited by Arvid Brodersen, 274–76. Vol. 2 of *Collected Papers*. The Hague: Martinus Nijhoff, 1964.

———. "Some Leading Concepts of Phenomenology." In *The Problem of Social Reality*, edited by Maurice Natanson, 99–117. Vol. 1 of *Collected Papers*. The Hague: Martinus Nijhoff, 1962.

———. "Some Structures of the Life-World." In *Studies in Phenomenological Philosophy*, edited by Ilse Schutz, 116–32. Vol. 3 of *Collected Papers*. The Hague: Martinus Nijhoff, 1966.

———. "The Stranger: An Essay in Social Psychology." In *Studies in Social Theory*, edited by Arvid Brodersen, 91–105. Vol. 2 of *Collected Papers*. The Hague: Martinus Nijhoff, 1964.

———. *Studies in Phenomenological Philosophy*. Edited by Ilse Schutz. Vol. 3 of *Collected Papers*. The Hague: Martinus Nijhoff, 1966.

———. *Studies in Social Theory*. Edited by Arvid Brodersen. Vol. 2 of *Collected Papers*. The Hague: Martinus Nijhoff, 1964.

———. "Symbol, Reality, and Society." In *The Problem of Social Reality*, edited by Maurice Natanson, 287–356. Vol. 1 of *Collected Papers*. The Hague: Martinus Nijhoff, 1962. First published in *Symbols and Society: Fourteenth Symposium of the Conference on Science, Philosophy, and Religion,* edited by Lyman Bryson, Louis Finkelstein, Hudson Hoagland, and R. M. MacIver, 135–202. New York: Conference on Science, Philosophy, and Religion in Their Relation to the Democratic Way of Life and Harper & Bros., 1955.

———. "Teiresias or Our Knowledge of Future Events." In vol. 4 *Collected Papers*, edited by Helmut Wagner and George Psathas in collaboration with Fred Kersten, 51–66. Dordrecht: Kluwer Academic Publishers, 1996.

———. *Theorie der Lebensformen: Frühe Manuskripte aus der Bergson-Periode*. Edited by Ilja Srubar. Frankfurt am Main: Suhrkamp, 1981. Translated by Helmut Wagner under the title *Life Forms and Meaning Structure* (see above).

———. "Tiresias, or Our Knowledge of Future Events." In *Studies in Social Theory*, edited by Arvid Brodersen, 277–93. Vol. 2 of *Collected Papers*. The Hague: Martinus Nijhoff, 1964.

———. "Toward a Viable Sociology." In vol. 4 of *Collected Papers*, edited by Helmut Wagner and George Psathas in collaboration with Fred Kersten, 75–83. Dordrecht: Kluwer Academic Publishers, 1996.

———. "T. S. Eliot's Concept of Culture." In vol. 5 of *Collected Papers*, edited by Lester Embree. In preparation.

———. "Type and Eidos in Husserl's Late Philosophy." In *Studies in Phenomenological Philosophy*, edited by Ilse Schutz Gurwitsch, 92–115. Vol. 3 of *Collected Papers*. The Hague: Martinus Nijhoff, 1966.

———. "Understanding and Acting in Political Economy and Other Social Sciences." In vol. 4 of *Collected Papers*, edited by Helmut Wagner and George Psathas in collaboration with Fred Kersten, 84–87. Dordrecht: Kluwer Academic Publishers, 1996.

———. "The Well-Informed Citizen: An Essay on the Social Distribution of Knowledge." In *Studies in Social Theory*, edited by Arvid Brodersen, 120–34. Vol. 2 of *Collected Papers*. The Hague: Martinus Nijhoff, 1964.

———. "William James's Concept of the Stream of Thought Phenomenologically Interpreted." In *Studies in Phenomenological Philosophy*, edited by Ilse Schutz, 1–14. Vol. 3 of *Collected Papers*. The Hague: Martinus Nijhoff, 1966.

Schutz, Alfred, and Aron Gurwitsch. *Philosophers in Exile: The Correspondence of Alfred Schutz and Aron Gurwitsch, 1939–1959*. Edited by Richard Grathoff. Translated by J. Claude Evans. Bloomington: Indiana University Press, 1989.

Schutz, Alfred, and Harold Laswell. "Report on the Discussions of Barriers to Equality of Opportunity for the Development of Powers of Social and Civic Judgment." In "The Ethical-Political Side of Schutz: His Contributions at the 1956 Institute on Ethics concerned with Barriers to Equality of Opportunity," by Lester Embree. In *Schutzian Social Science*, edited by Lester Embree, 297–311. Dordrecht: Kluwer Academic Publishers, 1999.

Schutz, Alfred, and Thomas Luckmann. *The Structures of the Life-World*, vol. 1. Translated by Richard M. Zaner and H. Tristram Engelhardt. Evanston, Ill.: Northwestern University Press, 1973.

———. *The Structures of the Life-World*. Vol. 2. Translated by Richard M. Zaner and David J. Parent. Evanston, Ill.: Northwestern University Press, 1989.

Schutz, Alfred, and Talcott Parsons. *The Theory of Social Action: The Correspondence of Alfred Schutz and Talcott Parsons*. Edited by Richard Grathoff. Bloomington: Indiana University Press, 1978.

Shaw, George Bernard. *Candida*. In *Plays, Pleasant and Unpleasant: The Four Pleasant Plays*, 111–92. Leipzig: Bernhard Tachnitz, 1914.

Smith, Barry. *Austrian Philosophy: The Legacy of Franz Brentano*. Chicago: Open Court, 1994.

Smith, F. J. Introduction to *In Search of Musical Method*, edited by F. J. Smith, 1–5. London: Gordon and Breach Science Publishers, 1976.

Sombart, Werner. *Die drei Nationalökonomien: Geschichte und System der Lehre von der Wirtschaft*. Munich: Duncker and Humblot, 1930.

Spiegelberg, Herbert. "A Defense of Human Equality." In *Steppingstones toward an Ethics for Fellow Existers: Essays, 1944–1983*, 131–53. Dordrecht: Martinus Nijhoff, 1986.

———. *The Phenomenological Movement*. 3rd ed. rev. and enl. 3 vols. The Hague: Martinus Nijhoff, 1982.

Sprondel, Walter M., and Richard Grathoff, eds. *Alfred Schütz und die Idee des Alltags in den Sozialwissenschaften*. Stuttgart: Ferdinand Enke, 1979.

Srubar, Ilja. "Alfred Schütz's Konzeption der Sozialität des Handelns." In *Alfred Schütz: Neue Beiträge zur Rezeption seines Werkes*, edited by Elisabeth List and Ilja Srubar, 145–56. Amsterdam: Rodopi, 1988.

———. "Einleitung: Schütz' Bergson-Rezeption." In *Theorie der Lebensformen: Frühe Manuskripte aus der Bergson-Periode*, edited by Ilja Srubar, 9–76. Frankfurt am Main: Suhrkamp, 1981.

———. *Kosmion: Die Genese der pragmatischen Lebenswelttheorie von Alfred Schütz und ihr anthropologischer Hintergrund*. Frankfurt am Main: Suhrkamp, 1988.

———. "Wertbeziehung und Relevanz zu Schütz' Weber-Rezeption." In *Phenomenology as a Dialogue*, a special issue of *Critique and Humanism*, edited by Kolyo Koev, 38–53. Sofia, Bulgaria: National Public Opinion Center, 1990.

———. "Where Does the Political Emerge From?" In *The Legacy of Alfred Schutz: International Conference on His Centennial*, edited by Hisashi Nasu, sixteenth paper, 1–22. Tokyo: Waseda University, 1999.

Stern, Gunther. "Toward a Solution of the Problem of Solipsism." *Philosophy and Phenomenological Research* 8 (1948): 679–87.

Treviño, A. Javier. Introduction to *Social Control through Law*, by Roscoe Pound. New Haven, Conn.: Yale University Press, 1942. Reprint, with a new introduction by A. Javier Treviño, New Brunswick, N.J.: Transaction, 1997.

Vaitkus, Steven. *How Is Society Possible? Intersubjectivity and the Fiduciary Attitude as Problems of the Social Group in Mead, Gurwitsch, and Schutz*. Dordrecht: Kluwer Academic Press, 1991.

van Breda, Hermann Leo. Preface to *The Problem of Social Reality*, edited by Maurice Natanson, Vol. 1 of *Collected Papers*. The Hague: Martinus Nijhoff, 1962.

Voegelin, Eric. *Anamnesis*. Translated and edited by Gerhart Niemeyer. Columbia: University of Missouri Press, 1978. Originally published as *Anamnesis: Zur Theorie der Geschichte und Politik* (Munich: R. Piper and Co., 1996).

———. *Autobiographical Reflections*. Edited by Ellis Sandoz. Baton Rouge: Louisiana State University Press, 1989.

———. *The Ecumenic* Age. Vol. 4 of *Order and History*. Baton Rouge: Louisiana State University Press, 1974.

———. "The German University and the Order of German Society: A Reconsideration of the Nazi Era." In *Published Essays, 1966–1985*, edited by Ellis Sandoz, 1–35. Vol. 12 of *The Collected Works of Eric Voegelin*, Baton Rouge: Lousiana State University Press, 1990.

———. *In Search of Order*. Vol. 5 of *Order and History*. Baton Rouge: Louisiana State University Press, 1987.

———. *Israel and Revelation*. Vol. 1 of *Order and History*. Baton Rouge: Louisiana State University Press, 1956.

———. *The New Science of Politics: An Introduction*. Chicago: The University of Chicago Press, 1952.

———. "The Origins of Totalitarianism." In *Published Essays: 1953–1965*, edited by Ellis Sandoz, 15–23. Vol. 11 of *The Collected Works of Eric Voegelin*, Columbia: University of Missouri Press, 1989.

———. "Siger de Brabant." *Philosophy and Phenomenological Research* 4 (1944): 507–25.

———. "Theory of Legal Science: A Review." *Louisiana Law Review* 4 (1942): 554–72.

———. *The World of the Polis*. Vol. 2 of *Order and History*. Baton Rouge: Louisiana State University Press, 1957.

Voegelin, Eric, and Leo Strauss. *Faith and Political Philosophy: The Correspondence between Leo Strauss and Eric Voegelin, 1934–1964*. Translated and edited by Peter Emberley and Barry Cooper. University Park: Pennsylvania State University Press, 1993.

Wagner, Helmut R. *Alfred Schutz: An Intellectual Biography*. Chicago: University of Chicago Press, 1983.

———. *A Bergsonian Bridge to Phenomenological Psychology*. With Ilja Scrubar. Washington, D.C.: Center for Advanced Research in Phenomenology and University Press of America, 1984.

———. "Editor's Note." In *Life Forms and Meaning Structures* by Alfred Schutz 121–23. London: Routledge and Kegan Paul, 1982.

———. "The Bergsonian Period of Alfred Schutz." *Philosophy and Phenomenological Research* 38 (1977): 187–99.

———. Course Listings for the New School for Social Research. Courtesy of Lester Embree.

———. "Marvin Farber's Contribution to the Phenomenological Movement." In *Philosophy and Science in Phenomenological Perspective*, edited by Kah Kyung Cho, 209–36. Dordrecht: Martinus Nijhoff, 1984.

Webb, Rodman G. *The Presence of the Past: John Dewey and Alfred Schutz on the Genesis and Organization of Experience*. Gainesville: University Presses of Florida, 1976.

Weber, Max. "The Concept of Following a Rule" In *Weber: Selections in Translation*. Edited by W. G. Runcimon and translated by Eric Mathews, 99–110. Cambridge: Cambridge University Press, 1978.

———. *Economy and Society: An Outline of Interpretive Sociology*, Edited by Guenther Roth and Cirus Wittich. Vol. 1. New York: Bedminster Press, 1968.

———. "Critical Studies in the Logic of the Cultural Sciences: A Critique of Edward Meyer's Methodological Views," In the *Methodology of the Social Sciences*, translated and edited by Edward A. Shils and Henry A. Finch. New York: Free Press, 1949.

———. *Hinduismus und Buddhismus*. In vol. 2 of *Gesammelte Aufsätze zur Religionssoziologie*, edited by Maia Tobler, 363–78. 2d ed. Tübingen: J. C. B. Mohr (Paul Siebeck), 1923. Translated by Eric Matthews under the title "The Religions of Asia" (see below).

———. "Kritischen Studien auf dem Gebiet der kulturwissenschaftlichen Logik: Zur Auseinandersetzung mit Edward Meyer." In *Gesammelte Aufsätze zur Wissenschaftslehre*, edited by Johannes Winckelmann, 215–90. 2d ed. 1917. Reprint, Tübingen: J. C. B. Mohr (Paul Siebeck), 1951. Translated by Shils and Finch under the title "Critical Studies in the Logic of the Cultural Sciences: A Critique of Eduard Meyer's Methodological Views" (see above).

———. *Max Weber: The Interpretation of Social Reality*. Edited by J. E. T. Eldridge. New York: Charles Scribner's Sons, 1971. *Max Weber: Selections in Translation.* Edited by W. G. Runciman. Translated by E. Matthews. Cambridge: Cambridge University Press, 1978.

———. "The Meaning of Ethical Neutrality in Sociology and Economics." In *The Methodology of the Social Sciences,* translated and edited by Edward A. Shils and Henry A. Finch. New York: Free Press, 1949.

———. "'Die 'Objektivität' sozialwissenschaftlicher und sozialpolitischer Erkenntnis.'" In *Gesammelte Aufsätze zur Wissenschaftslehre* edited by Johannes Winckelmann, 146–214. 2d ed. 1917. Reprint, Tübingen: J. C. B. Mohr (Paul Siebeck), 1951. Translated by Shils and Finch under the title "'Objectivity' in Social Science and Social Policy" (see below).

———. "Objectivity in Social Science and Social Policy." In *The Methodology of the Social Sciences,* translated and edited by Edward A. Shils and Henry A. Finch, 49–112. New York: Free Press, 1949.

———. "Politics as Vocation." In *Weber: Selections in Translation,* edited by W. G. Runciman and translated by Eric Matthews, 215–25. Cambridge: Cambridge University Press, 1978.

———. "Politik als Beruf." In *Gesammelte Politische Schriften*, edited by Johannes Winckelmann, 533–48. 2d ed. Tübingen: J. C. B. Mohr (Paul Siebeck), 1958. Translated by Eric Matthews under the title "Politics as Vocation" (see above).

———. "Prospects for Democracy in Tsarist Russia." In *Weber: Selections in Translation,* edited by W. G. Runciman and translated by Eric Matthews, 269–84. Cambridge: Cambridge University Press, 1978.

———. *The Protestant Ethic and the Spirit of Capitalism.* Translated by Talcott Parsons. London: Unwin University Books, 1930.

———. "R. Stammlers 'Überwindung' der materialistischen Geschichtsauffassung." In *Gesammelte Aufsätze zur Wissenschaftslehre,* edited by Johannes Winckelmann, 322–37. 2d ed. 1917. Reprint, Tübingen: J. C. B. Mohr (Paul Siebeck), 1951. Excerpt (322–37) translated by Eric Matthews under the title "The Concept of 'Following a Rule' " (see above).

———. The "Religions of Asia." In *Weber: Selections in Translation,* edited by W. G. Runciman and translated by Eric Matthews, 215–25. Cambridge: Cambridge University Press, 1978.

———. "Science as a Vocation." In From *Max Weber: Essays in Sociology,* translated and edited by H. H. Gerth and C. Wright Mills, 129–56. New York: Oxford U.P.. 1981.

———. "Der Sinn der 'Wertfreiheit' der soziologischen und ökonomischen Wissenschaften." In *Gesammelte Aufsätze zur Wissenschaftslehre,* edited by Johannes Winckelmann, 475–526. 2d ed. 1917. Reprint, Tübingen: Verlag J. C. B. Mohr (Paul Siebeck), 1951. Translated by Shils and Finch under the title "The Meaning of Ethical Neutrality in Sociology and Economics," in *The Methodology of the Social Sciences,* by Max Weber, edited by Edward A. Shils and Henry A. Finch. (New York: Free Press, 1949), 1–47.

———. "Socialism." In *Weber: Selections in Translation,* edited by W. G. Runciman and translated by Eric Matthews, 251–62. Cambridge: Cambridge University Press, 1978.

———. "Der Sozialismus." In *Gesammelte Aufsätze zur Soziologie und Sozialpolitik,* 500–511, 1918. Reprint, Tübingen: J. C. B. Mohr (Paul Siebeck), 1924. Translated by Eric Matthews under the title "Socialism" in *Weber: Selections in Translation* (see above).

———. *Wirtschaft und Gesellschaft.* Part 3 of *Grundriss der Sozialökonomik.* Tübingen: J. C. B. Mohr (Paul Siebeck), 1922. English translation by Ephraim Fischoff (and others) under the title *Economy and Society: An Outline of Interpretive Sociology* (see above).

———. "Wissenschaft als Beruf." In *Gesammelte Aufsätze zur Wissenschaftslehre,* edited by Johannes Winckelmann, 566–97. 2d ed. 1917. Reprint, Tübingen: J. C. B. Mohr (Paul Siebeck), 1951. Translated by Gerth and Mills under the title "Science as a Vocation." (see above).

———. "Zur Lage der bürgerlichen Demokratie in Russland." In *Gesammelte Politische Schriften,* edited by Johannes Winckelmann, 45–62. 2d ed. Tübingen: J. C. B. Mohr (Paul Siebeck), 1958. Translated by Eric Matthews under the title "Prospects for Democracy in Tsarist Russia" (see above).

Weiss, Gilbert. *Theorie, Relevanz, und Wahrheit: Eine Rekonstruktion des Brief wechsels zwischen Eric Voegelin und Alfred Schütz (1938–1959).* Munich: W. Fink, 2000.

Wiggins, Osbourne P., and Michael Alan Schwartz. "Psychiatric Diagnosis and the Phenomenology of Typification." In *Worldly Phenomenology: The Continuing Influence of Alfred Schutz on North American Human Science,* edited by Lester Embree, 202–30. Washington, D.C.: Center for Advanced Research in Phenomenology and University Press of America, 1988.

Williame, Robert. *Les fondements phénoménologiques de la sociologie compréhensive: Alfred Schutz et Max Weber.* The Hague: Martinus Nijhoff, 1973.

Winternitz, Emmanuel. *Musical Instruments and Their Symbolism in Western Art: Studies in Musical Iconology.* New Haven, Conn.: Yale University Press, 1979.

———. "The Role of Music in Leonardo's Paragone." In *Phenomenology and Social Reality: Essays in Memory of Alfred Schutz,* edited by Maurice Natanson, 270–96. The Hague: Martinus Nijhoff, 1970.

Wolff, Kurt, ed. *Alfred Schutz: Appraisals and Developments*. Dordrecht: Martinus Nijhoff, 1984. Reprint from *Human Studies,* no. 2 (1984).

———. "Before and after Sociology." In *Trying Sociology,* 262–73. New York: John Wiley & Sons, 1974.

———. "Discussion of Wagner, Imber, and Rasmussen." In *Alfred Schutz: Appraisals and Developments*, edited by Kurt Wolff, 27–33. Dordrecht: Martinus Nijhoff, 1984. Reprint from *Human Studies* 7(2) (1984): 133–39.

———. *Survival and Sociology: Vindicating the Human Subject*. New Brunswick, N.J.: Transaction, 1991.

———. *Transformation in the Writing: A Case of Surrender and Catch*. Dordrecht: Kluwer Academic Publishers, 1995.

Zaner, Richard M. Introduction to *Reflections on the Problem of Relevance,* by Alfred Schutz. Edited by Richard M. Zaner, New Haven, Conn.: Yale University Press, 1970.

———. "Making Music Together While Growing Older: Further Reflections on Intersubjectivity." *Human Studies* 25 (2002): 1–18.

Index